March 25–28, 2018
Monterey, CA, USA

Association for Computing Machinery

Advancing Computing as a Science & Profession

ISPD'18

Proceedings of the 2018 International Symposium on
Physical Design

Sponsored by:
ACM SIGDA

Technical Co-sponsored by:
IEEE Circuits and Systems Society

Supported by:
Cādence, IBM Research, Intel, Mentor Graphics, Synopsys, & Xilinx

**Association for
Computing Machinery**

Advancing Computing as a Science & Profession

The Association for Computing Machinery
2 Penn Plaza, Suite 701
New York, New York 10121-0701

ISBN: 978-1-4503-5626-8 (Digital)

ISBN: 978-1-4503-5881-1 (Print)

Additional copies may be ordered prepaid from:

ACM Order Department
PO Box 30777
New York, NY 10087-0777, USA

Phone: 1-800-342-6626 (USA and Canada)
+1-212-626-0500 (Global)
Fax: +1-212-944-1318
E-mail: acmhelp@acm.org
Hours of Operation: 8:30 am – 4:30 pm ET

Foreword

On behalf of the organizing committee, we are delighted to welcome you to the 2018 ACM International Symposium on Physical Design (ISPD), held at Seaside, California. Continuing the great tradition established by its twenty-six predecessors, which includes a series of five ACM/SIGDA Physical Design Workshops held intermittently in 1987-1996 and twenty one editions of ISPD in the current form since 1997. The 2018 ISPD provides a premier forum to present leading-edge research results, exchange ideas, and promote research on critical areas related to the physical design of VLSI and other related systems.

The regular papers in the ISPD 2018 program were selected after a rigorous, month-long, double-blind review process and a face-to-face meeting by the Technical Program Committee (TPC) members. The papers selected exhibit latest advancements in a variety of topics in physical design, including emerging challenges for current and future process technologies, FPGA architectures, placement, detailed routing, and application of machine-learning based techniques to physical design.

The ISPD 2018 program is complemented by two keynote addresses, eleven invited talks and a tribute session, all of which are delivered by distinguished researchers from both industry and academia. On Monday morning, Dr. Anthony Hill, fellow of Texas Instruments, Inc., will talk about challenges and opportunities in automotive, industrial, and IoT Physical Design. In the second keynote on Tuesday, Andreas Olofsson, DARPA's Microsystems Technology Office Program Manager, will discuss the next generation of silicon compilers. A commemorative session on Tuesday afternoon will pay tribute to Professor Te Chiang Hu. His collaborators will share with us Dr. Hu's exceptional contributions to research in physical design and VLSI applications, including his influential work on trees, flows, and networks. There will be other invited talks interspersed with the presentations of the regular papers. The topics of the invited papers range from advanced FPGA applications, high-speed processor design, logic computation, machine learning in EDA, interconnect optimization, to electromigration-aware physical design.

Since 2005, the ISPD has organized highly competitive contests to promote and advance research in placement, global routing, clock network synthesis, discrete gate sizing, and detailed routing-driven placement. The contest this year, organized by Cadence, focuses on detailed routing. Continuing the tradition of all the past contests, a new large-scale real-world benchmark suite for detailed routing has been specified using LEF/DEF and will be released in the ISPD website (http://www.ispd.cc). The contest evaluates the routing quality and the ability to connect all the nets of a design without design rule violations. It is expected to lead and motivate more research and contributions on the detailed routing of large integrated circuits.

We would like to take this chance to express our gratitude to the authors, the presenters, the keynote/invited speakers for contributing to the high-quality program, and the session chairs for moderating the sessions. We would like to thank our program committee and external reviewers, who provided insightful constructive comments and detailed reviews to the authors. We greatly appreciate the exceptional set of invited talks put together by the Steering Committee, which is chaired by Mustafa Ozdal. We also thank the Steering Committee for selecting the best paper. Special thanks go to the Publications Chair Bill Swartz and the Publicity Chair Jens Lienig for their tremendous services. We would like to acknowledge the team organizing the contest led by Wen-Hao Liu. We are also grateful to our sponsors. The symposium is sponsored by the ACM SIGDA (Special Interest Group on Design Automation) with technical co-sponsorship from the IEEE Circuits and Systems Society. Generous financial contributions have also been provided by (in alphabetical order): Cadence, IBM, Intel Corporation, Mentor Graphics, Synopsys, and Xilinx. Last but not least, we thank Lisa Tolles and others from Sheridan Communications for their expertise and enormous patience during the production of the proceedings.

The organizing committee hopes that you will enjoy ISPD. We look forward to seeing you again in future editions of ISPD.

Chris Chu
ISPD 2018 General Chair

Ismail Bustany
Technical Program Chair

Table of Contents

Statistical and Machine Learning-Based CAD

Session Chair: Ivan Kissiov *(Mentor, a Siemens Business)*

Three Shades of Placement!

Session Chair: Joseph Shinnerl *(Mentor, a Siemens Business)*

Commemoration for Professor Te Chiang Hu

Session Chair: Andrew B. Kahng *(University of California at San Diego)*

Interconnect Optimization and Detailed Routing Contest Results

Session Chair: Jackey Yan *(Cadence Design Systems Inc.)*

How to Make Your Foundry Happier?

Session Chair: Jiang Hu *(Texas A&M University)*

ISPD 2018 Symposium Organization

General Chair: Chris Chu *(Iowa State University)*

Technical Program Chair: Ismail Bustany *(Xilinx Inc.)*

Past Chair: Mustafa Ozdal *(Bilkent University)*

Steering Committee Chair: Mustafa Ozdal *(Bilkent University)*

Steering Committee: Chuck Alpert *(Cadence Corp.)*
Yao-Wen Chang *(National Taiwan University)*
Patrick Groeneveld *(Cadence Corp.)*
Jiang Hu *(University of Texas A&M)*
Noel Menezes *(Intel Corp.)*
Mustafa Ozdal *(Bilkent University)*
David Pan *(University of Texas at Austin)*
Martin Wong *(University of Illinois at Urbana-Champaign)*
Evangeline Young *(Chinese University of Hong Kong)*

Program Committee: Yongchan Ban *(GlobalFoundries Inc.)*
Ismail Bustany *(Xilinx Inc.)*
Nima Karimpour Darav *(Microsemi Corp.)*
Sabya Das *(Xilinx Inc.)*
Sheqin Dong *(Tsinghua University)*
Rickard Ewetz *(University of Central Florida)*
Mahesh Iyer *(Intel Corp.)*
Iris Hui-Ru Jiang *(National Chiao Tung University)*
Marcelo Johann *(Federal University of Rio Grande do Sul)*
Jens Lienig *(Dresden Univ. of Technology)*
Mark Po-Hung Lin *(National Chung Cheng University)*
Wen-Hao Liu *(Cadence Corp.)*
Ulf Schlichtmann *(Technical University of Munich)*
Joseph Shinnerl *(Mentor Graphic, a Siemens Business)*
Yasuhiro Takashima *(Kitakyu University)*
Hua Xiang *(IBM Corp.)*
Jae-Seok Yang *(University of Texas at Austin)*
Gary Yeap *(Synopsys Inc.)*
Bei Yu *(Chinese University of Hong Kong)*

Publication Chair: William Swartz *(TimberWolf Systems Inc. & University of Texas at Dallas)*

Publicity Chair: Jens Lienig *(Dresden University of Technology)*

Contest Chair: Wen-Hao Liu *(Cadence Corp.)*

Additional Reviewers:

Saurabh Adya
Steve Bigalke
Kalen Brunham
Marko Chew
David Chinnery
Aysa Fakheri Tabrizi
Robert Fischbach
Grigor Gasparyan
Tilman Horst
Dana How
Iris Jiang
Yi-Min Jiang
Andreas Krinke
Yuji Kukimo
Xiaolue Lai
Bao Liu
Hugo Lu
Dmitry Malafei
Pavlos Matthaiakis

Larry McMurchie
Sergii Osmolovskyi
Duaine Pryor
Tiago J. Reimann
Ned Saleh
Jinny Singh
Love Singhal
Nish Sinnadurai
Valeriy Sukharev
Vishal Suthar
Thorlindur Thorolfsson
Amr Toppozada
Ilhami Torunoglu
Robert Walker
Wei Ye
Chien-Chih Yu
Kai Zhu

ISPD 2018 Sponsors & Supporters

Sponsor:

Technical Co-sponsor:

Supporters:

IBM Research

Challenges and Opportunities in Automotive, Industrial, and IoT Physical Design

Anthony M. Hill
Texas Instruments, Inc.
ant@ti.com

ABSTRACT

Taping out modern, complex SOCs presents a myriad of challenges in physical design. Doing so for demanding markets such as automotive, industrial, and IoT multiplies that complexity. In this talk we will take a broad look across the physical design space and discuss what works, what doesn't work, and where the major gaps are today and evolving challenges for future devices. We will look at experiences gained over the last 20 years for devices in high volume production and devices in active development across a myriad of technologies including bulk CMOS, low-power nodes, and FinFET.

BIO

Anthony Hill is a Texas Instruments Fellow and Director of Technology Backplane for TI's Processors Business. His team has broad responsibilities including technology assessment and procurement, analog design, high-performance IP development and validation, and development of design implementation and signoff methodologies. Currently he is working on technology backplane development for automotive and industrial SOCs for TI's Jacinto™ and Sitara™ products.

He joined TI in 1996 after taking his BSEE from Oklahoma State University in 1992, and MSEE and PhD from the University of Illinois Urbana-Champaign in 1993 and 1996.

He has been with TI since 1996 and was elected Senior Member of Technical Staff in 2001, Distinguished Member of Technical Staff in 2007, and Fellow in 2016.

He has been involved in 8 generations of cutting-edge devices from 180nm to 16nm with TI's DSP and Processor business groups. He has been at the forefront of applying and driving EDA technologies including SI-based timing, multi-scenario signoff, and physical synthesis. He has been involved and driven numerous patents and publications in areas such as standard cell architecture and design, synthesis, place and route, timing signoff, and reliability.

ISPD'18, March 25–28, 2018, Monterey, CA, USA.
ACM ISBN 978-1-4503-5626-8/18/03.
DOI: https://doi.org/10.1145/3177540.3178455

Wot the L: Analysis of Real versus Random Placed Nets, and Implications for Steiner Tree Heuristics *

Andrew B. Kahng[1,2], Christopher Moyes[1], Sriram Venkatesh[1] and Lutong Wang[2]

[1]CSE and [2]ECE Departments, UC San Diego, La Jolla, CA 92093

{abk, cmoyes, srvenkat, luw002}@ucsd.edu

ABSTRACT

The NP-hard Rectilinear Steiner Minimum Tree (RSMT) problem has been studied in the VLSI physical design literature for well over three decades. Fast estimators of RSMT cost (which reflects routed wirelength) are a required ingredient of modern physical planning and global placement methods. Constructive estimators build heuristic RSMTs whose costs are used as wirelength estimates; notably, these include FLUTE [8]. Analytic and lookup table-based estimators include the methods of Cheng [7] and Caldwell et al. [3]; the latter is based on both the number of points and the aspect ratio of the pointset in the RSMT instance. We observe that the physical design literature has numerous evaluations of RSMT heuristics and estimators on random pointsets, and that the relative merits of heuristics and estimators have been determined based on this use of random pointsets. In this paper, we show that a pointset attribute which we call *L-ness* highlights the difference between real placements and random placements of net pins. We explain why placements of netlists in practice result in pointsets with much higher L-ness than random pointsets, and we confirm this difference empirically for both academic and commercial placement tools. We further present an improved lookup table-based RSMT cost estimator that includes an L-ness parameter. Last, we illustrate how differences between Steiner tree heuristics can change depending on whether real or random pointsets are used in the evaluation.

ACM Reference Format:
Andrew B. Kahng[1,2], Christopher Moyes[1], Sriram Venkatesh[1] and Lutong Wang[2]. 2018. Wot the L: Analysis of Real versus Random Placed Nets, and Implications for Steiner Tree Heuristics . In *Proceedings of 2018 International Symposium on Physical Design (ISPD'18)*. ACM, New York, NY, USA, 8 pages. https://doi.org/10.1145/3177540.3178238

1 INTRODUCTION

VLSI global placement seeks to minimize routed wirelength (WL) along with timing path delays, dynamic power and other design metrics, subject to the constraint that placeable instances do not overlap. Because signal nets are routed as Steiner trees, their routed wirelengths are ideally modeled as the costs of respective *Rectilinear Steiner Minimum Trees* (RSMTs) over pin locations. Since the RSMT problem is NP-hard, placement tools typically minimize the sum over all nets of the bounding box half-perimeter of pin locations – i.e., the *half-perimeter wirelength* (HPWL) objective [13]. An important element of efficient placer implementation is the fast estimation of RSMT costs, e.g., by weighting HPWL according to a lookup table of scaling factors [3][7].

---

*Merriam-Webster https://www.merriam-webster.com/dictionary/wot defines "wot" as the old English verb meaning "know (of)".

ISPD'18, March 25–28, 2018, Monterey, CA, USA
© 2018 Association for Computing Machinery.
ACM ISBN 978-1-4503-5626-8/18/03...$15.00
https://doi.org/10.1145/3177540.3178238

Our present work focuses on the qualitative difference between *real* pointsets corresponding to pin locations of placed nets, and *random* pointsets that have often been used to characterize the performance and relative merits of RSMT heuristics or RSMT cost estimators. As discussed below, placement tools will tend to move the pins of a net up against two adjacent edges of the net bounding box, as shown in Figure 4 below. This phenomenon is due to the HPWL objective in conjunction with each placeable instance having multiple incident nets. By contrast, with random pointsets, all point locations inside the pointset bounding box are equiprobable. We define the *L-ness* of a placed net's pin locations to capture how close they are to two adjacent edges of the net bounding box:

Definition: Given a pointset P, the *bounding box* of P is the minimum-area rectangle that contains all points of P; we use $B(P)$ to denote the bounding box area. The *L-ness* of P is measured as $R(P)/B(P)$, where $R(P)$ is the area of the *largest empty (isothetic) rectangle* that (i) is contained in the bounding box of P, (ii) contains one corner of the bounding box of P, and (iii) contains no points in P.

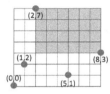

Figure 1: Illustration of largest empty (isothetic, i.e., with axis-parallel edges) rectangle. The L-ness of this 5-pin pointset is 24/56.

High $R(P)/B(P)$ ratio corresponds to large L-ness. If $B(P) = 0$, then we consider the L-ness of P to be 1. Figure 1 shows a pointset with $R(P)/B(P) = \frac{24}{56}$.

1.1 Motivation: Non-uniformity of Net Pin Placements

As a motivating study, we first confirm the non-uniform distribution of real placed pointsets (i.e., pins of signal nets). We use the leon3mp [15] and theia [20] design blocks mapped to a 28nm LP foundry enablement, with place-and-route performed using Cadence Innovus Implementation System version 15.2 [19]. Two types of placements are studied: *pseudo-1D* and *2D*. To obtain a pseudo-1D placement, we create a floorplan with width/height *aspect ratio* (AR) of 10:1 following the methodology described in [5]. We collect the point (pin) location distribution for each net along the x-axis, within a normalized range of 0 (left boundary of each given net) to 1 (right boundary of each given net). We categorize nets into three types – L, R, and O, defined as follows. A net n is of type L if, for each cell c of the net, no fanin/fanout net of c has a pin to the right of the rightmost pin of the net n, and at least one has a pin to the left of the leftmost pin of the net n. A net n is of Type R if for each cell c of the net, no fanin/fanout of c has a pin to the left of the bounding box (BBox) of net n, and at least one has a pin to the rightmost pin of net n. A net n is otherwise of type O. For example, in Figure 2, nets A and D are of type L; net B is of type R; and net C is of type O.

Figure 3 shows results of this empirical study on the designs mentioned above. We see that a "real" placement tool will clearly push cells (pins) of a type L net (respectively, a type R net) toward the left (respectively, right) boundary. There are virtually no cells in the middle, and only a few cells are pushed to the opposite boundary. From our study, we believe that there are two explanations for cells occurring at the opposite boundary: (i) we plot cell locations according to the center of the cell, which has error with respect to exact pin locations; and (ii) nets with short x-span can exhibit this behavior since the placer does not see a significant wirelength penalty for doing this. For a type O net, the cell distribution still shows preference to the bounding box boundary, indicating non-uniform distribution.

We have also performed the above experiment for 2D placements with floorplan height = width, i.e., aspect ratio = 1. In the y direction, "bottom" and "top" are respectively equivalenced to "left" and "right" in the x direction. Then, we sum up the pointset distribution in both directions. The results look similar to Figure 3. We see a very strong deviation from the uniform distribution that is seen with random pointsets.[1]

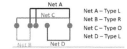

Figure 2: Illustration of L, R, and O types of nets.

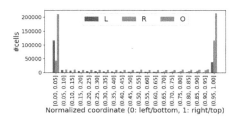

Figure 3: Empirical results from pseudo-1D placements.

Figure 4: Pins of a net from an industrial placer, clustered towards the left and bottom edges of the bounding box.

1.2 Related Works

Previous works have estimated RSMT cost based on characteristics of placed pin locations. Caldwell et al. [3] demonstrate how RSMT cost depends on both the cardinality and the aspect ratio of a pointset. This improves upon the earlier work of Cheng [7], which estimates RSMT cost based only on the pointset cardinality. Quite notably, Cheng [7] appears to point out the concept of L-ness in real placed pin locations when discussing the modeling of routing resource demand. However, this observation does not seem to have been followed up in the RSMT estimation or placement literatures.[2]

---

[1]While this motivating study uses the Cadence Innovus placer, Section III below shows similar non-uniformity across multiple academic and commercial placers' outputs.

[2]Section 3 of [7] states, "The high wiring probability at the top and bottom boundaries comes from the following two facts: (1) the probability of having two pins located at the same boundary is high because of bounding box. (2) when finding an optimal Steiner tree, either a left-L or a right-L is used to reduce the wire length of a minimum spanning tree."

In the computational geometry literature, Chazelle et al. [6] present an $O(n \log^3 n)$ divide-and-conquer algorithm which calculates the area of the largest empty (isothetic) rectangle in a set of n points. By using a semi-dynamic heap, Naamad et al. [14] calculate the largest empty rectangle in a set of n points in $O(s \log n)$ time where s is the number of possible empty rectangles.

With regard to RSMT heuristic constructions, Chu and Wong [8] give a well-known $O(n \log n)$ RSMT heuristic, FLUTE, which is the most accurate of the RSMT heuristics that we study in Section 4.1. The Prim-Dijkstra heuristic of Alpert et al. [1] "blends" classic minimum spanning tree and shortest-paths tree constructions using a weighting factor α to obtain a heuristic "shallow-light" spanning tree. Below, in our experimental studies, we augment the Prim-Dijkstra construction with the edge-overlapping method of Ho et al. [11] to obtain a heuristic RSMT from the Prim-Dijkstra spanning construction.

1.3 Contributions and Outline of This Paper

The main contributions of this paper are as follows.

- We propose a formal definition of *L-ness* of a pointset in the Manhattan plane.
- We empirically characterize a qualitatively significant difference in L-ness between real placed net pins and random pointsets. As seen in Section 3.1, real placed pointsets have significantly higher L-ness than random pointsets.
- We describe a pointset generator which can be used to generate more realistic pointsets with prescribed L-ness distribution. This can be used to assess RSMT heuristics and cost estimators with randomly generated pointsets that match AR and $R(P)/B(P)$ distributions (as well as RSMT costs - see Subsection 4.2) of real placed pointsets.
- We give a new lookup table-based RSMT cost estimator which improves over the method of [3] by adding L-ness as a parameter. Our implementation of this lookup table gives a non-dominated (speed, accuracy) option for RSMT cost estimation.

In the following, Section 2 presents notation and analyses of L-ness in planar pointsets. Section 3 describes empirical characterizations of real placed pointsets, contrasted with random pointsets. Section 4 discusses the impact of L-ness on the relative performance of various RSMT heuristics. Section 5 presents a new lookup table-based RSMT cost estimate that improves upon [3] by adding an L-ness dimension. Section 6 summarizes our results and concludes the paper.

2 PRELIMINARIES

In this section, we first give notations and facts used in this work. We then analyze different properties of pointsets, and discuss the relationship of L-ness to other pointset characteristics. Last, we provide methods to generate realistic pointsets, and an algorithm to compute $R(P)$ in $\Theta(n \log n)$ time.

2.1 Notations

Notations that we use in this paper are summarized in Table 1. The layout region is assumed to have lower-left corner $(0, 0)$ and upper-right corner (H, W). A *random p-pin pointset* consists of p points chosen randomly from a uniform distribution in the $H \times W$ layout region. As noted above, the *bounding box* of pointset P is the minimal isothetic (axis-parallel) rectangle that contains all points of P. The *half-perimeter* of a given bounding box is half the perimeter of the bounding box. For example, the half-perimeter of the bounding box in Figure 1 is 15, and its AR is $\frac{8}{7}$.

Our discussion furthermore assumes that points of a random pointset are in *general position*, i.e., all x-coordinates and all y-coordinates are distinct. To validate this assumption, we extract

Table 1: Notations.

Notation	Meaning
p	net degree (# pins of a signal net) ($p \geq 2$)
P	a net (pointset), $P = (x_1, y_1), \ldots, (x_p, y_p)$
$B(P)$	the area of the minimum bounding box of P
$R(P)$	the area of the largest empty rectangle of P
$RSMT(P)$	the rectilinear Steiner minimum tree over P
(H, W)	chip dimensions, i.e., height and width of the chip
AR	aspect ratio (W/H) of the bounding box
$R(P)/B(P)$	L-ness, the ratio of $R(P)$ divided by $B(P)$

Table 2: Probability that any two points in a pointset share the same x- or y-coordinate.

p	ICC/Innovus	Capo	ePlace
2	9.88%	7.48%	7.65%
3	10.98%	7.90%	7.46%
4	7.57%	6.84%	6.01%
5	8.03%	7.99%	6.32%
6	7.50%	7.69%	7.49%
7	7.45%	8.27%	5.28%
8	7.68%	4.86%	3.90%
9	8.48%	6.13%	4.37%
10	7.46%	4.35%	3.81%
11	6.78%	4.51%	3.59%
12	6.18%	4.27%	3.50%

placed pin coordinates from the placements of seven design blocks, including leon3mp and netcard from [15]; theia, jpeg, aes and mpeg from [20]; and an ARM Cortex A53 [18]. The placements are obtained using two leading commercial place-and-route tools, Cadence Innovus 15.2 [19] and Synopsys ICC L-2016.03-SP4 [22] with foundry enablements at 28nm and 16nm. We also extract the placements of the DAC-2012 benchmark suite [17] from two well-known academic placers, i.e., Capo [4] and ePlace [12]. These placements are collectively referred to as *real pointsets* in the rest of this paper. Table 2 shows that the percentage of any two points in a real pointset sharing the same x-coordinate or y-coordinate is less than 11%, supporting our assumption of distinct x- and y-coordinates.

We define *L-ness* of P as the ratio of $R(P)$ to $B(P)$, where $R(P)$ is the area of the *largest empty (isothetic) rectangle* that (i) is contained in the bounding box of P, (ii) contains one corner of the bounding box of P, and (iii) contains no points in P. High $R(P)/B(P)$ ratio corresponds to large L-ness.

2.2 Probability that k Points Define the Bounding Box

A bounding box can be represented by four extreme coordinate values, i.e., x_{min}, x_{max}, y_{min} and y_{max}. Given unique x- and y-coordinates, at most four points of a pointset can define the pointset's bounding box, where each of the points provides exactly one of the four extreme coordinates. Further, at least two points define the bounding box, where each of the points contains one extreme x-coordinate and one extreme y-coordinate. We use $Pr(p, k)$ to denote the probability that the bounding box of a pointset P (having cardinality p) is defined by k points ($k \in \{2, 3, 4\}$).

For $k = 2$, assume that points $p_1 = (x_1, y_1)$ and $p_2 = (x_2, y_2)$ define the bounding box. Then, x_1 (resp. y_1) must be x_{min} or x_{max} (resp. y_{min} or y_{max}) out of the p x-coordinates (resp. y-coordinates), and x_2 (resp. y_2) can only be the other extreme x (resp. y)-coordinate out of $p - 1$ x-coordinates (resp. y-coordinates). Thus, Equation (1) gives the probability $Pr(p, 2)$.

For $k = 4$, each of four points can define only one extreme coordinate of the bounding box. Assume that these points $p_1 = (x_{min}, \neg(y_{min} \vee y_{max}))$, $p_2 = (x_{max}, \neg(y_{min} \vee y_{max}))$, $p_3 = (\neg(x_{min} \vee x_{max}), y_{min})$, and $p_4 = (\neg(x_{min} \vee x_{max}), y_{max})$. Then, the probability that four points define the bounding box is as given in Equation (3). Supplemental equations using chain rules to derive probabilities are given in Equations (4)–(7). For example, $Pr(p_1)$ is computed by finding the probability that a point has the minimum x-coordinate and not an extreme y-coordinate. These probabilities are each computed separately and are then multiplied together since they are independent. The remaining probabilities in Equations (4)–(7) are computed in a similar fashion.

Table 3: $Pr(p, k)$ for $p \in [3, 10]$ and $k \in \{2, 3, 4\}$.

p	$Pr(p, k = 2)$	$Pr(p, k = 3)$	$Pr(p, k = 4)$
3	0.3333	0.6667	0.0000
4	0.1667	0.6667	0.1667
5	0.1000	0.6000	0.3000
6	0.0667	0.5333	0.4000
7	0.0476	0.4762	0.4762
8	0.0357	0.4286	0.5357
9	0.0278	0.3889	0.5833
10	0.0222	0.3556	0.6222

$$Pr(p, k = 2) = \binom{p}{2}\left(\frac{2}{p}\right)^2\left(\frac{1}{p-1}\right)^2 \tag{1}$$

$$Pr(p, k = 3) = 1 - Pr(p, k = 2) - Pr(p, k = 4) \tag{2}$$

$$Pr(p, k = 4) = 4!\binom{p}{4}Pr(p_1 \, p_2 \, p_3 \, p_4)$$

$$= 4!\binom{p}{4}Pr(p_1)Pr(p_2|p_1)Pr(p_3|p_1 p_2)Pr(p_4|p_1 p_2 p_3)$$

$$= \binom{p}{4}\left(\frac{4!}{(p^2)(p-1)^2}\right) \tag{3}$$

For the remaining case of $k = 3$, we can calculate the probability $Pr(p, 3)$ using Equation (2). Table 3 provides a lookup table for $Pr(p, k)$ for $k \in \{2, 3, 4\}$ and $p \in [3, 10]$.

$$Pr(p_1) = \left(\frac{1}{p}\right)\left(\frac{p-2}{p}\right) \tag{4}$$

$$Pr(p_2|p_1) = \left(\frac{1}{p-1}\right)\left(\frac{p-3}{p-1}\right) \tag{5}$$

$$Pr(p_3|p_1 \cdot p_2) = \left(\frac{p-2}{p-2}\right)\left(\frac{1}{p-2}\right) \tag{6}$$

$$Pr(p_4|p_1 \cdot p_2 \cdot p_3) = \left(\frac{p-3}{p-3}\right)\left(\frac{1}{p-3}\right) \tag{7}$$

We use this probability in Algorithm 2 to determine the parameter k. Subsequently, we use Algorithm 2 to create the *real'* pointsets, as described in Section 4.

2.3 Independence of AR and $R(P)/B(P)$

To justify the experimental methodology used below, we prove the intuitive claim that $R(P)/B(P)$ is preserved when a 2D pointset P is "stretched" (by scaling of x-coordinates and of y-coordinates) into a pointset P' that has a different aspect ratio. We refer to this property of pointsets as *independence* of AR and $R(P)/B(P)$. We show this independence of AR and $R(P)/B(P)$ by (i) exhibiting an appropriate 1-1 correspondence between pointsets P with bounding box area $B(P)$ and pointsets P' with bounding box area $B(P')$, then (ii) showing that the ratio $R(P)/B(P) = R(P')/B(P')$ is preserved by this correspondence. In Subsection 3.1, we measure $R(P)/B(P)$ without considering the effect of AR on L-ness of pointsets. Hence, we prove the independence of $R(P)/B(P)$ with AR below.

Fact 1. Scaling of x- and y-coordinates provides a (bidirectional) 1-1 mapping between pointsets P having unit square bounding box $B(P)$, and pointsets P', with $|P| = |P'|$ and bounding box B' having an arbitrary aspect ratio.

Fact 1 is established as follows. Denote the width and height of B' are w and h, respectively. We obtain pointset P' from P by scaling x- and y-coordinates of points in P by w and h, respectively. As a result, the x- and y-coordinates of the bounding box edges of P' are also scaled by w and h. The inverse scaling procedure can be applied to restore any such P' to the original P. The scaling of coordinates thus provides a 1-1 correspondence between pointsets having the same cardinality but different bounding box ARs.

Next, we say that the point (x_i, y_i) in P *corresponds* to a point (x_i', y_i') in P' if $(x_i', y_i') = (w \cdot x_i, h \cdot y_i)$. A bounding box-edge of P analogously *corresponds* to a scaled bounding box-edge of P'. For example, Figure 5(b) shows a pointset P' obtained by scaling P (in Figure 5(a)) by $(w, h) = (w, 1)$. From our definitions, we say that the point (x_i, y_i) in P corresponds to the point (x_i', y_i') in P', and the edge $x = x_{sp}$ of P corresponds to the edge $x = x_{sp}'$ of P'.

The following Fact 2 holds for pointsets (i) P with its largest empty rectangle defined by two edges of the bounding box, $x = x_{sp}$ and $y = y_{sp}$, and two points, (x_1, y_1) and (x_2, y_2); and (ii) P', which is created by scaling the x- and y-coordinates of points in P by w and h, respectively.

Fact 2. Given P and P', the edges and points that define $R(P)/B(P)$ correspond to edges and points that define $R(P')/B(P')$.

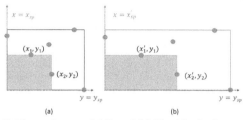

Figure 5: The pointsets (a) P and (b) P' with the largest empty rectangle colored green.

Fact 2 is established as follows. P contains p points, i.e., $P = \{(x_1, y_1), (x_2, y_2), \cdots, (x_p, y_p)\}$. Without loss of generality, we assume that the bounding box of P has $AR = 1$, and we only scale points in pointset P in the x-direction by w (i.e., $w > 0$, $h = 1$) to obtain P'. P' also contains p points, $P' = \{(x_1', y_1), (x_2', y_2), \cdots, (x_p', y_p)\}$, where $(x_j', y_j) = (w \cdot x_j, y_j)$ for $k \in [1, p]$. The following treats the case illustrated in Figure 5, namely, the case with the empty rectangle at the lower-left corner of the bounding box, i.e., $x_{sp} < x_1 < x_2$, and $y_{sp} < y_2 < y_1$. The other three cases are similarly analyzed. $R(P)$ is defined as

$$R(P) = (x_2 - x_{sp}) \cdot (y_1 - y_{sp}) \qquad (8)$$

Assume toward a contradiction that the edges $x = w \cdot x_{sp}$, $y = y_{sp}$, and the points (x_1', y_1) and (x_2', y_2) do not form the largest empty rectangle of P'. Then, there must exist an empty rectangle of P' such that

$$R(P') > w \cdot R(P) \qquad (9)$$

Suppose that the largest empty rectangle of P' is defined by the edges $w \cdot x_{sp}$ and y_{sp} and two points (x_m', y_m) and (x_n', y_n), with $\{n, m\} \neq \{1, 2\}$ and $x_{sp}' < x_m' < x_n'$ and $y_{sp} < y_n < y_m$. Then, $R(P')$ is calculated as

$$R(P') = (x_n' - x_{sp}') \cdot (y_m - y_{sp}) \qquad (10)$$
$$= (w \cdot x_n - w \cdot x_{sp}) \cdot (y_m - y_{sp}) \qquad (11)$$
$$= w \cdot (x_n - x_{sp}) \cdot (y_m - y_{sp}) \qquad (12)$$

According to the definition of $R(P)$, $(x_n - x_{sp}) \cdot (y_m - y_{sp}) \leq R(P)$. Therefore,

$$R(P') \leq w \cdot R(P) \qquad (13)$$

which contradicts Equation (9). This establishes Fact 2.

2.4 Efficient Calculation of $R(P)$

We now describe an efficient method to obtain $R(P)$. Each of the four corners of the bounding box may be the intersection of the two edges that form $R(P)$. For simplicity, we only describe our algorithm for the corner (x_{min}, y_{min}). The final result can be obtained by

invoking the algorithm on each corner of the bounding box of P with small modifications and then returning the largest value, at the cost of a constant-factor complexity increase.

Algorithm 1 describes the calculation of $R(P)$. The algorithm begins with pointset P sorted in ascending order of x-coordinates. Lines 1 and 2 perform initializations. In Lines 3 – 8, we check whether the current point has a smaller y-coordinate than the stored value of y_0. If so, the lower-left corner will form an empty rectangle, and we update the maximum known rectangle area. The same procedure is followed to compute the largest empty rectangle at the remaining corners. We step through the sorted list of points, check if each pair of points forms an empty rectangle, and if so, update the maximum known rectangle area. The time complexity of the algorithm is lower-bounded by the implied sorting step, which gives a $\Theta(p \log p)$ time complexity.

Algorithm 1 CalcRP (Assuming lower-left corner is selected).

Input: P with x-coordinates in ascending order
Output: $R(P)$
1: $R(P) = 0$
2: $y_0 = y_1$
3: **for** $i = 2$ to p **do**
4:    **if** $y_i \leq y_0$ **then**
5:       $R(P) \leftarrow \max(R(P), (x_i - x_{min}) \cdot (y_0 - y_{min}))$
6:       $y_0 \leftarrow y_i$
7:    **end if**
8: **end for**
9: **return** $R(P)$

---

3 REAL VS. RANDOM POINTSETS

In this section, we empirically demonstrate the significant difference in L-ness between real and random pointsets. We then present a method for generating pointsets with prescribed L-ness and aspect ratio.

3.1 L-ness of Real vs. Random Pointsets

We experimentally compare the $R(P)/B(P)$ distribution of 100K random pointsets with the $R(P)/B(P)$ distribution of real (placed net pins) pointsets. Figure 6 shows the distributions of $R(P)/B(P)$ in random and real pointsets. In each plot, the x-axis denotes the $R(P)/B(P)$ ratio and the y-axis denotes the fraction of nets for each $R(P)/B(P)$ value. From the figure, we see that the placements from commercial and academic placers result in pointsets with significantly larger L-ness (i.e., larger $R(P)/B(P)$ ratio) than random pointsets.[3] We also observe that the qualitative difference from random pointsets holds across academic and commercial placers.

We believe that this large L-ness arises due to the following reasons. Given a large chip area and a relatively small bounding box (b_0) area for any net n_0, it is intuitive that the other nets incident to the cells of net n_0 have their bounding boxes outside b_0. This causes the cells to get pulled towards the boundary, and extend the boundaries of net n_0 due to multiple inter-related nets (i.e., intersecting hyperedges of the netlist). Further, low net degrees usually result in a geometrically asymmetrical cell distribution, increasing the L-ness of a particular net.

To confirm the statistical difference for $p \in [3, 12]$, we perform two tests: (i) bootstrapping the mean with a 95% confidence interval [2], and (ii) Two-Sample Kolmogorov-Smirnov (KS) Test [16]. The bootstrap test provides a 0.95 confidence interval on the average of $R(P)/B(P)$ for 10000 random pointsets. We compare the means of $R(P)/B(P)$ values for real pointsets with the 0.95 confidence interval. Figure 7 shows that the means of real pointsets do not lie within the confidence intervals of random pointsets for

---

[3]We have separately extracted net pin locations from an advanced processor design from a leading semiconductor company, and confirmed that the $R(P)/B(P)$ distributions follow the same trend as in Figure 6.

Table 4: D_{nm} **for** $p \in [3, 12]$ **using ICC/Innovus, Capo and ePlace placers.**

p	ICC/Innovus	Capo	ePlace
3	3.363	6.160	3.256
4	3.788	6.204	3.926
5	5.159	6.913	4.240
6	4.641	5.605	3.341
7	3.658	5.150	2.884
8	3.219	4.500	2.481
9	1.737	2.953	2.747
10	4.754	3.413	3.777
11	5.790	3.987	3.162
12	7.106	4.028	4.708

any $p \in [3, 12]$. Hence, real pointsets have a statistically significant larger $R(P)/B(P)$ compared to random pointsets.

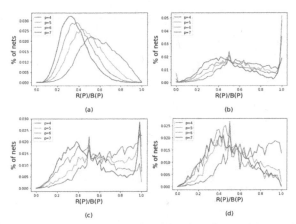

Figure 6: Distribution of $R(P)/B(P)$ **from (a) random pointsets, (b) ICC [22] and Innovus [19] placements, (c) Capo [4] placements, and (d) ePlace [12] placements.**

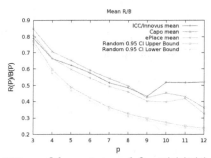

Figure 7: 95% confidence interval for $R(P)/B(P)$ **in random pointsets and mean** $R(P)/B(P)$ **for real pointsets.**

The Two-Sample Kolmogorov-Smirnov (KS) Test [2] states that for a confidence interval of 95%, we have a statistically significant difference if the KS statistic $D_{nm} > 1.36$. The KS statistic is computed as

$$D_{nm} = \sqrt{nm/(n+m)} \cdot sup|F(x) - G(x)| \qquad (14)$$

where n and m are sample sizes of random and real pointsets respectively, F and G are cumulative distribution functions (CDFs) (with 100 bins of width 0.01) of $R(P)/B(P)$ values of random and real pointsets respectively. sup is the maximum distance between F and G for $0 \leq x \leq 1$. Table 4 shows the KS statistics. We see that $D_{nm} > 1.36$ for all random versus real pointsets, again confirming the statistically significant difference between $R(P)/B(P)$ distributions of random and real pointsets.

Algorithm 2 GenRandPointset.

Input: $p, k, RPBP, \Delta_{err}, AR$
Output: P with $R(P)/B(P) \in [RPBP - \Delta_{err}, RPBP + \Delta_{err}]$
1: $P \leftarrow \varnothing$
2: $R(P)/B(P) \leftarrow 0$
3: $P \leftarrow getBBoxPts(P, k, RPBP, \Delta_{err}, AR)$
4: **while** $|P| < p$ **do**
5:      $P \leftarrow AddPoint(P)$
6:      **if** $calcRP(P) < RPBP - \Delta_{err}$ **then**
7:          $RemovePoint(P)$
8:      **end if**
9: **end while**
10: **if** $calcRP(P) \leq RPBP + \Delta_{err}$ **then**
11:      **return** P
12: **else**
13:      **return** -1
14: **end if**

3.2 Pointset Generation

Since random pointsets differ significantly from real placed pin locations, and since it is challenging to obtain real placement data, there is a need to generate pointsets with prescribed L-ness. Here, we present an algorithm (Algorithm 2) to generate a random pointset with prescribed $R(P)/B(P)$ (L-ness) and aspect ratio (AR). The inputs include #pins p, intended number of points k that define the bounding box (see Section 2.2), intended L-ness range [$RPBP - \Delta_{err}, RPBP + \Delta_{err}$], and aspect ratio AR. The output is a pointset P that satisfies the L-ness range constraint.

Lines 1 and 2 perform initializations. In Line 3, we generate k points on the bounding box. Since $R(P)/B(P)$ will monotonically decrease as we add one more point to an existing pointset, the function $getBBoxPts$ comprehends the desired L-ness range and always gives k points with $R(P)/B(P) \geq RPBP - \Delta_{err}$. These k points form a bounding box with area 1M x 1M and aspect ratio AR. In Lines $5 - 9$, we iteratively add one point with random location strictly inside the bounding box and check L-ness. If we do not meet the L-ness lower bound, the last added point is removed and reselected. The points are added with unique x- and y-coordinates, following the assumption of points in general position in Section 2.1. In Lines 11 and 12, we return the pointset satisfying the L-ness range constraint and discard the result otherwise. In our actual implementation, we can reuse discarded pointsets when generating for a different L-ness range – e.g., during the process of reproducing a distribution such as in Figure 6(b)-(d).

Algorithm 2 is qualitatively equivalent to randomly generating a pointset and checking if the pointset is valid, i.e., having $R(P)/B(P) \in [RPBP - \Delta_{err}, RPBP + \Delta_{err}]$. If we assume towards a contradiction that it does not, then at least one of the points we remove in Line 8 would contribute to a valid pointset. Since adding points within the bounding box cannot increase the $R(P)/B(P)$ value of a pointset, the points in this pointset cannot be part of a pointset with $R(P)/B(P)$ within the prescribed L-ness range. Hence, Algorithm 2 returns qualitatively the same pointsets as repeated generation of a pointset and checking whether the pointset has $R(P)/B(P)$ within the prescribed L-ness range. However, Algorithm 2 is much more efficient, e.g., we can produce 100K pointsets targeted to match the distribution of Figure 6(d) with $p = 7$ in 75.54 seconds with a 2.7 GHz Intel Xeon server.

4 IMPLICATIONS FOR RSMT HEURISTICS

In this section, we perform experiments to analyze the impact of L-ness on the performance (tree cost / wirelength estimation) of various RSMT heuristics. We first show how wirelength changes with different L-ness. Then, we show the RSMT cost difference between random and real pointsets.

4.1 Impact of L-ness on RSMT Heuristics

In this subsection, we study the change in wirelength with $R(P)/B(P)$ (L-ness). We generate 10K pointsets for each $R(P)/B(P)$ from 0.2

to 0.8, with a step of 0.1 and $\Delta_{err} = 0.02$. We use a fixed $B(P)$ size of 1M×1M. We evaluate the wirelength cost of four heuristics: (i) rectilinear MST implementation by Kahng et al. [21] using Prim's algorithm, (ii) Prim-Dijkstra (PD) [1] with $\alpha = 0.3$ (PD 0.3) and with $\alpha = 1.0$ (PD 1.0 constructs a shortest path tree, and is equivalent to Dijkstra's algorithm [9]), (iii) HVW [11] algorithm as a post-processing of PD 0.3 (HVW 0.3) and PD 1.0 (HVW 1.0), and (iv) FLUTE [8].

Figure 8 shows the wirelength values. The x-axis denotes the $R(P)/B(P)$ ratio and the y-axis represents the total wirelength for all 10K pointsets per each $R(P)/B(P)$. Each row of figures represents a particular value of $AR = \{1, 2, 4\}$; each column represents a value of $p = \{4, 5, 7\}$. We see that wirelength decreases as $R(P)/B(P)$ increases, indicating that we should expect lower wirelength for real pointsets which tend to have larger $R(P)/B(P)$ than random pointsets. Also, difference in wirelength among heuristics decreases with increase in $R(P)/B(P)$. Although PD 0.3 and HVW 0.3 have different optimization objectives (i.e., radius and wirelength balance) from FLUTE, wirelength follows the same trend with $R(P)/B(P)$ for all heuristics. These results suggest that assessments of cost or accuracy benefit versus runtime overhead when using these heuristics may have been misguided by the use of random pointsets in experimental studies, and that random pointsets might not give sufficient insight into the benefits of RSMT heuristics. We also observe that crossovers between heuristics tend to decline as AR increases.

4.2 RSMT Cost on Real Pointsets

Previous works [1][11] use random pointsets to verify the accuracy of RSMT heuristics. However, we reevaluate their accuracy and show their performance difference considering L-ness in real pointsets. We first generate *real' pointsets* with $R(P)/B(P)$ and AR distributions of *real pointsets* from academic and commercial placements, and show that our Algorithm 2 generates statistically similar pointsets to real placements. We then use *real' pointsets* to analyze the accuracy of heuristic WL estimation.

To generate real' pointsets, we extract the distributions of $R(P)/B(P)$ and AR from real pointsets for $p \in [3, 12]$ and use these distributions to create 10K real' pointsets for each p. We run FLUTE on all pointsets and perform the two-sample Kolmogorov-Smirnov test (KS) test on the wirelength distributions with a 95% confidence interval, using 50 bins to generate the CDFs. Table 5 shows that eight of nine values are smaller than the minimum D_{nm} value in Table 4. This shows that real' pointsets give a good representation of real pointsets for most cases. Figure 9 shows one case with a Kolmogorov-Smirnov failure. However, the probability distributions of wirelengths from real' and real pointset distributions are still similar in appearance.

Table 5: D_{nm} for wirelengths on real and real' pointsets.

p	4	5	6	7	8	9	10	11	12
D_{nm}	1.189	1.063	1.402	1.788	1.690	1.621	1.026	1.086	1.601

We use the above real' pointsets to evaluate the accuracy of each heuristics. Tables 6 and 7 report the errors of these heuristics versus FLUTE[4], and compare the differences in errors for real and random pointsets. A positive value in Table 6 means a larger wirelength is given compared to FLUTE.

Table 7 reports the percentage difference for each heuristic between real and random pointsets as $Error_{real} - Error_{random}$. A negative value means a smaller error when using real pointsets, and a positive value means a larger error, compared to using random pointsets. Hence, Tables 6 and 7 show that the errors of heuristics

---

[4]Errors are calculated relative to FLUTE, since FLUTE is optimal for $p \leq 9$ and introduces on average 0.16% RSMT error for $p \in [10, 17]$ [8].

Table 6: Percent error of heuristics vs. FLUTE for random and real pointsets.

p	Percent error of heuristics vs. FLUTE on random pointsets				
	HVW 0.3	RMST	PD 0.3	HVW 1.0	PD 1.0
4	1.93%	10.41%	12.35%	13.57%	44.05%
5	2.76%	11.15%	13.94%	16.14%	51.22%
6	3.38%	11.46%	14.96%	19.00%	56.94%
7	3.91%	11.52%	15.44%	21.08%	61.72%
8	4.47%	11.68%	16.02%	23.06%	65.29%
9	4.80%	11.77%	16.44%	24.72%	68.69%
10	5.07%	11.72%	16.71%	26.04%	71.06%
11	5.49%	11.80%	17.20%	27.34%	73.57%
12	5.57%	11.73%	17.24%	28.55%	75.81%
p	Percent error of heuristics vs. FLUTE on real pointsets				
	HVW 0.3	RMST	PD 0.3	HVW 1.0	PD 1.0
4	1.54%	8.96%	10.43%	15.29%	50.04%
5	1.92%	9.03%	10.90%	18.09%	58.06%
6	2.35%	9.31%	11.64%	20.37%	63.56%
7	2.99%	9.86%	12.77%	22.52%	68.10%
8	3.37%	10.19%	13.42%	24.42%	72.17%
9	4.01%	10.75%	14.58%	26.05%	74.38%
10	3.93%	10.38%	14.18%	28.00%	78.88%
11	4.19%	10.46%	14.44%	29.78%	82.00%
12	4.57%	10.60%	15.05%	30.89%	83.70%

Table 7: Difference in % error between heuristics and FLUTE for real and random pointsets.

p	Difference in % error between real and random pointsets				
	HVW 0.3	RMST	PD 0.3	HVW 1.0	PD 1.0
4	-0.39%	-1.45%	-1.92%	1.72%	5.99%
5	-0.84%	-2.12%	-3.04%	1.95%	6.84%
6	-1.03%	-2.15%	-3.32%	1.37%	6.62%
7	-0.92%	-1.66%	-2.67%	1.44%	6.38%
8	-1.10%	-1.49%	-2.60%	1.36%	6.88%
9	-0.79%	-1.02%	-1.86%	1.33%	5.69%
10	-1.14%	-1.34%	-2.53%	1.96%	7.82%
11	-1.30%	-1.34%	-2.76%	2.44%	8.43%
12	-1.00%	-1.13%	-2.19%	2.34%	7.89%

HVW 0.3, RMST and PD 0.3 are overestimated, whereas the errors of heuristics HVW 1.0 and PD 1.0 are underestimated. Since FLUTE is the most accurate of these heuristics and wirelength can only be overestimated when constructing spanning trees, all values in the tables are positive.

Table 7 can also be seen as a lookup table to improve the accuracy of existing RSMT cost estimators. For a given heuristic, more accurate wirelength values can be obtained by subtracting the errors reported in Table 7 from the wirelength of random pointsets.

5 AN IMPROVED WL ESTIMATION LOOKUP TABLE

In this section, we present a lookup table (LUT) for improved wirelength estimation. Previously, Caldwell et al. [3] constructed a lookup table indexed with p and AR. We build upon this table and add $R(P)/B(P)$ as a third parameter dimension for improved accuracy of wirelength estimation, as shown in Section 4. We use FLUTE to obtain the RSMT wirelength (see Footnote 4).

Table 8 shows a portion of our lookup table. [5] In the table, we report three sets of values for each p. The first row ($W1$) shows the FLUTE wirelength value by generating and averaging the wirelength over 1000 pointsets with $AR = \{1, 2, 4\}$. These values are equivalent to the wirelength values reported by Caldwell et al. [3]. The second row ($W2$) shows the FLUTE wirelength with specific $R(P)/B(P) = \{0.2, 0.4, 0.6, 0.8\}$ (generated using Algorithm 2), averaged over 1000 pointsets. The third row ($W3$) is the percent error between $W1$ and $W2$, i.e., $\frac{W2-W1}{W1} \cdot 100\%$. For example, with $p = 6$ and $AR = 1$, we see that the $W1$ row contains the value 2.39; this is the single value for estimated RSMT cost given by [3]. The $W2$ row contains four values, 2.71, 2.37, 2.22 and 2.10; these are our estimated RSMT costs with $R(P)/B(P)$ ratios of 0.2, 0.4, 0.6 and 0.8, respectively. The $W3$ row gives the four corresponding percentage differences between the L-ness dependent estimates and the single

---

[5]The entire lookup table is available at http://vlsicad.ucsd.edu/~sriram/Final_WL_estimate_LUT.htm

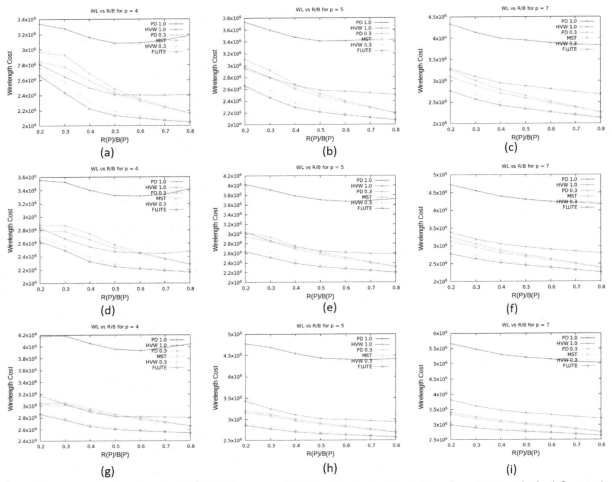

Figure 8: Change in wirelength with $R(P)/B(P)$ for nets with $AR = 1$ (a, b, c), $AR = 2$ (d, e, f) and $AR = 4$ (g, h, i) for $p \in \{4, 5, 7\}$.

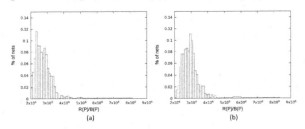

Figure 9: Wirelength distribution functions for (a) real pointsets and (b) real' pointsets for $p = 12$.

estimate of [3]. We omit estimates for $p \in [2, 3]$ since these RSMT costs are the half-perimeter wirelengths of the bounding boxes.

Runtime. We compare the runtime using different wirelength estimators: (i) FLUTE, (ii) our LUT, and (iii) rectilinear MST (RMST) implementation by Kahng et al. [21] using Prim's algorithm.[6] All algorithms are implemented using C and are executed on a 2.7 GHz Intel Xeon server with 8 threads. We evaluate using 500K real and random pointsets. Table 9 shows that our improved lookup table

runs significantly faster than FLUTE for all values of $p \in [2, 12]$ and faster than RMST except for $p = 4$. We believe that this significant speedup ($\sim 10\times$), at the cost of small loss of accuracy of WL estimation, can be beneficial in modern-day contexts that involve very large designs, highly iterative methods, and a requirement for reduced tool turnaround times.

Accuracy. Table 10 reports the percent error, along with standard deviation and maximum error in wirelength estimates compared to FLUTE, using our lookup table (LUT), Caldwell LUT [3] and RMST implementation [21]. Percent error is calculated as $Error = \left(\frac{WL_{heur} - WL_{FLUTE}}{WL_{FLUTE}}\right) \cdot 100\%$. Our lookup table dominates that of [3] in all error metrics evaluated. However, our improved lookup table does give a higher standard deviation and maximum absolute error for higher values of p when compared to RMST. We note that the LUT errors reported in Table 10 are the averages of absolute errors, whereas RMST error is always positive. Figure 10 shows error distributions for the LUT and RMST estimators for $p = 9$.

WL estimation for pointsets with $p \in [2, 3]$ using our LUT has no error. (In our studies, 68% of the nets in a 16nm implementation of ARM Cortex A53 have $p = 2$ or $p = 3$.) The WL estimation error using our LUT for $p \in [4, 12]$ is $1 - 2\%$ lower than the error using

---

[6]We use an $O(n^2)$ implementation since it runs much faster than other $O(n \log n)$ algorithms for small p.

Table 8: Wirelength lookup table using aspect ratio and $R(P)/B(P)$.

AR		1				2				4			
$R(P)/B(P)$		0.2	0.4	0.6	0.8	0.2	0.4	0.6	0.8	0.2	0.4	0.6	0.8
p=4	W1	2.14				2.25				2.60			
	W2	2.66	2.23	2.10	2.04	2.63	2.32	2.22	2.17	2.86	2.66	2.58	2.54
	W3	24.37	4.24	-2.03	-4.51	16.89	3.31	-1.48	-3.77	9.93	2.20	-0.76	-2.24
p=5	W1	2.27				2.36				2.69			
	W2	2.66	2.30	2.16	2.08	2.63	2.39	2.27	2.20	2.86	2.71	2.63	2.58
	W3	17.02	1.22	-4.80	-8.57	11.41	1.25	-3.67	-6.84	6.38	0.66	-2.12	-4.19
p=6	W1	2.39				2.48				2.78			
	W2	2.71	2.37	2.22	2.10	2.70	2.45	2.34	2.23	2.93	2.77	2.69	2.61
	W3	13.58	-0.90	-7.21	-12.00	8.95	-1.13	-5.81	-10.28	5.39	-0.30	-3.17	-6.21
p=7	W1	2.52				2.59				2.87			
	W2	2.78	2.44	2.27	2.13	2.77	2.53	2.39	2.26	3.00	2.82	2.73	2.64
	W3	10.13	-3.32	-9.84	-15.42	7.12	-2.38	-7.76	-12.70	4.56	-1.58	-4.73	-8.13
p=8	W1	2.63				2.69				2.96			
	W2	2.83	2.50	2.32	2.16	2.86	2.59	2.44	2.29	3.06	2.89	2.79	2.67
	W3	7.57	-4.81	-11.62	-17.96	6.18	-3.72	-9.30	-15.01	3.50	-2.33	-5.86	-9.96
p=9	W1	2.73				2.81				3.03			
	W2	2.90	2.57	2.37	2.18	2.92	2.67	2.49	2.32	3.13	2.95	2.83	2.69
	W3	6.35	-5.72	-13.07	-20.02	3.99	-5.14	-11.30	-17.51	3.34	-2.72	-6.49	-11.14
p=10	W1	2.84				2.91				3.13			
	W2	2.98	2.65	2.42	2.21	2.99	2.73	2.54	2.34	3.19	2.99	2.88	2.72
	W3	4.77	-6.80	-14.68	-22.07	2.79	-6.24	-12.71	-19.53	1.99	-3.70	-8.10	-13.16
p=11	W1	2.95				3.00				3.22			
	W2	3.03	2.71	2.47	2.24	3.07	2.79	2.59	2.37	3.27	3.07	2.91	2.75
	W3	2.65	-8.22	-16.15	-24.15	2.38	-6.85	-13.83	-21.04	1.64	-4.52	-9.48	-14.69
p=12	W1	3.04				3.09				3.30			
	W2	3.11	2.77	2.52	2.27	3.15	2.85	2.63	2.40	3.33	3.13	2.97	2.77
	W3	2.43	-8.85	-16.97	-25.45	1.80	-7.68	-14.89	-22.47	1.04	-5.14	-10.07	-15.97
p=13	W1	3.14				3.20				3.39			
	W2	3.18	2.84	2.56	2.29	3.21	2.92	2.68	2.42	3.40	3.19	3.02	2.80
	W3	1.14	-9.56	-18.48	-26.94	0.17	-8.70	-16.25	-24.27	0.44	-5.80	-11.02	-17.28
p=14	W1	3.23				3.27				3.48			
	W2	3.24	2.90	2.62	2.32	3.28	2.97	2.73	2.44	3.47	3.25	3.05	2.83
	W3	0.45	-10.08	-19.00	-28.17	0.27	-8.82	-16.49	-25.32	-0.43	-6.64	-12.22	-18.76
p=15	W1	3.34				3.38				3.55			
	W2	3.32	2.97	2.66	2.35	3.35	3.04	2.77	2.48	3.54	3.29	3.10	2.86
	W3	-0.60	-11.01	-20.45	-29.62	-0.86	-10.06	-18.19	-26.71	-0.31	-7.20	-12.75	-19.51

Table 9: Execution time (seconds) for 0.5M pointsets with $p \in [2, 12]$.

p	Random pointsets			Real pointsets		
	FLUTE	Impr. LUT	RMST	FLUTE	Impr. LUT	RMST
2	0.051	0.003	0.012	0.050	0.003	0.012
3	0.185	0.004	0.023	0.254	0.006	0.040
4	0.229	0.047	0.045	0.295	0.065	0.050
5	0.262	0.060	0.061	0.240	0.061	0.063
6	0.299	0.077	0.095	0.328	0.116	0.109
7	0.352	0.093	0.135	0.318	0.089	0.130
8	0.431	0.111	0.173	0.368	0.104	0.171
9	0.576	0.127	0.216	0.492	0.119	0.223
10	1.192	0.146	0.258	1.248	0.134	0.259
11	1.761	0.164	0.303	1.241	0.152	0.314
12	1.804	0.184	0.378	1.607	0.166	0.360

Table 10: Error for $p \in [2, 12]$ with real pointsets.

p	Absolute Error			Std. Dev. of Abs. Error			Max. Absolute Error		
	Impr. LUT	Cald-well	RMST	Impr. LUT	Cald-well	RMST	Impr. LUT	Cald-well	RMST
3	0.00%	0.00%	6.13%	0.00%	0.00%	7.81%	0.00%	0.00%	33.31%
4	4.06%	5.61%	6.01%	3.62%	3.67%	6.49%	24.51%	28.19%	46.17%
5	4.47%	7.14%	6.20%	3.76%	4.48%	6.01%	24.94%	23.44%	42.73%
6	4.70%	8.07%	6.48%	3.95%	5.44%	5.66%	25.53%	25.24%	36.02%
7	4.93%	8.75%	6.82%	4.04%	6.41%	5.36%	28.20%	25.71%	34.60%
8	5.17%	9.85%	7.15%	4.21%	7.66%	5.14%	27.56%	31.46%	32.25%
9	5.28%	9.81%	7.73%	4.21%	7.88%	4.90%	30.95%	37.03%	32.13%
10	5.75%	11.38%	7.35%	4.69%	9.39%	4.76%	32.94%	42.16%	28.06%
11	6.00%	12.47%	7.14%	4.85%	10.37%	4.59%	37.01%	46.94%	27.46%
12	6.46%	12.62%	7.18%	5.32%	10.82%	4.58%	40.35%	52.94%	28.25%

RMST as an estimate. Thus, in terms of speed and accuracy, the new LUT provides a non-dominated wirelength estimate.[7]

6 CONCLUSION

In this paper, we have given a formal definition of the concept of *L-ness*, that is, the phenomenon that a net's pin locations within a real placement tend to be clustered towards two adjacent edges of

---

[7]For $p \in [10, 12]$ our LUT is approximately 10 times faster than FLUTE and twice as fast as RMST.

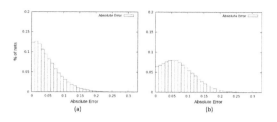

Figure 10: Error distributions with (a) lookup table and (b) RMST estimators for $p = 9$.

the net's bounding box. We have provided empirical data showing the extent to which real pointsets have larger L-ness values than random pointsets. This data suggests at least the possibility that previous usage of random pointsets may have led to inaccurate assessments of RSMT heuristics and RSMT cost estimators. With this in mind, we describe a pointset generation function which can produce artificial pointsets that are similar to real placed pointsets. We furthermore present an improved lookup table for RSMT cost estimation that is sensitive to L-ness of a pointset; its implementation gives a speed-accuracy tradeoff point between FLUTE [8] and a fast rectilinear MST implementation [21].

Our ongoing and future works seek ways to exploit the L-ness attribute to achieve better estimates of routed WL or FLUTE heuristic RSMT costs – e.g., after placement and without any running of global/detailed routers. We are also exploring the direct optimization of an L-ness-aware wirelength estimate during placement. A high-fidelity wirelength predictor, congestion- and DRC-aware wirelength predictor, as well as hierarchical placement-based predictors are also of interest. Other future directions include tree topology generation considering L-ness and objectives such as timing or power, as well as comprehension of driver vs. sink pin locations.

7 ACKNOWLEDGMENTS

We thank the authors of ePlace [12] for providing the executable that we used in our experiments. ABKGroup research is supported by NSF, Samsung, Qualcomm, NXP, Mentor Graphics and C-DEN.

REFERENCES

[1] C. J. Alpert, T. C. Hu, J. H. Huang, A. B. Kahng and D. Karger, "Prim-Dijkstra Tradeoffs for Improved Performance-driven Routing Tree Design", *IEEE TCAD* 14(7) (1995), pp. 890-896.
[2] J. Bloom and J. Orloff, *18.05 Introduction to Probability and Statistics*, Cambridge, Massachusetts Institute of Technology: MIT OpenCourseWare, 2014. https://ocw.mit.edu
[3] A. E. Caldwell, A. B. Kahng, S. Mantik, I. L. Markov and A. Zelikovsky, "On Wirelength Estimations for Row-Based Placement", *IEEE TCAD* 18(9) (1999), pp. 1265-1278.
[4] A. E. Caldwell, A. B. Kahng and I. L. Markov, "Can Recursive Bisection Alone Produce Routable Placements", *Proc. DAC*, 2000, pp. 477-482.
[5] W.-T. J. Chan, A. B. Kahng and J. Li, "Revisiting 3DIC Benefit with Multiple Tiers", *Proc. SLIP*, 2016, pp. 6:1-6:8.
[6] B. Chazelle, R. L. Drysdale and D. T. Lee, "Computing the Largest Empty Rectangle", *SIAM J. Computing* 15(1) (1986), pp. 300-315.
[7] C. L. Cheng, "RISA: Accurate and Efficient Placement Routability Modeling", *Proc. ICCAD*, 1994, pp. 690-695.
[8] C. Chu and Y. Wong, "FLUTE: Fast Lookup Table Based Rectilinear Steiner Minimal Tree Algorithm for VLSI Design", *IEEE TCAD* 27(1) (2008), pp. 70-83.
[9] E. W. Dijkstra, "A Note on Two Problems in Connexion with Graphs", *Numerische Mathematik* 1 (1959), pp. 269-271.
[10] A. E. Dunlop and B. W. Kernighan, "A Procedure for Placement of Standard-Cell VLSI Circuits", *IEEE TCAD* 4(1) (1985), pp. 92-98.
[11] J. Ho, G. Vijayan and C. K. Wong, "New Algorithms for the Rectilinear Steiner Tree Problem", *IEEE TCAD* 9(2) (1990), pp. 185-193.
[12] J. Lu, H. Zhuang, P. Chen, H. Chang, C.-C. Chang, Y.-C. Wong, L. Sha, D. Huang, Y. Luo, C.-C. Teng and C.-K. Cheng, "ePlace-MS: Electrostatics based Placement for Mixed-Size Circuits", *IEEE TCAD* 34(5) (2015), pp. 685-698.
[13] I. L. Markov, J. Hu and M.-C. Kim, "Progress and Challenges in VLSI Placement Research", *Proc. ICCAD*, 2015, pp. 1985-2003.
[14] A. Naamad, D. T. Lee and W. L. Hsu, "On the Maximum Empty Rectangle Problem", *Discrete Applied Mathematics* 8(3) (1984), pp. 267-277.
[15] M. M. Ozdal, C. Amin, A. Ayupov, S. Burns, G. Wilke and C. Zhuo, "The ISPD-2012 Discrete Cell Sizing Contest and Benchmark Suite", *Proc. ISPD*, 2012, pp. 161-164.
[16] D. Panchenko, *18.650 Statistics for Applications*, Cambridge, Massachusetts Institute of Technology: MIT OpenCourseWare, 2004. https://ocw.mit.edu
[17] N. Viswanathan, C. J. Alpert, C. C. N. Sze, Z. Li and Y. Wei, "The DAC 2012 Routability-driven Placement Contest and Benchmark Suite", *Proc. DAC*, 2012, pp. 774-782.
[18] ARM Cortex A53 Processor. https://developer.arm.com/products/processors/cortex-a/cortex-a53
[19] Cadence Innovus User Guide.
[20] OpenCores: Open Source IP-Cores. http://www.opencores.org
[21] RMST-Pack: Rectilinear Minimum Spanning Tree Algorithms [Source code]. http://vlsicad.ucsd.edu/GSRC/bookshelf/Slots/RSMT/RMST
[22] Synopsys IC Compiler User Guide.

Prim-Dijkstra Revisited: Achieving Superior Timing-driven Routing Trees

Charles J. Alpert[1], Wing-Kai Chow[1], Kwangsoo Han[1,2], Andrew B. Kahng[2,3],

Zhuo Li[1], Derong Liu[1] and Sriram Venkatesh[3]

[1]Cadence Design Systems, Inc., Austin, TX 78759
[3]CSE and [2]ECE Departments, UC San Diego, La Jolla, CA 92093
{kwhan, abk, srvenkat}@ucsd.edu, {alpert, wkchow, kwangsoo, zhuoli, derong}@cadence.com

ABSTRACT

The Prim-Dijkstra (*PD*) construction[1] was first presented over 20 years ago as a way to efficiently trade off between shortest-path and minimum-wirelength routing trees. This approach has stood the test of time, having been integrated into leading semiconductor design methodologies and electronic design automation tools. *PD* optimizes the conflicting objectives of wirelength (WL) and source-sink pathlength (PL) by blending the classic Prim and Dijkstra spanning tree algorithms. However, as this work shows, *PD* can sometimes demonstrate significant suboptimality for both WL and PL. This quality degradation can be especially costly for advanced nodes because (i) wire delays form a much larger component of total stage delay, i.e., timing-driven routing is critical, and (ii) modern designs are severely power-constrained (e.g., mobile, IoT), which makes low-capacitance wiring important. Consequently, achieving a good timing and power tradeoff for routing is required to build a market-leading product[2]. This work introduces a new problem formulation that incorporates the total detour cost in the objective function to optimize the detour to every sink in the tree, not just the worst detour. We then propose a new *PD-II* construction which directly improves upon the original *PD* construction by *repairing* the tree to simultaneously reduce both WL and PL. The *PD-II* approach achieves improvement for both objectives, making it a clear win over *PD*. *PD-II* is a spanning tree algorithm (which is useful for seeding global routing); however, since Steiner trees are needed for timing estimation, this work also includes a post-processing algorithm called *DAS* to convert *PD-II* trees into balanced Steiner trees. Experimental results demonstrate that this construction outperforms the recent state-of-the-art academic tool, SALT [36], for high-fanout nets, achieving up to 36.46% PL improvement with similar WL on average for 20K nets of size ≥ 32 terminals from DAC 2012 contest benchmark designs[37].

ACM Reference Format:
Charles J. Alpert[1], Wing-Kai Chow[1], Kwangsoo Han[1,2], Andrew B. Kahng[2,3], Zhuo Li[1], Derong Liu[1] and Sriram Venkatesh[3]. 2018. Prim-Dijkstra Revisited: Achieving Superior Timing-driven Routing Trees. In *ISPD '18: 2018 International Symposium on Physical Design, March 25–28, 2018, Monterey, CA, USA.* ACM, New York, NY, USA, 8 pages. https://doi.org/10.1145/3177540.3178239

1 INTRODUCTION

In recent technology nodes, wire capacitance has become a key challenge to design closure, and this problem only worsens with each successive technology node[2]. Today, a digital implementation flow cannot simply use minimum wirelength (WL) trees for routing estimates in placement and optimization, nor can they be used for timing-driven routing of critical nets. Routing an advanced-node design with minimum WL trees leads to untenable source-to-sink distances, yielding high delays for many nets. On the other hand, one cannot afford to use a shortest path tree which achieves optimal source-to-sink pathlength (PL) for each sink, due to the increased WL which degrades dynamic power and worsens routing congestion. For these reasons, timing-driven tree construction that trades off WL and PL becomes a critical technology for modern designs.

The Prim-Dijkstra (*PD*)[1] construction is generally regarded as the best available spanning tree algorithm for achieving this tradeoff and has the additional advantage of simplicity[4].[1] This algorithm has been used for over 20 years to construct high-performance routing trees in leading semiconductor design methodologies and electronic design automation (EDA) tools, as can be seen by related patents assigned to IBM, Synopsys, Cadence and other entities ([25] [26] [27] [28] [29] [30] [31] [32]). Further, the authors of [9] performed an evaluation that compared *PD* to other spanning tree constructions such as BRBC[10], KRY[11], etc. in 2006; they concluded that *PD* obtained the best tradeoff between WL and PL. That paper [9] argues that the *PD* wirelength cost is minimal enough to be practically free. However, this claim is now suspect because today's designs are significantly more power-sensitive than a decade ago: now, a 1% reduction in power is viewed as a big win for today's design teams performing physical implementation. Consequently, even a small WL savings with similar timing can have a high impact on value. A deeper discussion of prior art is given in Section 2.

The *PD* construction balances between WL and source-to-sink PL by blending the Prim and Dijkstra spanning tree constructions[5][6] via a weighting factor, α. When $\alpha = 0$, *PD* is identical to Prim's algorithm[5] and constructs a minimum spanning tree (MST). As α increases, *PD* constructs a tree with higher WL but better PL; when $\alpha = 1$, *PD* is identical to Dijkstra's algorithm[6] and constructs a shortest-path tree (SPT). *PD* begins with a tree consisting just the source node, then iteratively adds the edge e_{ij} that minimizes $d_{ij} + \alpha \cdot l_i$, where node v_i is in the current tree and v_j is not in the current tree, d_{ij} is the distance between nodes v_i and v_j, and l_i is the PL from the source to v_i in the current tree.

One problem with the *PD* algorithm is that it greedily adds edges, which becomes problematic with higher fanout trees. Once an edge is added, it is never removed from the final solution, making it

---

[1]For global routing, spanning trees are often preferred to Steiner trees since global routing commonly decomposes multi-fanout nets into two-pin nets. A spanning tree provides the router with an obvious decomposition. However, Steiner trees are not well-suited for this because the Steiner points become unnecessary constraints that restrict the freedom of the router to resolve congestion.

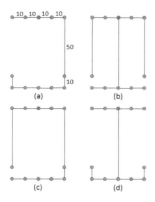

Figure 1: An example instance showing suboptimality of *PD*. The red node is the source. (a) shows the MST obtained when $\alpha = 0.2$, (b) shows the SPT obtained when $\alpha = 0.8$, and (c) shows the solution when $\alpha = 0.4$. The tradeoff in (c) is clearly suboptimal in both WL and PL, as compared to (d).

impossible for *PD* to recover from a potentially poor choice. This can lead to trees that are suboptimal in both WL and maximum PL. Figure 1 shows such an example. When α is small (0.2), *PD* obtains the MST solution (a) with $WL = 150$ and $PL = 130$. When α is large (0.8), *PD* obtains the SPT solution (b) with $WL = 240$ and $PL = 80$. However, when $\alpha = 0.4$, *PD* obtains the solution (c) with suboptimal values of both WL and PL ($WL = 190$ and $PL = 120$). This solution (c) is inferior for both objectives than the solution (d) with $WL = 160$ and $PL = 90$. Thus, $\alpha = 0.4$ generates a poor solution for both WL and PL.

This paper makes the following contributions:

- To fix the shortcomings in *PD*, one needs to directly optimize PL in the tree construction, which requires a new problem formulation. We propose incorporating total *detour cost*, the amount of suboptimal PL for each node, into the tradeoff. The correct formulation of the objective is paramount since it drives any optimization which follows. This work seeks to optimize the detour cost to all sinks instead of just the worst one, as proposed in prior works [36].
- Next, a new algorithm, which we call *PD-II*, is proposed. The idea is to recover the tree, that has any edges poorly chosen by *PD*, using an iterative improvement method according to the proposed objective function.
- Since Steiner trees are most commonly useful for timing prediction and physical synthesis, an algorithm for converting balanced spanning trees into balanced Steiner trees is proposed. The resulting *Detour-Aware Steinerization* (DAS) algorithm optimizes both WL and detour cost to achieve a tree with similar properties to those obtained by the *PD-II* spanning tree algorithm.
- Finally, three sets of experiments are presented. The first shows that *PD-II* is able to meaningfully shift the Pareto curve obtained by the *PD* algorithm, obtaining up to 18% improvement in PL for the same WL. The second experiment demonstrates the value of the *DAS* algorithm versus more standard Steinerization methods. The third experiment shows that the proposed Steiner construction outperforms those of SALT [36] for medium- and high-fanout nets, a recent state-of-the-art academic tool, achieving up to 36.48% PL improvement for similar WL.

The remainder of this paper is organized as follows. Section 2 briefly reviews related works in the areas of spanning and Steiner tree constructions. Section 3 presents the proposed problem formulation that incorporates both WL and detour cost. Section 4 presents the *PD-II* heuristic for spanning tree optimization, and Section 5 presents the *DAS* heuristic for Steiner tree optimization. Section 6 reports our experimental results, and Section 7 concludes the paper.

2 PREVIOUS WORK

There is a rich history on spanning tree and Steiner tree constructions. Many focus on minimizing WL or minimizing longest PL. (Our present work studies constructions that consider both metrics.)

Spanning Tree Constructions. As discussed previously, the Prim and Dijkstra constructions achieve optimal WL and PL, respectively. Spanning tree algorithms that optimize both are called *shallow-light* constructions [10] [12]; they seek to optimize WL and PL simultaneously to within constant factors of optimal. Shallow-light constructions have in many ways been a "holy grail" in VLSI CAD literature for over 25 years. The *PD* algorithm is "shallow-light in practice", but no such formal property has ever been established[1]. Cong et al.[13] give the Bounded Prim (BPRIM) extension of Prim's MST algorithm[5], which produces trees with low average WL and bounded PLs, but possibly unbounded WL. The BRBC algorithm of Cong et al.[10] produces a tree that has WL no greater than $1 + 2/\epsilon$ times that of an MST, and radius no greater than $1 + \epsilon$ times that of an SPT. Khuller et al.[12] contemporaneously develop a method similar to BRBC.

Minimum WL Heuristic Steiner Tree Constructions. Several works describe heuristic algorithms for Steiner tree constructions with minimized WL. Kahng and Robins[15] give the iterated 1-Steiner (I1-S) heuristic which greedily constructs a Steiner tree through iterative Steiner point insertion, resulting in trees with close to optimal WL. Ho et al.[7] propose an algorithm (HVW) to optimally edge-overlap *separable* MSTs to obtain Steiner trees, while Borah et al.[16] present a greedy heuristic (BOI) to convert spanning trees to RSMTs with performance similar to the I1-S heuristic. Chu and Wong[33] propose FLUTE which uses pre-computed lookup tables for Steiner construction to find solutions more efficiently than the prior art.

Rectilinear Steiner Arborescence (RSA) Constructions. The NP-complete[17] *rectilinear Steiner arborescence* (RSA) problem seeks to find a minimum-WL tree in the Manhattan plane that achieves optimal PL for every sink. Rao et al.[3] present the first heuristic for the RSA problem. Cong et al.[18] address the construction of RSAs with the A-tree algorithm, while Kahng and Robins[19] give a simple adaptation of their Iterated 1-Steiner algorithm to the RSA problem.

Steiner Constructions that Optimize WL and PL. Recently, Scheifele[35] has proposed a method to construct Steiner trees for which Elmore delays are bounded. Given an RMST solution (i.e., FLUTE), [35] iteratively finds the vertex that breaks its ϵ-based metric, and reroutes the vertex to the source via a shortest path, which indirectly balances between RMST and RSA. On the other hand, Elkin and Solomon[34] propose a more direct shallow-light Steiner tree construction method (ES). The main idea is to identify breakpoints and reconnect those breakpoints to the root directly by a Steiner SPT so that there is no detour from the root to the breakpoints. The authors of [34] build a Hamiltonian path and check the accumulated distance along the Hamiltonian path to find proper breakpoints, such that the final Steiner tree meets the given shallowness and lightness criteria. Recently, Chen et al.[36] present SALT, which further improves the ES method[34]. The key contributions are (i) tighter criteria to identify breakpoints, and (ii) using an MST instead of a Hamiltonian path. With some post-processing such as L-shape flipping, the method shows superior tradeoffs between pathlength and wirelength compared to any state-of-the-art spanning/Steiner tree construction methods. Comparisons to the method of [36] are included in Section 6 below.

Table 1: Notation

Notation	Meaning
V	signal net, $V = \{v_0, v_1, ... v_{n-1}\}$ having $n-1$ sinks
G	routing graph in the spanning tree context
T	routing tree, which is a spanning subgraph of G
v_0	source node of the signal net V, which is the root of T
e_{ij}	edge from node v_i to v_j
$par(v_i)$	parent node of v_i
l_j	cost of the unique v_0 to v_j path in a tree, $v_0, v_j \in T$
d_{ij}	cost of the edge e_{ij}
m_{ij}	Manhattan distance from node v_i to v_j
W_T	total wirelength of a tree
Q_i	detour cost of node v_i, $Q_i = l_i - m_{i0}$
Q_T	detour cost of a tree, $= \sum_{n-1}(Q_i)$
C	weighted cost of a tree, $= \alpha \cdot Q_T + (1-\alpha) \cdot W_T$
$\Delta C_{e,e'}$	the change in the weighted cost that results from removing edge e and adding e', used in *PD-II*
α	weighting factor used in *PD* and *PD-II*
D	flipping distance used in *PD-II*
P_T	sum of pathlengths of a tree, $= \sum_{n-1}(l_j)$

3　PROBLEM FORMULATION

A *signal net* $V = \{v_0, v_1, ..., v_{n-1}\}$ is a set of n terminals, with v_0 as the *source* and the remaining terminals as *sinks*. We define the underlying routing graph to be a connected weighted graph $G = (V, E)$, where each edge $e_{ij} \in E$ has a cost d_{ij}. We are concerned with the case where G is a complete graph with each e_{ij} having cost equal to the Manhattan distance d_{ij}. A *routing tree* $T = (V, E')$ is a spanning subgraph of G with $|E'| = n - 1$.[2] Given a routing tree T, the cost of the unique $v_0 - v_i$ path in T is l_i, the *radius* of T is $r(T) = max_{1 \le i \le n-1} l_i$, and the *wirelength* (WL) of T is $W_T = \sum_{e_{ij} \in T} d_{ij}$. All notations used in our work are listed in Table 1.

Initially, the tree consists only of v_0. The *PD* algorithm iteratively adds edge e_{ij} and sink v_i to T, where v_i and v_j are chosen to minimize

$$(\alpha \cdot l_j) + d_{ij} \quad s.t. \ v_j \in T, \ v_i \in V - T \qquad (1)$$

The *PD* algorithm can result in trees with either large WL or PL, as shown in Figure 1. To alleviate this issue, conventional *shallow-light* tree constructions[10][13][36] focus on bounding the *shallowness* and *lightness* to optimize the tree cost. Lightness η means that the WL of a tree is at most η times of the MST WL. A tree has shallowness ζ if PL to each sink in the tree is at most ζ times the source-to-sink Manhattan distance (MD). However, shallowness alone does not adequately represent the quality of a routing tree. Figure 2 shows two examples that have the same shallowness and lightness. It is clear that Figure 2(b) is preferable to Figure 2(a) since the left sinks have shorter PLs, but shallowness does not capture the difference.

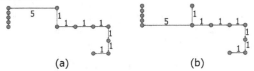

(a)　　　　　　　　　　(b)

Figure 2: Two routing trees that have the same lightness and shallowness.

With the above in mind, we define a new *detour cost* metric as follows. Detour cost Q_i of a sink v_i is the difference between PL from v_0 to v_i in T and the Manhattan distance from v_0 to v_i. The detour cost of the tree T, denoted by Q_T, is the sum of the detour cost values of all the sinks in the tree, i.e., $Q_T = \sum_{1 \le i \le n-1} Q_i$.

---

[2]Our use of G and T pertains to the spanning tree context. In the rectilinear Steiner tree context, the underlying routing graph would be the Hanan grid [20], and a Steiner routing tree would be a spanning tree over $\{V \cup S\}$, where S is a set of Steiner points taken from the Hanan grid. For simplicity, as long as meanings are obvious, we will use terms from the spanning tree context in the Steiner tree context as well.

Since *PD* iteratively adds edges and nodes to the growing tree, if a sink v_j close to the source incurs high detour, then all downstream sinks (descendants of v_j) will also have high detour and hence long PL. We therefore propose the following formulation to capture the problem of simultaneously reducing WL and detour cost of a spanning tree:

Simultaneous WL and Detour Cost Reduction (SWDCR) Problem. Given a spanning tree $T = (V, E)$, minimize the weighted sum of WL and detour cost of the tree.

$$\text{Minimize } \alpha \cdot \sum Q_i + (1 - \alpha) \cdot W_T \qquad (2)$$

where $0 \le \alpha \le 1$. We present a heuristic algorithm *PD-II* in Section 4 for tackling the SWDCR problem.

Once the spanning tree construction is converted into a Steiner tree, there is a change in the tree topology. We propose and address the following formulation to further optimize the detour cost of a Steiner tree:

Detour Cost Reduction in Steiner Trees (DCRST) Problem. Given a Steiner tree, minimize the tree detour cost.

$$\text{Minimize } Q_T \qquad (3)$$

$$\text{s.t. } W_{T,new} \le W_{T,init} \qquad (4)$$

$$Q_{T,init} \ge Q_{T,new} \qquad (5)$$

To address the DCRST problem, we present our algorithm *DAS* below in Section 5.

4　THE *PD-II* SPANNING TREE CONSTRUCTION

This section presents the *PD-II* algorithm that performs iterative edge-swapping which simultaneously improves the detour cost and WL. The key idea of the *PD-II* algorithm is to start with a spanning tree and swap edges to improve the tradeoff between detour cost and WL. The algorithm can take any spanning tree as input, but it makes sense to start with the *PD* solution since it should already be relatively strong for both objectives. We note that while *PD* can be quite slow for higher-fanout nets, it can be sped up significantly by using a sparsified nearest-neighbor graph instead of the complete graph.

We initially populate the *neighbors* of each node using the following method. We say that v_i is a *neighbor* of v_j if the smallest bounding box containing v_i and v_j contains no other nodes. The worst-case number of neighbor nodes for each node is $\Theta(n)$. For example, every red point in Figure 3 is a neighbor of every green point, and vice versa. However, Naamad et al.[23] show that the expected number of maximal empty boxes amidst n random points in a plane is bounded above by $O(n \log n)$, so it is reasonable to expect the average number of neighbors per node to be $O(\log n)$.

Figure 3: Example showing $\Theta(n^2)$ asymptotic worst-case complexity of the number of *neighbor* relationships. Each green node is a neighbor to each red node.

Analysis of random placements of net sinks show this to be true. The number of neighbors for 100K random point sets of size 16, 32, and 64 yields an average number of neighbors per node of 6.3, 8.7 and 11.3, respectively. Real placements should generally have even fewer neighbors, since cells tend to align horizontally or vertically. For the testcases described in Section 6.1, the average number of neighbors is 2.58, 4.27, 6.15 and 8.24 for small, medium, large and huge nets, respectively. Hence, in practice, runtime complexity of iterating through the neighbors of a node has logarithmic complexity.

An $O(n \log n)$ runtime complexity can be obtained for *PD* using a binary heap implementation and an adaptation of Scheffer's MST code[21][22]. Since *PD* solutions are generally good, though sometimes suboptimal, it makes sense to post-process the *PD* solution to obtain a better one. The key technique for *PD-II* is *edge flipping*, whereby one edge is removed from the original tree and replaced with a new one. Figure 4(a) shows an example tree, represented as a DAG, representing a topological ordering starting at the source. Figure 4(b) shows an example transform in which one edge is removed and replaced with a new red edge, thereby obtaining a different tree. Note that one of the directed edges in the new (rooted) tree is reversed from its previous orientation in order to maintain a well-formed rooted tree. This approach recalls the iterative improvement operation used in BOI[16], but the application of *flipping* is more restricted to focus on WL vs. PL improvements.

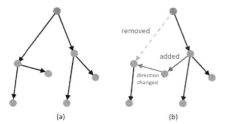

Figure 4: Illustration of *PD-II* edge *flipping*.

For each edge pair, we define the *flip cost* as the cost associated with edge flipping, i.e., the cost of removing edge e_{ij} and adding edge $e_{i'j'}$. Flip cost $\Delta C_{e,e'} = \alpha \cdot (Q_{T_{i'j'}} - Q_{T_{ij}}) + (1 - \alpha) \cdot (d_{i'j'} - d_{ij})$, where α is a weighting factor;[3] $Q_{T_{ij}}$ and $Q_{T_{i'j'}}$ are the detour costs of the trees before and after edge flipping, respectively; and d_{ij} and $d_{i'j'}$ are the lengths of edges being removed and inserted, respectively.

Pseudocode for *PD-II*, Algorithm 1 is given below. Essentially, *PD-II* takes an input tree and searches for edge flips that improve flip cost.[4] If the flip cost improves, the swap is taken. Considering all pairs of possible swaps could be expensive, so we define the *flipping distance D* to be equal to the number of edges in the DAG that require a change in direction to preserve topological ordering, i.e., rooted orientation. For the swap in Figure 4, $D = 1$. In practice, using $D > 1$ has little benefit (but more runtime) compared to $D = 1$, so we use $D = 1$ for all experiments.

Line 3 of Algorithm 1 initializes the best flip cost to zero. Line 5 computes the set of candidate edges E_e that can be flipped with edge e, as restricted by the flipping distance D. For each candidate edge $e' \in E_e$, we calculate the flip cost for the edge pair (e, e') and find the edge pair (e_{best}, e'_{best}) with lowest flip cost in Lines 6-12. These edges are swapped if the lowest flip cost is less than zero (Lines 14-16). The algorithm continues until no more flip-cost improvement is obtained (Line 17).

The number of candidates for edge flipping can be very large when D is unbounded. The worst-case number of edges is $(n/2)^2$, giving Algorithm *PD-II* a worst-case time complexity of $O(n^3)$,

---

[3]The parameter α can be determined by the timing constraints. If a net is critical, a higher value of α can be used to achieve lower delays, but if arcs through the net have positive slacks, α can be small to save wirelength. Hence, α allows topology optimization and can be chosen to best satisfy the design specifications on a per-net basis.

[4]Flipping cannot be added into the original PD cost function since the flip cost objective cannot be correctly computed until an entire tree is constructed. Hence, we propose PD-II as a post-processing algorithm which improves a given spanning tree.

Algorithm 1 Algorithm *PD-II*

Input: Spanning tree $T_{in} = (V, E_{in})$, with $E_{in} \subseteq E$
Output: Spanning tree $T_{out} = (V, E_{out})$, with $E_{out} \subseteq E$
1: Initialize $T_{out} \leftarrow T_{in}$
2: **repeat**
3:    Initialize largest detour cost reduction, $\Delta C_{best} \leftarrow 0$
4:    **for all** $e \in E_{out}$ **do**
5:       $E_e \leftarrow candidateEdges(e, D)$
6:       **for all** $e' \in E_e$ **do**
7:          $\Delta C_{e,e'} \leftarrow flipCost(e, e')$
8:          **if** $\Delta C_{e,e'} < \Delta C_{best}$ **then**
9:             $\Delta C_{best} \leftarrow C_{e,e'}$
10:             $e_{best} \leftarrow e ; e'_{best} \leftarrow e'$
11:          **end if**
12:       **end for**
13:    **end for**
14:    **if** $\Delta C_{best} < 0$ **then**
15:       Remove e_{best}, insert e'_{best} and change direction of associate edges
16:    **end if**
17: **until** $\Delta C_{best} == 0$

---

where n is the number of sinks. However, with the distance restriction, the complexity reduces to $O(D \cdot n^2)$, and in practice it converges rapidly. To show this, we take two large blocks from an industrial design and run a production Steiner package on an Intel Xeon 2.7GHz machine (CPU E5-2680), using RHEL5. The first design has 1.9 million datapath nets, and the total runtime for the Steiner package which uses *PD* for its spanning tree construction requires 59.3 seconds. Adding *PD-II* to the Steiner package increases the runtime to 62.7 seconds, for a net penalty of 3.4 seconds. The second design with 4.0M datapath nets requires 124.0 seconds for running the default Steiner package. Adding *PD-II* to the Steiner package increases the runtime from 124.0 seconds to 125.8 seconds, for a net penalty of 1.8 seconds. Consequently, the runtime cost of using *PD-II* is negligible, averaging less than one additional second of runtime per million nets.

5 THE DETOUR-AWARE STEINERIZATION ALGORITHM (*DAS*)

For global routing, spanning tree constructions such as *PD-II* are sometimes preferred to Steiner trees since global routing commonly decomposes multi-pin nets into two-pin nets. However, for timing estimation, congestion prediction, or general physical synthesis optimization, a Steiner tree is required since spanning trees will have too much WL. The previous spanning tree formulation can easily be extended to Steiner trees; the definitions of WL and PL do not change. However, since finding the minimum wirelength Steiner is NP-complete, FLUTE WL is used as a proxy for minimum Steiner tree cost.

To transform a spanning tree into a Steiner tree, the linear-time algorithm of [7] is invoked. It maximizes edge-overlaps in the spanning tree by creating a Steiner node. We call the algorithm *HVW* after the algorithm's creators: Ho, Vijayan, and Wong. *HVW* traverses the tree from the leafs and iteratively maximize overlaps with the currently visited edge and its immediate children edges. However, this basic construction can be inefficient both in terms of WL and PL. Hence a new Steinerization algorithm, called *DAS* for Detour-Aware Steinerization is proposed below.

DAS has two phases of optimization. The first phase seeks to reduce WL while minimizing the detour cost penalty (Lines 1-14). This phase does a bottom-up tree traversal and makes edge swaps which reduce WL. For each edge e_{ji} in the Steiner tree, the edge e_{ji} is removed from the tree and replaced with e_{ki} where v_k is a nearest neighbor of v_i if the WL improves and the PL is not overly degraded. (i.e., $p_i \leq 0.5 \cdot p_T^{max}$).

After the first phase, since PL (or detour cost) is not targeted, there still may be room to improve for that dimension. Hence,

Algorithm 2 The Detour-Aware Steinerization Algorithm (*DAS*)

Input: Steiner tree $T_{St,in}$
Output: Improved Steiner tree $T_{St,out}$
1: //First phase: wire recovery at the cost of small additional PL
2: $p_T^{max} \leftarrow$ maximum PL of the Steiner tree
3: Do Breadth-First Search (BFS) from the leaf node
4: **for all** v_i **do**
5:     $v_j \leftarrow par(v_i)$; $d_{ji} \leftarrow$ edge length to v_i;
6:     $o_{ji} \leftarrow$ overlap length with other edges to v_i
7:     $\Delta d_{ji} \leftarrow d_{ji} - o_{ji}$
8:     **for all** v_k in {all *neighbors* of v_i} **do**
9:         $\Delta d_{ki} \leftarrow d_{ki} - o_{ji}$; $p_i \leftarrow$ PL to node v_i
10:         **if** ($\Delta d_{ki} < \Delta d_{ji}$ && ($p_i \leq 0.5 \cdot p_T^{max}$) **then**
11:             Disconnect v_i to v_j and reconnect v_i to v_k
12:         **end if**
13:     **end for**
14: **end for**
15: //Second phase: detour cost reduction with bounded WL
16: $W_{T,init} \leftarrow$ Init. Steiner tree WL; $Q_{T,init} \leftarrow$ Init. Steiner tree detour cost
17: Do Breadth-First Search (BFS) from the source node
18: **for all** v_i **do**
19:     $v_j \leftarrow par(v_i)$; $d_{ji} \leftarrow$ Initial edge length to v_i
20:     **for all** v_k in {all *neighbors* of v_i} **do**
21:         $e_{ki} \leftarrow$ Edge from v_k to v_i; $d_{ki} \leftarrow$ Edge length from v_k to v_i
22:         $W_{T,new} \leftarrow W_{T,init} + d_{ki} - d_{ji}$
23:         $Q_{T,new} \leftarrow$ detour cost tree with edge e_{ki}
24:         **if** ($W_{T,new} \leq W_{T,init}$) && ($Q_{T,new} < Q_{T,init}$) **then**
25:             Disconnect v_i to v_j and reconnect v_i to v_k
26:             $W_{T,init} \leftarrow W_{T,new}$; $Q_{T,init} \leftarrow Q_{T,new}$
27:         **end if**
28:     **end for**
29: **end for**

a second phase (Lines 15-29) seeks to optimize detour cost Q_T without degrading WL. This second phase performs a *top-down* tree traversal to minimize Q_T. This is because the detour cost Q_i to a node v_i affects not only the PL to the node, but also the PL to the downstream nodes of v_i. Thus, more opportunity for large Q_T reductions exists in the edges near the source v_0. For each edge e_{ji} in the Steiner tree, the edge e_{ji} is removed and replaced with e_{ki}, where v_k is the possible parent among the nearest neighbors of v_i, to reduce Q_T without degrading WL. This process is repeated for all the nodes in the tree with non-zero detour cost.

Algorithm *DAS* has a worst-case time complexity of $O(n^2)$. However, with the sparsified nearest neighbor graph implementation described in Section 4, *DAS* runs much faster than $O(n^2)$ and is closer to $O(n \log n)$ in practice. For 100K nets, *DAS* runs in 0.86 seconds for 16-terminal nets, 1.71 seconds for 32-terminal nets and 4.83 seconds for 64-terminal nets.

6 EXPERIMENTAL SETUP AND RESULTS
6.1 Experimental Setup
The algorithms described above are implemented in C++. The following experiments are performed on a 2.7 GHz Intel Xeon server with 8 threads. Testcases are generated from the DAC 2012 contest benchmarks[37], with pin locations for each net are extracted from ePlace placement solutions[38]. Since finding a solution with optimal WL and PL is trivial for two- and three-pin nets, our experiments focus on nets with fanout larger than two. The roughly 749K total nets are divided into four groups (small, medium, large, huge) by their terminal count, as shown in Table 2.

Table 2: Net Statistics for Superblue Benchmark Designs

	small	medium	large	huge
$|V|$	$4-7$	$8-15$	$16-31$	$32+$
#nets	533029	128463	46486	20853

While our algorithms optimize Q_T, Q_T itself does not adequately capture the quality of the tree. Instead, results are reported based

on two normalized metrics, W_{Tnorm} (normalized WL) and P_{Tnorm} (normalized PL). W_{Tnorm} is defined as the ratio of the tree WL to the MST WL for spanning trees. P_{Tnorm} is defined as the ratio of sum of PLs of each node in the tree to the sum of Manhattan distances from source to each node. The optimal value any tree could have for either metric is one, which makes the corresponding Pareto curve more intuitive.

6.2 Experiment I - Spanning Tree Results
In the following results, *PD* and *PD-II* refer respectively to the *spanning trees* constructed using the *PD* and *PD-II* algorithms. Figure 5 shows normalized WL and PL tradeoff curves for *PD* and *PD-II*, for the 46486 large nets. Each point in the curves represents the average (W_{Tnorm}, P_{Tnorm}) over all the nets for a particular value of α. We sweep α from 0.05 to 0.95, in steps of 0.05, to obtain both the *PD* and *PD-II* curves. We observe that the blue *PD-II* Pareto curve is clearly better than the red *PD* curve.

The Pareto curve makes the improvement trend clear, but makes it difficult to measure the degree of improvement of *PD-II*. To compare the two algorithms more robustly, we analyze the results in the following way; (1) select different percentages of permissible WL degradation with respect to MST WL (i.e., WL thresholds = 1%, 2%, 4%, 7%, 10% and 15%), and (2) for each net, find the minimum P_{Tnorm} solution that meets the WL threshold across all solutions with different α. The results are averaged across all the nets and summarized in Table 3. Each entry in the table corresponds to the normalized PL P_{Tnorm}. To find the percentage improvement, one is subtracted from each value, since 1.0 is a lower bound. For example, a reduction from 1.15 to 1.12 results in an improvement of 20%, i.e., $(1 - (1.12 - 1.0)/(1.15 - 1.0)) \cdot 100\%$.

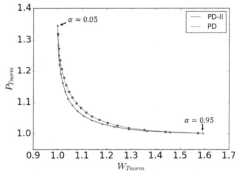

Figure 5: WL and PL tradeoff for various α.

Table 3: Comparisons of the best P_{Tnorm} for *PD* and *PD-II* across different WL thresholds.

$|V|$	Method	WL threshold					
		1%	2%	4%	7%	10%	15%
small	PD	1.0972	1.0927	1.0819	1.0680	1.0569	1.0427
	PD-II	1.0970	1.0923	1.0812	1.0672	1.0561	1.0420
	Imp. (%)	0.26	0.42	0.78	1.15	1.36	1.63
med.	PD	1.1888	1.1746	1.1483	1.1189	1.0974	1.0723
	PD-II	1.1870	1.1706	1.1423	1.1122	1.0909	1.0668
	Imp. (%)	0.93	2.33	4.07	5.66	6.62	7.68
large	PD	1.2981	1.2698	1.2216	1.1723	1.1390	1.1006
	PD-II	1.2895	1.2545	1.2025	1.1533	1.1219	1.0870
	Imp. (%)	2.89	5.66	8.64	11.00	12.32	13.52
huge	PD	1.3952	1.3550	1.2873	1.2210	1.1777	1.1302
	PD-II	1.3758	1.3238	1.2526	1.1876	1.1488	1.1056
	Imp. (%)	4.91	8.79	12.06	15.14	16.27	18.87

We observe the following:
- *PD-II* gives better results than *PD* for all classes of nets. This makes sense since it strictly improves upon an existing *PD* solution.

- Small nets obtain relatively small improvement, ranging from 0.26% to 1.63%; however, huge nets show significant improvements, ranging from 4.91% to 18.87%. Trends for medium and large nets lie in between. This is because the detour cost is close to optimal for smaller nets, but is much larger for bigger nets. For example, with a 1% WL threshold, the average normalized PL for *PD-II* is 1.097 for small nets but 1.376 for large nets.
- When the WL threshold is tight (such as 1% or 2%), the improvement of *PD-II* is much smaller as compared to looser constraints of 10% or 15%. This makes sense because a looser constraint gives the algorithms more freedom to reduce PL. A threshold of 1% means the topology cannot deviate much from the minimum-length spanning tree.

6.3 Experiment II - Steiner Tree Results

Our next experiments compare (*PD + HVW + DAS*) and a baseline flow (*PD + HVW*) to show the value of *DAS*. *HVW* refers to the Steiner tree obtained after performing edge-overlapping as described by Ho et al.[7], and *DAS* refers to the Steiner tree after applying *DAS* algorithm to the *HVW* tree. Figure 6 shows the normalized WL and PL tradeoff comparison for the two flows for the set of large nets. Steiner tree W_{Tnorm} is defined as the ratio of total WL of the tree to the FLUTE WL[5][33] and P_{Tnorm} is defined as the ratio of sum of PLs of all sinks in the tree to the sum of source-to-sink Manhattan distances. Each point in the curve represents the average (W_{Tnorm}, P_{Tnorm}) over all nets, for a particular value of α. It is clear that *DAS* adds significant value to the Steiner construction, pushing its Pareto curve further left and down compared to the one from the baseline.

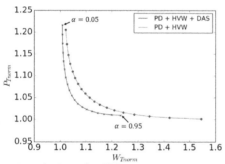

Figure 6: WL and PL tradeoff for Steiner tree constructions.

Table 4: Comparisons of the best P_{Tnorm} for (1) *PD + HVW* and (2) *PD + HVW + DAS* across different WL thresholds.

$|V|$	Method	\multicolumn{6}{c}{WL threshold}					
		1%	2%	4%	7%	10%	15%
small	(1)	1.0233	1.0241	1.0250	1.0249	1.0236	1.0202
	(2)	1.0126	1.0115	1.0097	1.0073	1.0054	1.0033
	Imp. (%)	**46.14**	**52.31**	**61.15**	**70.85**	**77.30**	**83.67**
med.	(1)	1.0786	1.0821	1.0828	1.0757	1.0649	1.0489
	(2)	1.0665	1.0629	1.0532	1.0385	1.0277	1.0168
	Imp. (%)	**15.43**	**23.30**	**35.78**	**49.07**	**57.24**	**65.58**
large	(1)	1.1637	1.1644	1.1547	1.1275	1.1026	1.0728
	(2)	1.1440	1.1347	1.1087	1.0760	1.0553	1.0357
	Imp. (%)	**12.01**	**18.07**	**29.73**	**40.36**	**46.08**	**50.93**
huge	(1)	1.2278	1.2091	1.1606	1.1107	1.0812	1.0538
	(2)	1.228	1.209	1.161	1.111	1.081	1.054
	Imp. (%)	**8.36**	**15.14**	**27.82**	**36.36**	**39.74**	**41.69**

Similarly to Table 3, Table 4 shows normalized PL across a range of permissible WL degradations for *HVW* versus *HVW+DAS*. We observe the following:

- DAS always obtains better results than HVW. Again, this makes sense since DAS starts with an HVW solution and further refines it to improve both WL and PL.
- Improvements for DAS can be quite significant, ranging from 8.36% to 83.67%.
- DAS improves results more significantly for smaller fanout nets than for larger ones. This may suggest there is still further room for improvement in Steinerization.
- Larger WL thresholds correspond to larger normalized PL improvements, which again is likely due to more freedom for the algorithm to find a solution that reduces detour cost.

6.4 Experiment III - Comparison with SALT[36]

Our final set of experiments compares the best combined flow (*PD-II + HVW + DAS*) with the results from the state-of-the-art academic Steiner tree construction, SALT[36]. SALT uses FLUTE [33] to generate its initial input and improves the initial construction to reduce PL. For nets with less than 10 terminals, FLUTE produces the optimal WL and may also produce excellent or even optimal PL, in which case running SALT is not even necessary. Hence, the cases for which FLUTE produces excellent PL are in some sense uninteresting. If FLUTE produces a good tradeoff curve, then SALT simply returns the FLUTE solution. Our approach can do something similar using the following simple metaheuristic: (1) run both FLUTE and (*PD-II + HVW + DAS*) in parallel; (2) if FLUTE is better than (*PD-II + HVW + DAS*) for both WL and PL, return the FLUTE solution, else return the (*PD-II + HVW + DAS*) solution. Essentially, the metaheuristic returns a solution identical to SALT's when the FLUTE solution is dominant. Note that for large and huge nets, the FLUTE solution almost never is dominant.

Figure 7 shows normalized WL and PL tradeoff curves for the metaheuristic flow and SALT for (a) small, (b) medium, (c) large and (d) huge nets. For small nets, SALT actually achieves better solutions than the metaheuristic until the normalized WL is about 2.3% higher than optimal.[6] However, for medium, large and huge nets, the Pareto curve for the metaheuristic outperforms the one from SALT, especially as nets increase in size. For huge nets, SALT achieves $W_{Tnorm} = 1.0370$, $P_{Tnorm} = 1.141$ for $\epsilon = 1.281$, which is its knee point in the tradeoff curve. The knee point in the metaheuristic's tradeoff curve corresponds to $W_{Tnorm} = 1.024$ and $P_{Tnorm} = 1.121$ at $\alpha = 0.35$, which achieves 35.13% WL and 14.18% PL improvements compared to SALT at its $\epsilon = 1.281$.

Since SALT optimizes shallowness and not detour cost, Figure 8 presents the same set of data but using SALT's proposed metrics. SALT dominates our method according to the shallowness metric. Thus, SALT is superior with respect to its proposed metric, while *PD-II + HVW + DAS* is superior with respect to its metric.

Finally, Table 5 compares our best recipe to SALT using the same methodology as Tables 3 and 4. Note that we use FLUTE WL as a lower bound. We observe the following:

- For small nets, and WL thresholds below 10%, SALT outperforms the proposed approach. SALT is also better on medium nets with WL thresholds below 2%. This makes sense since trees in this space will closely resemble FLUTE constructions. SALT starts with a FLUTE construction and iteratively improves it, so in the space where FLUTE obtains good trees for WL and PL, such an approach outperforms the algorithm proposed in this work. Note that the magnitude of the improvement is still small. For example, for small nets and a 1% threshold, SALT is 0.99% away from the optimal normalized path length, while our approach is 1.26% away.

---

[5]FLUTE constructs optimal RSMTs for nets with terminal sizes up to 9, and near-optimal RSMTs for nets with higher terminal counts.

[6]For {small, medium, large, huge} nets, FLUTE results for {55.6, 7.9, 0.03, 0}% of nets have smaller WL and PL than our results. As expected, FLUTE results are dominant for small nets, but our algorithm gives better PL for large and huge nets.

- For large and huge nets, and for medium nets with thresholds larger than 2%, the proposed approach performs better, reaching a peak of 36.46% improvement for huge nets with a 10% threshold. This is the domain for which the optimal tradeoff can be considerably different from FLUTE. These arguably form the class of more interesting instances where the tradeoff between WL and PL becomes increasingly important.
- As WL threshold increases, the improvement of our approach vs. SALT improves too, especially around the 7% and 10% WL threshold ranges. However, for large and huge nets the improvement is somewhat less at the 15% threshold.

Table 5: Comparisons of the best P_{Tnorm} for (1) SALT and (2) PD-II + HVW + DAS across different WL thresholds.

$|V|$	Method	WL threshold					
		1%	2%	4%	7%	10%	15%
small	(1)	1.0099	1.0093	1.0082	1.0067	1.0053	1.0036
	(2)	1.0126	1.0115	1.0097	1.0073	1.0054	1.0033
	Imp. (%)	-27.29	-23.85	-17.98	-8.80	-0.86	7.90
med.	(1)	1.0652	1.0619	1.0547	1.0435	1.0337	1.0213
	(2)	1.0665	1.0629	1.0532	1.0385	1.0277	1.0168
	Imp. (%)	-1.95	-1.66	2.76	11.32	17.63	21.15
large	(1)	1.1564	1.1475	1.1261	1.0961	1.0720	1.0432
	(2)	1.1440	1.1347	1.1087	1.0760	1.0553	1.0357
	Imp. (%)	7.91	8.66	13.77	20.92	23.09	17.31
huge	(1)	1.2744	1.2574	1.2205	1.1688	1.1277	1.0763
	(2)	1.2278	1.2090	1.1606	1.1107	1.0811	1.0536
	Imp. (%)	17.01	18.79	27.18	34.44	36.46	29.71

Runtime. For the benchmarks studied, SALT's total runtime is 2762 seconds. By contrast, the *PD-II + HVW + DAS* algorithms, as implemented and optimized within a commercial EDA tool's code base, take 361 seconds in total. Thus, PD-II today runs more than 7 times faster than SALT.

Delay. Below, we show the impact of WL and PL improvement on delay. We estimate delays of nets produced by our algorithms and by SALT, based on the Elmore delay model with resistance of 37.318Ω per micron of wire, capacitance of 0.228fF per micron of wire, and 0.67fF pin capacitance per sink. For the solutions produced by our approach and SALT with WL threshold 2%, we calculate the sum of all sink delays for each net, and the average of this sum across all nets. For {small, medium, large, huge} nets, the average sum of sink delays from PD-II is lower than the average sum of sink delays from SALT by {-0.0005, 0.24, 1.54, 5.62}%. As seen with the WL and PL comparison, our algorithm has slightly larger delays for small nets and smaller delays for higher-fanout nets.

In summary, while our approach does not uniformly outperform SALT, it does provide a superior tradeoff for the most interesting class of nets that are far from optimal in terms of PL and WL.[7]

7 CONCLUSION

This work shows that the classic *PD* spanning tree algorithm that balances between Prim's and Dijkstra's algorithm can have a bad tradeoff that ends up with both WL and PL being highly suboptimal. A new spanning tree heuristic *PD-II* is demonstrated to significantly improve both WL and total detour cost compared to *PD*. Further, this work extends the construction to Steiner tree with the *DAS* algorithm that directly improves trees according to both objectives. The algorithms are shown to be fast and practical. They are also suitable for integration into existing commercial routers, and can be applied in conjunction with any existing spanning and Steiner tree constructions for simultaneous WL and PL improvements. Compared to the recent SALT algorithm, our construction generates clear improvements according to the proposed metrics, especially for medium-size and larger nets. Future research includes (i) revisiting the still-open question of worst-case detour from a *PD* construction; (ii) learning-based estimation of the best α for any

---

[7]The PD-II algorithm has been released as part of a leading commercial tool, with demonstrated improvements of timing and wirelength.

given instance (i.e., set of pin locations of a signal net); and (iii) extending the detour cost objective to encompass sink criticality, "global" radius, and other additional criteria.

8 ACKNOWLEDGMENTS

We thank Mr. Gengjie Chen and the other authors of SALT [36] for their kindness in performing studies with their code so that we could report comparisons with SALT. We also thank the authors of [38] for making their ePlace executable available for us to gather placement data. ABKGroup research is supported by NSF, Samsung, Qualcomm, NXP, Mentor Graphics and C-DEN.

REFERENCES

[1] C. J. Alpert, T. C. Hu, J. H. Huang, A. B. Kahng and D. Karger, "Prim-Dijkstra Tradeoffs for Improved Performance-driven Routing Tree Design", *IEEE TCAD* 14(7) (1995), pp. 890-896.
[2] ITRS 2013 Edition Report - Interconnect, *https://www.semiconductors.org/clie ntuploads/Research_Technology/ITRS/2013/2013Interconnect.pdf*, 2013.
[3] S. K. Rao, P. Sadayappan, F. K. Hwang and P. W. Shor, "The Rectilinear Steiner Arborescence Problem", *Algorithmica* 7(2) (1992), pp. 277-88.
[4] C. J. Alpert, *Personal Communication*, Nov. 2016.
[5] R. C. Prim, "Shortest Connecting Networks and Some Generalizations", *Bell System Tech. J.* 36 (1957), pp. 1389-1401.
[6] E. W. Dijkstra, "A Note on Two Problems in Connexion with Graphs", *Numerische Mathematik* 1 (1959), pp. 269-271.
[7] J. M. Ho, G. Vijayan and C. K. Wong, "New Algorithms for the Rectilinear Steiner Tree Problem", *IEEE TCAD* 9(2) (1990), pp. 185-193.
[8] J. B. Kruskal Jr., "On the Shortest Spanning Subtree of a Graph and the Traveling Salesman Problem", *Proc. Amer. Math. Soc.* 7(1) (1956), pp. 48-50.
[9] C. J. Alpert, A. B. Kahng, C. N. Sze and Q. Wang, "Timing-driven Steiner Trees are (Practically) Free", *Proc. DAC*, 2006, pp. 389-392.
[10] J. Cong, A. B. Kahng, G. Robins and M. Sarrafzadeh, "Provably Good Performance-driven Global Routing", *IEEE TCAD* 11(6) (1992), pp. 739-752.
[11] G. Kortsarz and D. Peleg, "Approximating Shallow-light Trees", *Proc. SODA*, 1997, pp. 103-110.
[12] S. Khuller, B. Raghavachari and N. Young, "Balancing Minimum Spanning Trees and Shortest-path Trees", *Proc. SODA*, 1993, pp. 243-250.
[13] J. Cong, A. B. Kahng, G. Robins, M. Sarrafzadeh and C.K. Wong, "Performance-driven Global Routing for Cell Based ICs", *Proc. ICCD*, 1991, pp. 170-173.
[14] A. Lim, S.-W. Cheng and C.-T. Wu, "Performance Oriented Rectilinear Steiner Trees", *Proc. DAC*, 1993, pp. 171-175.
[15] A. B. Kahng and G. Robins, "A New Class of Iterative Steiner Tree Heuristics with Good Performance", *IEEE TCAD* 11(7) (1992), pp. 893-902.
[16] M. Borah, R. M. Owens and M. J. Irwin, "An Edge-based Heuristic for Steiner Routing", *IEEE TCAD* 13(12) (1994), pp. 1563-1568.
[17] W. Shi and C. Su, "The Rectilinear Steiner Arborescence Problem is NP-complete", *SIAM J. Comp.* 35(3) (2006), pp. 729-740.
[18] J. Cong, K. S. Leung and D. Zhou, "Performance-driven Interconnect Design Based on Distributed RC Delay Model", *Proc. DAC*, 1993, pp. 606-611.
[19] A. B. Kahng and G. Robins, *On Optimal Interconnections for VLSI*, Kluwer Academic Publishers, 1995.
[20] M. Hanan, "On Steiner's Problem with Rectilinear Distance", *SIAM J. Appl. Math.* 14(2) (1966), pp. 255-265.
[21] L. Scheffer, Bookshelf RMST code, http://vlsicad.ucsd.edu/GSRC/bookshelf/Slots/RSMT/RMST/.
[22] L. J. Guibas and J. Stolfi, "On Computing All Northeast Nearest Neighbors in the L1 Metric", *Information Processing Letters* 17 (1983), pp. 219-223.
[23] A. Naamad, D. T. Lee and W.-L. Hsu, "On the Maximum Empty Rectangle Problem", *Discrete Applied Mathematics* 8 (1984), pp. 267-277.
[24] J. Griffith, G. Robins, J. S. Salowe and T. Zhang, "Closing the Gap: Near-optimal Steiner Trees in Polynomial Time", *Proc. TCAD*, 1994, pp. 1351-1365.
[25] L. He, S. Yao, W. Deng, J. Chen and L. Chao, "Interconnect Routing Methods of Integrated Circuit Designs", *US Patent 8386984*, Feb. 2013.
[26] S. Bose, "Methods and Systems for Placement and Routing", *US Patent 8332793*, Dec. 2012.
[27] R. F. Hentschke, M. de Oliveira Johann, J. Narasimhan and R. A. de Luz Reis, "Methods and Apparatus for Providing Flexible Timing-driven Routing Trees", *US Patent 8095904*, Jan. 2012.
[28] G. M. Furnish, M. J. LeBrun and S. Bose, "Tunneling as a Boundary Congestion Relief Mechanism", *US Patent 7921393*, Apr. 2011.
[29] G. M. Furnish, M. J. LeBrun and S. Bose, "Node Spreading Via Artificial Density Enhancement to Reduce Routing Congestion", *US Patent 7921392*, Apr. 2011.
[30] P. Saxena, V. Khandelwal, C. Qiao, P-H. Ho, J. C. Lin and M. A. Iyer, "Interconnect-driven Physical Synthesis using Persistent Virtual Routing", *US Patent 7853915*, Dec. 2010.
[31] C. J. Alpert, J. Hu and P. H. Villarrubia, "Practical Methodology for Early Buffer and Wire Resource Allocation", *US Patent 6996512*, Feb. 2006.
[32] C. J. Alpert, R. G. Gandham, J. Hu, S. T. Quay and A. J. Sullivan, "Apparatus and Method for Determining Buffered Steiner Trees for Complex Circuits", *US Patent 6591411*, Jul. 2003.
[33] C. Chu and Y.C. Wong, "FLUTE: Fast Lookup Table Based Rectilinear Steiner Minimal Tree Algorithm for VLSI Design", *IEEE TCAD* 27(1) (2008), pp.70-83.
[34] M. Elkin and S. Solomon, "Steiner Shallow-light Trees are Exponentially Lighter than Spanning Ones", *SIAM J. Comp.* 44(4) (2015), pp. 996-1025.
[35] R. Scheifele, "Steiner Trees with Bounded RC-delay", *Algorithmica* 78(1) (2017), pp. 86-109.
[36] G. Chen, P. Tu and E. F. Y. Young, "SALT: Provably Good Routing Topology by a Novel Steiner Shallow-Light Tree Algorithm", *Proc. ICCAD*, 2017.
[37] N. Viswanathan, C. J. Alpert, C. C. N. Sze, Z. Li and Y. Wei, "The DAC 2012 Routability-driven Placement Contest and Benchmark Suite", *Proc. DAC*, 2012, pp. 774-782.
[38] J. Lu, H. Zhuang, P. Chen, H. Chang, C.-C. Chang, Y.-C. Wong, L. Sha, D. Huang, Y. Luo, C.-C. Teng and C.-K. Cheng, "ePlace-MS: Electrostatics based Placement for Mixed-Size Circuits", *IEEE TCAD* 34(5) (2015), pp. 685-698.

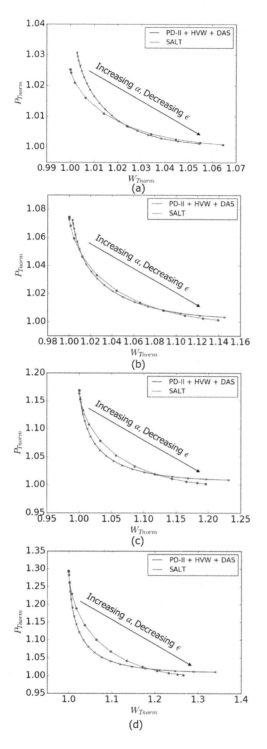

Figure 7: Normalized WL and PL for our metaheuristic and SALT on nets with $|V|$ = (a) 4 to 7, (b) 8 to 15, (c) 16 to 31 and (d) 32+.

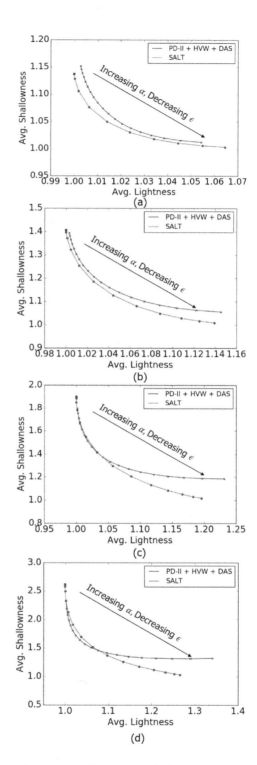

Figure 8: Average shallowness and lightness for our metaheuristic and SALT on nets with $|V|$ = (a) 4 to 7, (b) 8 to 15, (c) 16 to 31 and (d) 32+.

Construction of All Rectilinear Steiner Minimum Trees on the Hanan Grid*

Sheng-En David Lin
Washington State University
Pullman, Washington
slin3@eecs.wsu.edu

Dae Hyun Kim
Washington State University
Pullman, Washington
daehyun@eecs.wsu.edu

ABSTRACT

Given a set of pins, a Rectilinear Steiner Minimum Tree (RSMT) connects the pins using only rectilinear edges with the minimum wirelength. RSMT construction is heavily used at various design steps such as floorplanning, placement, routing, and interconnect estimation and optimization, so fast algorithms to construct RSMTs have been developed for many years. However, RSMT construction is an NP-hard problem, so even a fast RSMT construction algorithm such as GeoSteiner [7] is too slow to use in electronic design automation (EDA) tools. FLUTE, a lookup-table-based RSMT construction algorithm, builds and uses a routing topology database to quickly construct RSMTs [5]. However, FLUTE outputs only one RSMT for a given set of pin locations. In this paper, we develop an algorithm to build a database of all RSMTs on the Hanan grid for up to nine pins. The database will be able to help minimize routing congestion and maximize the routability in the design of modern very-large-scale integration layouts.

CCS CONCEPTS

• **Hardware → Wire routing**;

KEYWORDS

Rectilinear Steiner Minimum Tree, RSMT, Routing, Wirelength, Congestion

ACM Reference Format:
Sheng-En David Lin and Dae Hyun Kim. 2018. Construction of All Rectilinear Steiner Minimum Trees on the Hanan Grid. In *ISPD '18: 2018 International Symposium on Physical Design, March 25–28, 2018, Monterey, CA, USA.*. ACM, New York, NY, USA, Article 4, 8 pages. https://doi.org/10.1145/3177540.3178240

1 INTRODUCTION

The Rectilinear Steiner Minimum Tree (RSMT) construction problem is finding an Rectilinear Steiner Tree (RST) having the minimum length. Since there could be infinitely many RSMTs for a given set of pin locations, the RSMT construction problem is generally limited to finding an RSMT on the Hanan grid [9]. RSMT construction is

---

*Produces the permission block, and copyright information

heavily used in many very-large-scale integration (VLSI) computer-aided design (CAD) tools at various steps such as floorplanning, placement, routing, and interconnect estimation and optimization. Thus, several fast algorithms have been proposed in the literature to construct an RSMT for a given set of pin locations [5, 7]. However, the RSMT construction problem is NP-hard [6], so several papers proposed Rectilinear Minimum Spanning Tree (RMST) or RST construction algorithms for practical use [1, 7, 8, 10–12, 17].

FLUTE builds a database of potentially optimal wirelength vectors (POWVs) and potentially optimal Steiner trees (POSTs) and constructs an RSMT in no time for a given set of pin locations using the database for up to nine pins. FLUTE achieves the shortest wirelength on average for all the 18 IBM benchmarks among five RSMT and one RMST construction algorithms in [5]. In addition, its runtime is 5.56× to 64.92× shorter than the runtimes of all the other RSMT algorithms compared in [5].

One of the applications heavily using RSMT construction in VLSI CAD tools is global routing, in which RSMTs are used for routing topologies. For example, BoxRouter [4], DpRouter [2], Archer [14], MaizeRouter [13], FastRoute [16], GRIP [15], and NTHU-Route [3] use FLUTE for routing topology generation. If there are multiple POWVs having the same minimum wirelength for given pin locations, FLUTE can also construct multiple RSMTs. However, FLUTE constructs only one POST for each POWV, so there is no guarantee that the multiple RSMTs constructed by FLUTE look quite different.

In this paper, we propose an efficient algorithm constructing all RSMTs on the Hanan grid for given pin locations. The algorithm builds a database of all POSTs on the Hanan grid for each POWV for up to nine pins so that applications can use the database to quickly obtain all RSMTs. For more than nine pins, we use the proposed algorithm with a wirelength vector found by FLUTE to construct all RSTs in a reasonable amount of time. Various applications such as global routing and congestion estimation can use the proposed algorithm to quickly generate meaningfully different routing topologies.

2 THE ALGORITHM OF FLUTE

Our all RSMT construction algorithm is based on FLUTE, so we briefly review the idea of FLUTE in this section.

2.1 Position Sequence (Pin Group)

Let $P = \{p_1, p_2, ..., p_n\}$ be a set of n pins and assume that all the pins have distinct x- and y- coordinates. In other words, if the location of p_i is (x_{p_i}, y_{p_i}), $x_{p_i} \neq x_{p_j}$ and $y_{p_i} \neq y_{p_j}$ for any i and j ($i \neq j$). Then, the Hanan grid constructed for the n pins has n horizontal lines and n vertical lines. Let x_i be the x-coordinate of the i-th vertical line from the left and y_i be the y-coordinate of the

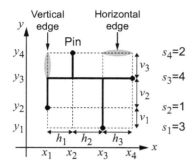

Figure 1: Four pins on the Hanan grid, their position sequence (3142), and an RSMT constructed on the Hanan grid.

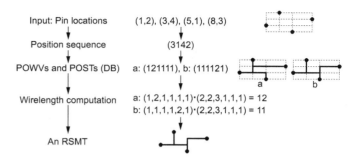

Figure 2: Four pins located on the Hanan grid and its position sequence.

i-th horizontal line from the bottom on the Hanan grid as shown in Figure 1. If the n pins are placed on the Hanan grid, we can characterize the distribution of the pins on the Hanan grid using a *position sequence (pin group)* as follows. Suppose the x-coordinate of the pin whose y-coordinate is y_i is x_{s_i}. Then, the distribution of the pins on the Hanan grid has a position sequence $(s_1 s_2 ... s_n)$. Figure 1 shows four pins, the Hanan grid constructed for them, and its position sequence (3142). Notice that the position sequence is based on not the actual x- and y-coordinates, but the relative locations of the pins. Thus, any set of pin locations can be mapped into one of the $n!$ position sequences for n pins.

2.2 Potentially Optimal Wirelength Vector

The Hanan grid constructed for a position sequence can be decomposed into horizontal and vertical edges as shown in Figure 1. A horizontal edge is a horizontal segment $([x_i, x_{i+1}], y_j)$ and a vertical edge is a vertical segment $(x_k, [y_m, y_{m+1}])$. The length of the horizontal edge whose end points are (x_i, y_j) and (x_{i+1}, y_j) is $h_i = x_{i+1} - x_i$. Similarly, the length of the vertical edge whose end points are (x_k, y_m) and (x_k, y_{m+1}) is $v_m = y_{m+1} - y_m$. Then, any RST constructed on the Hanan grid can be decomposed into horizontal and vertical edges. For example, the RSMT shown in Figure 1 uses one h_1, one h_2, one h_3, one v_1, two v_2, and one v_3 edges on the Hanan grid. The wirelength of the RSMT is

$$L = 1 \cdot h_1 + 1 \cdot h_2 + 1 \cdot h_3 + 1 \cdot v_1 + 2 \cdot v_2 + 1 \cdot v_3, \quad (1)$$

which can also be expressed as a dot product between $(1, 1, 1, 1, 2, 1)$ and $(h_1, h_2, h_3, v_1, v_2, v_3)$. We call $(h_1, h_2, h_3, v_1, v_2, v_3)$ the *edge length vector* of the given set of pin locations. The edge length vector is dependent on the actual pin locations, but the coefficient vector $(1, 1, 1, 1, 2, 1)$ is dependent only on the RSMT topology. When two coefficient vectors $A = (a_1, ..., a_n)$ and $B = (b_1, ..., b_n)$ are given, if $a_i < b_i$ holds for at least one $i = 1, ..., n$ and $a_j \le b_j$ holds for all the other $j = 1, ..., n$, the dot product $A \bullet H$ between A and an edge length vector H is always less than $B \bullet H$. We denote this relation by $A < B$. However, if $a_i < b_i$ holds for some i and $a_j > b_j$ holds for some j ($j \ne i$), $A \bullet H$ is greater or less than $B \bullet H$ depending on H. We denote this relation by $A \leftrightarrow B$. FLUTE finds the set of all coefficient vectors C for each position sequence such that any two coefficient vectors c_i and c_j in C are in the $c_i \leftrightarrow c_j$ relation and there is no c_k in C such that $c_k < c_i$ or $c_k < c_j$. Each element

in C is called a *potentially optimal wirelength vector (POWV)* because it can be a candidate for an RSMT.

FLUTE builds a database of all POWVs for each position sequence. Then, when the locations of n pins are given, FLUTE finds the position sequence of the pins and obtains all the POWVs from the database. Since the actual wirelength is the dot product between a POWV and the edge length vector for the given pins, FLUTE computes the wirelength for each POWV by computing the dot product between the POWV and the edge length vector and finds a POWV having the shortest wirelength.

2.3 Potentially Optimal Steiner Tree

Since FLUTE returns an RSMT for a given set of pin locations, FLUTE has to construct an actual RSMT. Thus, FLUTE also stores a topology corresponding to each POWV in the FLUTE database. A topology stored for each POWV is called a *potentially optimal Steiner tree (POST)*. Figure 2 shows an example. For given four pins located at (1, 2), (3, 4), (5, 1), and (8, 3), FLUTE extracts the position sequence (3142) and obtains two POWVs (1, 2, 1, 1, 1, 1) and (1, 1, 1, 1, 2, 1) from the database. The POSTs corresponding to the POWVs are also shown in the figure. Then, FLUTE computes the wirelength of each POWV and returns the POST corresponding to a POWV having the minimum wirelength. We refer readers to [5] for the details of the FLUTE database construction.

3 CONSTRUCTION OF ALL RSMTS

A POST becomes an RSMT if the POWV of the POST has the minimum wirelength for given pin locations. Thus, constructing all RSMTs on the Hanan grid means constructing all POSTs for all POWVs so that we can return all POSTs of all POWVs having the minimum wirelength for the given pin locations. In this section, we explain our algorithm to construct all POSTs on the Hanan grid for a given set of pin locations.

3.1 Terminologies and Notations

Figure 3 shows the Hanan grid constructed for n pins. There exist $n(n-1)$ horizontal edges, $n(n-1)$ vertical edges, and n^2 vertices. If a vertex is a pin, we call the vertex a *pin vertex*. A vertex is connected to two, three, or four edges. We call these edges the *neighboring edges* of the vertex and denote the set of all the neighboring edges of vertex d by $NE(d)$. An edge connects two vertices. If edge e_i

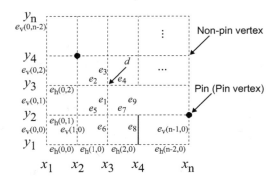

Figure 3: The Hanan Grid for n pins.

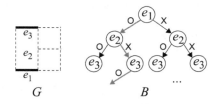

Figure 4: A rectilinear graph G constructed on the Hanan grid and a binary tree B corresponding to G. The red path shows a decision sequence. e_2 is removed in G because the red path traverses through the right arrow of e_2. O and X mean the edge is used or removed in G, respectively.

connects vertices d_j and d_k, we call $NE(d_j) \cup NE(d_k) - \{e_i\}$ the set of the neighboring edges of edge e_i and denote it by $NE(e_i)$. In Figure 3, $NE(d)$ is $\{e_1, e_2, e_3, e_4\}$ and $NE(e_1)$ is $\{e_2, e_3, e_4, e_5, e_6, e_7\}$.

A horizontal edge connects two vertices, one on the left and the other on the right. We denote the left and right vertices of horizontal edge e_i by $V_L(e_i)$ and $V_R(e_i)$, respectively. Similarly, we denote the top and the bottom vertices of vertical edge e_i by $V_T(e_i)$ and $V_B(e_i)$, respectively. Thus, for example, $NE(V_L(e_i))$ is the set of all the neighboring edges connected to the left vertex of horizontal edge e_i. We denote each horizontal edge by $e_h(i, j)$ where i and j are the indices to locate the edge and each vertical edge by $e_v(i, j)$. The indices are shown in Figure 3.

If a vertex of an edge is not a pin vertex and is not connected to any other edges, the edge is *dangling*. For example, if $NE(V_L(e)) - \{e\}$ is the empty set and $V_L(e)$ is not a pin vertex for edge e, e is dangling. If an edge is dangling, it cannot be a part of a POST.

An edge on the Hanan grid can be *available*, *used*, or *removed*. An available edge is an edge that is not used nor removed, but we will decide to use or remove it to construct a POST. e_1 and e_2 in Figure 3 are available edges. A used (or removed) edge is an edge that we have decided to use (or remove) to construct a POST. e_8 is a used edge and e_9 is a removed edge in Figure 3. $powv(e)$ for given edge e is the POWV element corresponding to e. If a POWV is $(q_1, q_2, ..., r_1, r_2, ...)$ where q_k is for the horizontal edges and r_k is for the vertical edges, $powv(e_h(i, j))$ is q_{i+1} and $powv(e_v(i, j))$ is r_{j+1}. We also denote the set of all edges whose POWV element is k by $PE(k)$. For example, $PE(powv(e_h(0, 0)))$ is $\{e_h(0, 0), ..., e_h(0, n-1)\}$.

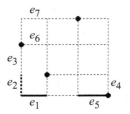

Figure 5: Must-use and must-remove edges.

3.2 Binary Tree-Based POST Construction

We construct a rectilinear graph G on the Hanan grid using a binary tree B to find all POSTs for a given position sequence and a POWV as follows. An internal node in B corresponds to an edge in the Hanan grid. The left and right arrows of an internal node means that we decide to use or remove the edge in G, respectively. Figure 4 shows an example. When we traverse B starting from the root node e_1, we decide to use or remove e_1 in G. When we reach a leaf node, we evaluate the graph G, i.e., we check whether all the pins in G are connected through the used edges. We use the breadth-first search (BFS) algorithm to evaluate a graph.

An exhaustive POST construction algorithm using B uses the in-order traversal to traverse B and evaluates each graph G constructed by B whenever it reaches a leaf node because each leaf node corresponds to a decision sequence ($e_h(0, 0) = O, e_h(0, 1) = X, ...$) where O and X denote that the edge is used and removed, respectively. However, the exhaustive POST construction algorithm is too slow. The Hanan grid constructed for n pins has $2n(n - 1)$ edges, so the total number of leaf nodes in the complete binary tree constructed for n pins has $2^{2n(n-1)}$ leaf nodes. Since we use the BFS algorithm for evaluation of G and there are $2n(n - 1)$ edges, the complexity to check whether all pins are connected is $O(n^2)$. Thus, the complexity of the exhaustive POST construction algorithm is $O(n^2 2^{2n(n-1)})$.

When we construct all POSTs, however, we use the binary tree with various pruning criteria to reduce the search space. Although the runtime of the algorithm still seems to increase exponentially, it can find all POSTs for up to nine pins in a reasonable amount of time.

3.2.1 Pruning by Zero POWV Elements. When element q in a POWV becomes zero, we can remove all the available edges in $PE(q)$ from graph G. For example, if the position sequence for four pins is (3142) as shown in Figure 1 and a given POWV is $(1, 2, 1, 1, 1, 1)$, taking the left arrow of node $e_h(0, 0)$ in B uses the edge in G and decreases the first element of the POWV by 1, so the POWV becomes $(0, 2, 1, 1, 1, 1)$. Since the first element of the POWV is zero, $e_h(0, 1)$, $e_h(0, 2)$, and $e_h(0, 3)$ in Figure 1 should be removed from G, which also means we remove the left arrows of all the nodes corresponding to these three edges in B.

3.2.2 Pruning by Must-Use and Must-Remove Edges. When an edge on the Hanan grid is used or removed, there might be edges that should also be used or removed. We call the edges that should be used *must-use* edges and the edges that should be removed *must-remove* edges. The reason that there exist must-use and must-remove edges are as follows.

First, suppose we decide to use edge e_1 in Figure 5. If $N_L(e_1)$ is not a pin vertex, we should use e_2 too, otherwise e_1 becomes a dangling edge. Thus, e_2 becomes a must-use edge. Notice that this does not guarantee that e_1 and e_2 will be included in a POST. Rather, we reduce the search space in the binary tree by removing the right arrows of all the nodes corresponding to e_2 in B.

Second, suppose we remove an edge from G. In this case, some of the neighboring edges of the removed edge might become dangling, so we also have to remove them. For example, suppose we remove e_1 in Figure 5, which causes e_2 to be dangling, so e_2 becomes a must-remove edge and should be removed. If we remove e_2, e_3 also becomes a must-remove edge, so we remove e_3 too. We can remove multiple edges consecutively in this way.

Using or removing an edge can cause some of its neighboring edges to be must-use or must-remove edges. For example, if $powv(e_1)$ is 1 and we use e_1 in Figure 5, e_2 becomes a must-use edge and e_6 and e_7 become must-remove edges. If we remove e_1, e_2 becomes a must-remove edge. If we remove e_4, however, e_5 becomes a must-use edge because e_5 is the only edge connecting pin p_1.

3.2.3 Conditions for POST Evaluation. Evaluation of G checks whether G on the Hanan grid connects all the pins. However, evaluating graphs too often increases the runtime meaninglessly. Thus, we evaluate G only when 1) the current POWV becomes a zero vector or 2) we reach a leaf node in B.

3.2.4 Intermediate Connectivity Check. In many cases, using or removing edges occurs consecutively as explained above. Using edges decreases the POWV elements corresponding to them, so some of the POWV elements might become zero if many edges become must-use edges during pruning. If some POWV elements become zero, all the available edges corresponding to the POWV elements become must-remove edges, so we remove them. If many edges are removed, G is highly likely to be disconnected. Thus, we also check whether all the pins are still connected through the used and available edges in G during the pruning if the number of used and removed edges at a pruning step is greater than a pre-determined threshold value[1].

3.2.5 Binary Tree Construction and Traversal. We construct a binary tree for given pin locations and POWV as follows. The root node (at level 0) is $e_h(0,0)$ and the two child nodes (at level 1) of the root node are $e_h(0,1)$. In general, the nodes at level k are $e_h(\lfloor k/n \rfloor, k \bmod n)$ if $k < n(n-1)$ and $e_v(k \bmod n, \lfloor k/n \rfloor - (n-1))$ if $k >= n(n-1)$. Although we used a binary tree above to explain the proposed algorithm, we implemented the algorithm using a recursive function call without explicitly constructing a binary tree to reduce the memory usage.

3.3 Overall Algorithm

Algorithm 1 shows the overall algorithm for constructing all POSTs for given pin locations and a POWV. We first prepare an ordered set (array) E of all the edges (Line 1). The edges are sorted in the traversal order, so E is $(e_h(0,0), e_h(0,1), ..., e_h(1,0), ..., e_h(n-2, n-1), e_v(0,0), e_v(1,0), ..., e_v(n-1, n-2))$. Array R will contain all the POSTs for the given pin locations and POWV (Line 2). Then, we call

___
[1]We use the number of pins for the threshold.

Input: Pin locations and a POWV (powv).
```
 1: Ordered set E = (e_h(0, 0), ..., e_v(n − 1, n − 2));
 2: R = {};
 3: Call recursive_construction (powv, E, R, 0);
 4: Return R;
Function: recursive_construction (powv, E, R, index)
 5:   if powv == 0 or index == E.size then
 6:       if Current graph G connects all the pins then
 7:           Insert G into R;
 8:       end if
 9:       return;
10:   end if
11:   e = E[index];
12:   if e is a used or removed edge then
13:       Call recursive_construction (powv, E, R, index+1);
14:       return;
15:   end if
16:   if powv(e) > 0 then
17:       Call use_or_remove_and_prune (e, NULL, powv);
18:       if # must-use and must-remove edges ≥ threshold then
19:           if Current graph G connects all the pins then
20:               recursive_construction (powv, E, R, index+1);
21:           end if
22:       else
23:           recursive_construction (powv, E, R, index+1);
24:       end if
25:       Roll back the must-use and must-remove edges.
26:   end if
27:   Call use_or_remove_and_prune (NULL, e, powv);
28:   if # must-use and must-remove edges ≥ threshold then
29:       if Current graph G connects all the pins then
30:           recursive_construction (powv, E, R, index+1);
31:       end if
32:   else
33:       recursive_construction (powv, E, R, index+1);
34:   end if
35:   Roll back the must-use and must-remove edges.
```
Algorithm 1: Construction of all POSTs for given pin locations and POWV.

function *recursive_construction* with the current POWV, E, R, and the edge index 0 (Line 3). Once the recursive function call finishes, we return R (Line 4).

At the beginning of function *recursive_construction*, we check whether the current POWV is equal to the zero vector or the edge index has reached the end of E (Line 5). If the condition is true, we check whether the current graph G connects all the pins by performing a BFS starting from a pin only through the used edges (Line 6). If G is connected, it is a POST, so we insert G into R (Line 7) and finish the current function call because there is no reason to explore using/removing edges further (if the POWV is zero) or there is no more edge to process (if the current node is a leaf node).

If the POWV is not equal to the zero vector and there are remaining edges to process (Line 11), we keep constructing POSTs as follows. If the current edge e is a used or removed edge (Line 12), we move on to the next edge (Line 13), which is the same as immediately taking the left or the right arrow at the node corresponding to e in B if it is a used or removed edge, respectively. If e is an available edge, we check whether $powv(e)$ is greater than zero (Line 16). If it is greater than zero, we try using e (which is traversing through the left arrow of the node corresponding to e in B) and prune additional edges (Line 17). Notice that we also try removing e from G (which is traversing through the right arrow of the node) and prune additional edges (Line 27). Once the pruning is done, we perform intermediate connectivity check (Line 18 and 19) when the number of must-use and must-remove edges is greater or equal to a threshold number. In this case, if we can reach all the pins in G through the used and available edges, we call function *recursive_construction* to continue to construct POSTs. If the number of must-use and must-remove edges is less than the threshold number, we just call function *recursive_construction* to move on to the next edge. If G is not connected, we immediately roll back all the changes by restoring G to its previous state (Line 25). Line 27 to Line 35 tries removing edge e from G.

Algorithm 2 shows the proposed algorithm for pruning must-use and must-remove edges after using or removing a given edge. First, insert given edge u into set U (Line 1) and insert given edge m into set M (Line 2). Then, we keep repeating processing must-use edges (from Line 4 to Line 16) and must-remove edges (from Line 17 to Line 26). For each edge e in U, we check whether e is a removed edge or $powv(e)$ is zero (Line 6). If e is a removed edge or $powv(e)$ is zero, we cannot use e in G because it is contradictory, so the current graph G cannot be a POST. Thus, if any of the two conditions is true, we stop processing the must-use edge and return *invalid_topology* (Line 7). Otherwise, we use e (Line 9) and decrease $powv(e)$ by 1 (Line 10). If $powv(e)$ becomes zero, we insert all the available edges in $PE(powv(e))$ into M so that we can remove the edges later (Line 12). Then, we check whether any of the edges in $NE(e)$ are must-use edges. If any, we insert them into U (Line 14) so that we can process them later.

Once we process all the must-use edges in U, we move on to the must-remove edges in M (Line 17). If e in M is a used edge (Line 19), removing e from G leads to a contradiction. Thus, we stop processing the must-remove edge and return *invalid_topology* (Line 20). Otherwise, we remove e from G (Line 22). Then, we insert all dangling edges and must-use edges in $NE(e)$ into M (Line 23) and U (Line 24), respectively, to process them later.

3.4 Example

Figure 6 shows an example. In Figure 6(a), four pins, their position sequence (4123), and a POWV (121111) are given. Starting with edge e_1, $powv(e_1)$ is 1, so we try using it first by marking it used and reducing $powv(e_1)$ by 1 in Figure 6(b). In this case, e_1 will be a dangling edge if e_{13} is not used, so e_{13} becomes a must-use edge. In addition, e_2, e_3, and e_4 become must-remove edges because the POWV element corresponding to the edges is zero. In Figure 6(c), we use e_{13} in G and decrease $powv(e_{13})$ by 1, so the POWV becomes (021011). Since $powv(e_{13})$ becomes zero, e_{16}, e_{19}, and e_{22} become must-remove edges. In Figure 6(d), we remove e_2, e_3, and e_4 in this order. If we remove e_4, e_{15} becomes a must-remove edge. In Figure 6(e), $powv(e_{13})$ is zero, so we remove e_{16}, e_{19}, and e_{22}. Then, we remove e_{15} in Figure 6(f), which causes e_{14} to be dangling, so we remove e_{14} too. However, e_{13} is not dangling when we remove e_{14} because the top vertex of e_{13} is a pin vertex.

```
Function: Use_or_remove_and_prune (u, m, powv)
Input:  (Edge u to use, Edge m to remove, a POWV (powv)).
 1:  U = {u};
 2:  M = {m};
 3:  while U.size + M.size > 0 do
 4:      while U.size > 0 do
 5:          for each e ∈ U do
 6:              if e is a removed edge or powv(e) == 0 then
 7:                  return invalid_topology;
 8:              end if
 9:              Use e in G;
10:              powv(e) = powv(e) - 1;
11:              if powv(e) == 0 then
12:                  Insert all available edges in PE(powv(e)) into M;
13:              end if
14:              Insert all must-use edges in NE(e) into U.
15:          end for
16:      end while
17:      while M.size > 0 do
18:          for each e ∈ M do
19:              if e is a used edge then
20:                  return invalid_topology;
21:              end if
22:              Remove e from G;
23:              Insert all dangling edges in NE(e) into M;
24:              Insert all must-use edges in NE(e) into U;
25:          end for
26:      end while
27:  end while
```

Algorithm 2: Use or remove a given edge and process must-use and must-remove edges.

When we remove e_{16} in Figure 6(e), e_5 becomes a must-use edge because e_1 will be dangling if e_5 is not used. Similarly, when we remove e_{19} and use e_5 after removing e_{16}, e_9 becomes a must-use edge because e_5 will be dangling if e_9 is not used. Thus, e_5 and e_9 become must-use edges. We use these two edges in Figure 6(g) and decrease $powv(e_5)$ and $powv(e_9)$ by 1, so the POWV becomes (010011). Since the third element of the POWV is zero, e_{10}, e_{11}, and e_{12} become must-remove edges, so we remove them in Figure 6(h). Removing the three edges causes e_{23} and e_{24} to be dangling as shown in Figure 6(h), so we remove them in Figure 6(i). Figure 6(j) shows the result of using e_1.

Overall, using e_1 leads to using three additional edges (e_5, e_9, e_{13}) and removing 13 edges (e_2, e_3, e_4, e_{10}, e_{11}, e_{12}, e_{14}, e_{15}, e_{16}, e_{19}, e_{22}, e_{23}, e_{24}). Since the total number of must-use and must-remove edges at this step is 16, which is greater than the total number of pins (four), we perform the intermediate connectivity check. Since the pins are disconnected, using e_1 will not generate POSTs. Thus, we roll back all the used and removed edges and try removing e_1 from the graph in Figure 6(k). e_{13} becomes dangling in this case, so we remove e_{13} too in Figure 6(l). Then, we move on to e_2.

4 SIMULATION RESULTS

In this section, we present various simulation results obtained from the construction of all POSTs on the Hanan grid. We implemented the proposed algorithm using C/C++ and ran all simulations in a

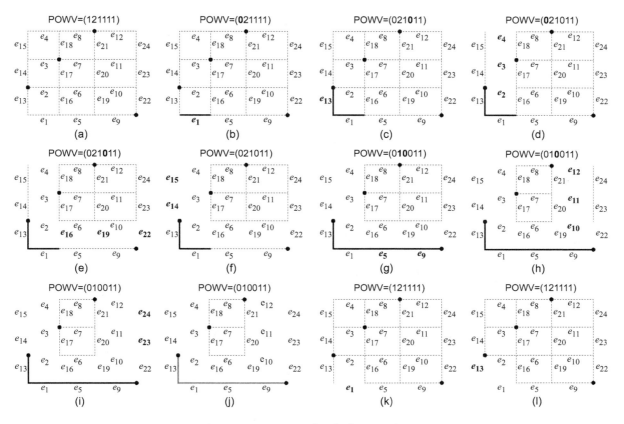

Figure 6: An example of edge pruning.

Table 1: Statistics of the construction of all POSTs. "Con. time" is the construction time for all the POSTs for each pin count and "Con. eff." is the construction efficiency measured by the number of total POSTs over the construction time (in seconds).

# pins (n)	# pin groups ($n!$)	# POWVs in a group			# POSTs for a POWV			# POSTs	Con. time	Con. eff.	Table size
		Min.	Avg.	Max.	Min.	Avg.	Max.				
2	2	1	1	1	2	2	2	4	0.0 s	–	0 MB
3	6	1	1	1	2	2.667	4	16	0.0002 s	80,000	0 MB
4	24	1	1.667	2	2	7.100	12	284	0.0035 s	81,142	0 MB
5	120	1	2.467	3	4	14.392	38	4,260	0.079 s	53,924	0.1 MB
6	720	1	4.433	8	4	37.661	216	120,212	3.72 s	32,315	3.5 MB
7	5,040	1	7.932	15	4	98.080	852	3,920,832	254 s	15,436	141 MB
8	40,320	1	15.251	33	6	289.972	6,558	178,313,916	9.06 hr	5,465	7.7 GB
9	362,880	1	30.039	79	8	929.600	52,010	10,133,050,012	1,700 hr	1,656	525 GB

3.3GHz Intel Core i5-3550 system with 32GB memory. We used only one core to build the database of all POSTs.

4.1 POWVs and POSTs

Table 1 shows various statistics about the construction of all POSTs for up to nine pins. The number of pin groups is the number of position sequences for a given pin count (n). The total number of POSTs for each pin count and the average number of POSTs per POWV increase exponentially. The construction time is almost negligible for up to five pins, but then it increases exponentially,

3.72 seconds for six pins, 254 seconds for seven pins, 9.06 hours for eight pins, and approximately 1,700 hours for nine pins. We also show the construction efficiency measured by the total number POSTs divided by the construction time in seconds. As shown in the table, the construction efficiency goes down exponentially as the pin count goes up. However, the proposed algorithm can still construct 5,465 POSTs per second for eight pins and 1,656 POSTs per second for nine pins on average.

Since the database has all POWVs and POSTs, we can construct all RSMTs for given pin locations as follows. First, we obtain all

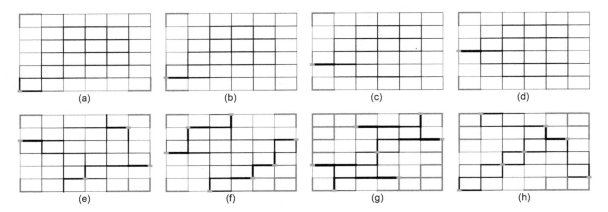

Figure 7: Statistics of POSTs for seven pins. The red edges are not used at all in any POSTs. Thicker edges are used in more POSTs than thinner edges. Green rectangles are pins. Position sequences are as follows. (a) (1XXXXXX), (b) (X1XXXXX), (c) (XX1XXXX), (d) (XXX1XXX), (e) (X47X16X), (f) (3561724), (g) (2514736), which is one of the position sequences having the fewest POSTs, (h) (1734652), which is one of the position sequences having the most POSTs. X is a don't-care.

the POWVs of the position sequence for the pin locations from the database. Then, we compute a dot product between each POWV and the edge length vector $(h_1, ..., v_1, ...)$ and obtain all POWVs having the minimum wirelength. Then, we return all POSTs belonging to the POWVs from the database.

4.2   Statistics of POSTs

In this simulation, we investigate how many times each edge is used in all POSTs for given pin locations. The simulation methodology is as follows. We first come up with a position sequence for seven pins. Each position sequence can be an exact sequence such as (1234567) or include some don't-cares (X). For example, position sequence (12345XX) includes two position sequences (1234567) and (1234576). Then, we search the database to find all POSTs matching the position sequence and count how many times each edge is used in the POSTs. This statistics help estimate whether we can route a given net through non-congested area. If an edge is used in most of the POSTs for given pin locations, for example, it would be hard to route the net without using the edge.

Figure 7 shows eight examples for seven pins. In the figure, the thickness of a black edge is proportional to the number of times it is used. Red edges are not used at all. Green rectangles are pins. First, Figure 7(a) shows the usage of the edges for (1XXXXXX), i.e., when a pin is located at (0,0). As the figure shows, the two edges adjacent to vertex (0,0) are used in almost all POSTs. The edges in the middle area are also used in many POSTs, which means that it would not be possible to route through the middle area if the position sequence of a seven-pin net is (1XXXXXX). Figure 7(b) shows the edge usage for (X1XXXXX), i.e., when a pin is located at (0,1). In this case, none of the POSTs uses edges $e_h(0,0)$, $e_v(0,0)$, $e_h(0,6)$, and $e_v(0,5)$ no matter where the other six pins are located. Similarly, position sequences (XX1XXXX) and (XXX1XXX) do not use the same four edges and heavily use the right edge of the pin vertex and the edges in the middle of the grid as shown in Figure 7(c) and (d). Figure 7(e) shows the usage for position sequence (X47X16X), which we picked randomly. For this position sequence, some edges such as $e_h(1,3)$,

Table 2: Effectiveness (runtime in seconds) of the pruning algorithms. All: Enabling all pruning algorithms. The other four columns are disabling (1) zero POWV elements, (2) must-use edges, (3) must-remove edges, and (4) intermediate connectivity check.

		All	(1)	(2)	(3)	(4)
6 pins	3.72	13.58	3,850	22.39	9.15	
	Ratio (1.00)	3.65×	1,035×	6.02×	2.46×	
7 pins	254	2,837	∞	6,973	964	
	Ratio (1.00)	11.17×	-	27.45×	3.80×	

$e_h(4,2)$, and $e_v(5,4)$ around the middle of the grid are used in many POSTs. Figure 7(f) shows the usage of an exact position sequence (3561724). Since the pins are distributed around the boundaries of the grid, the edges in the middle of the grid are used many times. Figure 7(g) shows the usage for (2514736), which is one of the position sequences having the fewest POSTs and Figure 7(h) shows the usage for (1734652), which is one of the position sequences having the most POSTs.

4.3   Effectiveness of the Pruning Algorithms

We use four pruning algorithms, 1) pruning by zero POWV elements, 2) pruning by must-use edges, 3) pruning by must-remove edges, and 4) intermediate connectivity check, to reduce the POST construction time. Thus, we measured the effectiveness of each algorithm by disabling each of them while enabling all the other techniques. Table 2 shows that pruning by must-use edges is the most effective technique and pruning by must-remove edges is also effective when the pin count goes up. However, the other two pruning techniques also help reduce the runtime considerably, especially when the pin count goes up. For example, if the intermediate connectivity check is disabled, finding all POSTs for the nine-pin case would take more than 8,500 hours instead of 1,700 hours.

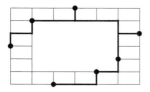

Figure 8: A POST not using specific edges for position sequence (3561724).

4.4 Application – POSTs Using/Not Using Specific Edges

A representative application of the proposed algorithm is multiple routing topology generation for global routing. Generating multiple RSMTs for each net can effectively reduce routing overflows, minimize routing congestion, and reduce the total coupling capacitance. In this section, we show how to use the database of all POSTs to avoid non-preferred (such as congested) area and/or preferred (such as non-congested) area. Suppose a set of pin locations and non-preferred region are given. Then, we search the POST database to find all POWVs belonging to the position sequence of the given pin locations. For each POWV, we compute the wire length by the dot product between the POWV and the edge length vector. Then, we find all POWVs having the shortest wire length. For each POST belonging to the POWVs, we check whether the POST uses any edges in the non-preferred region. Finally, we return all the POSTs not using any edges in the non-preferred region. Figure 8 shows an example for position sequence (3561724) shown in Figure 7(f). We searched for POSTs not containing the removed edges in Figure 8. The POST in the figure shows one of the POSTs satisfying the condition.

The search time consists of 1) finding the position sequence, 2) finding the set P all the POWVs belonging to the position sequence and having the shortest wire length, 3) going through all the POSTs in P and checking whether each POST contains specific edges. The runtime of the first step is negligible and the complexity of the second step is approximately $O(n \cdot 2^n)$ where n is the number of pins. The exponential term comes from the total number of POWVs belonging to a position sequence as shown in Table 1 and the multiplication factor n comes from the total number of multiplications for the dot product computation. The complexity of the third step is approximately $O(k \cdot 3^n)$ where n is the number of pins. The exponential term comes from the total number of POSTs for a POWV and k is the number of edges in the non-preferred and/or preferred regions.

Notice that this does not solve the obstacle-avoiding RSMT construction problem that finds RSTs having the minimum wirelength for given pin locations and obstacles. Rather, we return all POSTs (or RSMTs if their POWVs have the minimum wirelength) that use and/or do not use specific edges.

4.5 Multiple RSTs For More Than Nine Pins

Although it might be inefficient or impossible (due to the large database size) to build and use a database for nets having more than nine pins, if a set of pin locations is given, we can run FLUTE to construct an RST, obtain its wirelength vector (WV), and run the proposed algorithm to obtain multiple RSTs having the same WV. Notice that the proposed algorithm is not limited to constructing RSMTs. Rather, if pin locations and a wirelength vector are given, the proposed algorithm can construct all RSTs satisfying the given WV. Thus, we tried constructing multiple RSTs using FLUTE for a few cases. Constructing all Steiner trees (STs) for a 10-pin, a 11-pin, and a 12-pin cases (each with one WV) found 324, 6,390, and 870 STs in 10.38 seconds, 72.99 seconds, and 7.91 seconds, respectively. The 12-pin case had a smaller search space than the 10- and 11-pin cases, so it took only 7.91 seconds.

5 CONCLUSION

In this paper, we proposed an efficient algorithm to construct all RSMTs for up to nine pins using a lookup table and FLUTE. The generation time and table size are reasonable for up to nine pins, but the number of POSTs, the database generation time, and the database size increase exponentially as the number of pins goes up. Using the database of all POSTs, we investigated several properties of the POSTs. The proposed algorithm and the database of all POSTs will help various VLSI CAD software optimize layouts more efficiently.

ACKNOWLEDGMENTS

This work was supported by the Defense Advanced Research Projects Agency Young Faculty Award under Grant D16AP00119 and the New Faculty Seed Grant (125679-002) funded by the Washington State University.

REFERENCES

[1] Manjit Borah, Robert Michael Owens, and Mary Jane Irwin. 1994. An Edge-Based Heuristic for Steiner Routing, Vol. 13. 1563–1568.
[2] Zhen Cao, Tong Jing, Jinjun Xiong, Yu Hu, Lei He, and Xianlong Hong. 2007. DpRouter: A Fast and Accurate Dynamic-Pattern-Based Global Routing Algorithm. 256–261.
[3] Yen-Jung Chang, Yu-Ting Lee, Jhih-Rong Giao, Pei-Ci Wu, and Ting-Chi Wang. 2010. NTHU-Route 2.0: A Robust Global Router for Modern Designs, Vol. 29. 1931–1944.
[4] Minsik Cho and David Z. Pan. 2007. BoxRouter: A New Global Router Based on Box Expansion and Progressive ILP, Vol. 26. 2130–2143.
[5] Chris Chu and Yiu-Chung Wong. 2008. FLUTE: Fast Lookup Table Based Rectilinear Steiner Minimal Tree Algorithm for VLSI Design, Vol. 27. 70–83.
[6] M. R. Garey and D. S. Johnson. 1979. *Computers and Intractability: A Guide to the Theory of NP-Completeness*. New York: Freeman.
[7] GeoSteiner. [n. d.]. Software for Computing Steiner Trees. http://www.geosteiner.com. ([n. d.]).
[8] J. Griffith, G. Robins, J. S. Salowe, and Tongtong Zhang. 1994. Closing the Gap: Near-Optimal Steiner Trees in Polynomial Time, Vol. 13. 1351–1365.
[9] M. Hanan. 1966. On Steiner's Problem with Rectilinear Distance. In *SIAM Journal on Applied Mathematics*, Vol. 14. 255–265.
[10] F. K. Hwang, D. S. Richards, and P. Winter. 1992. *The Steiner Tree Problem*. Elsevier.
[11] Andrew B. Kahng, I. I. Mandoiu, and A. Z. Zelikovsky. 2003. Highly Scalable Algorithms for Rectilinear and Octilinear Steiner Trees. 827–833.
[12] Ion I. Mandoiu, Vijay V. Vazirani, and Joseph L. Ganley. 2000. A New Heuristic for Rectilinear Steiner Trees, Vol. 19. 1129–1139.
[13] Michael D. Moffitt. 2008. MaizeRouter: Engineering an Effective Global Router, Vol. 27. 2017–2026.
[14] Muhammet Mustafa Ozdal and Martin D. F. Wong. 2007. Archer: A History-Driven Global Routing Algorithm. 488–495.
[15] Tai-Hsuan Wu, Azadeh Davoodi, and Jeffrey T. Linderoth. 2009. GRIP: Scalable 3D Global Routing Using Integer Programming. 320–325.
[16] Yue Xu, Yanheng Zhang, and Chris Chu. 2009. FastRoute 4.0: Global Router with Efficient Via Minimization. 576–581.
[17] Hai Zhou. 2004. Efficient Steiner Tree Construction Based on Spanning Graphs, Vol. 23. 704–710.

Challenges in Large FPGA-based Logic Emulation Systems

William N. N. Hung
Synopsys
Mountain View, California
William.Hung@synopsys.com

Richard Sun
Synopsys
Mountain View, California
Richard.Sun@synopsys.com

ABSTRACT

Functional verification is an important aspect of electronic design automation. Traditionally, simulation at the register transfer-level has been the mainstream functional verification approach. Formal verification and various static analysis checkers have been used to complement specific corners of logic simulation. However, as the size of IC designs grow exponentially, all the above approaches fail to scale with the design growth. In recent years, logic emulation have gained popularity in functional verification, partly due to their performance and scalability benefits. There are two main approaches to logic emulation: ASIC and commercial field-programmable gate array (FPGA). In this paper, we focus on commercial FPGA based logic emulation and present various challenging problems in this area for the academic community.

CCS CONCEPTS

• **Hardware → Reconfigurable logic and FPGAs; Hardware accelerators; Reconfigurable logic applications;**

KEYWORDS

Logic emulation; field-programmable gate array

ACM Reference Format:
William N. N. Hung and Richard Sun. 2018. Challenges in Large FPGA-based Logic Emulation Systems. In *ISPD '18: 2018 International Symposium on Physical Design, March 25–28, 2018, Monterey, CA, .* ACM, New York, NY, USA, 8 pages. https://doi.org/10.1145/3177540.3177542

1 INTRODUCTION

Murphy's Law states "if anything can go wrong, it will." The hi-tech industry is a good testimony to this ancient adage. From the Intel Pentium floating-point division bug [8], to NASA's Mars space craft crash due to metric confusion [9], disasters one after another showcase brilliant engineering projects marred by trivial mistakes. They may be big designs, but their verification tasks failed to catch some of the most obvious problems. The importance of verification cannot be over-emphasized. A well-known fact is that nowadays verification cost in an IC design team occupies 60-80% of the entire working resources and efforts. Consequently, functional verification has been the focus of the EDA industry for the last several

ISPD '18, March 25–28, 2018, Monterey, CA,
© 2018 Association for Computing Machinery.
ACM ISBN 978-1-4503-5626-8/18/03...$15.00
https://doi.org/10.1145/3177540.3177542

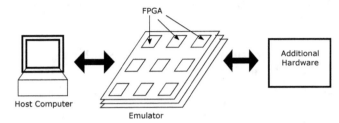

Figure 1: Emulator connected to host computer and other hardware adapted from [3, 24]

years. Although there has been a lot of progress on formal and static verification in the past decades, scalability is still a major concern in formal verification and related methods. At present, simulation is still the mainstream approach to functional verification. As the hardware companies work on increasingly larger designs, even simulation is struggling to tackle runtime and memory problems. In recent years, logic emulation has emerged as the dominant approach to address design size explosion problems. There are three main hardware chips used in logic emulation: (1) customized processor chips, (2) customized FPGA and processor chips, and (3) commercial FPGA chips. It should be noted that (1) and (2) are both application specific integrated circuits (ASIC), but (3) is not ASIC. There has been some analysis [4, 22] of the pros and cons of ASIC and commercial FPGA-based logic emulation. In this paper, we focus on the challenges in commercial FPGA based logic emulation.

The idea of using multiple FPGAs for logic emulation was introduced in [12] as an application of reconfigurable computing [10]. The basic concept of FPGA-based logic emulation was described in [3, 24]. A logic emulation system consists of one or more emulation boards. Each board can contain multiple FPGAs as well as other ICs such as memory chips [14]. These emulation boards can connect to a host computer. A traditional simulation on a computer can be accelarated using an emulation system, whereas the FPGAs on the emulation boards replace a part of the design to be simulated, and software on the host computer complete the remaining simulation tasks. To achieve high speed emulation, many people utilize a transaction-based emulation [20, 23] approach to reduce the coupling between the emulated design and host computer so that emulation and the computer software can separately proceed without frequently waiting for each other. The emulator can further connect to other hardware systems. The overall emulation system is illustrated in Figure 1. Other approaches [5, 17–19, 25] have also been used to leverage FPGA for logic emulation.

2 SOFTWARE FLOW

In order to emulate a design, we typically start from the hardware description which is written in Verilog, SystemVerilog or VHDL. The overall flow involves a number of steps: translation, partitioning, global placement, global routing, pin assignment, technology mapping, FPGA placement and routing, until it finally generates the bitstream for each FPGA.

(1) Translation: The hardware description is translated into circuit representation using EDA tools. Some logic restructuring is needed to translate certain non-synthesizable portion of the design to synthesizable circuitry. For example, assertions in SystemVerilog need to be compiled into circuit. Hardware description language semantic interactions with external environment such as DPI functions, system tasks or system functions can be converted to special circuits using well-defined emulator interfaces such as the SCE-MI [1].

(2) Partitioning and Global Placement: The circuit is divided into multiple pieces such that each leaf-level partition can fit into individual FPGA by the global placer.

(3) Global Routing: Signals connecting different partitions are routed using the wires between various FPGAs.

(4) Pin Assignment: Since each FPGA has only a limited number of pins, the physical connection between FPGAs are very limited. Multiplexing of signals through physical wires [3] can be used to achieve the desired connectivity.

(5) Technology Mapping: The partitioned circuit on each FPGA is mapped to the FPGA vendor's logic primitives.

(6) FPGA placement and routing: The technology mapped netlist for each FPGA is being placed and routed within each FPGA. This is typically done using proprietary tools from the FPGA vendor.

There is a debate between two school of thoughts regarding where technology mapping should happen. One school of thought follows the flow of [12] which is shown in Figure 2(a). Their reasoning is technology mapping should be deferred just before FPGA place and route step, when all the circuit partitions for each FPGA and their inter-chip connectivity have been determined. At this point, the technology mapping tool only need to focus on optimizing within the FPGA with known set of hardware resources from the chip. Another school of thought follows the flow of [3] which is shown in Figure 2(b). They argue that technology mapping should happen before partitioning such that accurate resource utilization information can be given to the partitioner. Ultimately this is a chicken-and-egg problem: the partitioner needs the resource utilization information from the technology mapper, and the technology mapper needs the circuit boundary defined by the partitioner. However, notice that circuit before technology mapping can retain more high level information from the original hardware description. After technology mapping, most of these information will be lost or difficult to retain.

3 SYSTEM ARCHITECTURAL CHALLENGES

In this section, we will start with a discussion of two commonly adopted architecture topologies of multi-FPGA logic emulation systems. They are 2-dimensional mesh and hierarchical network.

Then, we will review the concept of I/O TDM which is a critical enabler for logic emulation as an FPGA application.

3.1 Architectural Topology

To emulate a DUT that is larger than a single FPGA, multiple FPGAs have to be used to accommodate the DUT logic. The topology used to interconnect these FPGAs is essential for the quality of routing the signals spanning multiple FPGAs. Among others, one topology to connect multiple FPGAs is 2-dimensional mess shown in Figure 3. This topology was commonly adopted in earlier commercial emulation systems due to its simplicity for PCB layout. When counting the distance between two FPGAs, it also has the advantage of possessing rectilinear metric which is the underlying distance model of modern placement algorithms. This nice property enables the potential usage of the existing 2-dimensional ASIC placement algorithms to partition DUT into these regularly arranged FPGAs. However, this topology suffers from the long routing delay if the driver of a timing critical net is placed in an FPGA that is not in the proximity of the FPGAs containing its targets. A clear analogy of such a problem is the long delay issue in providing only the unit-length wire segments inside Xilinx's FPGAs in which lies a 2-dimensional mesh of Configurable Logic Blocks (CLBs). The unit-length wire segments provide the most flexibility in routing. However, the resultant performance has to be improved by the introduction of longer wire segments such as the hex lines and the long lines to reduce the route delay. Because of this long routing delay issue, the 2-dimensional mesh topology is mainly used for hardware prototyping systems and small emulation systems. For designs of multiple billions of gates, hundreds of FPGAs have to be used to accommodate such big designs. These FPGAs are usually divided into groups and those belonging to the same group are interconnected in PCBs through PCB traces. Multiple PCBs can be connected together via backplane connectors to form a unit of larger capacity and, multiple of units can also be connected via cable lines in order to accommodate designs with even larger sizes. Such a topology of hierarchical network as shown in Figure 4 has the advantages of better performance scalability and higher potential parallelism in compiling parts of the DUT independently. Therefore, we shall assume the architecture of network topology in the remaining discussions.

3.2 Input/Output Time-Division Multiplexing

To maximize logic emulation speed, it is natural to favor FPGAs with large capacity in order to minimize the number of signals propagating across FPGA boundaries as the off-chip delay is much higher than the routing delay inside an FPGA. However, the number of I/O pins available in each FPGA is so limited that the FPGA logic utilization for logic emulation applications is upper bounded by 20% if we honor the limitation of I/O pin count [2]. In order to increase the logic utilization to achieve higher performance, Time-Division Multiplexing (TDM) is applied to I/O pin-pair, allowing multiple DUT signals to share the same I/O pin-pair between two connecting FPGAs [2]. The implementation of I/O TDM relies on a fast clock that controls the transmission of the DUT signals to cross the boundary sequentially. The frequency of the fast clock must be higher than that of the emulation clock frequency and

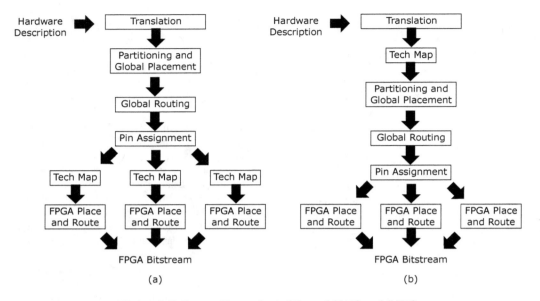

Figure 2: Software Flow adapted from (a)[12] and (b)[3]

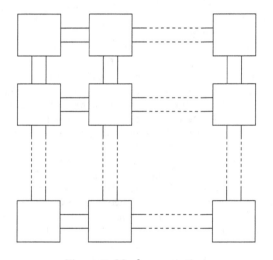

Figure 3: Mesh connection

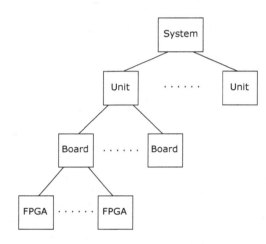

Figure 4: Hierarchical connection

thus is dependent on the frequency of the emulation clock. In one I/O implementation (the "ordered approach") the design signals are ordered and statically scheduled for TDM transmission based on their relative arrival times and signal dependencies [24]. This ordered I/O TDM scheduling can improve system performance. However, the explicit TDM scheduling of all DUT signals together with the performance-driven partitioning and routing makes the timing optimization problem very computationally complex and difficult to solve. To mitigate the complexity of the performance optimization problem, one idea is to ignore the TDM scheduling during partitioning and routing and consider TDM scheduling only after partitioning and routing processes are done. However, this two-separate-step approach could likely lead to a back-end compilation with sub-optimal performance quality. Moreover, FPGA

P&R tools have to ensure the approximated signal arrival time is achievable for each TDM signal, which is, in general, difficult. An alternative I/O TDM implementation uses an order-agnostic approach. The order-agnostic approach schedules design signals in any TDM time slot without regard to signal dependencies or relative arrival times. Instead, the order-agnostic TDM scheduling considers only the TDM-ratio (the number of signals sharing the same pin-pair) and assumes the same worst-case delay for all signals. Thus, specific ordering of TDM signals is no longer necessary and the transmission delay is a function that only depends on the TDM ratio, the number of signals sharing the same pin-pair. With this approach, each signal sharing the same pin-pair with TDM ratio equal to x is assumed to have the same TDM delay, which is equal to the time to transmit all x signals. This worst-case delay value for each signal involved in I/O TDM ensures that each signal has enough time to propagate through regardless of its relative arrival time. This approach simplifies the performance optimization problem during partitioning and routing. However, it eliminates the possibility of optimizing the emulation speed by scheduling the TDM signals based on their arrival times.

4 COMPILE CHALLENGES

The compile process converts the hardware description language into its implementation in multi-FPGA logic emulation system with hierarchical network topology. In this section, we present details in optimization challenges when maximizing performance and minimizing compilation time in each step of this compile process.

4.1 Technology Mapping Challenges

FPGA-based logic emulation present many challenges for technology mapping. In this section, we focus our discussion on two main challenges: clock domain and control set reduction.

4.1.1 Clock Domain. The original hardware design for logic emulation typically come from ASIC designers. There are some fundamental differences between designing for ASIC and designing for FPGA. The physical design process for ASIC has the flexibility to implement complex clock structures and could guarantee low clock skew. FPGA relies on dedicated clock routing resources to guarantee low clock skew. Since these dedicated clock resources are limited in FPGAs, the number of clocks that can be supported are also limited. When we use FPGA to emulate a design that was originally written for ASIC purpose, we typically encounter a lot of derived clocks, including combinatorial gated clocks, sequential generated clocks, etc. This problem is exasperated by low power design, where many clocks are further gated by power down circuitry. A classic way [6] of handling combinatorial power-down gated clock is to find out which signal is the clock and which signal contains the power-down enable, the enable signal can then be moved to the data path of the register enable path, as shown in Figure 5. However, this approach require the user to differentiate the clock signal from the enable signal to the EDA tool. On large designs, there are too many clocks, it is necessary for the EDA tool to automatically handle such scenarios. This is a generic problem that still needs to be improved.

4.1.2 Control Set. Many FPGAs have pre-arranged grouping of LUTs and flip-flops. For example, the Xilinx Virtex 7 FPGA uses the SLICE concept. Each SLICE in Virtex 7 has 4 LUTs and 4 Flip-flops. These flip-flops share the same clock signal, the same clock synchronous enable signal, and the same set/reset signal. We refer to these signals (clock, synchronous enable, set/reset) as the control set of the SLICE.

Similar arrangement can be found in the Altera Stratix FPGA family, which uses the LAB concept instead of SLICE. Each LAB contains numerous Adaptive Logic Modules (ALMs). Each ALM contains a fixed number of LUTs and flip-flops. There are very few unique clock, enable, and set/reset signals for the entire LAB.

The control set presents a problem if the technology mapped netlist has too many flip-flops with unique clocks, enables, or set/reset signals. These distinct control set signals will prevent these flip-flops from sharing the same SLICE. Hence, too many unique

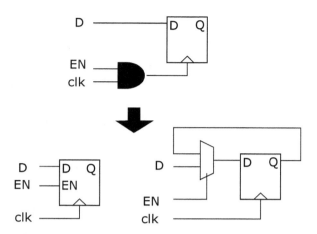

Figure 5: Gated clock conversion adapted from [6]

control set may require a blow-up of SLICE usage and present a place and route problem.

4.2 Partitioning

The partitioning problem is to partition the DUT into hundreds of pieces such that each piece can be implemented inside an FPGA without exceeding the pre-specified logic utilization. The objective of partitioning is traditionally to minimize the cut sizes, which is considered in both academia and industry as effectively solved by hMetis [16]. Therefore, we shall list the challenges of the partitioning problem specific in FPGA-based logic emulation as follows.

(1) For DUTs with billions of gates, it is mandatory to leverage as much design hierarchy as possible when constructing the hyper-graph for partitioning. A design instance of a reasonable size and with the minimum number of interfacing signals is usually selected as an indivisible block and represented as a node in the hyper-graph for partitioning. For logic emulation emphasizing performance optimization, this block selection criterion has to be extended to consider the performance aspect. However, identifying timing critical blocks without already forming a partitioning requires an effective timing estimate that correlates well with the final timing.

(2) For logic emulation emphasizing high performance, cut size is not an accurate indicator of the emulation performance. The delay associate with each signal in the cut depends on two factors. The first factor is the how many inter-FPGA hops this cut signal routes through. The longer inter-FPGA hops usually imply a larger delay. The second factor for the delay is the TDM ratio of each inter-FPGA hop in the route of this cut signal. Unfortunately, the exact values of both factors are not available until routing is done. An accurate enough delay estimate needs to be invented for partitioner to optimize toward performance goals. Moreover, the calculation of this delay estimate should be fast enough so that it will not slow down the partitioning time significantly.

(3) A reasonable logic utilization constraint for partitioning is needed for FPGA P&R success. However, this is often not

sufficient to guarantee FPGA P&R success. Therefore, it is desirable to find a partitioning with as even area distribution as possible, at the expense of degradation in partitioning quality such as an increase in cut size. Such an FPGA-P&R-friendly partitioning should be obtained without much increase in the partitioning time.

(4) Logic replication has been proved to be effective in improving performance [11]. Given a partitioning result, we could perform timing analysis, extract the critical path information, and decide the logic to replicate for better performance, subject to the logic utilization constraint for FPGA P&R. Techniques of performance-driven logic replication [7, 11] can be applied here. In addition, further improvement could be possible if the partitioner is able to foresee the potential of logic replication for performance optimization and consider logic replication impacts on performance during partitioning.

4.3 Placement

Placement can be considered as a separate step after partitioning if the partitioner only partitions the DUT into multiple logical partitions without assigning a physical FPGA location for each logic partition. Challenges of placement problem specific in FPGA-based logic emulation for large designs are listed as follows.

(1) Placement problem can be considered as an extension of the partitioning problem, where the logic belonging to the same logical partition is further constrained to be placed together at a location decided in the solution. In other words, we need to decide not only the logic instances belonging to a partition, but the location FPGA these logic instances of a partition will be implemented. Therefore, all the challenges in optimizing performance discussed in the partitioning section need to be addressed here.

(2) A bridging FPGA is a physical FPGA which connects with FPGAs in different boards or in different units. Intuitively, the router has to route signals connecting to other boards or units through bridging FPGAs. Therefore, generally speaking, bridging FPGAs have more routes hopping through and, consequently, could potentially have more FPGA routing congestion for FPGA P&R. Therefore, it is desirable to place partitions with less logic at bridging FPGA locations to avoid FPGA P&R difficulty. However, placing a partition with more signals connecting to other boards or units tends to reduce one routing hop for such signal routes. Therefore, a trade-off between the performance optimization and the ease of FPGA P&R needs to be decided. Unfortunately, the optimization in such a trade-off is difficult because the FPGA routability is difficult to predict without the actual P&R execution and the performance benefit in reducing one FPGA hop is also not known until the actual routing (described next) is performed.

4.4 Routing

After the placement is finished, a netlist connecting FPGAs, which are already placed at physical FPGA locations according to the placement results, can be extracted. The routing problem is to find a route for each net using the physical FPGAs available in the

emulation systems and the pre-routed PCB traces, each of which connects a pair of LVDS pins belonging to two physical FPGAs. The PCB-trace connectivity between physical FPGAs can be described as a graph where a node represents a physical FPGA and an edge with an edge weight w means the two physical FPGAs represented by the two end nodes of the edge are connected by w LVDS pin pairs. Note that although some regularity of the connectivities among local physicacl FPGAs can be observed in practice, we should assume the connectivity graph is irregular in general and the amount of LVDS pin pairs connecting two physical FPGAs varies. To simplify our subsequent discussion of challenges in optimizing performance during routing, we adopt the asynchronous I/O TDM clocking scheme, where all signals involved in TDM sharing have the same delay whose value only depends on the TDM ratio. Also, we assume each FPGA has a fixed internal delay since the FPGA internal delay is not yet known before FPGA netlist is decided and compiled using FPGA vendor's software.

The challenges in optimizing performance during routing starts with the construction of the routing graph, which is the underlying graph that the routing algorithm traverses through to find connecting paths. Intuitively, each node in the routing graph corresponds to a physical FPGA. A route going through a node means it goes through the corresponding physical FPGA as a hop. It is, however, not as trivial to represent the connectivity between physical FPGAs in the routing graph. If an edge corresponds to an LVDS pin-pair between two physical FPGAs, say u and v, then the number of edges connecting nodes corresponding to u and v is equal to the number of LVDS pin-pairs connecting physical FPGAs represented by u and v. Treating each such an LVDS pin-pair as a separate edge slows down Dijkstra's shortest-path expansion without giving much benefit as these LVDS pin-pairs are functionally equivalent. However, using one edge to represent all of them is not sufficient, as some of them will be shared by routes going from physical FPGA represented by u to the one represented by v and the rest will be shared by routes going in the opposite direction. In order to optimize performance, the pin-pairs shared by routes going in the same direction between physical FPGAs represented by u and v need to be further split into groups so that pin-pairs of the same group are shared by routes with a similar timing criticality in that direction. This splitting is important because we would like a timing critical route to go through a pin-pair with a smaller TDM ratio value so that the delay added to the route delay can be smaller. Similarly, a less timing-critical route can go through a pin-pair with a larger TDM ratio as it is less disruptive in the overall performance. Despite of the need to split pin-pairs for better performance, we cannot afford to split pin-pairs into too many groups either to avoid slowing down Dijkstra's shortest path algorithm. Therefore, the decision on the number of groups we should split pin-pairs into for different timing criticalities is a trade-off between performance and routing compile time. What is more challenging is each rip-up and re-route reduces the TDM ratios of the pin-pairs used by the ripped route and increases the TDM ratios of the pin-pairs used by the newly created route. Therefore, splitting of pin-pairs needs to be adjusted during each route-ripping and re-routing in order to actually reflect the delay changes caused by the route changes. However, the compile time increase needs to be taken into consideration for the dynamic adjustment of pin-pair splitting during each rip-up and re-route.

Performance instability is another challenge in solving the routing problem with TDM'ed routing resources. The performance instability challenge comes from the fact that whenever the pin-pair splitting changes, the resultant TDM ratios of the affected pin-pair groups could fluctuate by much. This is because TDM raio = # of routes/# of pin-pairs and incrementing or decrementing the denominator, which is usually at least one order of magnitude smaller than the enumerator, could cause the quotient to change by a larger amount. Therefore, the resultant performance tends to be unstable in routing optimization.

One unique nature of our routing problem is that there is no capacity constraint on the routing resources since each LVDS pin-pair can accommodate as many routes as possible. The number of routes using the same pin-pair should be limited only for the performance reason. Consequently, the existing negotiation-based routing algorithm [21], which exhibits a negotiation process between meeting capacity constraint and maximizing performance, cannot be applied directly. Moreover, the fact that all the routes sharing the same pin-pair have the same TDM delay implies that the ripping of a route, say x, could reduce the delays of all existing routes that shared pin-pair with x, and that the rerouting of x could increase the delays of all existing routes that become sharing pin-pair with x. In other words, an existing route that was routed successfully to meet certain minimum speed requirement might not meet the same requirement anymore after some newly routed signal starts sharing a pin-pair with it. This fact of changing the route delays of all the routes sharing pin-pairs also causes the incremental timing update not as effective as its applicability in the traditional routing problem, because there are usually multiple route delays that need to be updated, instead of only the route delay of the signal that is being ripped-up and re-routed. Note that the property where the delay of a route depends on other routes also applies to the ASIC routing problem with crosstalk consideration [13]. However, it is not clear how an ASIC crosstalk routing algorithm which concerns mainly the proximity of routes in a two-dimensional space can be applied to solve our routing problem where the routes are limited to use the edges of an irregular routing graph.

4.5 Pin Assignment

Pin assignment happens after all the nets of the netlist constructed for routing are routed. The routing result for each net consists of

- a route tree where each node is a physical FPGA and the edges describe precisely the route of the net constructed as the routing result;
- a TDM ratio wherever the route enters or leaves a physical FPGA.

The pin assignment problem can be stated using an example as follows. Consider a pair of physical FPGAs connected by LVDS pin-pairs as shown in Figure 6. Suppose the routing step produces 16 routes of TDM raio 8, 4 routes of TDM raio 4, and 6 routes of TDM ratio 6, through this pair of physical FPGAs. There are 4 pin-pairs needed to propagate these routed signals through the two FPGAs, 2 for TDM raio 8, 1 for TDM raio 4, and 1 for TDM raio 6. In such an example, pin assignment has to divide the 16 routes

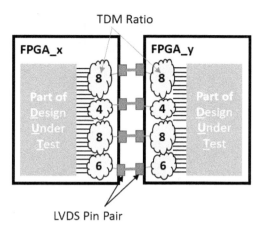

Figure 6: Pin Assignment

of TDM ratio 8 into two groups evenly, and routes in each group share the same LVDS pin-pair. This task is called *signal grouping*. Other than signal grouping, pin assignment also decides which physical LVDS pin-pair should be used to propagate through the signals in each signal group. This 1-to-1 mapping betweeen physical pins and signal groups is called *pin mapping*. Note that in order to do pin mapping, we need to know the locations of LVDS pins inside a physical FPGA and the connectivity of the physical LVDS pin-pairs between two connected physical FPGAs. We use Xilinx's Virtex-7 2000T as an example. This device has 4 dies arranged linearly inside the same package as shown in Figure 7. For each two physical FPGAs connected by LVDS pin-pairs, there are totally 16 possible die pairs, each pair with one die from each of the two FPGAs. However, the LVDS pin-pairs are only available in some, not all, die pairs due to the routability limitations of PCB routing. For instance, FPGA 1 and FPGA 2 in Figure 7 has only 3 die pairs with LVDS pin-pairs connecting these two FPGAs. They are (FPGA1-die0, FPGA2-die0), (FPGA1-die1, FPGA2-die1), and (FPGA1-die2, FPGA2-die3). Given a route from FPGA 0 to FPGA 4 in this figure, we need to decide which die of FPGA 0 and FPGA 4 the driver and the target of this route should be placed, respectively. Also, for each intermediate FPGA in the route, we need to decide which LVDS pin-pair should be used to enter the FPGA and which to leave. Given a route produced in the routing step, these decisions uniquely define a die-level route. For instance, the pin mapping result shown in brown color results in 9 crossings of die boundary, whereas the one in purple results in no crossing of die boundary. In practice, each crossing of a die boundary incurs propagation delay of the route and could potentially slow down the emulation performance if this route is part of the most critical path. Therefore, as part of the pin assignment step, partitioning DUT inside each physical FPGA into 4 dies and pin mapping to minimize the number of crossings of die boundary are both important in maximizing the emulation performance.

The pin mapping example above illustrates a simplified case where only 1 route is considered. Note that this route belongs to one signal group (decided by the signal grouping decision described

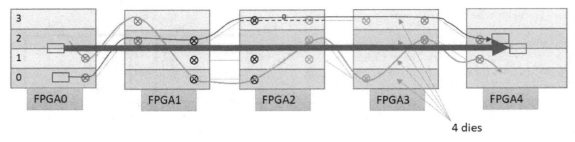

Figure 7: Inter FPGA die crossing?

above) between each pair of consecutive physical FPGAs in the route path. All the routes belonging to the same signal group as this route choose the same LVDS pin-pair to propagate their signals through the corresponding pair of connected physical FPGAs. Therefore, the pin mapping decision needs to be based on the consideration of all the routes in the same signal group. In general, there are n FPGAs and m pairs of physical FPGAs connected by LVDS pin-pairs. It is non-trivial to decide the best sequence of signal groups to perform pin assignment in order to maximize the overall performance. For a design requiring a large number of the largest Xilinx FPGAs, performing pin assignment in parallel is required. It is difficult to have the multi-threading strategy to achieve the maximum parallelism with the least performance compromise. Moreover, building a complete timing graph for such a large design and updating timing is very time-consuming. Timing budgeting might be a must to solve the parallel pin assignment problem.

Similar to the partitioning, placement, and routing steps, pin assignment results should ensure a high probability of FPGA P&R success rate. For instance, we should not assign too many signal groups with high TDM ratios to use LVDS pins in close proximity within any physical FPGA in order to avoid local routing congestion during FPGA P&R.

4.6 FPGA P&R

FPGA P&R is the last step of backend implementation, during which FPGA vendor's software is used to implement the netlist for each FPGA. As the FPGA size doubles every two years, FPGA P&R time has become the most dominating part in the entire backend implementation time. Therefore, it is essential to ensure a successful FPGA P&R in the backend implementation. However, guaranteeing a successful FPGA P&R requires an accurate routability prediction, which requires an accurate characterization of the following three important factors:

- FPGA internal routing fabric architecture;
- FPGA vendor's packing, placement, and routing algorithms;
- netlist properties that affect the routability such as average fanouts, reconvergent fanouts, Rent's constant and exponent, etc.

Recently, there are efforts in using machine learning techniques in predicting timing closure of FPGA implementation [15][26]. To our best knowledge, there exists no effective methods that can predict the routability of commercial FPGAs with high confidence.

5 CONCLUSION

In this paper, we present various challenges in FPGA based logic emulation: various software flows, handling clock domains, impact on control sets in FPGAs, connectivity between FPGAs, time domain multiplexing, partitioning, placement and routing, pin assignment, FPGA P&R. Some of these problems have been studied before, but many prior published solutions are still not perfect for industrial deployment. We hope to give better exposure of the various problems to the academic community and inspire more research in this challenging and fast growing field.

REFERENCES

[1] Accellera. 2016. *Standard Co-Emulation Modeling Interface (SCE-MI) Reference Manual* (2.4 ed.).
[2] Jonathan Babb, Russell Tessier, and Anant Agarwal. 1993. Virtual wires: Overcoming pin limitations in FPGA-based logic emulators. In *FPGAs for Custom Computing Machines, 1993. Proceedings. IEEE Workshop on.* IEEE, 142–151.
[3] Jonathan Babb, Russell Tessier, Matthew Dahl, Silvina Zimi Hanono, David M. Hoki, and Anant Agarwal. 1997. Logic Emulation with Virtual Wires. *IEEE Transactions on CAD* 16, 6 (June 1997).
[4] Brian Bailey. 2010. Emulator, accelerator, prototype âĂŞ whatâĂŹs the difference? (Nov. 2010). Retrieved November 26, 2017 from https://www.eetimes.com/author.asp?section_id=36&doc_id=1284694
[5] Dinesh Baviskar and Dinesh Baviskar. 2009. A pipelined simulation approach for logic emulation using multi-FPGA platforms. In *Proceedings of the IEEE International Symposium on Circuits and Systems.* 1141 – 1144.
[6] Drazen Borkovic and Kenneth S. McElvain. 2001. Reducing clock skew in clock gating circuits. U.S. Patent US7082582B1, granted on July 25, 2007. (Dec. 2001).
[7] Sao-Jie Chen and Chung-Kuan Cheng. 2000. Tutorial on VLSI partitioning. 11 (01 2000).
[8] Barry Cipra. 1995. How number theory got the best of the Pentium chip. *Science* 267, 5195 (Jan. 1995).
[9] CNN. 1999. NASA's metric confusion caused Mars orbiter loss. (Sept. 1999). http://www.cnn.com/TECH/space/9909/30/mars.metric/
[10] Katherine Compton and Scott Hauck. 2002. Reconfigurable Computing: A Survey of Systems and Software. *Comput. Surveys* 34, 2 (June 2002), 171–210.
[11] Wen-Jong Fang and Allen C.-H. Wu. 1998. Performance-driven multi-FPGA Partitioning Using Functional Clustering and Replication. In *Proceedings of the 35th Annual Design Automation Conference (DAC '98).* 283–286.
[12] Scott Hauck. 1996. *Software Techniques for Reconfigurable Systems.* Technical Report. Northwestern University.
[13] Tsung-Yi Ho, Yao-Wen Chang, Sao-Jie Chen, and D. T. Lee. 2003. A Fast Crosstalk- and Performance-Driven Multilevel Routing System. In *Proceedings of the 2003*

IEEE/ACM International Conference on Computer-aided Design (ICCAD '03). IEEE Computer Society, Washington, DC, USA, 382–. https://doi.org/10.1109/ICCAD.2003.3

[14] Kohei Hosokawa, Katsunori Tanaka, and Yuichi Nakamura. 2007. Efficient Memory Utilization for High-Speed FPGA-Based Hardware Emulators with SDRAMs. IEICE Trans. Fundam. Electron. Commun. Comput. Sci. E90-A, 12 (Dec. 2007), 2810–2817. https://doi.org/10.1093/ietfec/e90-a.12.2810

[15] Nachiket Kapre, Harnhua Ng, Kirvy Teo, and Jaco Naude. 2015. InTime: A Machine Learning Approach for Efficient Selection of FPGA CAD Tool Parameters. In Proceedings of the 2015 ACM/SIGDA International Symposium on Field-Programmable Gate Arrays (FPGA '15). ACM, New York, NY, USA, 23–26. https://doi.org/10.1145/2684746.2689081

[16] George Karypis, Rajat Aggarwal abd Vipin Kumar, and Shashi Shekhar. 1999. Multilevel Hypergraph Partitioning: Applications in VLSI Domain. IEEE Transactions on VLSI Systems 7, 1 (March 1999).

[17] Mohammed A. S. Khalid and Jonathan Rose. 2000. A Novel and Efficient Routing Architecture for multi-FPGA Systems. IEEE Transactions on VLSI 8, 1 (Feb. 2000), 30–39.

[18] Helena Krupnova and Gabriele Saucier. 2000. FPGA-Based Emulation: Industrial and Custom Prototyping Solutions. In Proceedings of the The Roadmap to Reconfigurable Computing, 10th International Workshop on Field-Programmable Logic and Applications (FPL '00). Springer-Verlag, 68–77.

[19] Yangfan Liu, Peng Liu, Yingtao Jiang, Mei Yang, Kejun Wu, Weidong Wang, and Qingdong Yao. 2010. Building a multi-FPGA-based emulation framework to support networks-on-chip design and verification. International Journal of Electronics 97, 10 (2010), 1241–1262.

[20] Paul McLellan. 2014. Transaction-based Emulation. (Aug. 2014). Retrieved September 24, 2017 from https://www.semiwiki.com/forum/content/3762-transaction-based-emulation.html

[21] Larry McMurchie and Carl Ebeling. 1995. PathFinder: A Negotiation-based Performance-driven Router for FPGAs. In Proceedings of the 1995 ACM Third International Symposium on Field-programmable Gate Arrays (FPGA '95). ACM, New York, NY, USA, 111–117. https://doi.org/10.1145/201310.201328

[22] Lauro Rizzatti. 2014. WhatâĂŹs The Difference Between FPGA And Custom Silicon Emulators? (April 2014). Retrieved September 24, 2017 from http://www.electronicdesign.com/fpgas/what-s-difference-between-fpga-and-custom-silicon-emulators

[23] Synopsys. 2014. Transaction-Based Emulation. (Aug. 2014). Retrieved September 24, 2017 from https://www.synopsys.com/verification/emulation/transaction-based-emulation.html

[24] Russel Tessier. 2008. Reconfigurable Computing. Elsevier, Chapter Multi-FPGA Systems: Logic Emulation, 637–669.

[25] Xilinx. 2017. ASIC Prototyping and Emulation. (2017). Retrieved November 26, 2017 from https://www.xilinx.com/applications/asic-prototyping/asic-prototyping-emulation-solution.html

[26] Que Yanghua, Chinnakkannu Adaikkala Raj, Harnhua Ng, Kirvy Teo, and Nachiket Kapre. 2016. Case for Design-Specific Machine Learning in Timing Closure of FPGA Designs. In Proceedings of the 2016 ACM/SIGDA International Symposium on Field-Programmable Gate Arrays (FPGA '16). ACM, New York, NY, USA, 169–172. https://doi.org/10.1145/2847263.2847336

Flexibility: FPGAs and CAD in Deep Learning Acceleration

Gordon R. Chiu
Intel Corporation
gordon.chiu@intel.com

Andrew C. Ling
Intel Corporation
andrew.ling@intel.com

Davor Capalija
Intel Corporation
davor.capalija@intel.com

Andrew Bitar
Intel Corporation
andrew.bitar@intel.com

Mohamed S. Abdelfattah
Intel Corporation
mohamed.abdelfattah@intel.com

ABSTRACT

Deep learning inference has become the key workload to accelerate in our AI-powered world. FPGAs are an ideal platform for the acceleration of deep learning inference by combining low-latency performance, power-efficiency, and flexibility. This paper examines the flexibility aspect, and its impact on FPGA design methodology, physical design tools and CAD. We describe the degrees of flexibility required for creating efficient deep learning accelerators. We quantify the varying effects of precision, vectorization, and buffering on both performance and accuracy, and show how the FPGA can yield superior performance through architecture customization tuned for a specific neural network. We describe the need for abstraction and propose solutions in modern FPGA design flows to enable the rapid creation of these customized accelerator architectures for deep learning inference acceleration. Finally, we examine the implications on physical design tools and CAD.

KEYWORDS

Deep Learning; FPGAs; High-Level Design; Physical Design

ACM Reference Format:
Gordon R. Chiu, Andrew C. Ling, Davor Capalija, Andrew Bitar, and Mohamed S. Abdelfattah. 2018. Flexibility: FPGAs and CAD in Deep Learning Acceleration. In *ISPD '18: 2018 International Symposium on Physical Design, March 25–28, 2018, Monterey, CA, USA.* ACM, New York, NY, USA, 8 pages. https://doi.org/10.1145/3177540.3177561

1 INTRODUCTION

Over the past few years, deep learning techniques have been increasingly applied to solve problems in many fields, starting with computer vision and speech recognition, but growing to include natural language processing, machine translation, autonomous vehicles and smart medicine. As of 2016, analytics was the fastest growing workload in the datacenter, and predicted to be the largest workload by compute cycles in 2020, mostly due to the rapid increase in adoption and deployment of deep learning. [4]

Unlike deep learning training, which is predominantly hosted in data-centers and the cloud, deep learning inference – the scoring of a trained neural network model against unknown input data – is often performed in-line with data collection, which could either be in a data-center context (for web-scale analytics, image or media processing) or in an embedded context (within autonomous driving systems or surveillance systems). In both contexts, system architects are looking to offload inference compute cycles from valuable CPUs, leveraging in-line or off-load compute accelerators, such as General-Purpose Graphics Processing Units (GPGPUs), FPGAs, or fixed-function ASICs. The enhanced data parallelism available in an accelerator can both improve power-efficiency as well as reduce compute latency. This reduced latency manifests in better system performance (such as response time to a user request over the web, or reaction time to external events in an autonomous driving system).

When data scientists look to solve a problem with deep learning, they typically begin with a "standard" neural-network topology (typically an ILSVRC [10]-winning network, such as GoogLeNet [9] or ResNet [13]) and iterate from there. With the rapid change in this space, the final network is often not defined at the beginning of the project, and can morph as compute, accuracy, and application requirements change. While general-purpose compute technologies such as CPUs are flexible enough to adapt to neural-network topology changes, the performance of an fixed-function accelerator varies profoundly with the choice of topology. This leads to a phase-ordering problem, as the acceleration hardware and design in a system is often locked down well before the workload is finalized, leading to subpar accelerator performance.

As research continues, the industry may consolidate on key standard network topologies. Until then, with new topologies and innovations emerging on a daily basis, flexibility in the accelerator is critical for supporting a wide gamut of network topologies. This flexibility has large implications on the physical design flows, tools, and CAD required to efficiently define and create accelerators.

1.1 Why FPGAs for Deep Learning Acceleration?

The FPGA architecture is naturally amenable for deep learning inference acceleration. Arithmetic datapaths can be synthesized and mapped to reconfigurable logic, for greater power-efficiency and lower latency than executing instructions temporally on a CPU or GPGPU. System integration options through flexible I/O interfaces allow tighter native integration into embedded or streaming applications (such as directly processing the output of a camera module). Most importantly, flexibility in the reconfigurable logic and routing enables many different accelerator architectures to

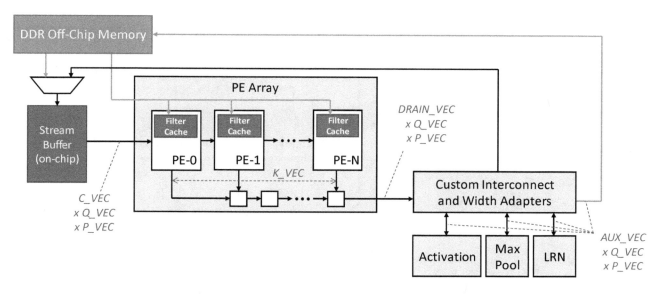

Figure 1: System-level diagram of our neural-network inference accelerator.

be efficiently implemented on the same FPGA fabric. This paper focuses on this flexibility argument for FPGAs, argues the need for higher-level design, and presents implications on CAD (both high-level and physical):

- **Flexibility inherent in the FPGA fabric** enables many accelerator architectures to be constructed. The optimization upside from using a bespoke acceleration architecture, tuned to a specific network, can outweigh the cost of the reconfigurable fabric of the FPGA. This exposes a very large design space.
- **High- and higher-level design solutions** are required to take full advantage of this architecture flexibility and large design space. Our current solution comprises of an acceleration stack, and a high-level synthesis compiler, providing good abstraction. Further abstraction is necessary for arbitrary accelerator generation.
- **New challenges for CAD and Physical Design** are exposed by the higher levels of design abstraction and the domain's high performance requirements. We describe some of our solutions to problems seen today, as well as motivate and propose areas of future research.

The remainder of the paper is organized as follows. Section 2 describes our Deep Learning Accelerator (DLA) architecture. Section 3 examines the various degrees of flexibility present when implementing an accelerator on an FPGA, and quantitatively analyzes the benefit of customizing accelerator to specific deep learning workloads (as opposed to a fixed-function accelerator). Section 4 describes our current high-level design abstraction for creating the Deep Learning Accelerator, and proposes future higher-levels to enable success in this space. Finally, Section 5 details some of the challenges in mapping generated designs to physical implementations, along with some workarounds employed as well as proposals for areas of future research.

2 FPGA DEEP LEARNING ACCELERATOR

In [2], we presented an architecture and implementation for high-performance on-FPGA execution of deep learning inference acceleration. The system implemented on-FPGA is summarized in Figure 1. An accelerator core reads input image and filter data from external (DDR) memory, and stores the data in caches built of on-chip block RAMs. Data is read from on-chip caches and fed to a set of parallel Processing Elements (PEs), which perform, in parallel, the dot product calculations that comprise the bulk of the workload. A drain network collects the output of the dot product, which is fed to *auxiliary kernels* that perform the non-linear computations (such as activation, pooling, and normalization). The resulting output is either fed as input to the next layer of convolution (executed sequentially), or written as an output back to external memory.

3 DEGREES OF FLEXIBILITY

Though our original work focused on a single optimized instance of an accelerator for the AlexNet neural network topology [2], our architecture is flexible enough for high-performance acceleration of other network topologies. The design can be parameterized to create a class of neural network accelerator designs that can be specialized for specific network topologies. In this section, we examine a few of the degrees of flexibility available, and quantify the benefit provided by the FPGA flexibility, across some example axes of compute precision, accelerator geometry, and memory architecture.

3.1 Compute Precision

Deep Learning applications often have large memory requirements, which pose a hurdle to their acceleration. Recent work has shown that reducing the accelerator's precision from full-precision floating-point can shrink the neural network model size while maintaining its required accuracy.

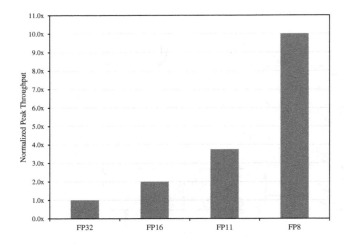

Figure 2: Normalized peak chip throughput vs. floating-point precision on Intel® Stratix® 10 FPGA

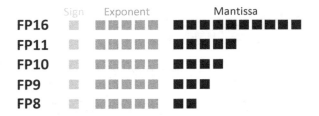

Figure 3: Reduced-precision floating point sign/exponent/mantissa breakdown.

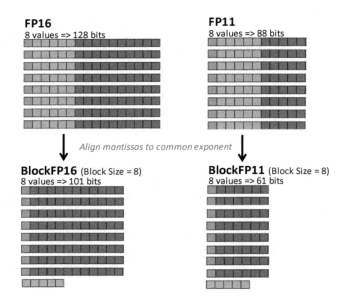

Figure 4: Organizing floating-point numbers in "blocks".

Fixed-point representation has been employed by NVIDIA [8], Xilinx [12], and Google's TPU [18] for CNN and RNN acceleration, while Microsoft has recently announced the use of a reduced-precision floating point on Intel® Stratix® 10 FPGAs in their acceleration of GRUs [7]. In Figure 2, we measure the impact of reduced-precision floating-point on overall compute performance available for a given Intel® Stratix® 10 FPGA. With reduced precision, fewer FPGA resources are required per compute unit.

While there have been many proposed solutions for achieving good accuracy at low precisions, there is no one-precision-fits-all solution. The ability to trade off precision for performance is heavily application- and topology-dependent. Every application has its own accuracy requirements, and thus values performance-accuracy tradeoffs differently. The different topologies used in these applications have different tolerance levels to reduced data precision. For example, SqueezeNet was designed to achieve AlexNet-level accuracies while reducing the model-size by 50× [14]; it is unsurprising that it is more sensitive to accuracy losses at reduced precision compared to AlexNet (see Figure 5). With its fine-grained, bit-level customizability, the FPGA platform can provide flexibility to employ a tuned precision-accuracy tradeoff that suits individual applications and topologies.

The DLA architecture leverages the FPGA platform to provide a reduced precision data representation with a tunable mantissa width (Figure 3). In addition to the ability to reduce the data width, the DLA architecture uses the FPGA fabric's bit-level granularity to improve resource usage efficiency by organizing floating-point numbers in "blocks" [2], defined as a group of FP numbers sharing a single common exponent. The "block size" is a tunable parameter that defines the number of mantissas sharing the common exponent. Placing a number into a block requires bit-shifting the mantissa such that it can use the block's common exponent, which may result in some precision loss. As can be seen in Figure 4, this loss of precision comes with the benefit of better resource utilization, as the storage requirements shrink when more numbers are placed

in a block. The block size can be tuned to trade off accuracy for performance.

To investigate their accuracy impact, different precision and block sizes were tested on AlexNet, GoogleNet, SqueezeNet, ResNet-18 and VGG-16 [16]. As can be seen in Figure 5 and 6, each topology can tolerate different levels of precision loss. This illustrates how different topologies can benefit from reduced precision and bigger block sizes to varying degrees. By leveraging the flexibility of the FPGA, DLA can be tuned to the level of precision that best suits an application.

At a specific precision, there remains the challenge of implementing a PE architecture that maximizes throughput per area for that precision. The optimal PE for each precision-level is dependent on the FPGA platform; DSP and Logic Element (LE) architecture strongly influence how a PE can be designed to achieve the highest throughput at the lowest area cost. Choosing the right combination of DSPs and LEs for a certain precision is a complex problem that can be facilitated by CAD tools, as will be described in Sections 4 and 5.1. Scaling the design, once a precision and PE architecture is chosen, is done through compute parallelism, which is explored in the next section.

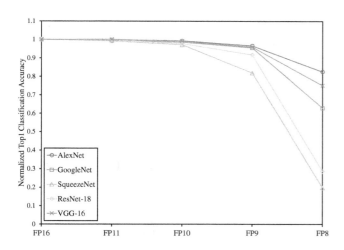

Figure 5: NN graphs have different tolerance levels to reduced precision. Accuracy numbers reported here are measured using a block size of 8.

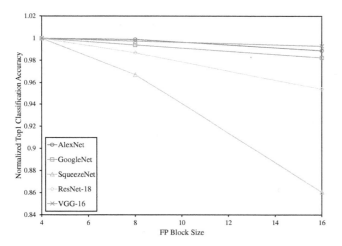

Figure 6: Increasing block size improves resource usage efficiency, but may cost accuracy depending on the graph used. Accuracy numbers reported here are measured using BlockFP9 precision.

3.2 Accelerator Geometry & Customization

To leverage the flexibility of FPGAs, we can customize the accelerator *vectorization* (degree of parallelism) to suit different classes of neural networks. A change to the vectorization manifests in a different accelerator *geometry* – the number of processing elements and the widths of databuses between them. Figure 1 shows the degrees of parallelism available in the accelerator, configurable via vectorization.

The problem size at each convolution stage is defined by the neural network topology:

- W, H, C are the input tensor width, height and depth.
- S, R, C are the filter width, height and depth.

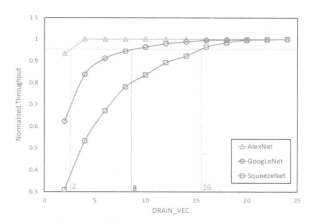

Figure 7: Effect of drain network vectorization on the throughput of GoogLeNet and SqueezeNet NNs, normalized to maximum performance.

- Q, P, K are the output tensor width, height and depth.

Architectural parameters in the accelerator control the degree of parallelism employed in the core compute, which impact both the number of compute units used as well as the width of datapaths:

- Q_VEC, P_VEC, and K_VEC define the window of the output tensor computed in parallel.
- C_VEC defines the depth of the input tensor read and used in parallel.
- S_VEC and R_VEC are the filter width and height read and computed in parallel.
- DRAIN_VEC is the width of the drain network from the PE array. This determines the subset of K_VEC that can be extracted from the PE array in one clock cycle.
- Each auxiliary kernel has an AUX_VEC, which describes the subset of the DRAIN_VEC that is processed in one clock cycle in each of the auxiliary kernels.

For each of our marquee neural networks, we customize the architecture to maximize throughput-per-area. We then analyze the geometry considerations for architectures tuned for various different graphs.

3.2.1 Smaller Filters Require Faster Drains. Each of the PEs consists of Q_VEC×P_VEC dot-product operations (each of which multiplies and sums C_VEC data items together), followed by accumulators. The accumulators keep accumulating the result of the dot products until it has iterated over the entire filter tensor; after which, a single output pixel is produced from a PE. Therefore, depending on the filter size and PE-array vectorization, the speed of producing results from the PEs differ – it depends on the ratio between the filter size and the vectorization of each PE.

Between the GoogLeNet and SqueezeNet networks, SqueezeNet has, on average, smaller filters. This causes convolution results to be produced more quickly from the PE array, and therefore requires a higher-bandwidth drain network. Figure 7 shows the effect of increasing the drain network parallelism (DRAIN_VEC) on the AlexNet, GoogLeNet and SqueezeNet networks. While GoogLeNet throughput saturates at DRAIN_VEC of 8, SqueezeNet requires DRAIN_VEC of 16 for 95% of maximum throughput. AlexNet only needs a DRAIN_VEC of 2 to achieve 95% performance since its filters are the largest. Scaling DRAIN_VEC beyond these values yields diminishing returns as the plot shows. Supporting increased drain network parallelization also requires scaling up the area of the auxiliary kernels. Table 1 presents the area cost of scaling DRAIN_VEC. With a fixed function accelerator, a designer has to choose apriori between an additional 21% area penalty (across all networks) or a 70% performance penalty on SqueezeNet-like networks. With a reconfigurable device like an FPGA, the designer can only instantiate the larger DRAIN_VEC when required by the network being accelerated.

Table 1: Area cost of increasing DRAIN_VEC.

DRAIN_VEC	Aux Kernels Area (% of Full System)
2	4%
8	14%
16	25%

3.2.2 Interconnect Customization and Width Adapters Allow Building Only What is Needed. Another degree of flexibility exists in the auxiliary kernels domain – the flexible interconnect allows building only exactly what is needed for each graph. For example, the SqueezeNet Graph has no Local Response Normalization (LRN) layers, so we can remove that kernel completely. The interconnection pattern within the interconnect is also customizable based on the order of the auxilliary operations. For example, the AlexNet graph has both MaxPool and LRN layers, but LRN always comes first; whereas the GoogLeNet graph has some layers in which MaxPool precedes LRN, so we need to support both these connection patterns by adding more muxing and arbitration logic. The width of each of the auxiliary kernels can be customized separately based on how much bandwidth is required of each operation. Finally, DLA can also leverage FPGAs enhanced with hardened interconnects – such as embedded Networks-on-Chip [1, 3] – for high-bandwidth inter-kernel communication.

3.2.3 Balance Vectorization to Minimize Quantization Inefficiencies. In general, scaling up the tensor vectorization increases throughput at the expense of more area. Initially, the design was scaled by increasing K_VEC – this was relatively simple, since increasing K_VEC only entails adding more PEs. However, this method of scaling saw diminishing returns, as quantization inefficiencies can become more pronounced as vectorization dimensions increase. For example, if the output depth (K) of a layer is 96, and K_VEC is 64, this will require 2 complete iterations, and so the output depth will be snapped up to 128, with only 96/128 (75%) useful computations. On the other hand, if K_VEC is 32, the output depth divides perfectly into 3 iterations at 100% efficiency. To mitigate this quantization effect, it is possible to balance the scaling of the design across multiple different dimensions besides just K_VEC (e.g. P_VEC, Q_VEC, C_VEC, etc). The optimal balance of vectorization depends on the graph's layer dimensions. Figure 8 demonstrates this point by comparing throughput at two architectures of similar area for multiple different graphs. As can be seen in the figure, the optimal balance of scaling the design between P_VEC and K_VEC

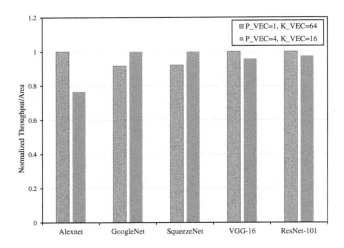

Figure 8: Throughput/Area on two architectures with different P_VEC and K_VEC vectorization.

varies based on the neural network topology being used. With a flexible FPGA platform, a custom instance of a deep learning accelerator can be can be generated, with vectorization parameters tuned for each application.

3.3 Memory Architecture

With their different models and layer sizes, neural networks have a wide range of memory requirements, and creating an efficient design around these requirements poses a complex problem. To support such requirements, the DLA architecture uses both the on-chip and off-chip memory provided by the FPGA platform.

On-chip memory provides a fast means to store and access data, avoiding the relatively long latency of communicating with off-chip memory. DLA uses on-chip memory for both filter and tensor data (Figure 1). Filter data is stored in a "filter cache" (FC) contained in each PE. While the PEs compute data, filters are pre-loaded from external memory into the filter caches for the next set of PE computation. The "stream buffer" is used to store intermediate tensors between layers on-chip. If the stream buffer is too small to hold a given tensor, then DLA falls back to using external memory. Given a limited DDR bandwidth, excessive use of external memory can bottleneck the performance of the design.

The balance between using on-chip and off-chip memory creates an important design tradeoff. Using more on-chip memory for the stream buffer alleviates DDR bottlenecks but consumes more chip resources that could have been used for more PEs. On the other hand, reducing on-chip memory used in the stream buffer, in favor of more PEs, provides more compute power at the cost of heavily relying on off-chip memory. The optimal balance of resources between on-chip memory and processing elements that maximizes performance is dependent on the graph's compute and memory requirements. Finding this optimal point requires accurate design modelling as well as knowledge of the target neural network and platform.

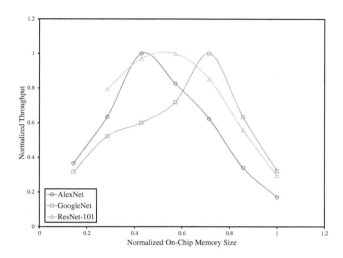

Figure 9: Impact of stream buffer memory vs. compute trade-off on AlexNet, GoogleNet and ResNet-101.

To illustrate this trade-off, we modelled the performance of AlexNet, GoogleNet and ResNet-101 at different stream buffer memory and PE sizes for a given FPGA platform. As can be seen in Figure 9, the optimal allocation of resources to memory and compute differs across each of the different graphs. This highlights the benefit of having a flexible FPGA fabric capable of specifically tailoring a design to achieve the optimal performance for a given application. A tradeoff that is optimal for one neural network can cause 40% or more performance degradation for a second neural network.

3.4   Implications of Flexibility

In general, one size does not fit all when designing deep learning accelerators. Using a flexible accelerator on a flexible FPGA platform can improve performance, with architecture parameters (compute precision, accelerator geometry, and memory architecture) tuned for a specific neural network topology. We have presented several dimensions of flexibility (by no means an exhaustive list); customization can deliver a performance benefit (or area savings) on each dimension. In aggregate, the benefit across the fully customized FPGA accelerator can outweigh the cost of the programmable fabric.

Flexibility of the deep learning acceleration architecture must be matched with flexible design-entry flow and CAD tools, to allow designers to specify optimized deep learning accelerators quickly.

4   HIGH- AND HIGHER-LEVEL DESIGN

With the large design space of possible architecture parameterizations, it becomes infeasible for a designer to manually configure the Deep Learning Accelerator using traditional FPGA RTL design techniques. We propose an extra level of abstraction to enable automatic specification and generation of custom deep learning acceleration. In Section 5, we discuss some of the implications on Physical Design when using such high-level design entry.

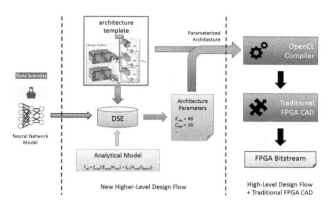

Figure 10: Design flow for neural network accelerators.

4.1   Abstracting Design Entry with OpenCL™

To achieve the desired flexibility, our Deep Learning Accelerator architecture is described in a generic form that can be easily modified with a set of architectural parameters. We describe our architecture using a set of pre-defined kernels written in OpenCL™, that can be modified with specific architectural parameters such as vectorization parameters, stream buffer dimensions, memory port widths, number of processing elements, and configuration of auxiliary kernels. The combination of these kernels form a generic architecture template. Once configured, the resulting architecture is compiled and executed through the Intel® FPGA SDK for OpenCL™. This design flow is illustrated on the right side of Figure 10.

High-level design tools like the Intel® FPGA SDK for OpenCL™ compile untimed, unscheduled OpenCL language into optimized RTL implementations, applying optimizations (pipelining, vectorization, compute unrolling) as necessary according to predicted system performance and knowledge of the physical FPGA architecture. [11] This abstraction is invaluable when creating complex, parameterizable, designs such as the Deep Learning Accelerator as it alleviates the need for time-consuming detailed physical design optimization and verification across a wide parameterization space.

4.2   Future Work: Even Higher-Level Design

Once we have an architecture template that can accept a wide range of architectural parameters to modify its structure, we envision that future users of the Deep Learning Accelerator will rely on even higher-level design techniques to select and configure appropriate architectures. An additional design space exploration (DSE) step is envisioned, to find the optimal architecture to run a given neural network model. The DSE step can be automated using traditional objective-optimization CAD techniques [15]. This would require a high-fidelity model to represent the physical characteristics of a given architecture and the resulting performance. Using the model, the DSE flow would efficiently search the architecture parameter space to identify the most optimal configuration for a given neural network model.

Each design point (a unique instance of the Deep Learning Accelerator) can be accurately modeled because our architecture is deterministic in nature, where all memory accesses, data movements, and compute times can be calculated apriori. The deterministic architecture and analytical model is presented in [2], where both the resource utilization of the FPGA and the final performance of the design can be calculated prior to runtime.

An illustration of this proposed future approach is shown on the left side of Figure 10. Here, the DSE tool is provided the neural network model, architecture template, analytical model architecture, and objective function (such as performance or latency). The DSE tool would compile the neural network into a graph and map it to the architecture template core primitives. After sweeping through a wide range of architecture parameters, and generating performance estimates from the model architecture, a final set of parameters is chosen to satisfy the objective function. The chosen architecture parameters can be used to configure the architecture template, and the resulting design can be compiled through the OpenCL and traditional FPGA compilers to generate a bitstream for the FPGA.

This higher-level design flow, where neural network models are compiled to generate custom FPGA-based accelerators, has many implications on FPGA CAD, and introduces several new challenges that need to be resolved to ensure high-performance while enabling flexibility.

5 PHYSICAL DESIGN IMPLICATIONS

Today, the state of the art FPGA CAD tools provide automated placement, routing and packing of homogeneous resources– the three foundational CAD algorithms that account for the physical aspects of the FPGA fabric. Hierarchical physical design techniques, such as floorplanning, packing of heterogeneous resources, and partitioning are currently done manually by the designer. We study the manual application of these hierarchical techniques to our DLA architecture, and show the benefit. Consequently, we advocate for automation of these techniques, in future work on FPGA CAD (both high-Level design and traditional). This automation is required to support automatic exploration of large accelerator design spaces exposed by our higher-level design tools.

Our study shows the following benefits:

- Significantly improved Quality of Results (QoR), with improved scalability to larger circuits, higher performance, and lower resource utilization.
- Improved repeatability of compilation results, through the reduction of seed noise.
- Improved designer productivity on a large design via reuse of partitions and incremental compilations.

In the following sections, we describe the techniques that we have manually prototyped in our physical design study that we applied to DLA.

5.1 Packing of Heterogeneous Resources for Efficient Implementation of PEs

The PEs occupies the majority of the area of the FPGA. The first challenge is to achieve high utilization of heterogeneous resources within that area, i.e., utilize nearly all available Logic Elements (LEs), DSP Blocks (DSPs) and block memory (M20Ks) in that area. To achieve this, each PE (or a small number of PEs) should consume a mix of LE, DSP and M20K resources that matches the resources within the physical region where they are implemented. Alternatively, this challenge can be formulated as a packing problem:

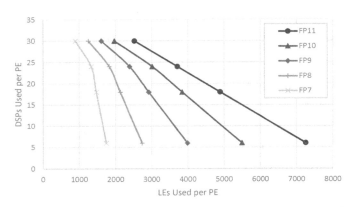

Figure 11: LE vs. DSP Resource Trade-off Curves for Equivalent Implementations of PEs, Across Different Precisions

given a mix of heterogeneous resource in a small region of a device, maximize the number of PEs that can be packed into that region.

One approach employed in order to address this challenge utilizes multiple variants of dot products, which are the building blocks of PEs. Each dot product variant uses a different tradeoff of LE and DSP resources. Figure 11 shows the tradeoff curves available when looking at multiple variants of equivalent dot products at different precisions. We can then solve an integer linear programming problem to select a mix of dot product variants that maximize the available resources given a region constraint. Today, the design of the different dot product variants is done manually at specific architecture design points, as well as the formulation of the linear system.

In order to enable the higher-level abstractions described in Section 4, next-generation tools should strive to automate this process– from the user's description of the dot product mathematics, the tool should generate and optimize a mix of dot product variants that maximizes resource usage, transparently to the user.

5.2 Systolic Arrays for Scalable Circuits

The use of systolic arrays and mesh-like strcuctures on FPGAs is motivated by the need to exploit the massive parallelism of modern FPGAs in a scalable manner [5, 17, 20]. Systolic arrays are circuits with regular structure and nearest-neighbor connections, primarily used in algorithms where the same piece of data needs to be broadcast and reused in a large number of PEs. In our DLA systolic array design, the broadcast structure is designed as a linear data forwarding pipeline in which data flows from one PE to another. This avoids a large fan-out of a wide data-path from a central location, and efficiently leverages local routing without introducing routing congestion.

In current tools, the user manually expresses the systolic array structure explicitly in their code by designing the data forwarding mechanism between the neighboring PEs. Future work could explore techniques for inferring large broadcast structures in user code, and automatically converting these structures to systolic arrays, to support the large design spaces of accelerators.

5.3 Floorplanning for Improving Performance of Large Circuits

Although the systolic array of PEs are a regular and repeated structure, we observe inefficiencies when compiling large systolic arrays which fill entire FPGA devices. The analysis of the placement of PEs by the CAD tool shows that in some cases the neighboring PEs are not placed close to each other. This results in long routes between PEs and a drop in frequency and performance.

We can address this challenge by manually creating floorplans for the systolic array, which are feasible due to its regular structure. Our floorplans comprise of a number of physical regions, we can then assign PEs to physical regions such that any two neighboring PEs are either in the same region or in two adjacent regions. This results in localized placement of PEs and mitigates the drop in performance for larger systolic arrays. We measure, on average, a 30% difference in performance for unfloorplanned designs versus a design floorplanned in this fashion. A similar benefit of floorplanning has been shown in a earlier work on floorplanning of mesh-of-functional-units overlay floorplanning [6].

Although manual floorplanning is feasible for a single architecture parameterization on a single FPGA device, it is not feasible across the full architecture design space and target devices. Automating this class of manual floorplanning effort remains a key outstanding physical design challenges for us, and research efforts that show promise have already started in academia [19].

5.4 Designer Productivity: Partitioning, Reuse and Incremental Compilation

As the sizes of FPGAs grow exponentially, the size of circuits implemented on the FPGA grow at the same pace. In addition to the QoR scaling challenges, these large sizes lead to long compile times, which can be up to a day. This poses two significant challenges for designer productivity. The first is development cycle, as the designer can only do a single iteration per day. The second is a reduced repeatability of results, as even a small design change can result in performance changes, due to seed noise inherently present in the CAD tool.

To enable scale, we employ approaches that leverage design partitioning. The DLA is composed of multiple OpenCL kernels, each encapsulating a distinct functionality of the design. The use of design partitioning can improve designer productivity by both reducing compile time and improving repeatability. By preserving the post-place-and-route netlists of partitions that have not been modified, only the kernels that the designer modified need to be re-compiled. Since in most cases only a small part of the design needs to be re-compiled, it is more likely that a single-seed compile will close timing.

When considering the large DLA architecture design space, the ideal partitioning may not be possible to define apriori, due to changing kernel size and number across all the architecture variants. Further research on automating the process of dynamic design partitioning (for an arbitrary set of interconnected kernels of varying sizes) is a key direction for future work. In addition to improving the development speed and repeatability of QoR, it would relieve designers from the burden of manual design partitioning.

6 CONCLUSION

We have shown through a case study of our Deep Learning Accelerator that flexibility to customize an architecture is essential to create future-proof accelerators. The resulting design space requires higher-level abstractions for efficient design and exploration. We advocate for new FPGA design flows that generate custom architectures from a high-level neural network description, and improved physical design flows to infer systolic arrays, optimize for resource constraints, and automate floorplanning and partitioning. With these future enhancements, FPGAs can continue to scale, and be an accelerator of choice for applications such as deep learning.

REFERENCES

[1] Mohamed S Abdelfattah, Andrew Bitar, and Vaughn Betz. 2015. Take the highway: Design for embedded NoCs on FPGAs. In *Proceedings of the 2015 ACM/SIGDA International Symposium on Field-Programmable Gate Arrays*. ACM, 98–107.

[2] Utku Aydonat, Shane O'Connell, Davor Capalija, Andrew C. Ling, and Gordon R. Chiu. 2017. An OpenCL™Deep Learning Accelerator on Arria 10. In *Proceedings of the 2017 ACM/SIGDA International Symposium on Field-Programmable Gate Arrays (FPGA '17)*. ACM, New York, NY, USA, 55–64.

[3] Andrew Bitar, Mohamed S Abdelfattah, and Vaughn Betz. 2015. Bringing programmability to the data plane: Packet processing with a NoC-enhanced FPGA. In *Field Programmable Technology (FPT), 2015 International Conference on*. IEEE, 24–31.

[4] Diane M. Bryant. 2016. Keynote at Intel Developer's Forum 2016, San Francisco. (August 2016). https://newsroom.intel.com/chip-shots/2016-idf-keynotes-innovation-drives-technology-future-artificial-intelligence/

[5] D. Capalija and T. S. Abdelrahman. 2013. A high-performance overlay architecture for pipelined execution of data flow graphs. In *2013 23rd International Conference on Field programmable Logic and Applications*. 1–8.

[6] D. Capalija and T. S. Abdelrahman. 2014. Tile-based bottom-up compilation of custom mesh-of-functional-units FPGA overlays. In *2014 24th International Conference on Field Programmable Logic and Applications (FPL)*. 1–8.

[7] Eric et. al Chung. 2017. Accelerating persistent neural networks at datacenter scale. HotChips.

[8] NVidia Corporation. 2017. NVidia TensorRT. (2017).

[9] C. Szegedy et al. 2015. Going deeper with convolutions. In *2015 IEEE Conference on Computer Vision and Pattern Recognition (CVPR)*. 1–9.

[10] Olga Russakovsky et al. 2015. ImageNet Large Scale Visual Recognition Challenge. *International Journal of Computer Vision (IJCV)* 115, 3 (2015), 211–252.

[11] T. S. Czajkowski et al. 2012. From opencl to high-performance hardware on FPGAS. In *22nd International Conference on Field Programmable Logic and Applications (FPL)*. 531–534.

[12] Yao et. al Fu. 2016. Deep Learning with INT8 Optimization on Xilinx Devices. *white paper of Xilinx* (2016).

[13] K. He, X. Zhang, S. Ren, and J. Sun. 2016. Deep Residual Learning for Image Recognition. In *2016 IEEE Conference on Computer Vision and Pattern Recognition (CVPR)*. 770–778.

[14] Forrest N et al. Iandola. 2016. SqueezeNet: AlexNet-level accuracy with 50x fewer parameters and< 0.5 MB model size. *arXiv preprint arXiv:1602.07360* (2016).

[15] Jacopo Panerati, Donatella Sciuto, and Giovanni Beltrame. 2017. *Handbook of Hardware/Software Codesign: Optimization Strategies in Design Space Exploration*. Springer, Netherlands.

[16] Karen Simonyan and Andrew Zisserman. 2014. Very deep convolutional networks for large-scale image recognition. *arXiv preprint arXiv:1409.1556* (2014).

[17] Xuechao et al. Wei. 2017. Automated Systolic Array Architecture Synthesis for High Throughput CNN Inference on FPGAs. In *Proceedings of the 54th Annual Design Automation Conference 2017 (DAC '17)*. ACM, New York, NY, USA, Article 29, 6 pages.

[18] Yonghui et al. Wu. 2016. Google's neural machine translation system: Bridging the gap between human and machine translation. *arXiv preprint arXiv:1609.08144* (2016).

[19] Xiaodong Xu, Qi Xu, Jinglei Huang, and Song Chen. 2017. An Integrated Optimization Framework for Partitioning, Scheduling and Floorplanning on Partially Dynamically Reconfigurable FPGAs. In *Proceedings of the on Great Lakes Symposium on VLSI 2017 (GLSVLSI '17)*. ACM, New York, NY, USA, 403–406.

[20] Jialiang Zhang and Jing Li. 2017. Improving the Performance of OpenCL-based FPGA Accelerator for Convolutional Neural Network. In *Proceedings of the 2017 ACM/SIGDA International Symposium on Field-Programmable Gate Arrays (FPGA '17)*. ACM, New York, NY, USA, 25–34.

Exploration and Tradeoffs of different Kernels in FPGA Deep Learning Applications

Elliott Delaye, Ashish Sirasao, Ehsan Ghasemi
Xilinx Inc., San Jose, CA

Abstract

In the field of deep learning, efficient computational hardware has come to the forefront of the large scale implementation and deployment of many applications. In the process of designing hardware, various characteristics of hardware platforms have been studied in order to best implement the high computational demand, high memory bandwidth, and flexibility of networks. In addition to design space exploration of kernels, kernel design must be seen in the context of full system architectures or in terms of the combination of deep learning and other types of applications whether video encoding/decoding or analytics, speech recognition, or the multitude of potential applications combining deep learning kernels with tightly integrated coprocessor architectures. Kernel sizes, on-chip and off-chip memories, numeric datatypes and efficient compute architectures all must be merged into optimal design choices for both performing computations with maximum efficiency as well as programmable flexibility.

ACM Reference Format:

Elliott Delaye, Ashish Sirasao, Ehsan Ghasemi. 2018. Exploration and Tradeoffs of different Kernels in FPGA Deep Learning Applications. In ISPD '18: 2018 International Symposium on Physical Design, March 25–28, 2018, Monterey, CA, USA. ACM, New York, NY, USA, 6 pages. https://doi.org/10.1145/3177540.3177559

Introduction

Deep learning fundamentally has grown from earlier work in neural networks and machine learning but developed into a field where orders of magnitude increases in computational cost have shown their effectiveness in area from image classification[1], object detection[2], speech recognition[3], video analytics[4] and many other fields which were once the domain of highly specialized feature engineering.

One of the enablers has been the development of specialized hardware highly capable of performing the large amount of arithmetic operations present in various forms whether in convolution, matrix-matrix multiplications, matrix-vector operations and various combinations these components. The rapid development of deep learning algorithms has brought flexible high performance computing hardware such as FPGAs into the forefront of understanding how best to apply these machine learning techniques into products and services. Three broad areas of deep learning computations can be described as convolutional networks (CNN), multi-layer perceptrons (MLP), and recurrent neural networks (RNN).

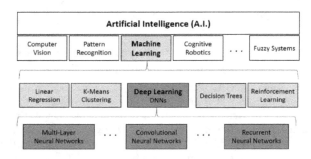

Figure 1 Context of Deep Learning in AI

All areas have many aspects in common and without diving into a great amount of detail they all fundamentally share many similar computations, the most common being the multiply-accumulate operation. Many of these areas can be directly or indirectly transformed into sequences of matrix multiplications which as a computational problem has been researched for decades because of its utility in areas far beyond deep learning. Additionally significant efforts to optimize matrix multiplications over past decades of computational acceleration provides a backdrop for understanding some of the present and future developments in deep learning hardware architectures. Although CNNs, MLPs, and RNNs all have various ways of using the computational data, first seeing them from the perspective of matrix multiplications is useful. This paper will often refer to matrix multiplication as an abstraction for various potential implementations of deep learning kernels in order to explore area, frequency, bandwidth, and efficiency tradeoffs. Additionally today where deep learning networks push the envelopes of computational hardware and artificial intelligence, we can still find shadows of earlier research almost 30 years old that is still relevant today in optimizing deep learning kernels for fixed point FPGAs[5].

With the variety of deep learning applications, one of the primary questions is which characteristics of computational kernels in particular take advantage of FPGA hardware and how should analysis of these architectures be performed during a design phase. In addition a further question is how do characteristics of the designs solve particular requirements of the full system application. We can first look at earlier work that has utilized FPGA for various applications specific to deep learning to understand how choices were made based on the particular hardware used.

FPGA Architectures

As one of the few truly open hardware platforms for architecture prototyping, there are many variations of deep learning architectures build on FPGAs ranging from very general compute engines to highly optimized single network optimized designs. We will first mention a few key points on representative work of deep learning architectures optimized for FPGAs.

1. In presented work from Baidu[6] an architecture was described for performing matrix multiplications on an FPGA with a combination of multiple 32x32 compute arrays along with 512x512 tiles of the input matrices. In this application they used floating point datatypes and made use of all the DSPs in the Xilinx K7 480t device running at 300MHz. The architecture they proposed had less theoretical GFLOPS performance than their comparison GPU however the latency which is the real world advantage of this architecture exceeded the GPUs by 2.5x to 4x. In addition to using DSPs, 75% of the BRAM resources were used primarily for buffering. The particular FPGA used two DDR3 interfaces which had a bandwidth of 8533MB/s each. As will be seen in other examples, larger FPGAs with more DSP resources can saturate even DDR4 bandwidth unless intelligent buffering and architectures are designed. The Xilinx UltraScale+ VU13P device for example has 12,228 DSPs with the potential to run over 800MHz. In the section about memory bandwidth we will talk about memory bandwidth and compute efficiency. Additionally the use

of fixed point datatypes instead of the floating point datatypes used in this work would bring many interesting potential improvements in performance and efficiency.

2. In other work covering LSTM networks, the ESE engine[7] architecture has been demonstrated that is more application specific. The work focuses on quantization and very low bit widths using table lookups which are very efficient operations in FPGAs as the FPGA fabric itself is made of lookup tables. Being able to build custom datatypes is one of the great advantages of FPGAs and has been fruitful in both experiments in very low bit width fixed datatypes as well as very low bit width floating datatypes[14]. In addition to the quantization example this work demonstrates a pipelined architecture with many parallel processing elements. In various examples of FPGA deep learning kernels one may find larger granularity pipelines as well as very fine granularity pipelines. This representative work operates at a higher level of abstraction. Within the pipeline stages however there are still potentials to implement fine grained systolic or pipeline internal computations. A final useful result of this work is the demonstration of model pruning which can reduce the complexity of a model and by building custom FPGA kernel this work demonstrates how to reduce a model by 10x. One of the key features of using FPGAs is the ability to create these custom optimized structures and run them on hardware which is how the ESE load balancing scheduler can operate in close coordination to the actual processing elements.

3. Another example of optimizing kernels on FPGA is work from Xilinx[8] discussing how to optimize dot products in specific for a particular characteristics of an FPGA. In the work on 8-bit dot product acceleration, Xilinx demonstrates a method of using cascaded DSPs to implement both the multiplication and addition parts of dot products using dedicated FPGA hardware. This example is a technique that may not necessarily be a kernel by itself but can be one of the major architecture features useful in both matrix multiplications and other CNN and RNN applications. The main FPGA feature being demonstrated here are both the possibility of using the DSP as an 8-bit SIMD multiply accumulate as well as demonstrating using the direct DSP to DSP cascaded interconnect. FPGAs have both a fully programmable interconnect fabric as well as hardened connections between DSPs and building kernels around the hardened features can greatly improve the efficiency of kernels.

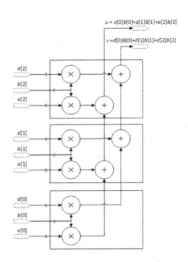

Figure 2 - Adder Cascade for 8-bit Operands

All of these architectural examples make efficient uses of the FPGA architecture because while the FPGAs are highly programmable, they also have specialized hardware features which can be utilized for higher frequencies, more efficient computation and more scalable full chip designs.

Compute Bandwidth

In deep learning architectures one of the most important aspects for deciding performance is the choices of datatypes. While most training on deep learning occurs with single precision floating point, the most efficient inference architectures rely on fixed point computations. In comparison between a fixed point and floating point algorithm, a dramatic reduction in latency, area as well as power can be measured.

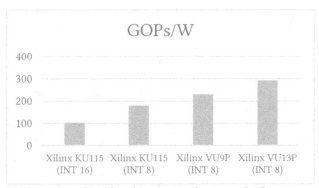

Figure 3 – Scaling fixed precision datatypes[15]

In more detail we can observe that going beyond typical 8 bit representations can change the task of DSP mapping into a technology mapping onto the variety of LUTs and adder hardware spread across the entire FPGA

fabric. In terms of accuracy, many successful experiments have demonstrated accuracy of 8 bit fixed point models as well as lower precision models [22].

Table 1 - Deep Learning Quantization [22]

	Layer Output Width	Conv Param Width	FC Width	32bit Floating Point	Fixed Point
LeNet (exp 1)	4 bits	4 bits	4 bits	99.10%	99.00%
Lenet (exp 2)	4 bits	2 bits	2 bits	99.10%	98.80%
Full CIFAR-10	8 bits	8 bits	8 bits	81.70%	81.40%
SqueezeNet Top-1	8 bits	8 bits	8 bits	57.70%	57.10%
CaffeNet Top-1	8 bits	8 bits	8 bits	56.90%	56.00%
GoogLeNet Top-1	8 bits	8 bits	8 bits	68.90%	66.60%

In fact far lower bit widths have been demonstrated with binary neural networks proven to be as accurate as floating point networks in certain situations [14].

Kernel Types

One common and among the most simple of kernel architectures that may use DSPs is a traditional systolic array. The definition of a systolic array is a grid of inter-communicating processing elements which can pass data, results or control signals to neighboring processing elements through the array. This technique is popular especially for creating complex algorithms from very simple nodes and is an efficient way to implement computation in hardware due to the lack of complex control systems which is often required in other computational architectures. It is also very easy to describe these arrays in RTL or HLS languages. In FPGAs the support for systolic arrays originates in the ability to create small local and regular connections between array nodes which can avoid many of the routing problems of more random or non-uniform logic.

An interesting characteristic of systolic arrays is that the majority of bandwidth supporting the processing elements are very small local connections and external bandwidth is effectively amortized across the width and height of the arrays. In more details we can model the operations/second performance as the product of the width and height.

$$OP_{MAX}=2\cdot(w\cdot h)\cdot freq$$

Whereas the input bandwidth requirement feeding the array is the sum of the width and height

$$OP_{MAX}=2\cdot(w\cdot h)\cdot freq$$

In the section about memory bandwidth we will formulate an integer linear program for maximizing the computation in a systolic array under limitations of bandwidth and FPGA DSP counts.

Kernel Sizes

While designing architectures one important choice is sizing the kernel both at the coarse grain level as well as the internal process-element (PE) level. At the high level of abstraction, an application could be designed to fully utilize an FPGA for a single deep learning problem at a time. This would let the kernel use all DSPs, all memory interfaces, and would minimize latency and generally make the software level interface on the CPU quite simple. On the other hand, sizing a kernel to the full chip has a significant number of drawbacks. First on a large modern FPGA the FPGA is not a uniform placeable area. It has holes and partitions that makes it challenging for designing a monolithic kernel from the actual design implementation. Additionally operating a single input at a time means there may be points in time where the FPGA cannot be fully utilized if parts of the hardware are idle for example if a maxpool operation means the convolution engine must be unused.

Creating multiple smaller kernels allow both batching as well as performing multiple different networks simultaneously. For example an application can be built as a pipeline of an object detection network followed by an image classification network. In a typical Xilinx UltraScale and UltraScale+ devices partitioning kernels across multiple super logic regions (SLRs) has problem to be a very effective technique for building deep learning systems.

With varying sizes of FPGAs it is desirable to build parameterizable kernels that can be built in different configurations to scale for the size of the FPGA available or to add multiple kernels into a single FPGA. In this manner for configurations c_0, c_1, ... c_n with respective DSP counts d_0, d_1, ... d_n a configuration of the maximum DSP count can be described as an integer constraint on

the number of each configuration simultaneously placeable on the FPGA

$$OP_{MAX}=2\cdot(w\cdot h)\cdot freq$$

And using this constraint the maximization objective is the number of operations per cycle which is a direct function of the total number of DSPs

Maximize $\sum x_i \cdot d_i$

As will be explained in the section on memory bandwidth this simple model by itself naively skips the effect memory bandwidth has on actual DSP efficiency and the integer programming model is not complete.

Memory Bandwidth

Deep learning kernels can have vastly different memory bandwidth requirements based on the types of operations that area being performed. Depending on the memory bandwidth, certain configurations of kernels may exceed available bandwidth. Towards the high end of bandwidth requirements are algorithms that require new data to be loaded into the kernel every cycle. Examples of these algorithms may be dense matrix operations. For a processing element in matrix multiplications, the total number of elements sent to each DSP or multiplier is directly related to the size of matrices being used. This is in contrast to a convolutional type operation used in CNNs where a sliding window and constant weight values means the potential bandwidth of a well designed architecture can be a fraction of the equivalently described matrix-matrix multiplication. In terms of convolutional windows the input data bandwidth is reduced by the data reuse scaled by the factor of stride. In this manner, a kernel designed with convolution in mind can greatly outperform one designed solely for dense matrix multiplication. In these situations we can initially model kernel efficiency as peak operations per second using a simple systolic array. Using the maximum bandwidth available to the FPGA can product an efficiency scaling factor that when multiplied by the DSP ops at a specific frequency can predict the actual DSP ops per second.

$$Efficiency=\max(\frac{BW_{FPGA}}{BW_{MAX}},1)$$

As the kernel efficiency based on bandwidth is included in the operations per second maximization and interesting result appears which is that smaller kernels while more flexible and more easily able to fit in constraint FPGA placements, due to the memory bandwidth requirements, the highest operations per second comes from large monolithic kernels.

Kernel Efficiency in Convolutions

Designing kernels for convolutions illustrates some key aspects of kernel tradeoffs. A typical convolutional kernel is performing a convolution on a variable size window typically anywhere from 1x1 up to approximately 7x7 although the range 1x1 to 5x5 is currently the most common in CNNs. As was already discussed in the context of memory bandwidth, kernel stride has a dramatic effect on memory bandwidth requirements. The complementary factor in stride is filter size. In the figure shown, various filter sizes are demonstrated from an experimental kernel developed on Zynq+ ZCU102 device.

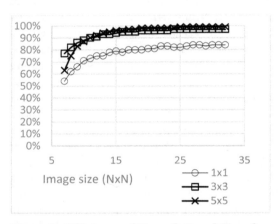

Figure 4 - Efficiency of Convolutional Kernels

There are multiple reasons why DSP efficiency can reduce for small images sizes and smaller convolutional filters. In this particular example low efficiency is directly related to requiring frequent memory loads. In small 1x1 filters, there is no memory reuse between windows as the window slides across the image data. Also for small images such as the 7x7 which is the smallest datapoint shown, a 5x5 window must perform a full image sample reload after 7 output pixels have been generated. In kernels designed for throughput and latency, much of these drawbacks can be reduced by proper buffering and reuse of image data across multiple rows of an image.

Conclusions

Designing architectures for deep learning kernels is a multi-faceted problem with many ways of using FPGA fabrics. Each type of application has targets for throughput or latency from the initial application requirement and in addition the conversion of an application into throughput or latency is dependent on the computational or memory requirements of the application. From MLPs to CNNs, RNNs and other techniques or hybrids of techniques the characteristics of the computations greatly vary. Certain applications best described as matrix operations can benefit from emphasis on the buffering to mask as much as possible memory bandwidth limitations. Other applications such as CNNs must emphasize the compute portion and the problem formulation. For FPGAs in particular, the efficient use of the DSP connectivity and resources as well as the tight coupling between memory and the DSPs provides one of the most effective techniques for both maximizing memory bandwidth to the DSPs as well as allowing the DSPs to run at very high frequencies for best throughput and latency.

References

[1] A. Krizhevsky, et al., Imagenet classification with deep convolutional neural networks, Neural Information Processing Systems 2012

[2] W. Liu, et al., SSD: Single Shot MultiBox Detector, Proceedings of the European Conference on Computer Vision 2016

[3] G. Hinton, et al., Deep Neural Networks for Acoustic Modeling in Speech Recognition: The Shared Views of Four Research Groups, IEEE Signal Processing Magazine Vol 29, Issue 6, Nov 2012.

[4] Y. H. Ng, et al., Beyond short snippets: Deep networks for video classification. In Proceedings of the IEEE Conference on Computer Vision and Pattern Recognition 2015.

[5] P. C. Woodland, Weight limiting, weight quantisation and generalisation in multi-layer perceptrons, Proceedings of the First IEE International Conference on Artificial Neural Networks, 1989.

[6] Jian Ouyang et al., SDA: Software-Defined Accelerator for Large-Scale DNN Systems, HotChips 2014

[7] S. Han et al., ESE: Efficient Speech Recognition Engine for Compressed LSTM on FPGA, International Symposium on Field-Programmable Gate Arrays, 2017

[8] 8-bit Dot Product Acceleration https://www.xilinx.com/support/documentation/white_papers/wp487-int8-acceleration.pdf

[9] T. Sainath, Towards End-To-End Speech Recognition Using Deep Neural Networks, Invited Talk, International Conference on Machine Learning 2015

[10] A. Chang, Recurrent Neural Networks Hardware Implementation on FPGA, https://arxiv.org/abs/1511.05552v4

[11] Norman P. Jouppi et al., In-Datacenter Performance Analysis of a Tensor Processing Unit, International Symposium on Computer Architecture (ISCA), Toronto, Canada, June 26, 2017

[12] C. Szegedy, et al., Going deeper with convolutions, , ILSVRC 2014

[13] Kaiming He, Xiangyu Zhang, Shaoqing Ren, Jian Sun, Deep Residual Learning for Image Recognition, ILSVRC 2015

[14] Y. Umuroglu, et al., FINN: A Framework for Fast, Scalable Binarized Neural Network Inference, International Symposium on Field Programmable Gate Arrays, 2017

[15] Reduce Power and Cost by Converting from Floating Point to Fixed Point https://www.xilinx.com/support/documentation/white_papers/wp491-floating-to-fixed-point.pdf

[16] S. Gupta, et al., Deep Learning with Limited Numerical Precision, https://arxiv.org/abs/1502.02551 2015

[17] C. Zhang et al., Optimizing FPGA-based Accelerator Design for Deep Convolutional Neural Networks, International Symposium on Field-Programmable Gate Arrays, 2015

[18] C. Farabet, et al., Large-Scale FPGA-based Convolutional Networks, Scaling up Machine Learning: Parallel and Distributed Approaches, Cambridge University Press, 2011

[19] K. Negi, et al., Deep pipelined one-chip FPGA implementation of a real-time image-based human detection algorithm, International Conference on Field-Programmable Technology , 2011

[20] J. Qiu, Going Deeper with Embedded FPGA Platform for Convolutional Neural Network, International Symposium on Field Programmable Gate Arrays, 2016

[21] C. Couprie, et al., Indoor Semantic Segmentation using depth information, International Conference on Learning Representations 2013

[22] F. Iandola, Squeezenet: Alexnet-Level Accuracy with 50x fewer Parameters and <0.5MB Model Size, https://arxiv.org/abs/1602.07360

[22] P. Gysel et al., Hardware-oriented Approximation of Convolutional Neural Networks, International Conference on Learning Representations 2016

Architecture Exploration of Standard-Cell and FPGA-Overlay CGRAs Using the Open-Source CGRA-ME Framework

S. Alexander Chin
Dept. of ECE, University of Toronto
Toronto, Ontario, Canada
xan@ece.utoronto.ca

Kuang Ping Niu
Dept. of ECE, University of Toronto
Toronto, Ontario, Canada
kuangping.niu@mail.utoronto.ca

Matthew Walker
Dept. of ECE, University of Toronto
Toronto, Ontario, Canada
matthewjp.walker@mail.utoronto.ca

Shizhang Yin
Dept. of ECE, University of Toronto
Toronto, Ontario, Canada

Alexander Mertens
Dept. of ECE, University of Toronto
Toronto, Ontario, Canada

Jongeun Lee
School of ECE, UNIST
Ulsan, Korea
jlee@unist.ac.kr

Jason H. Anderson
Dept. of ECE, University of Toronto
Toronto, Ontario, Canada
janders@eecg.toronto.edu

ABSTRACT

We describe an open-source software framework, *CGRA-ME*, for the modeling and exploration of coarse-grained reconfigurable architectures (CGRAs). CGRAs are programmable hardware devices having large ALU-like logic blocks, and datapath bus-style interconnect. CGRAs are positioned between fine-grained FPGAs and standard-cell ASICs on the spectrum of programmability – they are less flexible than FPGAs, yet are more flexible than ASICs. With CGRA-ME, an architect can describe a CGRA architecture in an XML-based language. The framework also allows the architect to map benchmarks onto the architecture and provides automatic generation of Verilog RTL for the modeled architecture. This allows the architect to simulate for verification purposes, and perform synthesis to either an ASIC or FPGA-overlay implementation of the CGRA, assessing performance, area, and power consumption. In an experimental study, we use CGRA-ME to model, map benchmarks onto, and evaluate several variants of a widely known CGRA [24], considering both standard-cell and FPGA-overlay physical realizations of the CGRA.

CCS CONCEPTS

• **Hardware → Reconfigurable logic and FPGAs**;

KEYWORDS

Reconfigurable architectures, coarse-grained reconfigurable architectures, CGRAs, FPGA overlays

ISPD '18, March 25–28, 2018, Monterey, CA
© 2018 Association for Computing Machinery.
ACM ISBN 978-1-4503-5626-8/18/03...$15.00
https://doi.org/10.1145/3177540.3177553

ACM Reference Format:
S. Alexander Chin, Kuang Ping Niu, Matthew Walker, Shizhang Yin, Alexander Mertens, Jongeun Lee, and Jason H. Anderson. 2018. Architecture Exploration of Standard-Cell and FPGA-Overlay CGRAs Using the Open-Source CGRA-ME Framework. In *ISPD '18: 2018 International Symposium on Physical Design, March 25–28, 2018, Monterey, CA*. ACM, New York, NY, USA, 8 pages. https://doi.org/10.1145/3177540.3177553

1 INTRODUCTION

Coarse-grained reconfigurable arrays (CGRAs) are programmable hardware architectures with coarse-grained logic blocks, often resembling ALUs, and datapath-style interconnect, where buses of signals are routed together as a group. These attributes stand in contrast to fine-grained field-programmable gate arrays (FPGAs), which contain a mix of fine and coarse-grained blocks for implementing logic (e.g. look-up-tables and hardened DSP blocks), and where individual logic signals are routed in a singular manner. CGRAs are thus less flexible than FPGAs, affecting both the ease of application mapping, as well as the power/performance/cost, elaborated upon below. In this paper, we describe an open-source framework under active development at the University of Toronto called *CGRA-ME* [9] that permits the modeling and exploration of a wide variety of CGRA architectures, and also facilitates research on CGRA mapping algorithms. Here, we also detail two physical implementations of CGRAs and show the capabilities of the framework's mapper, demonstrating the effectiveness of CGRA-ME.

A CGRA can be physically realized in a number of ways: 1) as a custom chip, with manual layout, 2) as a standard-cell ASIC, or 3) on an FPGA as an *overlay*. We believe the first option to be prohibitively expensive, and therefore, we focus on the second and third options in this paper, which we refer to as a *standard-cell CGRA* and an *FPGA-overlay CGRA*, respectively. A standard-cell CGRA will have comparatively less silicon area dedicated to programmability than an FPGA, therefore offering better power/performance than an FPGA for applications whose computational and communication needs are aligned with the CGRA architecture's capabilities. Standard-cell CGRAs have been proposed by both academia (e.g. [15, 24]), and more recently, in industry [17, 29].

On the other hand, because an FPGA-overlay CGRA is a programmable platform implemented *on top* of a programmable platform (the underlying FPGA), the power/performance benefits versus the direct use of the underlying FPGA are less clear. If the FPGA-overlay CGRA is carefully implemented to make best-possible use of the underlying FPGA resources, then power/performance parity may be achievable. Despite this apparent weakness, we believe an important future usage scenario for FPGA-overlay CGRAs will be in the cloud/datacenter context, where FPGAs are deployed alongside standard processors, to be used as hardware application accelerators. Particularly, we envision the existence of libraries of pre-compiled FPGA-overlay CGRA architectures, where a given architecture is tailored towards a specific application domain (e.g. machine learning or finance), with an easy-to-use software API. A user would select the pre-compiled FPGA-overlay CGRA that best meets their application needs, and aim to achieve application acceleration over a standard CPU/GPU implementation.

Regardless of the physical manifestation, a key benefit of CGRAs versus FPGAs is in application mapping runtime. Owing to their reduced flexibility, CAD tools for CGRAs need to make fewer decisions, reducing CAD complexity significantly. This brings runtimes closer to software compilation, as opposed to the hours or days that may be required for application mapping to FPGAs. Moreover, applications targeted to CGRAs are typically specified at a higher abstraction level than traditional hardware design. Applications are specified as data-flow graphs or in software, as opposed to Verilog/VHDL RTL.

While open-source modeling and evaluation frameworks have long existed for traditional processors (e.g. [4]), GPUs [2], and fine-grain FPGAs [3], there is no analogous framework for CGRAs. With CGRA-ME, a wide variety of CGRA architectures can be modeled, by a human architect using an XML-based language. The CGRA-ME framework accepts the architecture description as input, as well as an application benchmark to be mapped into the CGRA. An in-memory device model of the CGRA is constructed and the application is mapped into the CGRA. Verilog RTL for the CGRA is produced automatically, along with a bitstream configuring the device for the given benchmark. The generated Verilog can be synthesized to a standard-cell ASIC or an FPGA-overlay CGRA implementation to assess power/performance of the architecture. The RTL and configuration bitstream can also be simulated for functional correctness. CGRA-ME is a thus powerful platform for CGRA architecture and CAD research that we believe will be useful to both the academic and industrial communities.

2 FRAMEWORK OVERVIEW

Figure 1 depicts the CGRA-ME framework, its internal components, and data-flow. Circled labels are shown on each component. The inputs to the framework are a C-language application benchmark ①, as well as a textual description of the CGRA architecture ②. The XML-based CGRA-ME architecture description language, *CGRA-ADL* is elaborated upon in Section 2.1. The CGRA-ADL is parsed by an architecture interpreter ③, producing an in-memory

device model of the CGRA ④. The benchmark is parsed and then optimized by the LLVM compiler [18]. One or more data-flow graphs are extracted from the input benchmark and input to the CGRA Mapper ⑥. The specific portions of the program for which data-flow graphs are extracted are based on user annotations to the source code. The CGRA mapper ⑥ receives the application data-flow graph as input, as well as uses the in-memory CGRA device model to map the application onto the CGRA. The mapping algorithm is described in more detail in Section 2.2.

The CGRA architecture interpreter ③ is also capable of generating Verilog RTL for the specified CGRA ⑦. The generated Verilog has several utilities. First, the Verilog, along with a configuration bitstream produced by the mapper, can be simulated to verify CGRA functionality ⑧. Second, the Verilog can be input into a standard-cell ASIC design flow ⑨, to realize a physical implementation, which can then inform performance/power/area models Ⓑ. Or third, the RTL can be input into an FPGA design flow Ⓒ to realize an FPGA-overlay CGRA implementation, and associated performance/power/area models Ⓒ. In Section 4, we demonstrate standard-cell and FPGA-overlay implementations of variants of the ADRES [24] CGRA architecture. Finally, physical performance/power/area models can be combined with the mapping results to analyze the specific input benchmark implemented on the modeled CGRA Ⓓ.

2.1 CGRA-ME Architecture Description Language

CGRA-ADL allows the textual specification of a CGRA architecture in a concise XML-based language. The complete language definition is available on the CGRA-ME website [8]; here, we overview a few aspects of the language at a high level.

Figure 2 illustrates the pieces of an architecture description at an abstract level. Line 1 opens the description. At line 2, an architect may optionally use the `definition` tag to define one or more constants. The `module` tag at line 3 opens the description of a CGRA module, which may have inputs (line 4) and outputs (not shown). A module may contain sub-modules (line 5), which are interconnected with one another (line 6), as elaborated upon below. Within the `cgra` tags, a module may be described in a hierarchical manner, composed of sub-modules, which may themselves contain sub-modules.

The definition of the CGRA is opened with the `architecture` tag (line 9, Figure 2). Here, the example shows a 4×4 CGRA architecture. Lines 10-13 define a pattern of modules that populate the 4×4 array. The language is flexible in that it allows both homogeneous and heterogeneous CGRA architectures to be described, with a variety of interconnect styles for interconnecting the blocks, as described below.

Figure 3 shows an example CGRA module, `moduleA`, which contains within a sub-module as well as programmable interconnect that permits selection from three top-level inputs to two internal sub-module inputs. The CGRA-ADL specification is given in Figure 4. Line 1 opens the description. Lines 2-5 define the module I/Os. Line 6 instantiates a sub-module, of type `FuncUnit` having an instance name `fu_inst`. Lines 7-10 define the multiplexed interconnect to the sub-module. Implicit in this description is the presence of

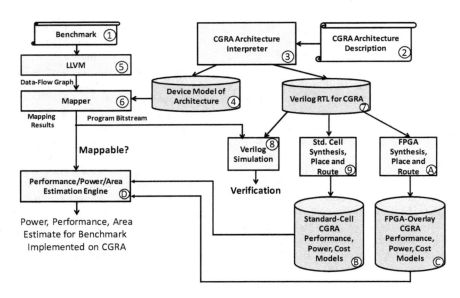

Figure 1: CGRA-ME framework overview showing the main components.

```
1   <cgra>
2       <definition .../>
3       <module name="blockA">
4           <input name="in"/>
5           <inst  module="fu"/>
6           <connection ... /> ...
7       </module>
8
9       <architecture row="4" col="4">
10          <pattern>
11              <block module="blockA"/>
12          </pattern> ...
13      </architecture>
14  </cgra>
```

Figure 2: High-level structure of a CGRA architecture description.

```
1   <module name="moduleA">
2       <input   name="in1"/>
3       <input   name="in2"/>
4       <input   name="in3"/>
5       <output name="out"/>
6       <inst    name="fu_inst" module="FuncUnit"/>
7       <connection select-from="this.in1 this.in2"
8           to="fu_inst.in1"/>
9       <connection select-from="this.in2 this.in3"
10          to="fu_inst.in2"/>
11      <connection from="fu_inst.out"
12          to="this.out"/>
13  </module>
```

Figure 4: CGRA-ADL module definition for moduleA depicted in Figure 3.

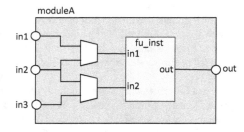

Figure 3: Example module within a CGRA.

```
1   <architecture rows="8" cols="8">
2   <pattern row-range="0 7" col-range="0 7"
3       row="2" col="2">
4       <block module="A"/> <block module="B"/>
5           <!-- row break -->
6       <block module="C"/> <block module="D"/>
7   </pattern>
8   </architecture>
```

Figure 5: CGRA-ADL for a heterogeneous CGRA with four block types.

SRAM configuration cells that drive the multiplexer-select signals. Lines 11-12 defines the interconnect from the sub-module output to the higher-level output. Line 13 closes the description.

With the architecture tag in Figure 2, a generic CGRA architectures can be composed, with varied functional unit architectures (homogeneous or heterogeneous) and a variety of different inter-block connectivity. Consider the example shown in Figure 5. Line 1 specifies an architecture with 8 rows and 8 columns. The pattern tag on line 2 opens a 2×2 pattern definition that applies repeatedly

to the entire 8×8 CGRA. Lines 4-6 specify that the 2×2 repeating pattern comprises 4 modules, A, B, C, and D, where A and B are on the first row; C and D are on the second row. Hence, the architecture is heterogeneous with 4 types of blocks, in an iterated 2×2 pattern. Although not shown in the example, the CGRA-ADL also contains syntactic sugar for common styles of inter-block CGRA interconnect, namely, North-South-East-West (NSEW) block connectivity, as well as NSEW+diagonal connectivity.

2.2 Mapping

2.2.1 Background. The process of implementing a benchmark onto a CGRA is called *mapping*. This process involves, at the highest level, a translation of a benchmark from a high-level software language such as C to a *data-flow graph* (DFG). A data-flow graph is an directed graph that contains a number of operations such as *add* or *mul* as nodes. Edges within the graph represent the flow of data from outputs to inputs of operations. This data-flow graph is then implemented on the CGRA through association of operations to functional units and ensuring routes for data between them, while accounting for registers and obeying a correct operation schedule.

To aid this association of operations with the physical CGRA, a device model of the CGRA is created. The Modulo Routing Resource Graph (MRRG) [23] is a representation that is commonly used to model CGRAs. This representation is used as the device model shown as ④ in Figure 1. This directed graph contains representations of functional units and routing resources as vertices with edges showing valid paths between resources. The MRRG is created by querying each module instance within the CGRA hierarchy to produce a graph sub-graphs of the MRRG, building the MRRG in a piece-meal fashion. The mapping problem is the finding an association of operation nodes in the DFG to functional units in the MRRG while ensuring values produced by operations are associated with a path over a number of routing resource nodes to the destination operation.

2.2.2 ILP Mapper. While other mappers have employed annealer-based [14, 23] or graph-based [7, 22] mapping techniques, in this work we use a constraint-based technique by formulating the graph association problem as an integer linear programming (ILP) problem. While our ILP mapper is not the first formulation to be applied to CGRAs [19, 25, 30, 31], the main difference with CGRA-ME's ILP formulation [8] is that the formulation is valid over any architecture that an MRRG can be generated, while other works are constrained to specific architectures or architectural templates.

Here we provide a brief discussion of the formulation. We refer to four sets of items: *FuncUnits*: every execution slot of every function unit within the architecture or one function node within the MRRG; *RouteRes*: every routing resource (wire or register) within the architecture or one routing node within the MRRG; *Ops*: every operation defined in the DFG that is to be mapped; *Vals*: every value output from an Operation in the DFG.

And we define two sets of binary variables. The first set of variables define the placement of operations onto functional units – a mapping from *Ops* to *FuncUnits*.

- $F_{p,q}$: functional-unit node p in the MRRG is used for implementing operation q in the DFG.

The second set of variables define the use of routing resources by values (a mapping from *Vals* to *RouteRes*).

- $R_{i,j}$: routing node i is used for routing value j.

A number of constraints are applied, some of which are outlined next.

Operation Placement: This ensures every operation in the DFG is placed on exactly one functional unit within the MRRG.

$$\sum_{p \in FuncUnits} F_{p,q} = 1, \forall q \in Ops \tag{1}$$

Functional Unit Exclusivity: This ensures each functional unit slot (represented by *FuncUnits*) is occupied by at most one DFG Operation (i.e. there is no multiple usage of a single functional unit slot).

$$\sum_{q \in Ops} F_{p,q} \leq 1, \forall p \in FuncUnits \tag{2}$$

Functional Unit Legality: This ensures that operations are only placed on functional units that can implement the operation (applies to reduced architectures).

$$F_{p,q} = 0$$
$$\forall p \in FuncUnits, q \in Ops$$
$$\text{where: } q \notin SupportedOps(p) \tag{3}$$

where $SupportedOps(p)$ is the set of operations that are supported by functional unit p.

Route Exclusivity: This ensures that each routing resource is occupied by *at most* one value (i.e. multiple DFG Values cannot be routed onto the same routing resource).

$$\sum_{j \in Vals} R_{i,j} \leq 1, \forall i \in RouteRes \tag{4}$$

Another set of constraints ensures that values between operations are routed from the source operations to the destination operations but a full discussion is omitted due to space limitations.

According to the aforementioned constraints, the following objective function is minimized to find the minimum number of routing resources used by the mapping:

$$Minimize \sum_{\forall i \in RouteRes, \forall j \in Vals} R_{i,j} \tag{5}$$

2.3 Verilog & Bitstream Generation

The in-memory objects representing modules are organized in a hierarchical manner. Each of these objects represent a logical hardware unit, and encapsulates its connections, ports, sub-modules, and configuration sub-modules. Each MRRG node also links to its module instance, enabling easy reverse mapping from node to module. A Verilog implementation of the architecture is automatically generated from the module tree: for each unique module type, a parameterized Verilog file is emitted with ports, sub-module declarations, and a generic implementation including connecting wires. Sub-modules containing configuration registers are also included, hooked up to the module they configure, and automatically linked together to form an inter-module scan chain.

A successful mapping associates all *Ops* and *Vals* with one or more MRRG nodes. The MRRG is iterated over and a map from module instance to a list of associated *Ops*, *Vals* and MRRG nodes is created. The configuration sub-modules are then walked in scan chain order, and the connected module instance is presented with its corresponding data stored in the map. The module then generates the configuration bits required by pattern matching and inspection of the *Ops*, *Vals*, and MRRG nodes. A Verilog file is produced, containing a module that will use the generated bitstream to program an instance of a top-level CGRA module, which was generated separately. The configuration generation and programming has been tested with ModelSim [10], and expected behaviour was verified at outputs.

3 PHYSICAL IMPLEMENTATION METHODOLOGY

3.1 Standard-Cell

In this work, we leverage the FreePDK45 [26] standard-cell library, an open-source 45 nm standard-cell library, for the experimental study using standard-cells. The tool-generated Verilog of the targeted architectures is used for physical implementation and is put through the following flow: Synopsys' Design Compiler is selected to perform technology mapping. Following technology mapping, we analyze area breakdown of targeted architectures. Architectures are mapped for minimum area and minimum delay. With the mapped design netlist as input, all architectures are pushed through standard-cell place and route, with Cadence's Innovus, which then produce accurate standard-cell placement, parasitic information (SPEF file), as well as total chip area. Given the design netlist and SPEF file, we perform static timing analysis with Synopsys' PrimeTime and determine designs' critical path. In Section 4.3.1, we demonstrate how user-specified architectures can be assessed for their design feasibility, at various stages of design flow: standard-cell technology mapping, place and route, and static timing analysis.

3.2 FPGA-Overlay

We also target the 45 nm Altera Stratix IV FPGA (same process node as the standard-cell implementation) using Altera/Intel's Quartus Prime ver. 16.1. A challenge that arose in the FPGA implementation pertains to floorplanning in the presence of CGRA blocks containing multipliers. It is desirable if the rows/columns of the CGRA's physical realization form a regular grid coherent with the CGRA's logical representation (e.g. CGRA blocks in column 2 are placed to the right of blocks in column 1, and so on). In the targeted Stratix IV FPGA, the DSP blocks containing hardened multipliers are arranged in columns that are relatively far apart. Interspersed among the DSP columns are comparatively numerous columns of standard LUT-based logic blocks, as well as occasional RAM-block columns. The floorplans of the CGRAs considered in Section 4.3.2 are thus defined primarily in relation to the DSP columns, with the LUT-based blocks between the DSPs being underutilized.

4 EXPERIMENTAL STUDY

4.1 Experimental Architectures

In this study we model two architecture variants resembling ADRES [24]. Figure 6 shows a high-level view of both architectures. The two targeted variants of ADRES are the "Full" and "Reduced" architecture, both are 4×4 grid of functional units; the Full architecture consists of functional units with a full set of operations: add, subtract, multiply, shifts, and, or, and xor, while also having torus connectivity between top and bottom rows, and between leftmost

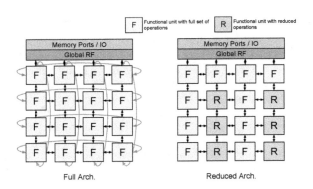

Figure 6: "Full" and "Reduced" variants of ADRES architecture

and rightmost columns; the Reduced architecture contains processing elements with only add and subtract capabilities in odd columns, and there are no torus connections.

4.2 Benchmarks & Mapping Results

The ILP mapper within CGRA-ME was used to map a combined set of synthetic and real benchmarks to the two architecture variants. Table 1 shows the benchmark set mapped to our two architecture variants. All benchmarks were able to be mapped into the Full architecture that contains 16 multipliers (one in each functional unit) and toroid connections. In the Reduced architecture, there are only 10 multipliers and no toroid connections. Not all benchmarks map to this architecture, especially ones with many multiplication operations. The benchmarks *cap*, *mac2*, *mults1*, and *mults2* are unable to be mapped to the reduced architecture. Though they all have less than 10 multiply operations, no feasible mapping exists as shown by the ILP mapper – due to constrained routing.

All benchmarks finished mapping in less than ~12 mins. The longest runtime for mapping is for *cap* on the Full architecture, followed by *mults1* and *mults2*. In these benchmarks, between 12 and 14 of the total 16 functional units are used. This high usage imposes a harder constraint problem to solve, leading to longer runtimes.

4.3 Physical Implementation

4.3.1 Standard-Cell. For the standard-cell implementation, both architecture variants are synthesized targeting minimum area, as well as minimum delay, producing four sets of results. Soft constraint floorplanning shown in Figure 8 is applied to generate more regular designs. All four implementations are given the same aspect ratio. After place and route, we are able to extract the total chip area of all four designs shown in Table 2. Figure 9 shows the chip layout of all four designs, while Figure 10 demonstrates where each sub-module is placed, which can be compared against the soft floorplan constraints in Figure 8.

Figure 7 presents the area breakdown of the four variants. Within the breakdown, the following categorization is used: multiplexers of any size are routing resources, registers storing configuration bits are configuration memory, data registers and register files are data memory, and functional units are computation resources.

	Architecture Mappability		Mapping Runtime [s]		Benchmark Statistics		
	Full Arch.	Reduced Arch.	Full Arch.	Reduced Arch.	Ops	Mults	I/O
accum	M	M	21.9	21.8	8	4	5
cap	M	U	727.6	1.8	12	9	4
conv2	M	M	3.4	3.4	7	5	3
conv3	M	M	21.4	109.9	11	7	4
mac	M	M	2.4	2.9	5	3	3
mac2	M	U	60.6	211.3	12	8	6
matmult	M	M	5.3	9.3	9	5	3
mults1	M	U	406.2	145.9	15	8	5
mults2	M	U	397.8	212.0	13	8	5
sum	M	M	0.3	0.3	3	1	2

Table 1: Mapping results for both Full and Reduced architectures. M indicates the benchmark was able to be mapped on the architecture. U indicates that the benchmark was unable to be mapped on the architecture. Mapping runtimes for each architecture and benchmark are also reported. Statistics for the benchmarks are also included listing the number of compute operations, number of multiplication operations, and the number of I/Os. Ops is the total number of operations including multiplications.

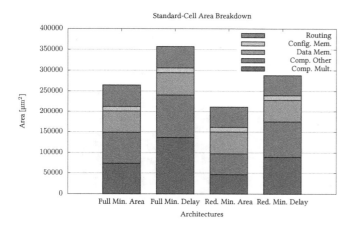

Figure 7: Standard-cell area breakdown of Full and Reduced architectures, when targeting minimum area and minimum delay.

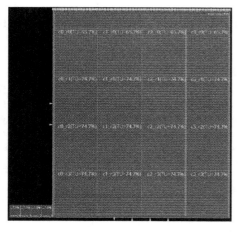

Figure 8: Floorplan for Cadence's Innovus place and route

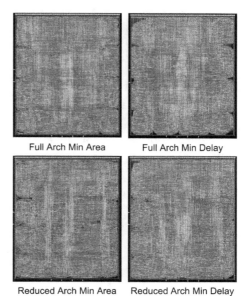

Full Arch Min Area Full Arch Min Delay

Reduced Arch Min Area Reduced Arch Min Delay

Figure 9: Standard-cell layout for all four designs in physical view

From Figure 7, we observe that routing, configuration memory, and data memory are nearly constant across the architecture and optimization variants. Also, increasing computation capabilities within the processing elements results in the largest impact to the overall area required. Additionally, between the minimum area and minimum delay architectures, the multiplier area sees the largest increase.

Static timing analysis (STA) is performed to determine the design's critical path using the SPEF file and netlist output from the place-and-route tool. Although the FMax generated using FreePDK45 may not be representative of an optimal design, comparisons of between architecture variants can still provide relative conclusions.

	Full Arch Min Area	Full Arch Min Delay	Reduced Arch Min Area	Reduced Arch Min Delay
Area [μm^2]	317927.0	403753.2	253239.8	327189.2
FMax [MHz]	140	164	142	192

Table 2: Standard-cell post-place-and-route area and performance of all four designs.

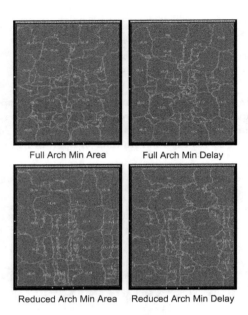

Full Arch Min Area   Full Arch Min Delay

Reduced Arch Min Area   Reduced Arch Min Delay

Figure 10: Standard-cell layout for all four designs in amoeba view

	Full Arch	Reduced Arch
Area [ALM]	8803	7192
FMax [MHz]	89	103

Table 3: FPGA area and performance for both architectures on Stratix IV.

From the STA results, the inter-processing-element routing multiplexers and the multipliers are the bottleneck of the designs. The Full architecture's torus routing multiplexers contribute to its lower FMax, compared to the Reduced architecture. Maximum operating frequencies of each design are shown in Table 2.

4.3.2 FPGA-Overlay. Figure 11 shows the layout of the two architectures implemented in Stratix IV. Area and performance results are reported in Table 3. Area numbers reflect Stratix IV ALMs (adaptive logic modules), each of which contains a dual-output fracturable 6-input LUT, carry-chain circuitry and two flip-flops. Logic blocks with multipliers use Stratix IV DSP blocks (not shown in the table).

Figure 12 shows an area breakdown of ALMs used on the FPGA. Here only the data memory and configuration memory stay constant and we see an increase in both the computation area as well as routing area between the Reduced architecture and Full architecture.

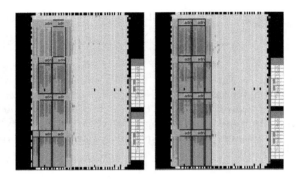

Figure 11: Floorplanned Stratix IV implementations of homogeneous CGRA with torus connections (left), and heterogeneous CGRA without torus connections (right).

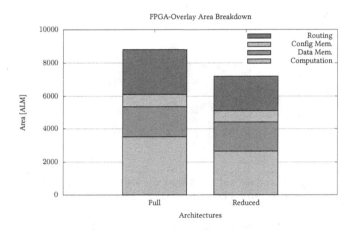

Figure 12: FPGA area breakdown for both architecture variants.

5 RELATED WORK

There are many different CGRA designs and mapping flows proposed in the past, the summary of which can be found in excellent survey articles [1, 11, 16, 27, 28]. One differentiating goal of the CGRA-ME framework is that it is able to generically model, map applications onto, and generate RTL designs for a wide range of architectures within a single framework, allowing for a 'level playing field'. Having all components including mapper and bitstream and RTL generator is essential to getting realistic performance numbers for specific benchmark applications.

Recent works have developed subsets of the CGRA-ME framework. CGADL [13] provides a modeling language to describe CGRA architectures but does not implement a way for application or benchmark mapping nor RTL output. Other works are focused on mappers such as DRESC [23], SPR [14] and others [7, 20, 22] but are not integrated into a larger generic architecture modeling framework. For physical design, there are a number of related works but they were not produced within a larger unifying framework, which again makes it difficult to compare different architectures in a holistic way. Other works also leverage standard-cells for implementation [12, 15, 21, 24]. And for FPGA overlays, Capalija et al. [5, 6] produced prototype designs with a custom mapping flow.

6 CONCLUSIONS AND FUTURE WORK

In this work we have demonstrated the capabilities of the CGRA-ME framework, encompassing architecture modeling, application mapping, and physical implementation. The CGRA-ADL language was shown to be capable of modeling complex patterns for our test architecture and from the use of the RTL generation through CGRA-ME, two different physical implementations were generated – one in standard-cells and as an FPGA-overlay. Area breakdowns and FMax for all implementations were reported, highlighting some of the design tradeoffs that can be made. The ILP based mapper within CGRA-ME was shown to quickly generate mappings for both architecture variants, reacting to the reduced routing and functional unit resources.

The CGRA-ME framework is open-source [8] and freely available for use by the academic research community – providing a basis for future CGRA research.

7 ACKNOWLEDGMENTS

The authors thank Dr. Qiang Wang and Taneem Ahmed from Huawei for their comments and suggestions on this research.

REFERENCES

[1] Hideharu Amano. 2006. A Survey on Dynamically Reconfigurable Processors. *IEICE Transactions* 89-B, 12 (2006), 3179–3187.

[2] Ali Bakhoda, G. L. Yuan, W. W. Fung, H. Wong, and T. M. Aamodt. 2009. Analyzing CUDA workloads using a detailed GPU simulator. In *Performance Analysis of Systems and Software, 2009. ISPASS 2009. IEEE Int'l Symposium on*. IEEE, Washington, DC, USA, 163–174. https://doi.org/10.1109/ISPASS.2009.4919648

[3] Vaughn Betz and J. Rose. 1997. VPR: A new packing, placement and routing tool for FPGA research. In *Int'l Workshop on Field Programmable Logic and Applications*. Springer, Berlin, Germany, 213–222.

[4] Nathan L. Binkert, B. M. Beckmann, G. Black, S. K. Reinhardt, A. G. Saidi, A. Basu, J. Hestness, D. Hower, T. Krishna, S. Sardashti, R. Sen, K. Sewell, M. S. B. Altaf, N. Vaish, M. D. Hill, and D. A. Wood. 2011. The gem5 simulator. *SIGARCH Computer Architecture News* 39, 2 (2011), 1–7.

[5] Davor Capalija and T. S. Abdelrahman. 2013. A high-performance overlay architecture for pipelined execution of data flow graphs. In *Field Programmable Logic and Applications, 2013 23rd Int'l Conference on*. IEEE, Washington, DC, USA, 1–8. https://doi.org/10.1109/FPL.2013.6645515

[6] Davor Capalija and T. S. Abdelrahman. 2014. Tile-based bottom-up compilation of custom mesh-of-functional-units FPGA overlays. In *Field Programmable Logic and Applications, 2014 24th Int'l Conference on*. IEEE, Washington, DC, USA, 1–8. https://doi.org/10.1109/FPL.2014.6927456

[7] Liang Chen and T. Mitra. 2014. Graph Minor Approach for Application Mapping on CGRAs. *ACM Trans. Reconfigurable Technol. Syst.* 7, 3, Article 21 (Sept. 2014), 25 pages. https://doi.org/10.1145/2655242

[8] S. Alexander Chin, S. Niu, S. Yin, A. Mertens, M. Walker, and J. Anderson. 2018. CGRA-ME. (2018). http://cgra-me.ece.utoronto.ca

[9] S Alexander Chin, N. Sakamoto, A. Rui, J. Zhao, J. H. Kim, Y. Hara-Azumi, and J. Anderson. 2017. CGRA-ME: A unified framework for CGRA modelling and exploration. In *IEEE 28th Int'l Conference on Application-specific Systems, Architectures and Processors 2017*. IEEE, Washington, DC, USA, 184–189. https://doi.org/10.1109/ASAP.2017.7995277

[10] Mentor Graphics Corporation. 2018. Modelsim. (2018). https://www.mentor.com/products/fpga/verification-simulation/modelsim/

[11] Bjorn De Sutter, P. Raghavan, and A. Lambrechts. 2013. *Coarse-Grained Reconfigurable Array Architectures*. Springer New York, New York, NY, 553–592. https://doi.org/10.1007/978-1-4614-6859-2_18

[12] Amin Farmahini-Farahani, J. H. Ahn, K. Morrow, and N. S. Kim. 2015. NDA: Near-DRAM acceleration architecture leveraging commodity DRAM devices and standard memory modules. In *High Performance Computer Architecture (HPCA), 2015 IEEE 21st Int'l Symposium on*. IEEE, Washington, DC, USA, 283–295. https://doi.org/10.1109/HPCA.2015.7056040

[13] Julio Oliveira Filho et al. 2009. CGADL: An Architecture Description Language for Coarse-grained Reconfigurable Arrays. *IEEE Trans. VLSI Syst.* 17, 9 (Sept. 2009), 1247–1259.

[14] Stephen Friedman, A. Carroll, B. Van Essen, B. Ylvisaker, C. Ebeling, and S. Hauck. 2009. SPR: An Architecture-adaptive CGRA Mapping Tool. In *Proc. of the ACM/SIGDA Int'l Symposium on FPGAs (FPGA '09)*. ACM, New York, NY, USA, 191–200. https://doi.org/10.1145/1508128.1508158

[15] Seth Copen Goldstein, H. Schmit, M. Moe, M. Budiu, S. Cadambi, R. R. Taylor, and R. Laufer. 1999. PipeRench: A Co/Processor for Streaming Multimedia Acceleration. *SIGARCH Comput. Archit. News* 27, 2 (May 1999), 28–39. https://doi.org/10.1145/307338.300982

[16] Reiner Hartenstein. 2001. Coarse grain reconfigurable architectures. In *Proc. of the ASP-DAC 2001*. IEEE, Washington, DC, USA, 564–569. https://doi.org/10.1109/ASPDAC.2001.913368

[17] Changmoo Kim, M. Chung, Y. Cho, M. Konijnenburg, S. Ryu, and J. Kim. 2014. ULP-SRP: Ultra Low-Power Samsung Reconfigurable Processor for Biomedical Applications. *TRETS* 7, 3 (2014), 22:1–22:15.

[18] Chris Lattner and V. Adve. 2004. LLVM: A Compilation Framework for Lifelong Program Analysis & Transformation. In *Proc. of the Int'l Symposium on Code Generation and Optimization (CGO '04)*. IEEE, Washington, DC, USA, 75–. http://dl.acm.org/citation.cfm?id=977395.977673

[19] Ganghee Lee, K. Choi, and N. D. Dutt. 2011. Mapping Multi-Domain Applications Onto Coarse-Grained Reconfigurable Architectures. *IEEE Transactions on Computer-Aided Design of Integrated Circuits and Systems* 30, 5 (May 2011), 637–650. https://doi.org/10.1109/TCAD.2010.2098571

[20] Hongsik Lee, D. Nguyen, and J. Lee. 2015. Optimizing Stream Program Performance on CGRA-based Systems. In *Proc. of the 52Nd Annual Design Automation Conference (DAC '15)*. ACM, New York, NY, USA, Article 110, 6 pages. https://doi.org/10.1145/2744769.2744884

[21] Cao Liang and X. Huang. 2008. SmartCell: A power-efficient reconfigurable architecture for data streaming applications. In *2008 IEEE Workshop on Signal Processing Systems*. IEEE, Washington, DC, USA, 257–262. https://doi.org/10.1109/SIPS.2008.4671772

[22] Lu Ma, W. Ge, and Z. Qi. 2012. *A Graph-Based Spatial Mapping Algorithm for a Coarse Grained Reconfigurable Architecture Template*. Springer Berlin Heidelberg, Berlin, Heidelberg, 669–678. https://doi.org/10.1007/978-3-642-25992-0_89

[23] Bingfeng Mei, S. Vernalde, D. Verkest, H. De Man, and R. Lauwereins. 2002. DRESC: A retargetable compiler for coarse-grained reconfigurable architectures. In *IEEE Int'l Conference on Field-Programmable Technology, 2002. Proceedings*. IEEE, Washington, DC, USA, 166–173. https://doi.org/10.1109/FPT.2002.1188678

[24] Bingfeng Mei, S. Vernalde, D. Verkest, H. De Man, and R. Lauwereins. 2003. *ADRES: An Architecture with Tightly Coupled VLIW Processor and Coarse-Grained Reconfigurable Matrix*. Springer Berlin Heidelberg, Heidelberg, Germany, 61–70. https://doi.org/10.1007/978-3-540-45234-8_7

[25] Tony Nowatzki, M. Sartin-Tarm, L. De Carli, K. Sankaralingam, C. Estan, and B. Robatmili. 2013. A General Constraint-centric Scheduling Framework for Spatial Architectures. *SIGPLAN Not.* 48, 6 (June 2013), 495–506. https://doi.org/10.1145/2499370.2462163

[26] James E. Stine, I. Castellanos, M. Wood, J. Henson, F. Love, W. R. Davis, P. D. Franzon, M. Bucher, S. Basavarajaiah, J. Oh, and R. Jenkal. 2007. FreePDK: An Open-Source Variation-Aware Design Kit. In *Proc. of the 2007 IEEE Int'l Conference on Microelectronic Systems Education (MSE '07)*. IEEE, Washington, DC, USA, 173–174. https://doi.org/10.1109/MSE.2007.44

[27] Vaishali Tehre and R. Kshirsagar. 2012. Survey on Coarse Grained Reconfigurable Architectures. *Intl. Jrnl. of Comp. Appl.* 48, 16 (2012), 1–7.

[28] Russell Tessier, K. Pocek, and A. DeHon. 2015. Reconfigurable Computing Architectures. *Proc. of the IEEE* 103, 3 (2015), 332–354.

[29] Takao Toi, N. Nakamura, T. Fujii, T. Kitaoka, K. Togawa, K. Furuta, and T. Awashima. 2013. Optimizing time and space multiplexed computation in a dynamically reconfigurable processor. In *Field-Programmable Technology (FPT), 2013 Int'l Conference on*. IEEE, Washington, DC, USA, 106–111.

[30] Jonghee W. Yoon, A. Shrivastava, S. Park, M. Ahn, R. Jeyapaul, and Y. Paek. 2008. SPKM: A Novel Graph Drawing Based Algorithm for Application Mapping Onto Coarse-grained Reconfigurable Architectures. In *Proc. of the 2008 Asia and South Pacific Design Automation Conference*. IEEE Computer Society Press, Los Alamitos, CA, USA, 776–782. http://dl.acm.org/citation.cfm?id=1356802.1356988

[31] Jonghee W. Yoon, A. Shrivastava, S. Park, M. Ahn, and Y. Paek. 2009. A Graph Drawing Based Spatial Mapping Algorithm for Coarse-Grained Reconfigurable Architectures. *IEEE Transactions on Very Large Scale Integration (VLSI) Systems* 17, 11 (Nov 2009), 1565–1578. https://doi.org/10.1109/TVLSI.2008.2001746

Concurrent High Performance Processor design: From Logic to PD in Parallel

Leon Stok
IBM Systems Group
2455 South Road, Poughkeepsie, NY
USA
leonstok@us.ibm.com

ABSTRACT

The design of a high-performance processor in an advanced technology node is a highly concurrent process. While most SoCs are designed with (fairly) stable IP, several trends are driving the design of the micro-architecture, the logic and the physical design of high-performance micro-processors to be an increasingly parallel process. Due to the slowdown of technology progress, a lot more innovation is coming from the micro-architecture. Fast evolving workloads lead to frequent additions of accelerators and instructions. Late security findings drive last minute updates. All these have a significant impact on the logic structure of the design and therefore implications to an efficient physical design.

On top of that, when designing in an advanced technology, the technology and its design rules are evolving at the same time. High-performance designs have many memories, register files and caches which are especially susceptible to sometimes small technology rule changes. Even a minimal design rule change can percolate up and have a substantial impact on the floorplan.

Fortunately, designers have an unprecedented amount of compute power available to them to conquer the challenges outline above and drive a massive concurrent design process. Especially design teams that harness the vast amount of data coming from the concurrent process can efficiently get to their design goals on time.

At IBM, we have divided the design flow into three distinct layers. Custom Block Design, Large Block design and Chip Integration. Significant physical design automation is applied to custom block design, to minimize the manual effort. The fact that the 7nm technology rules have become so elaborate and complicated but at the same time restrictive [1] allows for a new wave of interesting optimization algorithms to be applied. Large block synthesis(LBS) is the buffer in the middle of the design flow, designed to absorb all shocks from above and below. From above, micro-architectural changes need to be morphed into a modified floorplan with minimal change to the chip-integration fabric [2] [3]. From below, technology changes need to be prevented from rippling up the stack [4]. Chip Integration ensures the entire chip fabric comes together and deals with unique PD challenges [5] coming from the global pervasive design and the global clocks. Each of these layers and the interaction between them lead to unique logical and physical design optimization opportunities that will be discussed in this presentation.

During the entire design process, we need to maintain visibility in the state of the design across the entire hierarchy and across all key metrics. To that extend, an advanced analytics system [6] [7] is needed to represent the latest metrics of the design and show the deltas from earlier versions. This analytics system needs to be able to answer intricate questions about the design with respect to power, timing and physical design and help drive decisions and assertions for the next iteration. To connect the three layers across the hierarchy of the chip (in the space domain) and the entire design process (in the time domain), a graph database [8] based analytics system provides insight in key metrics to drive the next iteration in the design flow. This analytics system provides the data to enable Machine Learning to drive more automated iterations [9] [10].

By putting all these building blocks together, we are striving to provide an automated design and verification environment where we can take on increasingly complex processor designs with more last-minute specification changes with modest design efforts.

ACM Reference Format:
Leon Stok. 2018. Concurrent High Performance Processor design: From Logic to PD in Parallel. In ISPD '18: 2018 International Symposium on Physical Design, March 25–28, 2018, Monterey, CA, USA. ACM, New York, NY, USA, 1 page. https://doi.org/10.1145/3177540.3177556

References

[1] A. Lvov, G. Tellez and G.-J. Nam, "On Coloring and Colorability Analysis of Integrated Circuits with Triple and Quadruple Patterning Techniques," in *ISPD 2018*.

[2] W. Roesner, "Aspect-Oriented Design - Optimizing SoC Verification Via Separation of Concerns," in *51st Design Automation Conference*, Austin, 2014.

[3] M. H. Safieddine, F. A. Zaraket, R. Kanj and W. R. Ali Elzein, "Methodology for Separation of Design Concerns Using Conservative RTL Flipflop Inference," in *DVCon*, San Jose, 2015.

[4]   J. Jung, G.-J. Nam, L. Reddy, I. Jiang and Y. Shin, "OWARU: Free Space-Aware Timing-Driven Incremental Placement with Critical Path Smoothing",," *IEEE Transactions on Computer-Aided Design of Integrated Circuits and Systems*, 2018.

[5]   J. Hu, Y. Zhou, Y. Wei, S. Quay, L. Reddy, G. Tellez and G.-J. Nam, "Interconnect Optimization Considering Multiple Critical Paths," in *ISPD 2018*.

[6]   L. Stok, "EDA3.0: Implications to Logic Synthesis," in *Advanced Logic Synthesis*, R. D. André Inácio Reis, Ed., Springer Professional, 2018, pp. 1-20.

[7]   L. Stok, "The Next 25 Years in EDA: A Cloudy Future?," *IEEE Design & Test*, vol. 31, no. 2, pp. 40-46, April 2014.

[8]   K. Kalafala, "Advances in the use of Graph Databases to Aid in the Timing Analysis of the World's Fastest Microprocessors," in *TAU*, Monterrey, 2018.

[9]   M. M. Ziegler, H.-Y. Liu, G. Gristede, B. Owens, R. Nigaglioni and L. P. Carloni, "A synthesis-parameter tuning system for autonomous design-space exploration," in *DATE*, Dresden, 2016.

[10]   M. M. Ziegler, R. Bertran, A. Buyuktosunoglu and P. Bose, "Machine learning techniques for taming the complexity of modern hardware design," *IBM Journal of Research and Development*, vol. 61, no. 4, pp. 1-13, 2017.

Towards a VLSI Design Flow
Based on Logic Computation and Signal Distribution

André Reis
Institute of Informatics
UFRGS
Brazil
andre.reis@inf.ufrgs.br

ABSTRACT

This paper discusses directions for a VLSI design flow based on a novel paradigm of local logic computation and global signal distribution. In the last years there has been an increasing effort to perform a better integration between logic synthesis and physical design, with the aim to bring technology information into early design steps. The proposed paradigm shift can be very helpful to attain this integration.

CCS CONCEPTS

• **Hardware** → **Electronic design automation**; *Logic synthesis*; *Physical design (EDA)*; Physical synthesis; *Methodologies for EDA.*

KEYWORDS

Logic Computation, Signal Distribution.

ACM Reference format:
A. I. Reis. 2018. SIG Proceedings Paper in word Format. In *Proceedings of ACM International Symposium on Physical Design, March 25–28, 2018, Monterey, CA, USA, March 2018 (ISPD'18)*, 2 pages.
DOI: https://doi.org/10.1145/3177540.3177557

1 INTRODUCTION

In a previous work [1] we have discussed how to bring physical awareness to technology independent logic synthesis. Physical awareness can be understood in more than one sense. The most common sense is to perform logic synthesis already using the information from a cell library [2] designed for a given technology. A different sense is to have information about the placement of logic elements that form the circuit, even if they are still abstracted as logic gates. I think that the early placement

of logical elements plays a fundamental role to obtain an efficient VLSI design flow. In the following I will emphasize a solution that starts to place logic elements early on the VLSI design flow.

2 AIGS, K-CUTS AND KL-CUTS

Early steps of logic synthesis and optimization are usually performed on top of an And-Inverter-Graph (AIG) data structure (or some similar structure). An AIG is a data structure that is composed of four types of nodes: 2-input and gates, input nodes, output nodes and FFs. Inverters are not represented explicitly as gates, but as labels in the edges that connect cells that generate and consume signals.

As part of FPGA optimization techniques, the logic synthesis community developed the concept of K-cuts [3, 4], which are subgraphs that allow expressing a graph node as a Boolean function with at most K-inputs (to fit a look-up table). K-cuts have side-outputs that are not considered, meaning that the subgraph may have extra interconnection points with the main graph. We have proposed KL-cuts [3] as a means to know the complete interface of a sub-graph with the main graph. A KL-cut is a sub-graph where all K-inputs and all L-outputs are known and accounted for, allowing treating KL-cuts as sub-circuits that can be optimized independently. Notice that the maximum allowed value of K is usually constrained, so that the number of inputs for logic functions can be controlled.

3 KL-CUTS AND LOGIC COMPUTATION

KL-cuts are then sub-graphs of an AIG graph. As all the K-inputs and L-outputs are known, the content of a KL-cut can be locally treated independently of the main graph. This opens the way to: (1) perform local logic synthesis and optimization; (2) see a KL-cut as a logic container block. In this sense, if KL-cut computation is performed, and the complete AIG is covered with KL-cuts, each KL-cut can be seen as a logic computation block or sub-circuit. Notice that each KL-cut is still a sub-graph of an AIG graph, but as the type of elements (ands, FFs) are simple, the physical size of each KL-cut can easily computed, assuming that it will result in an essentially local circuit, where cell sizing will not increase area excessively. This way, the physical floor planning of the circuit can start still with an AIG version of the circuit. This is performed as placement of KL-cuts as boxes containing logic that will be implemented locally, without long interconnections. Long interconnections will happen among KL-cuts, and this is discussed in the next section.

4 1L-CUTS AND SIGNAL DISTRIBUTION

KL-cuts will have interconnections with different KL-cuts, and these will be potentially long interconnections. The question is how to avoid the increase on the size of the KL-cut due to the upsize of the internal cells to drive long interconnections. This can be done with a new type of cut, similar to KL-cuts, but with K=1. This new type of cut is a 1L-cut. Notice that 1L-cuts will have one source of signal (i.e, one input as K=1) and several consumers of signal (i.e, L outputs). The L outputs of a 1L-cut potentially drive distant consumers for the signals, located in distinct KL-cuts. So the design of a 1L-cut is the design of a signal distribution infrastructure. In the next section I will describe how to have a complete flow based on the proposed paradigm shift.

5 GLOBAL OVERVIEW

A minimally viable VLSI design flow based on this paradigm will require a sequence of tasks that I describe in this section. This will be described in a superficial way, more in order to have a global view of the whole process and the associated new problems that arise.

Initial Information. It is assumed that an initial netlist has already been generated and converted to a corresponding AIG. A corresponding design constraint (SDC) file specifying target frequency is also necessary. The same applies for library technology information that allows computing Elmore delays and cell delays for ands, inverters, buffers and FFs. Circuit floorplan and pin placement are also necessary, as well as available cell areas/sizes.

Initial evaluation. The first step is to compute the overall area of the AIG, and estimate the AIG physical size compared to the available space in the floorplan. The same is done to compare the delays of the AIG with the required times in the SDC.

Global AIG optimization. This action fixes global problems encountered in the initial evaluation. These two initial steps are necessary to have global optimization and some guarantee of feasibility.

KL-cut cover computation. The circuit is covered with KL-cuts to produce a hierarchical description. This process also estimates the total areas, delays and it produces a local SDC for each KL-cut. At this point, it is important to verify that the global SDC is still respected with sufficient slack for later including the 1L-cuts.

1L-cut logic design. This step creates 1L-cuts as separate elements, local SDC for the 1L-cuts are also created.

Global SDC verification. This task verifies that global SDC is still respected if all local KL and 1K cuts respect their SDCs.

KL-cut placement. This process performs a placement of KL-cuts. This will result in the placement of KL-cuts as local logic computation areas.

Definition of interface pins. This definition is necessary to place the input and output pins of KL cuts as well as to define capacitance restrictions to have and adequate coupling.

1L-cut physical design. This step creates the physical design of the routing trees for 1L-cuts as separate elements, guided by the SDC for each 1L-cut. When the task is finished, local SDC for the 1L-cuts are also re-evaluated. After completion, the global signal distribution infrastructure is frozen.

KL-cut local logic design. This step makes the logic design of KL-cuts, including technology mapping choosing cells from the library. Until now the KL-cuts contained a graph with area and delays estimated. Notice that the logic optimizations do not need to consider long wires as the connections are mostly local.

KL-cuts local physical design. Now the local physical design of KL-cuts can be done by local place and route of cells.

Local fixes. The modularity of the whole approach allows for local fixes. When violations cannot be resolved locally in a given cut, they can be propagated for resolution in neighboring cuts.

6 CONCLUSIONS

This talk presents the endeavors of constructing a VLSI design flow based in local logic computation (using KL-cuts) and global signal distribution (using 1L-cuts). Both problems (logic computation and signal distribution) can benefit from techniques used by the logic synthesis and physical design, meaning that a joint logic synthesis and physical design approach still makes sense. However, local logic computation and signal distribution are very different in nature. So I understand that there will distinct approaches to integrate logic synthesis and physical design for tasks related to local logic computation and global signal distribution.

ACKNOWLEDGMENTS

This work is partially supported by Brazilian funding agency CNPq (under grant 312086/2016-4).

REFERENCES

[1] Reis A.I., Matos J.M.A. (2018) Physical Awareness Starting at Technology-Independent Logic Synthesis. In: Reis A., Drechsler R. (eds) Advanced Logic Synthesis. Springer, Cham. DOI: https://doi.org/10.1007/978-3-319-67295-3_4
[2] Mayler Martins, Jody Maick Matos, Renato P. Ribas, André Reis, Guilherme Schlinker, Lucio Rech, and Jens Michelsen. 2015. Open Cell Library in 15nm FreePDK Technology. In Proceedings of the 2015 Symposium on International Symposium on Physical Design (ISPD '15). ACM, New York, NY, USA, 171-178. DOI: http://dx.doi.org/10.1145/2717764.2717783
[3] Peichen Pan and Chih-Chang Lin. 1998. A new retiming-based technology mapping algorithm for LUT-based FPGAs. In Proceedings of the 1998 ACM/SIGDA sixth int. symp. on Field program. gate arrays (FPGA '98). ACM, New York, NY, USA, 35-42. DOI=http://dx.doi.org/10.1145/275107.275118
[4] Jason Cong, Chang Wu, and Yuzheng Ding. 1999. Cut ranking and pruning: enabling a general and efficient FPGA mapping solution. In Proceedings of the 1999 ACM/SIGDA seventh international symposium on Field programmable gate arrays (FPGA '99). ACM, New York, NY, USA, 29-35. DOI=http://dx.doi.org/10.1145/296399.296425
[5] Osvaldo Martinello, Jr., Felipe S. Marques, Renato P. Ribas, and André I. Reis. 2010. KL-cuts: a new approach for logic synthesis targeting multiple output blocks. In Proceedings of the Conference on Design, Automation and Test in Europe (DATE '10). Pp. 777-782.

Power Grid Reduction by Sparse Convex Optimization

Wei Ye
ECE Department, UT Austin
weiye@utexas.edu

Meng Li
ECE Department, UT Austin
meng_li@utexas.edu

Kai Zhong
ICES, UT Austin
zhongkai@ices.utexas.edu

Bei Yu
CSE Department, CUHK
byu@cse.cuhk.edu.hk

David Z. Pan
ECE Department, UT Austin
dpan@ece.utexas.edu

ABSTRACT

With the dramatic increase in the complexity of modern integrated circuits (ICs), direct analysis and verification of IC power distribution networks (PDNs) have become extremely computationally expensive. Various power grid reduction methods are proposed to reduce the grid size for fast verification and simulation but usually suffer from poor scalability. In this paper, we present a convex optimization-based framework for power grid reduction. Edge sparsification is formulated as a weighted convex optimization problem with sparsity-inducing penalties, which provides an accurate control over the final error. A greedy coordinate descent (GCD) method with optimality guarantee is proposed along with a novel coordinate selection strategy to improve the efficiency and accuracy of edge sparsification. Experimental results demonstrate that the proposed approach achieves better performance compared with traditional gradient descent methods, and 98% accuracy and good sparsity for industrial benchmarks.

KEYWORDS

Power grid reduction; sparse convex optimization; greedy coordinate descent

1 INTRODUCTION

Power distribution network (PDN) provides power and ground voltage supply to on-chip components. Robust PDNs are essential to ensure reliable operations and high performance of chips. However, with the dramatic increase in the complexity of modern integrated circuits (ICs), direct analysis and verification of PDNs have become extremely computationally expensive. Therefore, fast and accurate modeling and verification techniques are necessary to assist power grid design.

The goal of power grid reduction is to reduce an original large power grid to a significantly smaller one for fast power grid analysis while preserving its electrical behavior and accuracy. However, power grid reduction faces the dilemma in which a reduced grid with a small number of nodes and edges is usually not accurate enough, and an accurate reduced grid may still be too large for power grid verification. Therefore, the primary difficulty with power grid reduction is how to explicitly control the trade-off between sparsity and accuracy. Moreover, the large size of modern power grids harms the efficiency of power grid reduction methods.

In recent years, power grid reduction has been widely studied [1–4]. The moment matching method PRIMA [1] projects the explicit moment space to Krylov subspace. This method is numerically stable but is not applicable to power grids with a large number of ports. TICER [2] based on Gaussian elimination removes the nodes with low degrees efficiently but introduces too many edges for mesh-like power grids. The multigrid method [3] reduces the original power grid to a coarser grid, solves the reduced grid directly, and then maps the solution back to the original grid. Although it can fast produce significantly small grids, it is not applicable to general irregular grids and the error is difficult to control.

To help achieve fast design closure and incremental analysis for PDNs, it is useful to preserve the physical information about the port nodes that are connected to C4 bumps or load devices in the power grid. Schur complement is a widely used technique for linear systems to keep these port nodes and eliminate the non-port nodes that only have internal connections without compromise on accuracy. However, as the number of non-port nodes is becoming much larger than that of port nodes, eliminating them by Schur complement tends to generate smaller but much denser reduced grids which are still intractable for power grid analysis [5]. To this end, edge sparsification is introduced to further sparsify the reduced models. Zhao et al. [5] propose a resistance-based port merging scheme to eliminate nodes and leverage a sampling-based spectral graph sparsification [6] to decrease the edge density of reduced grid blocks. However, the method eliminates most of the port nodes, which renders the reduced models less practical for further analysis. Besides, how to explicitly obtain a good trade-off between sparsity and accuracy is not well explored. Recently, Yassine et al. [7] propose an iterative power grid reduction framework, which eliminates an entire metal layer at one time and then remove edges topologically. However, the proposed heuristic approach to sparsify the reduced model lacks error guarantee. Wang et al. [8] formulate edge sparsification as a convex optimization problem which explores the current range information on the port nodes to achieve better sparsity and solve it by the stochastic gradient descent (SGD) algorithm. This approach has poor runtime and therefore cannot be directly applied to large graphs. Another major drawback is that the SGD algorithm usually spends most effort optimizing the edges

ISPD '18, March 25–28, 2018, Monterey, CA,
© 2018 Association for Computing Machinery.
ACM ISBN 978-1-4503-5626-8/18/03...$15.00
https://doi.org/10.1145/3177540.3178247

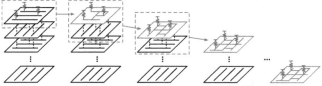

Figure 1: The proposed power grid reduction flow.

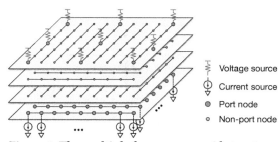

Voltage source
Current source
Port node
Non-port node

Figure 2: The multiple-layer power grid structure.

directly connected to the voltage sources under the mathematical formulation in [8] and ignores the errors at other port nodes, resulting in a significant overall error.

In this paper, we propose an efficient edge sparsification approach along with a holistic power grid reduction framework. By formulating the edge sparsification problem as a weighted sparse convex optimization problem, a greedy coordinate descent (GCD) algorithm with optimality guarantee is proposed to generate sparse and accurate solutions. To enable scalable power grid reduction, we propose an iterative reduction framework as illustrated in Figure 1, which reduces one layer at a time and eliminates all the internal layers incrementally from top to bottom. This reduction framework explicitly keeps all the port nodes in the topmost and bottommost layers. During the process of node elimination and edge sparsification for a middle layer, the nodes connected to the vias right below this layer are considered as pseudo external nodes, and their electrical properties are preserved with high accuracy. In this way, the reduced graph can be easily connected back to the next layer to process without loss of information, and the entire framework achieves a relatively small error for the final power grid model.

Our main contributions are summarized as follows:

- We propose a weighted convex optimization formulation with sparsity-inducing penalties for edge sparsification, which enables us to explicitly find a good trade-off between sparsity and accuracy. With the port nodes assigned different weights, this formulation provides an accurate control over the final error.
- We propose a novel GCD algorithm with optimality guarantee and runtime efficiency for edge sparsification. Besides, an efficient coordinate selection strategy is proposed for good convergence of GCD. A heap-based optimal coordinate search approach is proposed to improve the time complexity of iteration from $\mathcal{O}(n^2)$ to $\mathcal{O}(n \log n)$.
- Experimental results demonstrate that the proposed approach achieves significantly better accuracy and runtime compared with previous work [8] and the traditional coordinate descent method. The proposed reduction framework achieves 98% accuracy for industrial benchmarks and preserves their sparsity.

The rest of this paper is organized as follows. Section 2 reviews the background on power grid reduction. Section 3 and Section 4 illustrate the overall reduction flow and the node elimination method. Section 5 provides a detailed explanation of the proposed edge sparsification approach. Section 7 demonstrates the effectiveness of our approaches with comprehensive results, followed by conclusion in Section 8.

2 PRELIMINARIES

2.1 Notations

We first introduce some notations used in the paper. For any positive integers n, m, we use $[n]$ to denote the set $\{1, 2, \cdots, n\}$, and $[n, m]$ to denote the set $\{n, n + 1, \cdots, m\}$. Let $\mathbf{A}^\top$ denote the transpose of a given matrix $\mathbf{A}$, $\mathbf{A}_i$ denote the i-th column vector of matrix $\mathbf{A}$ and $A_{i,j}$ denote the entry in the i-th row and j-th column of matrix $\mathbf{A}$. Let $v_{k,i}$ denote the i-th element in vector $\mathbf{v}_k$. Let $\mathbf{u} \circ \mathbf{v}$ denote the Hadamard product between two vectors $\mathbf{u}$ and $\mathbf{v}$, i.e., $\mathbf{y} = \mathbf{u} \circ \mathbf{v}$ if $y_i = u_i v_i, \forall i$.

2.2 Power Grid Model and Reduction

A resistive power grid can be modeled as a weighted undirected graph $G(V, E, w)$, where edges represent the resistors connecting nodes. Weight $w(i, j)$ denotes the physical conductance between node i and node j, and $w(i, j) = 0$ if the two nodes are not directly connected through a metal segment. For any graph G, its connectivity can be encoded as a Laplacian matrix $\mathbf{L}$, with element (i, j) given by:

$$L_{i,j} = \begin{cases} \sum_{k, k \neq i} w(i, k), & \text{if } i = j \\ -w(i, j), & \text{if } i \neq j \text{ and } e(i, j) \in E \\ 0, & \text{otherwise.} \end{cases}$$

Let $\mathbf{v}$ be the vector of node voltages and $\mathbf{i}$ be the vector of currents entering the power grid through all the nodes. The Laplacian matrix $\mathbf{L}$ can be used to characterize the linear behavior between the input current vector $\mathbf{i}$ and the voltage vector $\mathbf{v}$ by

$$\mathbf{i} = \mathbf{L}\mathbf{v}. \tag{1}$$

Figure 2 illustrates the power grid structure that uses multiple layers of metal interconnects. Some nodes in the topmost layer are connected to C4 bumps for external voltage supplies, and the nodes in the bottommost layer are connected to load transistors which are modeled as ideal current sources. Here a port node is defined as a grid node that is electrically connected to a voltage or current source. All other nodes in the power grid are non-port nodes. Power grid analysis verifies the voltages arriving at load transistors and therefore requires calculating the voltages at all the port nodes by solving the linear system in Equation (1). The Laplacian matrices of power grids are typically large and computationally prohibitive to be solved directly. Therefore, in this work, we consider the power grid reduction problem defined as follows:

Problem 1 (Power Grid Reduction). Given an initial large power grid, we reduce it to a small and sparse power grid that contains

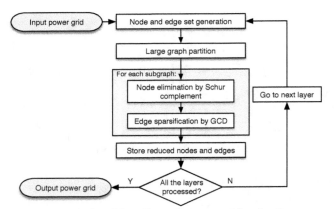

Figure 3: Algorithm flow of power grid reduction.

all the port nodes in the original power grid and preserves the accuracy in terms of the voltage drop error.

3 OVERALL FLOW

In this section, we introduce the overall flow for power grid reduction. The port nodes are required to be kept, while the non-port nodes in the middle layers will be eliminated for reduction of the grid size to the greatest extent. However, as the size of the power grid and the number of metal layers increase, the number of nodes in the middle layers increases dramatically [7]. The runtime and memory costs of removing all these non-port nodes at one time are not affordable anymore. In order to enable scalable power grid reduction, we propose an iterative layer-based node elimination and edge sparsification framework as shown in Figure 3.

The main idea is to perform node elimination and edge sparsification for one layer at a time, and remove all the middle layers incrementally from top to bottom. In each run, a new graph is created by combining the nodes and edges in the layer to be eliminated this time with the reduced graph obtained from the last run. If the combined graph is relatively large, we partition it into several small subgraphs. We explicitly keep the boundary nodes (the nodes connected to the vias below the layer) as well as the port nodes, and apply Schur complement to eliminate the rest of nodes (Section 4). Subsequently, we perform GCD to sparsify the smaller but much denser model (Section 5.2). Note that because the electrical behaviors of these boundary nodes are preserved as external nodes during Schur complement and GCD, the reduced graph can be easily combined with the lower layer through these boundary nodes for next run. Therefore, the layer-by-layer approach can achieve a small error for the reduced grid model.

4 NODE ELIMINATION

In this section, we introduce the elimination process of non-port grid nodes using the Schur complement method [9]. It should be noted that different from previous work [5], our elimination process explicitly keeps all the port nodes to be analyzed for power grid verification. Although the number of the remaining nodes is larger, the reduction result contains all the necessary physical information, which also benefits the design closure flow.

For each run of Schur complement, according to whether a node is going to be kept or removed, two different subsets of nodes are distinguished: external nodes V_{ext} and internal nodes V_{int}. Specifically, for the layer-by-layer reduction framework in Figure 3, the external nodes are the port nodes on the topmost and bottommost layers and the boundary nodes between layers. Assume $|V_{ext}| = n$ and $|V_{int}| = p$. Let i_{ext} (i_{int}) denote the vector for the current injected into external (internal) nodes, and v_{ext} (v_{int}) denote the column vector for voltage at external (internal) nodes. Then, we know that $i_{int}(a) = 0$ for $a \in V_{int}$, because no external current is injected into the internal node. Let $v = (v_{ext}, v_{int})$, and $i = (i_{ext}, i_{int}) = (i_{ext}, 0 \cdots 0)$. For a resistive network with its Laplacian given by $\widetilde{L}$, we can rewrite $\widetilde{L}v = i$ as follows:

$$\begin{bmatrix} \widetilde{L}_{11} & \widetilde{L}_{12} \\ \widetilde{L}_{12}^\top & \widetilde{L}_{22} \end{bmatrix} \begin{bmatrix} v_{ext} \\ v_{int} \end{bmatrix} = \begin{bmatrix} i_{ext} \\ 0 \end{bmatrix}, \qquad (2)$$

where $\widetilde{L}_{11} \in \mathbb{R}^{n \times n}$ represents the connections between the external nodes, $\widetilde{L}_{12} \in \mathbb{R}^{n \times p}$ represents the connections between the internal nodes and the external nodes, and $\widetilde{L}_{22} \in \mathbb{R}^{p \times p}$ represents the connections between the internal nodes.

We can derive $v_{int} = -\widetilde{L}_{22}^{-1}\widetilde{L}_{12}^\top v_{ext}$ from Equation (2), then for the external nodes,

$$(\widetilde{L}_{11} - \widetilde{L}_{12}\widetilde{L}_{22}^{-1}\widetilde{L}_{12}^\top)v_{ext} = i_{ext}.$$

Therefore, the Schur complement of $\widetilde{L}_{22}$ in $\widetilde{L}$ is given by

$$L = \widetilde{L}_{11} - \widetilde{L}_{12}\widetilde{L}_{22}^{-1}\widetilde{L}_{12}^\top.$$

Although L has a smaller dimension compared with $\widetilde{L}$, it is much denser. Hence, it is necessary to perform edge sparsification to further reduce the number of connections in the reduced model.

5 EDGE SPARSIFICATION

In this section, we give the details of the proposed edge sparsification techniques.

5.1 Mathematical Formulation

Graph sparsification refers to the approximation of a given graph with fewer nodes or edges. For a Laplacian matrix, the number of nonzero diagonal elements (i.e., ℓ_0-norm of diagonal elements) equals the number of nodes in the graph, and the number of nonzero elements off the diagonal (i.e., ℓ_0-norm of off-diagonal elements) indicates the number of edges. Therefore, the sparsity of the Laplacian matrix can act as a measure of the graph sparsity, and the goal of edge sparsification can be regarded as sparsifying the corresponding Laplacian matrix to reduce the nonzero elements off the diagonal.

Since ℓ_0-norm is non-convex and cannot be used directly as the sparsity penalty for edge sparsification, [8] relaxes ℓ_0-norm to ℓ_1-norm, the closest convex norm to it, and proposes a convex optimization-based edge sparsification formulation with ℓ_1-norm regularization. However, the formulation in [8] may not produce solutions that preserve the current behaviors of real-life circuits. The objective in [8] implies that all the port nodes are assigned the same weight. Typically, the currents flowing into the port nodes connected to voltage sources are much larger than the currents flowing out of other port nodes connected to current sources. Thus, the first term in the objective given by [8], the total error over all the port nodes, will be dominated by the errors associated with the port nodes connected to voltage sources. Gradient descent algorithms including SGD tend to spend considerable effort reducing these errors by repeatedly updating the edges connected to the voltage sources, and therefore cannot guarantee the accuracy of the currents flowing to current sources, which are undoubtedly more important for accurate power grid verification.

To overcome the drawback mentioned above, we propose a weighted sparse convex optimization formulation for edge sparsification. Given a Laplacian matrix $L \in \mathbb{R}^{n \times n}$, a set of vectors $v_1, v_2, \ldots, v_m \in \mathbb{R}^n$, a weight vector $w \in \mathbb{R}^n$ and a parameter $\lambda > 0$, we output a Laplacian matrix X with fewer edges by solving the following constrained problem:

$$\min_{X \in \mathbb{R}^{n \times n}} \frac{1}{2m} \sum_{k=1}^{m} \|((X - L)v_k) \circ w\|_2^2 + \lambda \sum_{i=1}^{n} X_{i,i} \quad (3)$$

$$\text{s.t. } X_{i,j} \leq 0, \qquad \forall i \neq j \quad (3a)$$

$$X_{i,j} = X_{j,i}, \qquad \forall i \neq j \quad (3b)$$

$$X_{i,i} = - \sum_{j \in [n] \setminus i} X_{i,j}, \qquad \forall i. \quad (3c)$$

Since Laplacian matrices are symmetric (Constraint (3b)) and have zero sum over rows or columns (Constraint (3c)), we can use the elements below (or above) the diagonal to represent the whole Laplacian matrix and drop these two constraints. The number of variables is also reduced from n^2 to $n(n-1)/2$. We define function $f : \mathbb{R}^{n(n-1)/2} \to \mathbb{R}$ such that

$$f(y) = \frac{1}{2m} \sum_{k=1}^{m} \|((X - L)v_k) \circ w\|_2^2 + \lambda \sum_{i=1}^{n} X_{i,i}, \quad (4)$$

where $X_{i,j} = X_{j,i} = y_{i,j}$, $X_{i,i} = - \sum_{j \neq i} y_{i,j}$, and $y_{i,j} \leq 0$, $\forall i \in [2, n]$, $j \in [i - 1]$.

Gradient methods can converge to the global solution of a convex function. The formulation proposed by [8] is convex. We next demonstrate the above function is also convex.

Lemma 1. *The function f defined in Equation (4) is strongly convex and coordinate-wise Lipschitz smooth.*

This lemma can be proved by calculating the Hessian matrix of f. The proof details are omitted here for lack of space.

The gradient of f at $y_{i,j}$ is

$$\frac{\partial f}{\partial y_{i,j}} = -\frac{1}{m}(w_i^2 (X - L)_i^\top - w_j^2 (X - L)_j^\top) \sum_{k=1}^{m} (v_{k,i} - v_{k,j}) v_k - 2\lambda.$$

For simplicity of notation, we define a gradient matrix $G \in \mathbb{R}^{n \times n}$ as in Equation (5).

5.2 GCD-based Algorithm

In this part, we introduce the GCD-based algorithm to solve the optimization problem in Formulation (4). The GCD optimization process starts from the initial solution $X^1 = 0$ and generates a sequence of matrices $\{X^t\}_{t=1}^{T+1}$ in T iterations [10]. At each iteration, the GCD method selects the coordinate along which maximum progress can be made, and updates the coordinate by minimizing

$$G = \begin{bmatrix} 0 & \frac{\partial f}{\partial y_{2,1}} & \cdots & \frac{\partial f}{\partial y_{n-1,1}} & \frac{\partial f}{\partial y_{n,1}} \\ \frac{\partial f}{\partial y_{2,1}} & 0 & \cdots & \frac{\partial f}{\partial y_{n-1,2}} & \frac{\partial f}{\partial y_{n,2}} \\ \vdots & \vdots & \ddots & \vdots & \vdots \\ \frac{\partial f}{\partial y_{n-1,1}} & \frac{\partial f}{\partial y_{n-1,2}} & \cdots & 0 & \frac{\partial f}{\partial y_{n,n-1}} \\ \frac{\partial f}{\partial y_{n,1}} & \frac{\partial f}{\partial y_{n,2}} & \cdots & \frac{\partial f}{\partial y_{n,n-1}} & 0 \end{bmatrix}. \quad (5)$$

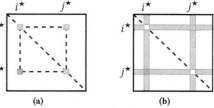

Figure 4: If select coordinate $(i^\star, j^\star)$ to update, we need to update (a) four elements in the Laplacian matrix X, and (b) two rows and columns in the gradient matrix G.

a single-variable subproblem. More specifically, for the edge sparsification problem, the initial solution is constructed as a graph that only consists of the nodes from the input graph as illustrated in Figure 5. Then the GCD method chooses the most important edge $e(i, j)$ at a time and adds the new edge in the graph (i.e., increases $w(i, j)$ from 0) or updates the weight on the existing edge (i.e., increases or decreases $w(i, j)$).

We first demonstrate how to determine the optimal coordinate to update, denoted (i^*, j^*). At each iteration GCD is supposed to select the coordinate direction with largest directional derivative; this is the same as choosing the largest (in absolute value) component of the gradient matrix G:

$$(i^*, j^*) = \operatorname*{arg\,max}_{(i,j) \in [n] \times [n]} |G_{i,j}|. \quad (6)$$

Next, we decide how far to move along the coordinate (i^*, j^*) for updating X^t to X^{t+1}. Since the objective function in Equation (4) is quadratic, we can apply exact coordinate optimization for better performance, i.e., updating the coordinate to the exact minimum point of the quadratic function as follows:

Claim 1. *Given the coordinate to update, (i, j), the next iterate for $y_{i,j}^t$ can be written as*

$$y_{i,j}^{t+1} = \operatorname*{arg\,min}_{y_{i,j} \in \mathbb{R}_{\leq 0}} f(y_{i,j}) = \min(0, y_{i,j}^t - \alpha_{i,j}), \quad (7)$$

where $\alpha_{i,j}$ is defined as

$$\frac{\partial f}{\partial y_{i,j}}\bigg|_{y_{i,j} = y_{i,j}^t} \cdot \left(\frac{1}{m}(w_i^2 + w_j^2) \sum_{k=1}^{m} (v_{k,i} - v_{k,j})^2 \right)^{-1}.$$

As illustrated in Figure 4(a), once we decide to update y_{i^*, j^*} by $\Delta y_{i^*, j^*}$, we will update four coordinates in X, i.e., $(i^\star, i^\star)$, $(i^\star, j^\star)$,

$(j^\star, i^\star)$ and $(j^\star, j^\star)$. Therefore, for each iteration $t \in [T]$, $|\text{supp}(\Delta \mathbf{X}^t)| = 4$. Besides, we update the entires in $\mathbf{G}$ in the following sense:

$$\Delta G_{r,c} = \begin{cases} \Delta y_{i^*,j^*} w_{i^*}^2 h(c, i^*, i^*, j^*), & \text{if } r = i^*, c \in [n] \\ \Delta y_{i^*,j^*} w_{j^*}^2 h(j^*, r, i^*, j^*), & \text{if } r \in [n], c = j^* \\ \Delta y_{i^*,j^*} w_{j^*}^2 h(j^*, c, i^*, j^*), & \text{if } r = j^*, c \in [n] \\ \Delta y_{i^*,j^*} w_{i^*}^2 h(r, i^*, i^*, j^*), & \text{if } r \in [n], c = i^* \\ -\Delta y_{i^*,j^*}(w_{i^*}^2 + w_{j^*}^2)h(i^*, j^*, i^*, j^*), & \text{if } r = i^*, c = j^* \\ 0, & \text{otherwise.} \end{cases} \quad (8)$$

where

$$h(i_1, j_1, i_2, j_2) = -\frac{1}{m}\sum_{k=1}^{m}(v_{k,i_1} - v_{k,j_1})(v_{k,i_2} - v_{k,j_2}). \quad (9)$$

Accordingly, the update in $\mathbf{X}$ only affects two rows (columns) in the gradient matrix $\mathbf{G}$ (Figure 4(b)). Therefore, the number of elements to update in $\mathbf{G}$ is $\mathcal{O}(n)$.

However, the GCD algorithm described above suffers from a high computational cost per iteration and sometimes even convergence failures. To achieve edge sparsification with better convergence and runtime, we propose an improved GCD algorithm. Our three key contributions are listed as follows.

Firstly, **efficient coordinate selection**. It is worth noting that Formulation (4) is constrained by $\mathbf{y} \leq \mathbf{0}$, which could make the selection rule in Equation (6) fail in some cases. For any coordinate (i, j), when other coordinates are fixed, $f(y_{i,j})$ is essentially a single-variable quadratic function. Sometimes the maximum absolute component of $\mathbf{G}$ given by Equation (6) has $y_{i^\star,j^\star} = 0$ and $G_{i^\star,j^\star} < 0$. For the quadratic function $f(y_{i^\star,j^\star})$ subject to $y_{i^\star,j^\star} \leq 0$, $y_{i^\star,j^\star} = 0$ is already the optimal solution when $G_{i^\star,j^\star} \leq 0$. Consequently, $y_{i^\star,j^\star}$ is updated to 0, and $\mathbf{X}$ and $\mathbf{G}$ are not changed. This selection strategy continues picking this coordinate in the following iterations because the gradient matrix is not changed, and therefore get stuck here. To this end, we propose an efficient coordinate selection strategy to avoid failure of GCD convergence as follows:

$$(i^*, j^*) = \underset{(i,j)\in[n]\times[n]}{\arg\max} \; |G_{i,j}| \; \text{s.t.} \; G_{i,j} > 0 \text{ or } y_{i,j} \neq 0. \quad (10)$$

Secondly, **heap-based optimal coordinate search**. In the straightforward implementation, at each iteration GCD needs to traverse $\mathcal{O}(n^2)$ elements to find the coordinate with the largest directional derivative, and it is as expensive as a full gradient evaluation. We observe that the structure of the gradient in Equation (4) enables an efficient implementation of the coordinate selection rule in Equation (10). More specifically, because each node has at most n neighbors, we can track the gradient of all the variables and use a max-heap data structure to fast search the optimal coordinate. Each node in the max-heap stores the coordinate index (i, j), the variable value $y_{i,j}$, and the absolute value of the gradient component $G_{i,j}$. In this way, we can directly get the largest element in the gradient matrix from the heap in $\mathcal{O}(1)$ time. Besides, we need to update at most $\mathcal{O}(n)$ nodes in the heap at the end of each iteration. In this way, the time complexity of each iteration in GCD is reduced from $\mathcal{O}(n^2)$ to $\mathcal{O}(n \log n)$ as proven in Section 6.1.

Thirdly, **lookup table-based gradient update**. It is clear that the calculation for updating any element in the gradient matrix $\mathbf{G}$ according to Equation (9) has a linear dependence on the sample size m, and it is not affordable as the size of voltage samples increases. To speed up the calculation of gradient update, we define function $r : \mathbb{N}^2 \to \mathbb{R}$ such that

$$r(i, j) = -\frac{1}{m}\sum_{k=1}^{m}v_{k,i}v_{k,j}, \quad \forall i \in [2, n], j \in [i-1].$$

Thus, we have

$$h(i_1, j_1, i_2, j_2) = r(i_1, i_2) - r(i_1, j_2) - r(j_1, i_2) + r(j_1, j_2). \quad (11)$$

It inspires that we can store the set of values for r in a lookup table (LUT), and simply add or subtract them to get the value of the element to update in $\mathbf{G}$ by Equation (11). In this way, the calculation cost of gradient update for each element decreases from $\mathcal{O}(m)$ to $\mathcal{O}(1)$.

Algorithm 1 summarizes the proposed GCD method. The algorithm takes as input the sparsity control parameter λ, the Laplacian matrix $\mathbf{L}$ of the input graph, the maximum number of iterations T, and a batch of sampled voltage vectors $\mathcal{V} = \{\mathbf{v}_k\}_{k=1}^{m}$ [8].

6 ALGORITHM ANALYSIS

6.1 Convergence and Runtime Analysis

The goal of this section is to prove our main theoretical results, Theorem 1 and Theorem 2.

Theorem 1. *GCD (Algorithm 1) converges to the global optimum.*

Theorem 1 demonstrates the correctness of our algorithm, and the proof is similar to [11] considering that function f is strongly convex (Lemma 1).

Before we prove Theorem 2, we first show a useful claim.

Claim 2. *For each iteration $t \in [T]$, for each nonzero element of $\Delta \mathbf{G}^t$, it requires $\mathcal{O}(\log n)$ time to update the position of the corresponding entry in the max-heap.*

PROOF. We use a max-heap to store $\mathbf{G}$. Once we update one certain node in this max-heap with $\mathcal{O}(n^2)$ elements, we also need to update the locations of some other nodes to make the heap still

---

Algorithm 1 GCD-based Edge Sparsification Algorithm

1: **procedure** GCD($\lambda, \mathbf{L}, \mathcal{V}, T$)
2:      $\mathbf{X}^1 \leftarrow \mathbf{0}$, initialize $\mathbf{G}^1$ according to $\mathbf{L}$ and $\mathcal{V}$;
3:      heap.init($\mathbf{X}^1, \mathbf{G}^1$);
4:      **for** $t = 1 \to T$ **do**
5:          $i^*, j^* \leftarrow$ heap.findMax();
6:          Compute $\Delta y_{i^*,j^*}$;   ▷ Equation (7)
7:          Compute $\Delta \mathbf{G}^t$;   ▷ Equation (8)
8:          Compute $\Delta \mathbf{X}^t$ by $\Delta y_{i^*,j^*}$;
9:          $\mathbf{X}^{t+1} \leftarrow \mathbf{X}^t + \Delta \mathbf{X}^t$;
10:         heap.update($\Delta \mathbf{X}^t, \Delta \mathbf{G}^t$);
11:      **end for**
12:      **return** $\mathbf{X}^{T+1}$;
13: **end procedure**

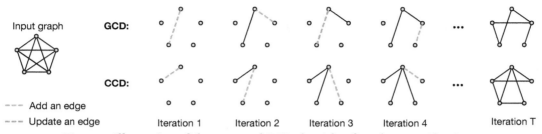

Figure 5: Illustration of the proposed GCD algorithm for edge sparsification.

valid. Because of the property of heap, we can finish the updates in $\mathcal{O}(\log n)$ time. □

Theorem 2. *GCD (Algorithm 1) takes $\mathcal{O}(Tn \log n)$ time and $\mathcal{O}(n^2)$ storage space. In particular, each iteration of GCD takes $\mathcal{O}(n \log n)$ time.*

Proof. It has been shown that at each iteration GCD takes $\mathcal{O}(1)$ time to update an element in $\mathbf{X}$ while $|\text{supp}(\Delta \mathbf{X})| = 4$, and GCD takes $\mathcal{O}(1)$ time to evaluate an element in $\mathbf{G}$ and $\mathcal{O}(\log n)$ time to update it in the heap while $|\text{supp}(\Delta \mathbf{G})| = \mathcal{O}(n)$. Therefore, each iteration of GCD takes $\mathcal{O}(n \log n)$ time. The overall running time is $\mathcal{O}(Tn \log n)$ if GCD runs T iterations. The storage cost of GCD comes from two parts. The first part is that we use $\mathcal{O}(n^2)$ space to store $\mathbf{X}$ in the array and $\mathcal{O}(n^2)$ space to store $\mathbf{G}$ in the heap for speedup. The second part is that after obtaining the training dataset, instead of storing each data individually, we calculate and store all possible values for r. Once r is known, it only requires $\mathcal{O}(1)$ time to compute h. □

6.2 Comparison with Other Algorithms

Various gradient descent methods can be applied to the convex optimization problem in Formulation (4). The stochastic gradient descent (SGD) algorithm chosen by [8] needs to update the entire Laplacian matrix $\mathbf{X}$ and its gradient at each iteration. Therefore, the computational cost for one SGD iteration is $\mathcal{O}(n^2)$, where n is the number of nodes in the graph, and the cost increases dramatically with the size of the input graph. Moreover, the SGD method has a slow convergence rate $\mathcal{O}(1/\epsilon^2)$. However, we observe that updating one edge in the graph only causes $\mathcal{O}(1)$ updates of elements in the Laplacian $\mathbf{X}$ and $\mathcal{O}(n)$ time to evaluate new gradients. This fact benefits the family of coordinate descent (CD) methods that minimize a single coordinate at a time.

There are several kinds of CD algorithms: cyclic gradient descent (CCD) [10] that goes through all coordinates repeatedly, randomized coordinate descent (RCD) [11] that randomly picks a coordinate each time, and GCD that selects the coordinate along which maximum progress can be made. It can be proved that these CD methods can achieve $\mathcal{O}(\log(1/\epsilon))$ convergence rate on the edge sparsification problem due to its strong convexity and coordinate-wise Lipschitz smoothness [12]. Nonetheless, their actual performance varies. Figure 5 illustrates the key difference between CCD and GCD. It is observed that the CCD (or RCD) method touches every coordinate and introduces too many edges. These edges usually have very small weights, and therefore the ℓ_1-norm regularization cost in f

is small. On the contrary, GCD selects the most significant coordinates to update and only adds a small number of edges to the output graph. In this way, GCD has the appealing advantage to produce a sparser graph than the other two methods and better preserves the ℓ_0-norm sparsity. In addition, GCD has a provably faster convergence rate for this problem with smoothness and strongly convexity [12, 13]. For the above reasons, the GCD method is chosen to solve Formulation (4). Furthermore, we improve the runtime complexity of GCD at each iteration from $\mathcal{O}(n^2)$ to $\mathcal{O}(n \log n)$ with the usage of max-heap and propose the efficient coordinate selection strategy (Equation (10)) as well as the fast LUT-based gradient update method (Equation (11)).

7 EXPERIMENTAL RESULTS

The proposed power grid reduction framework is implemented in C++ with Intel MKL library [14], and all experiments are performed on an 8-core 3.4GHz Linux machine with 32GB memory. METIS [15] is used for graph partition.

7.1 Edge Sparsification Comparison

The edge sparsification algorithm is tested on the dense synthetic benchmarks rand1-rand4. The node and edge count of each circuit are shown in columns "#Nodes" and "#Edges" in Table 1 and we normalize the maximum voltage drop in the circuit as listed in column "V_{drop}" to 100 mV by scaling the values of input current sources. For each benchmark, there is only one external voltage source and the node directly connected to it is labeled as the first node. To validate the effectiveness of the edge sparsification algorithm, we regard all the nodes as port nodes and do not perform node elimination on them.

In the first experiment, we examine the importance of the weight vector $\mathbf{w}$ in Formulation (4) on edge sparsification. We consider three weighting schemes: (1) $w_1 = w_i = 1, \forall i \in [2, n]$; (2) $w_1 = 1/n$, $w_i = 1, \forall i \in [2, n]$; (3) $w_1 = 0, w_i = 1, \forall i \in [2, n]$. In Scheme 1, all the port nodes are assigned the same unit weight and the formulation in this scenario is actually the same as the formulation in [8]. The GCD algorithm runs in the above schemes individually on the synthetic benchmarks for the same number of iterations and cross-validation is applied to choose the best λ. The results are listed in Table 1, where "I_{error}" gives the maximum relative current error over all the port nodes when given the voltage vector $\mathbf{v}$, and "V_{error}" gives the maximum error of voltage drop at all the nodes when given the current vector $\mathbf{i}$. As observed from Table 1, the runtime in the three schemes is nearly the same, and Scheme 2 and Scheme 3 have similarly accurate results, both of which are better

Table 1: Comparison of different weighting schemes on the synthetic benchmarks.

CKT	Bench. Stats.			Scheme 1: $w_1 = w_i = 1, \forall i \in [2,n]$				Scheme 2: $w_1 = 1/n, w_i = 1, \forall i \in [2,n]$				Scheme 3: $w_1 = 0, w_i = 1, \forall i \in [2,n]$			
	#Nodes	#Edges	V_{drop} (mV)	#Edges	I_{error} (%)	V_{error} (mV)	Time (s)	#Edges	I_{error} (%)	V_{error} (mV)	Time (s)	#Edges	I_{error} (%)	V_{error} (mV)	Time (s)
rand1	100	4×10^3	100	581	1.68	0.05	0.08	1063	1.17	0.03	0.08	1068	1.10	0.02	0.06
rand2	500	1×10^5	100	955	2.02	1.60	0.82	2690	1.22	0.01	0.88	2743	1.42	0.01	0.74
rand3	1000	4×10^5	100	1216	1.74	1.77	2.84	3821	1.04	0.02	3.26	3920	1.07	0.01	2.75
rand4	5000	1×10^7	100	4999	6.17	6.57	34.04	9436	1.88	1.34	36.00	10003	1.63	1.30	32.60
avg.				1937.8	2.90	2.50	9.45	4252.5	1.33	0.35	10.05	4433.5	1.31	0.34	9.04
ratio				0.44	2.21	7.35	1.05	0.96	1.02	1.03	1.11	1.00	1.00	1.00	1.00

Table 2: Comparison of three gradient descent methods for edge sparsification.

CKT	Ref. [8]				CCD				Ours			
	#Edges	I_{error} (%)	V_{error} (mV)	Time (s)	#Edges	I_{error} (%)	V_{error} (mV)	Time (s)	#Edges	I_{error} (%)	V_{error} (mV)	Time (s)
rand1	99	5.05	5.09	0.12	3169	4.22	0.07	0.01	1068	1.10	0.02	0.06
rand2	499	5.07	5.33	2.93	71548	3.24	0.05	1.92	2743	1.42	0.01	0.74
rand3	999	5.27	5.23	29.82	151106	2.42	0.03	19.09	3920	1.07	0.01	2.75
rand4	4999	7.00	7.52	144.43	304675	4.03	2.18	230.52	10003	1.63	1.30	32.60
avg.	1649	5.60	5.79	44.32	132624.5	3.48	0.58	62.89	4433.5	1.31	0.34	9.04
ratio	0.37	4.28	17.18	4.91	29.91	2.66	1.72	6.96	1.00	1.00	1.00	1.00

than Scheme 1. It is worth mentioning that the reduced graphs in Scheme 1 have much smaller edge counts than the other two schemes, which is aligned with our expectation: this weighting scheme emphasizes the node where the voltage source is attached due to the large current flowing from the voltage source, and the gradient descent method iteratively optimizes the edges having connections to the voltage source. We select Scheme 3 with slightly faster runtime in the following experiments.

We further study the trade-off between sparsity and accuracy for different sparsity control parameter λ during the GCD process. It is distinctly visible from Figure 6(a) that as the number of GCD iterations goes up, the voltage error decreases and the number of edges in the output graph increases as expected. We also run GCD for the same number of iterations with different λ as shown in Figure 6(b). It is shown that the smaller λ produces more accurate but denser results than the bigger λ, and therefore we can control the trade-off between the sparsity and accuracy of the reduced model by tuning the sparsity control parameter λ. Note that when λ is small enough ($\leq 10^{-4}$ in this case), it makes a negligible difference in the final accuracy and sparsity.

We compare our GCD algorithm with the SGD algorithm with its original formulation [8] and the CCD algorithm. Since the SGD algorithm in [8] was implemented in MATLAB and the voltage error was not reported, we implement it in C++ for a fair comparison. The results are summarized in Table 2, where "#Edges" denotes the edge count in the resultant graph, "V_{error}" is the maximum voltage drop error, and "Time" is the runtime in seconds. Table 2 shows that the SGD algorithm produces very sparse results but suffers from long runtime. Besides, the voltage error is not ideal because it uses only $n-1$ edges to connect n nodes. We set the same λ for running

CCD and GCD, and let them exit when the cost function value on the validation set is below the threshold or the maximum number of iterations is reached. It is clear from the edge value distributions in Figure 7, CCD produces much denser results than our GCD. As we have explained in Section 6.2, this is because CCD cycles through each coordinate and iteratively adds very small edges to the output graph; conversely, GCD only adds the most important edges. Besides, CCD has worse runtime than GCD because, even though CCD has less time complexity per iteration than GCD, it coverages much slower and wastes time on updating insignificant edges.

7.2 Reduction Framework Validation
Table 3 shows the experimental results of the proposed framework on the IBM power grid benchmarks [16]. "#L", "#V" and "#I" give the number of metal layers, voltage sources, and current sources in the circuit, respectively. "#Port nodes" gives the number of nodes that are directly connected to the external voltage/current sources, while "#Non-port nodes" gives that of nodes that only have internal connections. "#Edges" denotes the number of resistors in the power grid. "V_{drop}" denotes the maximum voltage drop in the power grid. It is important to remark that [5] deletes at least 50% of port nodes, whereas we do not allow elimination of any port nodes because all of the port nodes have important physical information for measurement and verification [7]. Therefore, the numbers of nodes and edges in [5] are not listed here. We also cannot perform a comparison with [7] due to unavailability of their benchmarks and binary.

The total number of the partitioned blocks for each circuit to facilitate reduction scalability is shown in column "#Blks", and

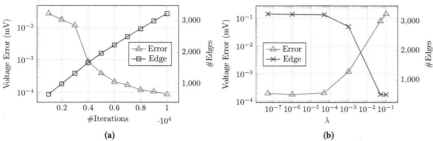

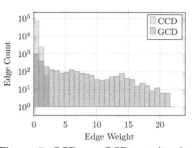

Figure 6: (a) Voltage error and edge count in the reduced circuit of `rand2` versus the number of iterations; (b) Accuracy and sparsity comparisons for different λ.

Figure 7: CCD v.s. GCD on circuit `rand2`.

Table 3: Experimental results on IBM power grid benchmarks.

CKT	Bench. Stats.							Ref. [5]		Ours						
	#L	#V	#I	#Port nodes	#Non-port nodes	#Edges	V_{drop} (mV)	V_{error} (mV)	Relative error (%)	#Blks	#Port nodes	#Non-port nodes	#Edges	V_{error} (mV)	Relative error (%)	Time (s)
ibmpg2	4	210	18963	19173	46265	106607	365.4	-	-	9	19173	0	48367	4.41	1.21	37.84
ibmpg3	5	461	100527	100988	340088	724184	181.8	1.4	0.77	68	100988	0	243011	1.32	0.73	105.71
ibmpg4	6	650	132972	133622	345122	779946	3.6	0.19	5.28	76	133622	0	284187	0.17	4.81	131.65
ibmpg5	3	177	270400	270577	311072	871182	42.9	1.2	2.80	40	270577	0	717026	0.96	2.23	122.81
ibmpg6	3	249	380742	380991	481675	1283371	114.1	2.4	2.10	56	380991	0	935322	2.23	1.96	281.25
avg.				181070	304844	753058					181070	0	445583			135.85

we observe from experiments that graph partitioning is usually necessary to process the lower layers because they contain a large number of vias or current sources. It is clear from Table 3 that the port nodes are kept in the reduced grids and all the non-port nodes are removed successfully. Moreover, the average sparsity of the reduced power grids is 0.01%. In terms of reduction accuracy, the voltage error on average is 2.19%, which is smaller than that of [5]. It is observed that as the number of remaining nodes increases, the runtime reported by [5] goes up. Our reduction framework intentionally keeps all the port nodes, and therefore the larger runtime than [5] makes sense.

8 CONCLUSION

In this work, we present a scalable power grid reduction framework. A weighted sparse convex optimization formulation for edge sparsification is proposed to reduce the number of connections in the power grid while preserving the electrical properties of the port nodes. A novel GCD method with optimality guarantee and runtime efficiency is proposed to leverage the sparsity of the reduced grids and offer a trade-off between the final accuracy and sparsity. The experimental results demonstrate that the proposed reduction framework efficiently reduces industrial power grids and preserves the accuracy and sparsity of these grids.

REFERENCES
[1] A. Odabasioglu, M. Celik, and L. T. Pileggi, "PRIMA: passive reduced-order interconnect macromodeling algorithm," in *IEEE/ACM International Conference on Computer-Aided Design (ICCAD)*, 1997, pp. 58–65.
[2] B. N. Sheehan, "TICER: Realizable reduction of extracted RC circuits," in *IEEE/ACM International Conference on Computer-Aided Design (ICCAD)*, 1999, pp. 200–203.
[3] H. Su, E. Acar, and S. R. Nassif, "Power grid reduction based on algebraic multigrid principles," in *ACM/IEEE Design Automation Conference (DAC)*, 2003, pp. 109–112.
[4] P. Li and W. Shi, "Model order reduction of linear networks with massive ports via frequency-dependent port packing," in *ACM/IEEE Design Automation Conference (DAC)*. ACM, 2006, pp. 267–272.
[5] X. Zhao, Z. Feng, and C. Zhuo, "An efficient spectral graph sparsification approach to scalable reduction of large flip-chip power grids," in *IEEE/ACM International Conference on Computer-Aided Design (ICCAD)*, 2014, pp. 218–223.
[6] D. A. Spielman and N. Srivastava, "Graph sparsification by effective resistances," *SIAM Journal on Computing (SICOMP)*, vol. 40, no. 6, pp. 1913–1926, 2011.
[7] A.-A. Yassine and F. N. Najm, "A fast layer elimination approach for power grid reduction," in *IEEE/ACM International Conference on Computer-Aided Design (ICCAD)*, 2016, p. 101.
[8] Y. Wang, M. Li, X. Yi, Z. Song, M. Orshansky, and C. Caramanis, "Novel power grid reduction method based on *l*1 regularization," in *ACM/IEEE Design Automation Conference (DAC)*, 2015, pp. 1–6.
[9] S. Boyd and L. Vandenberghe, *Convex Optimization*. Cambridge university press, 2004.
[10] S. J. Wright, "Coordinate descent algorithms," *Mathematical Programming*, vol. 151, no. 1, pp. 3–34, 2015.
[11] Y. Nesterov, "Efficiency of coordinate descent methods on huge-scale optimization problems," *SIAM Journal on Optimization (SIOPT)*, vol. 22, no. 2, pp. 341–362, 2012.
[12] J. Nutini, M. Schmidt, I. H. Laradji, M. Friedlander, and H. Koepke, "Coordinate descent converges faster with the gauss-southwell rule than random selection," in *International Conference on Machine Learning (ICML)*, 2015, pp. 1632–1641.
[13] A. Beck and L. Tetruashvili, "On the convergence of block coordinate descent type methods," *SIAM Journal on Optimization (SIOPT)*, vol. 23, no. 4, pp. 2037–2060, 2013.
[14] "Intel Math Kernel Library," http://software.intel.com/en-us/mkl.
[15] G. Karypis and V. Kumar, "A fast and high quality multilevel scheme for partitioning irregular graphs," *SIAM Journal on scientific Computing*, vol. 20, no. 1, pp. 359–392, 1998.
[16] S. R. Nassif, "Power grid analysis benchmarks," in *IEEE/ACM Asia and South Pacific Design Automation Conference (ASPDAC)*, 2008, pp. 376–381.

Machine Learning Applications in Physical Design: Recent Results and Directions

Andrew B. Kahng

CSE and ECE Departments, UC San Diego, La Jolla, CA 92093

abk@ucsd.edu

ABSTRACT

In the late-CMOS era, semiconductor and electronics companies face severe product schedule and other competitive pressures. In this context, electronic design automation (EDA) must deliver "design-based equivalent scaling" to help continue essential industry trajectories. A powerful lever for this will be the use of machine learning techniques, both inside and "around" design tools and flows. This paper reviews opportunities for machine learning with a focus on IC physical implementation. Example applications include (1) removing unnecessary design and modeling margins through correlation mechanisms, (2) achieving faster design convergence through predictors of downstream flow outcomes that comprehend both tools and design instances, and (3) corollaries such as optimizing the usage of design resources licenses and available schedule. The paper concludes with open challenges for machine learning in IC physical design.

ACM Reference Format:
Andrew B. Kahng. 2018. Machine Learning Applications in Physical Design: Recent Results and Directions. In *ISPD'18: 2018 International Symposium on Physical Design, March 25–28, 2018, Monterey, CA, USA*. ACM, New York, NY, USA, 6 pages. https://doi.org/10.1145/3177540.3177554

1 CONTEXT: THE LAST SCALING LEVERS

Semiconductor technology scaling is challenged on many fronts that include pitch scaling, patterning flexibility, wafer processing cost, interconnect resistance, and variability. The difficulty of continuing Moore's-Law lateral scaling beyond the foundry 5nm node has been widely lamented. Scaling boosters (buried interconnects, backside power delivery, supervias), next device architectures (VGAA FETs), ever-improving design-technology co-optimizations, and use of the vertical dimension (heterogeneous multi-die integration, monolithic 3D VLSI) all offer potential extensions of the industry's scaling trajectory. In addition, various "rebooting computing" paradigms – quantum, approximate, stochastic, adiabatic, neuromorphic, etc. – are being actively explored.

No matter how future extensions of semiconductor scaling materialize, the industry already faces a crisis: design of new products in advanced nodes costs too much.[1] Cost pressures rise when incremental technology and product benefits fall. Transitioning from 40nm to 28nm brought as little as 20% power, performance or area (PPA) benefit. Today, going from foundry 10nm to 7nm, or from 7nm to 5nm, the benefit is significantly less, and products may

---

[1] The 2001 *International Technology Roadmap for Semiconductors* [40] noted that "cost of design is the greatest threat to continuation of the semiconductor roadmap".

well realize only one – possibly two – of these PPA wins. The 2013 ITRS roadmap [40] highlighted a gap between scaling of *available* transistor density and scaling of *realizable* transistor density. This *design capability gap*, which adds to the spotlight on design cost, is illustrated in Figure 1 [20]. The recent DARPA Intelligent Design of Electronic Assets (IDEA) [38] program directly calls out today's design cost crisis, and seeks a "no human in the loop," 24-hour design framework for RTL-to-GDSII layout implementation.

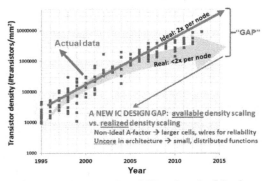

Figure 1: Design Capability Gap [40] [20].

More broadly, the industry faces three intertwined challenges: cost, quality and predictability. *Cost* corresponds to engineering effort, compute effort, and schedule. *Quality* corresponds to traditional power, performance and area (PPA) competitive metrics along with other criteria such as reliability and yield (which also determines cost). *Predictability* corresponds to the reliability of the design schedule, e.g., whether there will be unforeseen floorplan ECO iterations, whether detailed routing or timing closure flow stages will have larger than anticipated turnaround time, etc. Product quality of results (QOR) must also be predictable. Each of three challenges implies a corresponding "last lever" for scaling. In other words, reduction of design cost, improvement of design quality, and reduction of design schedule (which is the flip side of predictability; recall that Moore's Law is "one week equals one percent") are are all forms of *design-based equivalent scaling* [19] [20] that can extend availability of leading-edge technology to designers and new products. A powerful lever for this will be the use of machine learning (ML) techniques, both inside and "around" electronic design automation (EDA) tools.

The remainder of this paper reviews opportunities for machine learning in IC physical implementation. Section 2 reviews example ML applications aimed at removing unnecessary design and modeling margins through new correlation mechanisms. Section 3 reviews applications that seek faster design convergence through predictors of downstream flow outcomes. Section 4 gives a broader vision of how ML can help the IC design and EDA fields escape the current "local minimum" of coevolution in design methodology and design tools. Section 5 concludes with open challenges for ML in IC physical design. Since this paper shares its subject matter and was written contemporaneously with [23], readers are referred to [23] for additional context.

2 IMPROVING ANALYSIS CORRELATION

Analysis miscorrelation exists when two different tools return different results for the same analysis task (parasitic extraction, static timing analysis (STA), etc.) even as they apply the same "laws of physics" to the same input data. As illustrated in Figure 2, better accuracy always comes at the cost of more computation. [2] Thus, miscorrelation between two analysis reports is often the inevitable consequence of runtime efficiency requirements. For example, signoff timing is too expensive (tool licenses, incremental analysis speed, loops of timing window convergence, query speed, number of corners, etc.) to be used within tight optimization loops.

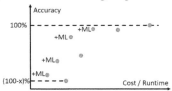

Figure 2: Accuracy-cost tradeoff in analysis.

Miscorrelation forces introduction of design guardbands and/or pessimism into the flow. For example, if the place-and-route (P&R) tool's STA report determines that an endpoint has positive worst setup slack, while the signoff STA tool determines that the same endpoint has negative worst slack, an iteration (ECO fixing step) will be required. On the other hand, if the P&R tool applies pessimism to guardband its miscorrelation to the signoff tool, this will cause unneeded sizing, shielding or VT-swapping operations that cost area, power and design schedule. Miscorrelation of timing analyses is particularly harmful: (i) timing closure can consume up to 60% of design time [12], and (ii) added guardbands not only worsen power-speed-area tradeoffs [3, 9, 12], but can also lead to non-convergence of the design.

Signoff Timer Correlation. Correlation to signoff timing is the most valuable target for ML in back-end design. Improved correlation can give "better accuracy for free" that shifts the cost-accuracy tradeoff (i.e. achieving the ML impact in Figure 2) and reduces iterations, turnaround time, overdesign, and tool license usage along the entire path to final design signoff.[3] [27] uses a learning-based approach to fit analytical models of wire slew and delay to estimates from a signoff STA tool. These models improve accuracy of delay and slew estimations along with overall timer correlation, such that fewer invocations of signoff STA are needed during incremental gate sizing optimization [34]. [16] applies deep learning to model and correct divergence between different STA tools with respect to flip-flop setup time, cell arc delay, wire delay, stage delay, and path slack at timing endpoints. The approach achieves substantial (multiple stage delays) reductions in miscorrelation. Both a one-time training methodology using artificial and real circuit topologies, as well as an incremental training flow from production usage, are described (Figure 3(a)). [30] achieves accurate (sub-10ps worst-case error in a foundry 28nm FDSOI technology) prediction of SI-mode timing slacks based on "cheaper, faster" non-SI mode reports. A combination of electrical, functional and topological parameters are used to predict the incremental transition times and arc/path delays due to SI effects. From this and other works, an apparent "no-brainer" is to use Hybrid Surrogate Modeling (HSM) [28] to combine predicted values from multiple ML models into final predictions (Figure 3(b)).

---

[2]The figure's y-axis shows that the error of the simplest estimates (e.g., "Elmore delay") can be viewed as having accuracy of $(100 - x)\%$. The return on investment for new ML applications would be higher when x is larger.
[3]Given that miscorrelation equates with margin, it is useful to note [18].

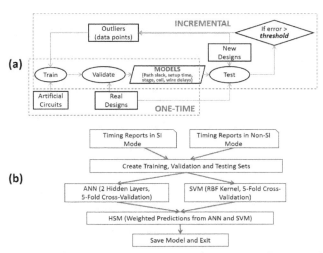

Figure 3: Flow and results for machine learning of STA tool miscorrelation: (a) [16]; (b) [30]. HSM approaches are described in [28] [29].

Next Targets. [23] identifies two near-term extensions in the realm of timer analysis correlation. **(1) PBA from GBA.** Timing analysis pessimism is reduced with *path-based analysis* (PBA), at the cost of significantly greater runtime than traditional *graph-based analysis* (GBA). In GBA, worst (resp. best) transitions (for max (resp. min) delay analyses) are propagated at each pin along a timing path, leading to conservative arrival time estimates. PBA calculates path-specific transition and arrival times at each pin, reducing pessimism that can easily exceed a stage delay. Figure 4 shows the frequency distribution of endpoint slack pessimism in GBA. This pessimism harms the design flow, e.g., when GBA reports negative slack when PBA slack is positive, schedule and chip resources are wasted to fix false timing violations; when both GBA and PBA report negative slack, there is waste from from over-fixing per the GBA report; etc. Similar considerations apply to accuracy requirements for prediction of PBA slack itself. **(2) Prediction of timing at "missing corners".** Today's signoff timing analysis is performed at 200+ corners, and even P&R and optimization steps of physical design must satisfy constraints at dozens of corners. [23] [24] note that prediction of STA results for one or more "missing" corners that *are not* analyzed, based on the STA reports for corners that *are* analyzed, corresponds to *matrix completion* in ML [6] - and that the outlook for this ML application is promising. An implicit challenge is to identify *or synthesize* the K timing corners that will enable the most accurate prediction of timing at all N production timing corners. Product teams can also inform foundries and library teams of these K corners, so that the corresponding timing libraries can be the first to be characterized.

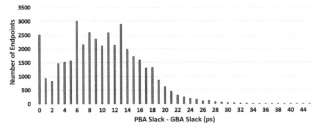

Figure 4: Frequency distribution of ((PBA slack) − (GBA slack)) at endpoints of *netcard*, 28FDSOI.

(3) Other analysis correlations. There are numerous other analysis correlation opportunities for ML. Often, these are linked with the prediction of tool and flow outcomes discussed below. Examples include correlation across various "multiphysics" analysis trajectories or loops [7] [22], such as those involving voltage droop or temperature effects in combination with normal signal integrity-aware timing. And, prominent among many parasitic estimation challenges is the prediction of bump inductance as early as possible in the die-package codesign process [22].

3 MODELS OF TOOLS AND DESIGNS

Convergent, high-quality design requires accurate modeling and prediction of downstream flow steps and outcomes. Predictive models (e.g., of wirelength, congestion, timing, etc.) become objectives or guides for optimizations, via a "modeling stack" that reaches up to system, architecture, and even project and enterprise levels. There is an urgent, complementary need for improved methods to (i) identify structural attributes of design instances that determine flow outcomes, (ii) identify "natural structure" in netlists (cf. [37]), and (iii) construct synthetic design proxies ("eye charts") [13][25][39] to help develop models of tools and flows. More broadly, tool and flow predictions are needed with increasing "span" across multiple design steps: the analogy is that we must predict what happens at the end of a longer and longer rope when the rope is wiggled.

Several examples of predictive models for tools and flows are reviewed in [23]. [8] demonstrates that learning-based models can accurately identify routing hotspots in detailed placement, and enable *model-guided optimization* whereby predicted routing hotspots are taken into account during physical synthesis with predictor-guided cell spreading. This addresses today's horrific divergence between global routing and final detailed routing, which stems from constraints on placement and pin access. Figure 5 [8] illustrates the discrepancy between routing hotspots (DRCs) predicted from global routing congestion, versus actual post-detailed routing DRCs. False positives in the former mislead routability optimizations and cause unnecessary iterations back to placement, while false negatives lead to doomed detailed routing runs. As with all other PD-related ML efforts thus far, the model of [8] incorporates parameters identified through domain expertise and multiple phases of model development. (Reducing this dependence could be a long-term goal for the field.) The work of [15] combines several simple predictions of layout and timing changes to predict clock buffer placement ECOs that will best improve clock skew variation across multiple timing corners. The work of [7] uses model parameters extracted from netlist, netlist sequential graph, floorplan, and constraints to predict post-P&R timing slacks at embedded memory instance endpoints. There are two clear takeaways from these experiences. First, there has been no escape from the need for deep domain knowledge and multiple, "highly curated" phases of model development. Second, results provide some optimism for the prospect of tool and flow prediction, based on models of both tools and design instances. The three reviewed works give a progression of "longer ropes": (i) from global/trial routing through detailed routing (and from ECO placement through incremental global/trial routing); (ii) from clock buffer and topology change through automated placement and routing ECOs, extraction, and timing analysis; and (iii) from netlist and floorplan information through placement, routing, optimization and IR drop-aware timing analysis.

Next Targets. [23] identifies two near-term targets for modeling of tools, flows and designs. **(1) Predicting doomed runs.** Substantial effort and schedule can be saved if a "doomed run" is avoided. Figure 6 shows four example progressions of the number of design rule

Figure 5: Post-route design rule violations (DRCs) predicted from global routing overflows (left); actual post-route DRCs (middle); overlay (right).

violations during the (default) 20 iterations of a commercial router. Unsuccessful runs are those that end up with too many violations for manual fixing (e.g., the red and orange traces); these should be identified and terminated after as few iterations as possible. However, ultimately successful runs (e.g., the green trace) should be run to completion. Tool logfile data can be viewed as time series to which hidden Markov models [35] or policy iteration in Markov decision processes (MDPs) [4] may be applied. For the latter, collected logfiles from previous successful and unsuccessful tool runs can serve as the basis for automated extraction of a "blackjack strategy card" for a given tool, where "hit" analogizes to continuing the tool run for another iteration, and "stay" analogizes to terminating the tool run.[4] **(2) Feeding higher-level optimizations.** As noted above, predictive models must provide new objectives and guidance for higher-level optimizations. [1] points out that the scope for application extends up to project- and enterprise-level schedule and resource optimizations, with substantial returns possible.

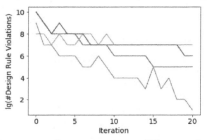

Figure 6: Four example progressions of the number of design rule violations (shown as a base-2 logarithm) with iterations of a commercial detailed router.

(3) Other Modeling and Prediction Needs. A first direction for future tool and flow modeling is to add confidence levels and probabilities to predictions. There is a trajectory of prediction from "can be achieved" to "will achieve" to "will achieve within X resources with Y probability distribution". A second direction is to improve the link between generation of data for model creation, and the model validation process. While physical design tools are not embedded in real-time, safety-critical contexts (i.e., impacts of poor modeling are likely limited to quality, cost and schedule), model accuracy must be as high as possible, as early as possible. Third, ML opportunities in physical design are clustered around "linchpin" flow steps: floorplan definition, logic synthesis, and handoff from placement to routing. For the logic synthesis step alone: since there is exactly one netlist handed off to implementation, what are the "magic" corners and constraints (including per-endpoint constraints [10]) that will induce the post-synthesis netlist that leads to best final implementation? Fourth, additional opportunities

---

[4]In the MDP paradigm, the *state space* used could consist of binned violation count and change in DRVs since a previous iteration; *actions* could be "go" or "stop", and *rewards* at each state used to derive the policy could include a small negative reward for a non-stop state, a large positive reward for termination with low number of DRVs, etc.

lie in finding the fixed point of a chicken-egg loop, as noted in [7] [22]. An example challenge today is to predict the fixed point for (non-uniform) power distribution and post-P&R layout that meets signoff constraints with maximum utilization.

4 SOC IMPLEMENTATION: A VISION

Physical design tools and flows today are unpredictable. A root cause is that many complex heuristics have been accreted upon previous complex heuristics. Thus, tools have become unpredictable, particularly when they are forced to *try hard*. Figure 7 (left), from implementation of the PULPino low-power RISC V core in a foundry 14nm enablement, shows that post-P&R area can change by 6% when target frequency changes by just 10MHz near the maximum achievable frequency. Figure 7 (right) illustrates that the statistics of this noisy tool behavior are Gaussian [32] [17]. Unpredictability of design implementation results in unpredictability of the design schedule. However, since product companies must strictly meet design and tapeout schedules, the design target (PPA) must be guardbanded, impacting product quality and profitability. Put another way: (i) our heuristics and tools are chaotic when designers demand best-quality results; and (ii) when designers want predictable results, they must aim low.

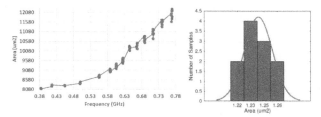

Figure 7: Left: SP&R implementation noise increases with target design quality. Right: Observed noise is essentially Gaussian.

SOC Design: Today. From Figure 7, a genesis of today's SOC physical implementation methodology can be seen, as illustrated in Figure 8(a). The figure illustrates that with unpredictable optimizers, as well as the perceived loss of "global optimization" of solution quality when the design problem is partitioned, designers demand as close to flat methodologies as possible. Hence, today's prevailing SOC methodology entails having as few large hard macros as possible. To satisfy this customer requirement in the face of Moore's-Law scaling of design complexity, EDA tools must add more heuristics so as to turn around ever-larger blocks in the same turnaround time. To recover design quality (e.g., in light of "aim low") designers seek as much flexibility as possible in their implementation tools.[5] This leads to poor predictability in design, which then leads to more iterations, and turnaround times become longer. Further, the lack of predictability induces larger design guardbands. As a result of these cause-effect relationships, the *achieved* design quality worsens, and the design capability gap grows. This is the unfortunate tale of coevolution between physical design tools and physical implementation methodology.

SOC Design: Future. To close the design capability gap, EDA and IC design together must "flip the arrows" of Figure 8(a). A vision for future SOC design is suggested in Figure 8(b). The physical implementation challenge is decomposed into many more small subproblems, by *hyperpartitioning* or "extreme partitioning"; this

---

[5]A modern P&R tool has thousands of, and even more than ten thousand, command-option combinations.

reduces the time needed to solve any given subproblem, and smaller subproblems can be better-solved (see [33]). At the same time, increasing the number of design partitions without undue loss of global solution quality demands new placement, global routing and optimization algorithms, as well as fundamentally new RTL partition and floorplan co-optimization capabilities. Further, *reducing design flexibility* by giving designers "freedoms from choice" with respect to RTL constructs, power distribution, clock distribution, global buffering, non-default wiring rules, etc. would increase predictability, leading to fewer iterations (ideally, single-pass design). Turnaround time is then minimized. Improved predictability and fewer iterations result in smaller design guardbands. The end result: improvement of *achieved* design quality, which shrinks the design capability gap. As pointed out in [24], achieving this vision of future SOC design methodology would improve quality, schedule and cost – i.e., "the last scaling levers". A number of new mindsets for tool developers and design flow engineers are implicit: (i) tools and flows should never return unexpected results; (ii) designers should see predictability, not chaos, in their tools and flows; (iii) cloud deployment and parallel search can help to preserve or improve achieved quality of results; and (iv) the focus of *design-based equivalent scaling* is on sustained reduction of design time and design effort.

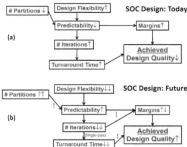

Figure 8: SOC design (a) today, and (b) in the future.

5 A ROADMAP FOR ML IN PD

This section describes a "roadmap" for the insertion of ML within and around physical design flow steps. Four high-level stages of insertion are described. Then, a list of specific, actionable challenges is given.

Four Stages of ML Insertion

Insertion of ML into and around physical design algorithms, tools and flows could be divided into four qualitatively distinct stages. Figure 9(a) conveys why IC implementation and design resource requirements are so challenging: there are thousands of potential options at each flow step (don't-use cells, timing constraints, pin placements, density screens, allowed netlist transforms, alternate commands-options and environment variables, ...), resulting in an enormous tree of possible flow trajectories. Today, even identifying a "best" among alternative post-synthesis netlists or physical floorplans to carry forward in the flow is beyond the grasp of human engineers. Thus, the likely **first stage** of ML insertion into IC will entail *creating robots*: mechanizing and automating (via expert systems, perhaps) 24/7 replacements for human engineers that reliably execute a given flow to completion.[6] Figure 10 shows

---

[6]This goes beyond today's typical 'make chip' flow automation in that real expertise and human-seeming smarts are captured within the robot engineer. As discussed below, robots will likely also fill in last-mile or small-market tasks that are unserved by available tools.

how primitive "multi-armed bandit" (MAB) sampling can achieve resource-adaptive commercial synthesis, place and route with no human involvement – in a "robotic" manner that is distinct from expert systems approaches. Past tool run outcomes are used by the MAB to estimate the probability of meeting constraints at different parameter settings; future runs are then scheduled that are most likely to yield the best outcomes within the given (licenses × schedule) design resource budget. The figure shows the evolution of sampled frequencies versus iterations in the MAB's "robotic" execution.

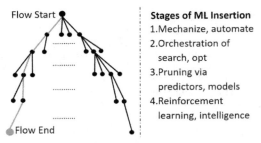

Figure 9: (a) Tree of options at flow steps. (b) Phases of ML insertion into production IC implementation.

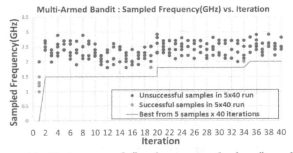

Figure 10: Trajectory of "no-human-in-the-loop" multi-armed bandit sampling of a commercial SP&R flow, with 40 iterations and 5 concurrent samples (tool runs) per iteration. Testcase: PULPino core in 14nm foundry technology, with given power and area constraints. Adapted from [21].

Once a robot engineer exists, the **second stage** of ML insertion is to optimally orchestrate N robot engineers that concurrently search multiple flow trajectories, where N can range from tens to thousands and is constrained chiefly by compute and license resources. Here, simple multistart, or depth-first or breadth-first traversal of the tree of flow options, is hopeless. Rather, it seems likely that strategies such as "go-with-the-winners" (GWTW) [2] will be applied. GWTW launches multiple optimization threads, and periodically identifies and clones the most promising thread while terminating other threads; see Figure 11(a). The GWTW method has been applied successfully in, e.g., [26]. Another promising direction may be *adaptive multistart* [5] [14], which exploits an inherent "big valley" structure in optimization cost landscapes to adaptively identify promising start configurations for iterative optimization. This is illustrated in Figure 11(b), where better start points for optimization are identified based on the structure of (locally-minimal) solutions found from previous start points.

The **third stage** will integrate *prediction* of tool- and design-specific outcomes over longer and longer subflows, so as to more surgically

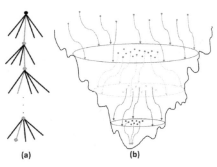

Figure 11: (a) Go-with-the-winners [2]. (b) Adaptive multistart in a "big valley" optimization landscape [5] [14].

prune, terminate, or otherwise not waste design resources on less-promising flow trajectories. Implicit in the third stage is the improvement of *predictability* and modelability for PD heuristics and EDA tools. Finally, the **fourth stage** will span from reinforcement learning to "intelligence". At this stage, there are many obstacles. For example, the latency and unpredictability of IC design tool runs (we can't play the IC design game hundreds of millions of times in a few days, as we would the game of chess), the sparsity of data (there are millions of cat and dog faces on the web, but not many 10nm layouts), the lack of good evaluation functions, and the huge space of trajectories for design all look to be difficult challenges. Hopefully, aspects of the vision for future SOC design given above, and solutions to the initial challenges given below, will provide help toward realization of the fourth stage.

Specific Initial Challenges

Following are several specific "initial challenges" for machine learning in physical design.

"Last-Mile" Robots. A number of today's time-consuming, error-prone and even trial-and-error steps in IC implementation should be automated by systems that systematically search for tool command sequences, and/or observe and learn from humans. (1) *Automation of manual DRC violation fixing.* After routing and optimization, P&R tools leave DRC violations due to inability to handle latest foundry rules, unavoidable lack of routing resource in a high-utilization block, etc. PD engineers today must spread cells and perform rip-up and reroute manually. (2) *Automation of manual timing closure steps.* After routing and optimization, several thousand violations of maxtrans, setup and hold constraints may exist. PD engineers today fix these manually at the rate of several hundred per day per engineer. (3) *Placement of memory instances in a P&R block.* (4) *Package layout automation.* The ML challenge is to be able to assess the post-routed quality (e.g., with respect to bump inductances) of floorplan and pin map in die-package codesign. From this will flow bump/ball placement and placement improvement; a possible prerequisite is the automation of manual package routing.

Improving Analysis Correlation. (1) *Prediction of the worst PBA path.* For a given endpoint, the worst PBA path is not necessarily among any the top k GBA paths: CCS loads on side fanouts, path topology and composition, GBA common path pessimism removal, etc. all affect the rank correlation between GBA and PBA results of timing paths. (2) *Prediction of the worst PBA slack per endpoint, from GBA analysis.* E.g., from all GBA endpoint slacks. (3) *Prediction of timing at "missing corners".* Given timing analysis reports at k corners, predict reports at $N - k$ corners, where $k << N$. Similarly, given a prediction accuracy requirement, find $k << N$ corners, with k as small as possible, that enable prediction of remaining corners with the required accuracy. (4) *Closing of multiphysics analysis loops.*

I.e., as in [22] [7], with early priorities being vectorless dynamic IR drop and power-temperature loops. (5) *Continued improvement of timing correlation and estimation* as in [16] [30]. Matching the golden tool earlier in the flow will more accurately drive optimizations and reduce ECO iterations.

Predictive Models of Tools and Designs. (1) *Prediction of the convergent point for non-uniform PDN and P&R.* The PDN is defined before placement, but power analysis and routability impact can be assessed only after routing. (2) *Estimation of the PPA response of a given block in response to floorplan optimizations.* Final PPA impacts of feedthroughs, shape, utilization, memory placement, etc. must be comprehended to enable floorplan assessment and optimization (within a higher-level exploration of design partitioning/floorplanning solutions). (3) *Estimation of useful skew impact on post-route WNS, TNS metrics.* See, e.g., [10]. A low-level related challenge: predicting buffer locations to optimize both common paths and useful skew. (4) *"Auto-magic" determination of constraints for a given netlist,* for given performance and power targets – i.e., best settings for maxtrans, maxcap, clock uncertainty, etc. at each flow stage. More generally, determine "magic" corners and constraints that will produce the best netlist to send into P&R. (5) *Prediction of the best "target sequence" of constraints through layout optimization phases.* I.e., timing and power targets at synthesis, placement, etc. such that best final PPA metrics are achieved. (6) *Prediction of impacts (setup, hold slack, max transition, power) of an ECO, across MCMM scenarios.* (7) *Prediction of the "most-optimizable" cells during design closure.* Many optimization steps are wasted on instances that cannot be perturbed due to placement, timing, power and other context. (8) *Prediction of divergence (detouring, timing/slew violations) between trial/global route and final detailed route.* (9) *Prediction of "doomed runs"* at all steps of the physical design flow.

And More. (1) *Infrastructure for ML in IC design.* Standards for model encapsulation, model application, IP-preserving model sharing, etc. are yet to be developed. (2) *Standard ML platform for EDA modeling.* Enablement of design metrics collection, tool and flow model generation, design-adaptive tool and flow configuration, prediction of tool and flow outcomes, etc. would realize the original vision of METRICS [36] [11] [31]. (3) *Development of more modelable algorithms and tools* with smoother, less-chaotic outcomes than present methods. (4) *Development of datasets to support ML.* This spans new classes of artificial circuits and "eyecharts", as well as sharing of training data and the data generation task across different design organizations.

6 ACKNOWLEDGMENTS

Many thanks are due to Dr. Tuck-Boon Chan, Dr. Jiajia Li, Dr. Siddhartha Nath, Dr. Stefanus Mantik, Dr. Kambiz Samadi, Dr. Kwangok Jeong, Ms. Hyein Lee and Mr. Wei-Ting Jonas Chan who, along with current ABKGroup students and collaborators, performed much of the research cited in this paper. I thank Professor Lawrence Saul for ongoing discussions and collaborations. Permission of coauthors to reproduce figures from works referenced here is gratefully acknowledged. Research at UCSD is supported by NSF, Qualcomm, Samsung, NXP, Mentor Graphics and the C-DEN center.

REFERENCES

[1] P. Agrawal, M. Broxterman, B. Chatterjee, P. Cuevas, K. H. Hayashi, A. B. Kahng, P. K. Myana and S. Nath, "Optimal Scheduling and Allocation for IC Design Management and Cost Reduction", *ACM TODAES* 22(4) (2017), pp. 60:1-60:30.
[2] D. Aldous and U. Vazirani, "Go With the Winners", *Proc. IEEE Symp. on Foundations of Computer Science*, 1994, pp. 492-501.
[3] S. Bansal and R. Goering, "Making 20nm Design Challenges Manageable", http://www.chipdesignmag.com/pdfs/chip_design_special_DAC_issue_2012.pdf
[4] D. Bertsekas, *Dynamic Programming and Optimal Control*, Athena, 1995.
[5] K. D. Boese, A. B. Kahng and S. Muddu, "New Adaptive Multistart Techniques for Combinatorial Global Optimizations", *Operations Research Letters* 16(2) (1994), pp. 101-113.
[6] E. J. Candes and B. Recht, "Exact Matrix Completion via Convex Optimization", *Foundations of Computational Mathematics* 9 (2009), pp. 717-772.
[7] W.-T. J. Chan, K. Y. Chung, A. B. Kahng, N. D. MacDonald and S. Nath, "Learning-Based Prediction of Embedded Memory Timing Failures During Initial Floorplan Design", *Proc. ASP-DAC*, 2016, pp. 178-185.
[8] W.-T. J. Chan, P.-H. Ho, A. B. Kahng and P. Saxena, "Routability Optimization for Industrial Designs at Sub-14nm Process Nodes Using Machine Learning", *Proc. ISPD*, 2017, pp. 15-21.
[9] T.-B. Chan, A. B. Kahng, J. Li and S. Nath, "Optimization of Overdrive Signoff", *Proc. ASP-DAC*, 2013, pp. 344-349.
[10] T.-B. Chan, A. B. Kahng and J. Li, "NOLO: A No-Loop, Predictive Useful Skew Methodology for Improved Timing in IC Implementation", *Proc. ISQED*, 2014, pp. 504-509.
[11] S. Fenstermaker, D. George, A. B. Kahng, S. Mantik and B. Thielges, "METRICS: A System Architecture for Design Process Optimization", *Proc. DAC*, 2000, pp. 705-710.
[12] R. Goering, "What's Needed to "Fix" Timing Signoff?", *DAC Panel*, 2013.
[13] P. Gupta, A. B. Kahng, A. Kasibhatla and P. Sharma, "Eyecharts: Constructive Benchmarking of Gate Sizing Heuristics", *Proc. DAC*, 2010, pp. 597-602.
[14] L. Hagen and A. B. Kahng, "Combining Problem Reduction and Adaptive Multi-Start: A New Technique for Superior Iterative Partitioning", *IEEE Trans. Computer-Aided Design of Integrated Circuits and Systems* 16(7) (1997), pp. 709-717.
[15] K. Han, A. B. Kahng, J. Lee, J. Li and S. Nath, "A Global-Local Optimization Framework for Simultaneous Multi-Mode Multi-Corner Skew Variation Reduction", *Proc. DAC*, 2015, pp. 26:1-26:6.
[16] S. S. Han, A. B. Kahng, S. Nath and A. Vydyanathan, "A Deep Learning Methodology to Proliferate Golden Signoff Timing", *Proc. DATE*, 2014, pp. 260:1-260:6.
[17] K. Jeong and A. B. Kahng, "Methodology From Chaos in IC Implementation", *Proc. ISQED*, 2010, pp. 885-892.
[18] K. Jeong, A. B. Kahng and K. Samadi, "Impacts of Guardband Reduction on Design Process Outcomes: A Quantitative Approach", *IEEE Trans. Semiconductor Manufacturing* 22(4) (2009), pp. 552-565.
[19] A. B. Kahng, "The Cost of Design", *IEEE Design & Test of Computers*, 2002.
[20] A. B. Kahng, "The ITRS Design Technology and System Drivers Roadmap: Process and Status", *Proc. DAC*, 2013, pp. 34-39.
[21] A. B. Kahng, DARPA IDEA Workshop presentation, Arlington, April 2017.
[22] A. B. Kahng, ANSYS Executive Breakfast keynote talk, June 2017. http://vlsicad.ucsd.edu/Presentations/talk/Kahng-ANSYS-DACBreakfast_talk_DISTRIBUTED2.pdf
[23] A. B. Kahng, "New Directions for Learning-Based IC Design Tools and Methodologies", *Proc. ASP-DAC*, 2018, pp. 405-410.
[24] A. B. Kahng, "Quality, Schedule, and Cost: Design Technology and the Last Semiconductor Scaling Levers". *keynote talk*, ASP-DAC, 2018. http://vlsicad.ucsd.edu/ASPDAC18/ASP-DAC-2018-Keynote-Kahng-POSTED.pdf
[25] A. B. Kahng and S. Kang, "Construction of Realistic Gate Sizing Benchmarks With Known Optimal Solutions", *Proc. ISPD*, 2012, pp. 153-160.
[26] A. B. Kahng, S. Kang, H. Lee, I. L. Markov and P. Thapar, "High-Performance Gate Sizing with a Signoff Timer", *Proc. ICCAD*, 2013, pp. 450-457.
[27] A. B. Kahng, S. Kang, H. Lee, S. Nath and J. Wadhwani, "Learning-Based Approximation of Interconnect Delay and Slew in Signoff Timing Tools", *Proc. SLIP*, 2013, pp. 1-8.
[28] A. B. Kahng, B. Lin and S. Nath, "Enhanced Metamodeling Techniques for High-Dimensional IC Design Estimation Problems", *Proc. DATE*, 2013, pp. 1861-1866.
[29] A. B. Kahng, B. Lin and S. Nath, "High-Dimensional Metamodeling for Prediction of Clock Tree Synthesis Outcomes", *Proc. SLIP*, 2013, pp. 1-7.
[30] A. B. Kahng, M. Luo and S. Nath, "SI for Free: Machine Learning of Interconnect Coupling Delay and Transition Effects", *Proc. SLIP*, 2015, pp. 1-8.
[31] A. B. Kahng and S. Mantik, "A System for Automatic Recording and Prediction of Design Quality Metrics", *Proc. ISQED*, 2001, pp. 81-86.
[32] A. Kahng and S. Mantik, "Measurement of Inherent Noise in EDA Tools", *Proc. ISQED*, 2002, pp. 206-211.
[33] A. Katsioulas, S. Chow, J. Avidan and D. Fotakis, "Integrated Circuit Architecture with Standard Blocks"', *U.S. Patent* 6,467,074, 2002.
[34] C. W. Moon, P. Gupta, P. J. Donehue and A. B. Kahng, "Method of Designing a Digital Circuit by Correlating Different Static Timing Analyzers", *US Patent* 7,823,098, 2010.
[35] L. R. Rabiner, "A Tutorial on Hidden Markov Models and Selected Applications on Speech Recognition", *Proc. IEEE* 77 (1989), pp. 257-286.
[36] The GSRC METRICS Initiative. http://vlsicad.ucsd.edu/GSRC/metrics/
[37] Partitioning- and Placement-based Intrinsic Rent Parameter Evaluation. http://vlsicad.ucsd.edu/WLD/RentCon.pdf
[38] "DARPA Rolls Out Electronics Resurgence Initiative", https://www.darpa.mil/news-events/2017-09-13
[39] Gate Sizing Benchmarks With Known Optimal Solution. http://vlsicad.ucsd.edu/SIZING/bench/artificial.html
[40] *International Technology Roadmap for Semiconductors.* http://www.itrs2.net/itrs-reports.html

Machine Learning for Feature-Based Analytics

Li-C. Wang
University of California
Santa Barbara, California
licwang@ece.ucsb.edu

ABSTRACT

Applying machine learning in Electronic Design Automation (EDA) has received growing interests in recent years. One approach to analyze data in EDA applications can be called feature-based analytics. In this context, the paper explains the inadequacy of adopting a traditional machine learning problem formulation view. Then, an alternative machine learning view is suggested where learning from data is treated as an iterative search process. The theoretical and practical considerations for implementing such a search process are discussed in the context of various applications.

CCS CONCEPTS

• **Hardware** → Software tools for EDA;

KEYWORDS

Machine Learning, Feature-Based Analytics, Learnable, Version Space, Occam's Razor, Design Automation

ACM Reference Format:
Li-C. Wang. 2018. Machine Learning for Feature-Based Analytics. In *ISPD '18: 2018 International Symposium on Physical Design, March 25–28, 2018, Monterey, CA, USA.* ACM, New York, NY, USA, 8 pages. https://doi.org/10.1145/3177540.3177555

1 INTRODUCTION

Applying machine learning in EDA applications can encounter different types of learning problems. For example, a popular type of analytics is based on two classes of samples. A set of k positive samples are in our interest to understand why. Then, the rest of samples are negative samples. It is also often that k is very small or in some situations, even $k = 0$. To learn, a set of n features $f_1, \ldots, f_n$ are available to describe each sample. The goal is to learn a model based on those features to differentiate one or more of the positive samples from the negative ones. A recent survey [24] discusses several applications that involve this type of analytics.

For example, Figure 1 illustrates an application in functional verification [5][23]. A testbench is instantiated through Constrained Random Test Generation (CRTG) into a set of functional tests. The design can be a SoC and each test can be a C program (or a sequence of instructions). Simulating the tests results in simulation traces

which are the data to be analyzed. Our interest concerns a point CP in the design and its coverage observed in the simulation. The goal of analytics is to help improve the coverage.

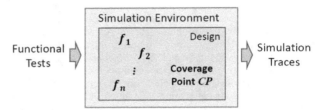

Figure 1: An application in functional verification

To apply analytics, we extract datasets from traces based on a set of features $f_1, \ldots, f_n$. Suppose each feature is a signal in the design which we know how to control from the CRTG perspective. For simplicity, suppose each sample is encoded based on the activities of these signals from each simulation cycle. Then, each sample can be represented as a vector of digital values. Each sample (x) is also associated with a label (y) based on the coverage status of CP. If in the cycle the coverage point CP is covered, then the sample is labeled as positive (+1). Otherwise, it is labeled as negative (−1). Such a dataset can be illustrated as Figure 2.

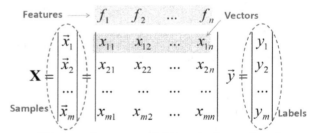

Figure 2: An extracted dataset to be analyzed

Usually, the coverage point CP is our concern because it receives very few or no coverage in the simulation. This means that in the dataset, there are very few or no positive samples. To improve its coverage, the goal of analytics is to discover what combination of feature values can lead to more coverage of CP.

Figure 3: Raster scan to extract layout snippets

In physical verification, a given layout can be scanned into a sequence of *snippets* [8], i.e. a small window of layout image, as illustrated in Figure 3. Each snippet can be characterized with a set of features, such as attributes related to shape, spacing, materials, etc. A positive sample can be defined as a snippet that potentially causes an issue (i.e. a hot-spot). Then, the rest are negative samples. Our interest is often in modeling (and predicting) the positive samples and such an application often encounters a dataset where there are many more negative samples than positive samples. Moreover, because different positive samples may be due to different reasons, it is likely that in a particular analysis, we are interested in modeling one or few selected positive samples.

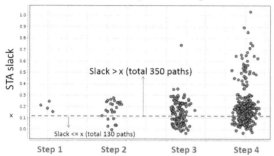

Figure 4: 350 critical paths not predicted by STA

In timing verification, samples are paths. For example, figure 4 shows critical paths collected from a silicon experiment [4] and their predicted slack from Static Timing Analysis (STA). For a path, its timing is measured on a set of process cores. The measurement is carried out by *frequency stepping* where step 1 has the lowest frequency. Each dot shown in the plot represents a path. For example, at step 1 there are four silicon critical paths.

In STA, the assumption is that if the path slack is less than a selected value x, then the path is reported as a STA-critical path. In the plot, the value of x is shown and it can be observed that 350 out of the 480 paths shown in the plot are not reported as STA-critical paths. In fact, based on x, the STA reports 21,589 STA-critical paths and only 130 paths show up in this plot.

To understand why a silicon-critical path is not a STA-critical path, one might be interested in starting the analytics by modeling the first four silicon-critical paths shown on the left of the plot. In this case, the positive samples are those 4 paths. The negative samples could be the remaining 21,459 (= 21589 − 130) STA-critical paths which do not show up as a silicon-critical path. To enable the analysis, a set of design-related features are developed for characterizing a path. These features can be based on, for example, the cells, the layout, the path location, and so on [4].

1.1 Limited number of positive samples

Refer back to the dataset illustration Figure 2. For the applications discussed above, a given dataset can be extremely unbalanced, i.e. with a large m but containing very few positive samples. In the case of functional verification, there can be no positive sample to begin with. The number of features n can be on the order of hundreds or more. Usually, the reason causing a positive sample can be described with only a few features (e.g. 1 to 3). Hence, the underlying problem can be thought of as searching in the large number of features for those few relevant ones.

1.2 Limited number of samples

For the applications discussed above, the limitation is on the number of positive samples. In other applications, the limitation can be on the total number of samples. In view of Figure 2, this means that we could have $m < n$.

For example, Figure 5 shows the maximum operation frequency (Fmax) characterized in system testing for 60 processor cores (in GHz). The frequency is determined in *frequency stepping* where two steps are separated by 0.02 GHz.

Because system testing is expensive, the goal is to develop a model to predict the Fmax of a processor core based on other inexpensive measurements. These other measurements can be the maximum delay measured at a flip-flop based on a set of transition test patterns, the maximum delay measured for a transition test pattern, and the maximum delay measured on a selected path. Therefore, a feature can be a flip-flop, a test pattern, or a path. In this context, a sample is a processor core. The label is the Fmax measured on the sample.

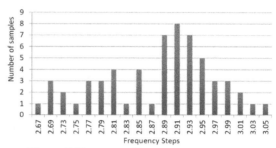

Figure 5: Fmax results across process cores

The learning problem can be treated as a regression problem [9]. However, since $m = 60$ and $n > m$ (there can be hundreds of features to consider), running a regression tool directly can lead to an *overfitting* model whose prediction accuracy on other samples not seen in the data is questionable. The core of the problem is again to search in the large number of features for those features relevant to the Fmax. There is another reason why identifying those relevant features is desirable. In practice, a Fmax predictor is more acceptable if one knows the features used to make the prediction and can verify the relevance of those features with domain knowledge.

1.3 An application with $m \sim O(n)$

In some applications, the number of samples m is on the same order as the number of features n and usually we can have $m > n$. However, even in this case the underlying problem can still be seen as a search problem for identifying those few relevant features.

For example, Figure 6 shows test results at two temperatures (cold and hot) for a sequence of wafers in production. The data were collected from an automotive SoC product line [18]. For every wafer, two vertical bars are shown, corresponding to the cold (blue) and hot (red) test results. Each bar shows the range of measured test values from dice on the respective wafer. This range is $[\mu - \sigma, \mu + \sigma]$ where μ stands for the mean and σ stands for the standard deviation. The upper and lower limits are shown as two horizontal dash lines. Observe that hot test values drift beyond the limit frequently. This means that on those wafers, many dice fail the hot test.

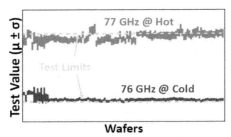

Figure 6: Yield issue observed on some wafers

The goal of the analytics can be to uncover a reason for those hot fails and more importantly, a recipe to reduce the number of failing dice so that the yield can be improved. In this example, a sample can be a wafer. The features can be those process-tunable parameters. There can be hundreds or thousands of wafers available for the analysis. The number of process-tunable parameters can be on the order of hundreds. The goal is to identify a few parameters to adjust in order to improve the yield (see, e.g. [20]).

1.4 Feature-based analytics

Analytics involved in the applications discussed above can be called *feature-based analytics* which means the underlying problem is to search for a small combination of features or feature values among a large set of features. This search problem is different from traditional *feature selection* studied in machine learning. A traditional feature selection algorithm is entirely data-driven. On the other hand, in feature-based analytics it is often that the data are insufficient to determine the relevance of all features when they are included in a dataset. As a result, applying a traditional feature selection algorithm on such a dataset is often not effective.

In feature-based analytics, it is not effective to run a learning tool with all n features included. As a result, the learning becomes an iterative search process [24].

2 ITERATIVE MODEL SEARCH

The iterative search process is illustrated in Figure 7. First, it is common that a tool from the machine learning toolbox (see, e.g. [10]) expects a dataset that is formatted as depicted in Figure 2. To produce such a dataset, three steps are performed: sample selection, feature selection, and dataset construction.

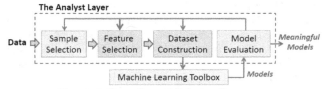

Figure 7: Iterative model search process

The sample selection step defines what a sample is and selects a set of m samples $\vec{x}_1, \ldots, \vec{x}_m$ for the analysis. For example, in functional verification a sample consists of signal activities in a simulation window. In physical verification, a sample is a layout snippet. In timing verification, a sample is a path. For Fmax prediction, a sample is a chip. In yield analysis, a sample can be a chip, a wafer or a lot. If the analysis is based on *supervised learning*, a label

value y_i is calculated for each sample $\vec{x}_i$. If it is for *unsupervised learning*, no label is required.

Calculating the label for a sample might need a separate analysis itself. For example, in yield analysis a wafer can be classified as good or bad and deciding this binary label can be based on outlier analysis [20] (i.e. a bad wafer has a yield number that is classified as an outlier). Furthermore, it is possible that a particular analysis does not use all samples. For example, after some initial analysis, it is decided that a subset of samples require a more focused analysis.

For feature selection, an initial set of features is provided. This feature set is often developed by consulting a domain expert. Then, in each iteration a subset of features $f_1, \ldots, f_n$ are selected. After this subset is determined, in the dataset construction step for each sample $\vec{x}_i$ its feature values $(x_{i1}, \ldots, x_{in})$ are computed. This computation might require running a machine learning tool also. For example, the original values of a feature might be divided into ranges and this division can be based on a clustering algorithm [3].

After a dataset is constructed, running a machine learning tool on the dataset can result in one or more models. For example, a tool can allow setting some parameter values to affect the optimization objective of the learning algorithm. With different parameter values, different models can be obtained. The models then go through a model evaluation step. In this step, the meaningfulness of a model is assessed in the context of the particular application. If model evaluation cannot determine a meaningful model, then a different dataset is required. This invokes a new iteration that can involve redoing one or more of the previous three steps.

2.1 The need for domain knowledge

In Figure 7, it is obvious that the effectiveness of the search is not determined solely by the effectiveness of the tools in the machine learning toolbox. For example, if relevant features are not included in a dataset, then no tool should produce a meaningful model. Consequently, automation of the entire search process requires automation of the four steps in the Analyst Layer shown above the machine learning toolbox. In practice, these four steps are mostly driven by domain knowledge [24] and usually performed with specific software scripts written by an analyst. This means that automation of these steps requires implementing a way to learn and incorporate the analyst's domain knowledge (see, e.g. [18]).

2.2 The expensive model evaluation step

In practice, the model evaluation step can be time consuming. For example, in functional verification, the step might involve modifying the testbench according to a learning model and generating new tests. Then, these new tests are simulated to decide if the model is meaningful. In other applications, the evaluation might involve meetings with the design team. In the context of yield analysis, the meetings could involve engineers from a foundry outside the company. Consequently, each search iteration can be delayed and this bottleneck is outside the machine learning toolbox.

2.3 The tool requirement

To speed up the process, ideally the search desires a machine learning tool that reports not only a model but also a quality measure of the model. This quality measure helps decide in the model evaluation step whether or not to go through the expensive evaluation.

In traditional machine learning, a tool is designed to output an "optimal" model based on a given dataset where the optimization objective depends on the learning algorithm. Then, the quality of the model is evaluated through *cross-validation*. In cross-validation, there are two datasets: a *training* set and a *validation* set. The model is learned with the training set and its accuracy is calculated by applying the model to the validation set. The accuracy seen on the validation dataset is supposed to represent how the model will perform on future unseen samples.

While cross-validation is a common practice, the no-free-lunch (NFL) theorem in machine learning [26] warns about its misuse in practice. Unless one can ensure that the validation set is somewhat a complete representation for the future unseen samples (which is often not the case in practice), cross-validation may provide little practical meaning in an application.

More importantly, for the applications mentioned before, cross-validation is often not a viable approach to assess the quality of a model. This is due to the limitation on the number of positive samples or on the total number of samples as discussed above. This means that in Figure 7, the quality of a model has to be assessed entirely in the model evaluation step. The only possible guarantee a learning tool can provide on its output models is that they are optimal with respect to some optimization objective. However, whether such an optimization objective has a meaning in the application context is usually difficult to decide.

In view of Fig. 7, ideally, the search desires a machine learning tool that can report a quality measure of the model without cross-validation. This requirement leads to the main challenge for the machine learning toolbox: How to assess the quality of a model without cross-validation?

In summary, there are two areas of concern for feature-based analytics: (1) How to provide a quality measure for the models entering the model evaluation step without cross-validation? (2) How to effectively incorporate the domain knowledge in the iterative search process. In the rest of the paper, the discussion will focus more on the first concern. Then, in section 7 we will briefly review two recent works [13][18] related to the second concern.

3 ASSUMPTIONS IN MACHINE LEARNING

To address the model quality concern, we need to understand why cross-validation is needed in the first place, i.e. why a machine learning algorithm does not guarantee its model accuracy and demands cross-validation to evaluate its model? To facilitate the discussion, Figure 8 illustrates a theoretical setup for *supervised learning*.

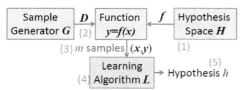

Figure 8: Five areas to make an assumption

In this setup, a hypothesis space H is assumed. H is a set of functions and one of them f is the target function to be learned. A sample generator G produces a set of samples $\vec{x}_1, \ldots, \vec{x}_m$ according to an unknown but fixed distribution D. For each sample $\vec{x}_i$, its label

y_i is calculated as $f(\vec{x}_i)$. Then, the dataset comprising the m pairs $(\vec{x}_i, y_i)$, is given to a learning algorithm L to learn. The algorithm L outputs its answer h. Ideally, if the answer is correct, we would have $\forall \vec{x}$ generated from G, $f(\vec{x}) = h(\vec{x})$.

In theory, f has to be *learnable* [16][21] in order for a learning algorithm to provide some sort of guarantee. To achieve learnability, some assumptions need to be made in view of the setup. There are five areas to make an assumption, as marked in Figure 8.

The first assumption concerns the hypothesis space H. It is intuitive that the learnability depends on the complexity of H, i.e. the more complex the H is, the more difficult the learning is (hence less learnable). If H is finite and enumerable, then its complexity can be measured more easily. For example, if H is the set of all Boolean functions based on n variables, then H contains 2^{2^n} distinct functions.

The difficulty is when H is infinite and/or uncountable. In this case, one cannot rely on counting to define its complexity. One theory to measure the complexity of H is based on its ability to fit the data. This concept is called the *capacity* of H which is characterized as the *VC dimension* [22]. The VC dimension (VC-D) also represents the minimum number of samples required to identify a f randomly chosen from H. To learn, one needs to make an assumption on the VC-D, for example VC-D should be on the order of $poly(n)$ (polynomial in n, the number of features). Otherwise, the number of required samples can be too large to be practical.

The second assumption concerns the sample generator G. The common assumption is that G produces its samples by drawing a sample randomly according to a fixed distribution D. Hence, as far as the learning concerns, all future samples are generated according to the same distribution.

The third assumption concerns the number of samples (m) available to the learning algorithm. This m has to be at least as large as the VC-D. Then, the fourth assumption concerns the complexity of the learning algorithm. Even though m is sufficiently large, learning the function f can still be computationally hard [16].

The computational hardness can be characterized in terms of the traditional NP-Hardness notion [16] or the hardness to break a cryptography function [15]. For example, learning a 3-term DNF (Disjunctive Normal Form) formula using the DNF representation is hard [16]. In fact, except for a few special cases, learning a Boolean functional class is usually hard [16]. Moreover, learning a simple neural network is hard [6]. The computational hardness for learning implies that in practice for most of the interesting learning problems, a learning algorithm can only be a heuristic. Consequently, its performance cannot be guaranteed on all problem instances.

The last assumption concerns how the answer h is evaluated. In the discussion of the other assumptions above, we implicitly assume that the "closeness" of h to f is evaluated through an error function $Err()$, for example $Err(h, f) = Prob(h(\vec{x}) \neq f(\vec{x}))$ for a randomly drawn $\vec{x}$. Notice that with such an $Err()$, the perfect answer does not require $h = f$. As far as the learning concerns, as long as their outputs are the same, h and f are the same. This is because the purpose of the learning is for prediction. However, in the applications discussed before, in many scenarios a learning model is for interpretation. For those scenarios, such an error function employed in a traditional learning algorithm can be misleading.

4 TRADITIONAL MACHINE LEARNING

When applying a machine learning algorithm, a practitioner is often instructed to pay attention to the model *overfitting* issue. Let D_T and D_V denote the training and validation datasets. Let $EmErr(h, D)$ be an error function to report an *empirical error rate* by applying a model h onto a dataset D. Let $e_T = EmErr(h, D_T)$ and $e_V = EmErr(h, D_V)$. In learning, a learning algorithm has only D_T to work on. Hence, the algorithm can try to improve on e_T but does not know what the resulting e_V might look like.

Figure 9: Underfitting Vs. Overfitting

Overfitting means that as the learning continues to improve on e_T, e_T and e_V deviate from each other and hence, the improvement does not translate to e_V. In contrast, *underfitting* means that e_T is high and hence there is still room for improvement. Fig. 9 illustrates these concepts where the x-axis can be thought of as the scale of "model improvement" based on D_T.

Refer back to Figure 8. A learning algorithm may have no knowledge regarding the actual hypothesis space H where the function f is drawn. For learning, the learning algorithm assumes its own hypothesis space H_L. When H_L is not properly assumed, for example its capacity is smaller than the capacity of H, it is possible that f is not included in H_L. In this case, there is no chance for $Err(h, f)$ to approach zero. This is another perspective to understand the concept of underfitting.

In practice, to avoid underfitting the learning begins with an assumed H_L whose capacity is as large as possible, for example as computationally-affordable as possible. This is because assuming a larger H_L usually means more computational overhead with the learning algorithm. Also, assuming a larger H_L means that more samples are needed to cover the entire hypothesis space. More importantly, with a H_L whose capacity is larger than the capacity of H, achieving a complete coverage on H_L might not be possible even with $|D_T| \rightarrow \infty$.

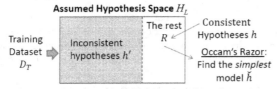

Figure 10: Occam's Razor in machine learning

For example, Figure 10 depicts such a situation. After a learning algorithm checks the hypotheses in the hypothesis space H_L against all samples in the training dataset D_T, the space can be divided into two subsets. The first includes all inconsistent hypotheses h', for example $EmErr(h', D_T) \neq 0$. Then, the rest R (called the *version space*) includes all consistent hypothesis h where $EmErr(h, D_T) = 0$. In overfitting, R contains more than one distinct answers even with $|D_T| \rightarrow \infty$ ("distinct" means existing one x where the two hypotheses result in two different y values). In practice R can contain a large number of distinct hypotheses after learning on D_T.

4.1 Occam's Razor

In machine learning, a common strategy to pick a model in R is based on the Occam's Razor principle, i.e. pick the "simplest" model as the answer. However, applying Occam's Razor requires a measure for model simplicity. Once this measure is defined, then picking the model in R becomes an optimization problem, i.e. optimizing the model according to the simplicity measure. Because such an optimization problem can be hard, a computationally-efficient heuristic is usually developed to tackle the problem.

In theory, there is some subtlety to apply the Occam's Razor principle in learning [25]. In practice, the definition of simplicity might or might not have a physical meaning in an application context. Hence, the simplest model does not guarantee on e_V. As a result, cross-validation is needed to evaluate the model even though it is considered as the optimal model by an algorithm.

4.2 Avoid overfitting

Ideally, avoiding underfitting and overfitting means to assume a H_L whose capacity is the same as H. However, this can be extremely difficult to accomplish in practice. In the context of feature-based analytics discussed before, underfitting can mean a required feature is not included in the initial feature set. Overfitting can mean there are features included where no data are available to tell their relevance. To avoid underfitting, one desires to begin with an initial feature set containing all possible features. However, this strategy can lead to a problem where there can be no sufficient data to find the exact answer (when all features are considered together).

From this perspective, the iterative search process in Figure 7 can be thought of as the search for the right hypothesis space H_L. Because the data are not sufficient for the search, the Analyst Layer is needed to assist the search based on domain knowledge.

5 ALTERNATIVE MACHINE LEARNING VIEW

As discussed in Section 4, a traditional machine learning algorithm is designed to find an optimal model that fits a dataset based on a given hypothesis space assumption. Such an approach provides little guarantee on its answer and hence, increases the burden of the model evaluation step in Figure 7. In addition, cross-validation is not a feasible option in most of the applications.

For feature-based analytics, the essence of the problem is finding the right hypothesis space assumption. From this perspective, it is desirable to design a machine learning tool that can automatically evaluate a hypothesis space assumption before finding a fitting model. With this in mind, an alternative view for the machine learning algorithm can be formulated as the following: To search for a *hypothesis space assumption* where there exists at least one hypothesis that can fit the samples in a given dataset but the assumption does not overfit the dataset.

It is interesting to note that in the traditional view, a machine learning algorithm can be for solving a constrained optimization problem. For example, in Figure 10, the constraints are due to the consistency requirement and the optimization objective is based on simplicity of the model. In the alternative view, the constraints are to fit the samples without overfitting. If there are multiple hypothesis spaces satisfying the constraints, choosing one could be based on a simplicity measure for the hypothesis spaces.

5.1 Search for a hypothesis space assumption

To implement a learning algorithm based on the alternative machine learning view, two definitions are required, a measure of simplicity for a given hypothesis space assumption, and a way to determine when overfitting occurs. Figure 11 illustrates the idea.

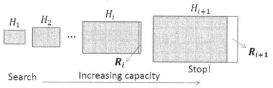

Figure 11: Search for a hypothesis space assumption

To implement a search, a sequence of hypothesis spaces H_1, H_2, $\ldots, H_i, H_{i+1}, \ldots$ are ordered with increasing capacity. The set R_i represents the set of consistent hypotheses (see Figure 10) in H_i based on a given dataset. In the figure, $R_1, \ldots, R_{i-1}$ are all empty, meaning that no hypothesis in those hypothesis spaces can be found to fit all the samples in the dataset (i.e. underfitting). H_i is the first hypothesis space where R_i is not empty. Depending on how overfitting is defined, the search may continue into H_{i+1}. For example, overfitting may be defined as $|R| > 10$, i.e. containing more than 10 consistent hypotheses. Then, if $|R_i| \leq 10$, the search continues to the next assumption H_{i+1}. When it is observed that $|R_{i+1}| > 10$ (i.e. overfitting), the search stops and the hypothesis space assumption H_i and its consistent hypotheses are reported.

A machine learning tool implementing the idea in Figure 11 can provide two advantages. First, the output includes a hypothesis space assumption used to derive the models. This provides an alternative measure for the quality of the models without cross-validation. Intuitively, the models are more reliable if the output hypothesis space is more complex. Second, it is possible that the tool results in a situation where R_{i-1} is empty and R_i is overfitting. In this case, the learning fails and no model is reported. This can be treated as an indication that the provided dataset is not appropriate for learning, and can immediately trigger another iteration in the search process in Figure 7, without involving the expensive model evaluation step.

6 AN INITIAL IMPLEMENTATION

One major challenge for implementing a learning tool following the idea presented in Figure 11 is to obtain an ordered sequence of hypothesis spaces. This ordering should be based on measuring the capacities of the hypothesis spaces. If a hypothesis space contains an infinite number of hypotheses, it is difficult to measure its capacity. In theory the capacity can be measured in terms of its VC dimension [22]. However, in practice the *effective capacity* of a hypothesis space is also limited by the learning algorithm [11], making its estimation quite difficult.

For applications discussed in Section 1, however, the number of features is limited. Moreover, the number of values a feature can take can be limited as well. Hence, for those applications we can assume that each feature has only a limited number of possible values. If we use a pseudo feature to represent a particular feature value, then we can further assume that all the features in use are binary, i.e. yes for the occurrence of the feature value and no otherwise.

Therefore, from a theoretical perspective the underlying learning problem can be treated as a Boolean learning problem.

6.1 Boolean learning

Given n features, the Boolean space contains 2^{2^n} Boolean functions. A hypothesis space is a set of Boolean functions in this space. Usually, a hypothesis space is specified with a representation. For example, a k-term DNF restricts the functions to those representable with k product terms. Each product term (also called a *monomial*) can have up to n literals (features in positive or negative forms).

For a given Boolean hypothesis space, its capacity can be measured in terms of the number of Boolean functions contained in the space. For example, in k-term DNF, let $B_1, \ldots, B_l$ be the hypothesis spaces representing 1-term DNF to l-term DNF, respectively. We see that $B_1 \subset B_2 \subset, \ldots, \subset B_l$, i.e. the larger the k is, the more general the hypothesis space is. Hence, focusing on a Boolean function representation enables us to implement the idea depicted in Fig. 11.

Assuming that the underlying learning problem is Boolean learning avoids the difficulty of measuring the capacity of an infinite hypothesis space. However, it does not avoid the computational hardness discussed in Section 3 before. For example, learning DNF formulas is as hard as solving a random K-SAT problem [7]. For k-term DNF, even for $k = 3$ the problem is hard [16] (hard to find a polynomial-time algorithm unless $\mathbf{RP} = \mathbf{NP}$. Note: $\mathbf{P} \subseteq \mathbf{RP} \subseteq \mathbf{NP}$ [17]). To avoid the known computational hardness, in our initial implementation we consider the simplest Boolean learning problem: learning *monomials*. From the perspective of Computational Learning Theory (CLT), monomials are efficiently learnable [16].

6.2 Monomial learning

Even though monomial learning is considered as an easy problem in CLT, it can still be a hard problem in view of Figure 11. In Fig. 8, consider that D is a uniform distribution. Suppose the true answer f is the monomial $f_1 \cdots f_j$ for a large j. It is likely that no positive sample is generated even for a large m, i.e. for all sample $\vec{x}$ produced by G we have $f(\vec{x}) = 0$. Consequently, the output model is simply the constant 0. From the CLT perspective, the constant 0 is a good model because the error probability for $f(\vec{x}) \neq 0$ on a randomly-drawn $\vec{x}$ is extremely low. However, in an application a constant 0 obviously means the learning has failed.

With the alternative learning view Figure 11, the concept of learnable is not based on an error function $Err()$. Instead, learnable can be viewed as achieving a small version space R_i (e.g. $|R_i| \leq 10$). With this change, monomial learning can be hard when the number of positive samples is small. In fact, if there is only one positive sample and many negative samples, finding the shortest monomial is NP-hard [12]. As mentioned in Section 1, some applications can have very few (or even zero) positive samples to learn from. Hence, the rest of discussion in this section will focus on the problem of learning monomials with few positive samples.

6.3 Hypothesis space pruning

By restricting the focus to monomial learning, the ordered sequence of hypothesis spaces in Figure 11 can be defined as $H_1, \ldots, H_n$ where n is the number of features. Each H_l comprises the monomials of length l. For example, H_1 comprises the monomials of length

1, i.e. $\{f_1, f'_1, f_2, f'_2, \ldots, f_n, f'_n\}$. H_2 comprises the monomials of length 2, which has $2^2 \binom{n}{2}$ monomials: For every pair of features f_i, f_j, where $i \neq j$, we have 2^2 monomials $\{f_i f_j, f'_i f_j, f_i f'_j, f'_i f'_j\}$. In general, H_l comprises $2^l \binom{n}{l}$ monomials.

For a given H_l and a dataset, our goal is to compute the version space R_l. This computation can be based on removing the monomials that are inconsistent with the samples. For example, suppose $n = 3$ and $l = 2$. A negative sample "001" removes the following hypotheses: $f'_1 f'_2, f'_1 f_3, f'_2 f_3$. A positive sample "100" removes all hypotheses except for: $f_1 f'_2, f_1 f'_3, f'_2 f'_3$. In general, a negative sample removes $\binom{n}{l}$ hypotheses while a positive sample removes all but the $\binom{n}{l}$ hypotheses. Therefore, the pruning power of a positive sample is larger than a negative sample.

Each sample can be treated as a constraint that removes a subset of hypotheses in a given space H_l. Suppose our definition of overfitting is that $|R_l| > 1$, i.e. the version space after the pruning can contain no more than one hypothesis. Then the pruning can be formulated as a Boolean Satisfiability (SAT) problem. A satisfiable assignment represents a monomial that is consistent with all samples. To check for overfitting, we need to invoke SAT twice. The first time is to find a satisfiable assignment A. Then, A is converted into a constraint to block itself. After this constraint is added to the SAT formula, if the result is unsatisfiable then we know A is the only satisfiable assignment. If not, we know $|R_l| > 1$.

6.4 SAT encoding

To convert the pruning problem into a SAT problem, we need three groups of CNF clauses: (1) clauses to constrain the monomial hypothesis space based on a given length l, (2) clauses to constrain the space based on negative samples, and (3) clauses to constrain the space based on positive samples. Let n be the number of variables, l be the length of monomial, m_p be the number of positive samples and m_n be the number of negative samples. Then, the encoding method described below results in a CNF formula with $\Theta(ln)$ symbols and $\Theta((l + m_p)n + m_n)$ clauses.

The key idea for the encoding is that each feature can appear in positive or negative, or does not appear in the monomial. Hence, three variables are used to represent these three cases for a feature:

- $X_{i,1}$ is True iff feature f_i appears in negative form
- $X_{i,2}$ is True iff feature f_i appears in positive form
- $X_{i,3}$ is True iff feature f_i does not appear

Since each feature can only be in one of the three cases, one-hot constraints are required to enforce the requirement:

$$\Pi_{i=i}^n (X_{i,1} + X_{i,2} + X_{i,3})(\neg X_{i,1} + \neg X_{i,2})$$
$$(\neg X_{i,1} + \neg X_{i,3})(\neg X_{i,2} + \neg X_{i,3})$$

For a given H_l, we need to constrain the space to contain only the monomial of length l. The performance of different encoding methods for a cardinality constraint can be found in [1]. In our implementation, we choose the sequential counter method [19] because its performance is comparable to other encoding methods and it has the unit propagation property[1]. The encoding for the cardinality constraint requires additional $l(n - 1)$ new symbols.

For each negative sample, one clause is used to encode its constraint. For example, suppose the negative sample is $f_1 f_2 f_3 = 001$. This means that the target monomial must have at least one feature

conflicting with this sample. In other words, the target monomial must satisfy at least one of the three cases: f_1 appear in positive form, or f_2 appear in positive form, or f_3 appear in negative form. Follow this observation, let $s_{i,j} \in \{0, 1\}$ be the value of feature f_j in sample i. The constraints from the m_n negative samples are encoded as m_n clauses:

$$\Pi_{i=1}^{m_n} (\Sigma_{j=1}^n X_{j, 2-s_{i,j}})$$

Similarly, suppose the positive sample is 100. Then the target monomial cannot have any of the three cases: feature f_1 appears in negative form, f_2 appears in positive form, and f_3 appears in positive form. Therefore, let $s_{i,j} \in \{0, 1\}$ be the value of feature f_j in sample i. The m_p positive samples are encoded as $m_p n$ clauses:

$$\Pi_{i=1}^{m_p} \Pi_{j=1}^n (\neg X_{j, 2-s_{i,j}}).$$

6.5 An experiment result

For detail of the implementation as well as other ideas to accomplish the search in the context of Boolean learning, please refer to [14]. In the following, we will use an experiment result to illustrate some of the interesting observations.

For the experiment, samples are generated uniformly randomly. The target monomial to learn is of length 5 and is chosen randomly from H_5. One of the recent SAT solvers is used [2]. Figure 12 shows the average run time (10 runs for each setup) by varying the n and l. The experiment is divided into three cases, with 0, 1, and 2 positive samples, respectively. The total number of samples is 1000.

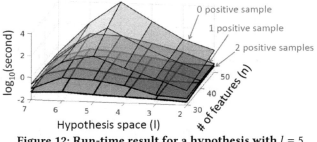

Figure 12: Run-time result for a hypothesis with $l = 5$

From the figure, we can observe the following: (1) The run time peaks at $l = 5$ which is the length of the target monomial. (2) The run time is affected significantly by the number of positive samples. (3) The number of features n also affects the run time but not as significant as the number of positive samples.

Overall, for all cases with $l < 5$, no satisfiable assignment is found. For all cases with $l > 5$, more than one satisfiable assignments can be found. For all cases with $l = 5$, the correct satisfiable assignment, corresponding to the target monomial, is identified. These results indicate that 1000 samples are more than enough to learn the target monomial. If we increase the target l and repeat the same experiment, in general we observe that learning a target monomial is limited not by the number of samples (assuming $n \geq 1000$), but by the SAT solver run time. In other words, for a large l, the run time could become unreasonable in practice (e.g. more than 12 hours). This means that computational resource can be more important for this type of learning than the number of samples. For more detailed discussion of this observation, please refer to [14].

7 LEARNING DOMAIN KNOWLEDGE

As discussed in Section 2.1, the Analyst Layer in Figure 7 relies on domain knowledge. To improve automation of the iterative model search process, learning the domain knowledge is required. For example, for functional verification the work in [13] develops an approach to identify important signal names and their relationships through text mining a design specification document. Those signal names can then be used to guide the feature selection step when Figure 7 is applied in the context of functional verification.

Another idea is presented in [18] where the analytic processes conducted by an analyst are recorded and learned. The result of this learning is a *process model* where each node in the model is an executable software script corresponding to a particular analytic task performed by the analyst. Figure 13 illustrates a process model learned from the analytic processes for the work described in [20]. An analytic task can be executed by following a path from the top node (start) to the bottom node (end).

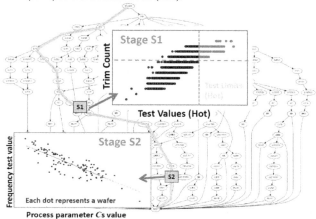

Figure 13: A process model capturing analyst's knowledge

For example, the figure shows two plots generated by a path executed from the process model. The application is to resolve the yield issue presented in Figure 6 before. In the first plot, each dot represents a chip. The first plot shows that all chips failing the hot test (red dots) have a high trim count. Because the trim count is known to be associated with a frequency test. The analysis continues based on the frequency test. In the second plot, it is shown that the frequency test values are highly correlated to a process parameter C. As a result, by pushing C to a larger value, we may reduce the frequency test value and consequently, reduce the trim count to avoid failing the hot test [18].

8 CONCLUSION

In this paper, we discuss a particular type of machine learning commonly employed in EDA applications, and give it the name *feature-based analytics*. Due to the various theoretical and practical reasons, feature-based analytics can be treated as an iterative model search process as depicted in Figure 7. The effectiveness of this search depends on the steps conducted in the Analyst Layer as well as on the design of the machine learning tools. For the machine learning tools, we explain the inadequacy to adopt a traditional machine learning problem formulation. Instead, an alternative machine learning view is proposed, and illustrated in Figure 11. The

initial idea to achieve this alternative learning view is presented. Then, to improve automation of the Analyst Layer, we introduce two ideas [13][18] for domain knowledge learning. More future research is required in order to fully automate the feature-based analytics approach for diverse EDA applications.

ACKNOWLEDGMENTS

This work is supported in part by National Science Foundation under grant No. 1618118 and in part by Semiconductor Research Corporation with project 2016-CT-2706.

REFERENCES

[1] Yael Ben-Haim, Alexander Ivrii, Oded Margalit, and Arie Matsliah. 2012. Perfect hashing and CNF encodings of cardinality constraints. In *International Conference on Theory and Applications of Satisfiability Testing*. Springer, 397–409.
[2] Armin Biere. 2013. Lingeling, Plingeling and Treengeling entering the SAT competition 2013. *Proceedings of SAT Competition* (2013).
[3] Nicholas Callegari, Dragoljub (Gagi) Drmanac, Li-C. Wang, and Magdy S. Abadir. 2013. Classification rule learning using subgroup discovery of cross-domain attributes responsible for design-silicon mismatch. *ACM/IEEE Design Automation Conference* (2013), 374–379.
[4] Janine Chen, Brendon Bolin, Li-C. Wang, Jing Zeng, Dragoljub (Gagi) Drmanac, , and Michael Mateja. 2010. Mining AC Delay Measurements for Understanding Speed-limiting Paths. *IEEE International Test Conference* (2010).
[5] Wen Chen, Li-C. Wang, and Jayanta Bhadra. 2013. Simulation Knowledge Extraction and Reuse in Constrained Random Processor Verification. *ACM/IEEE Design Automation Conference* (2013).
[6] Amit Daniely, Nati Linial, and Shai Shaleve-Shwartz. 2014. From average case complexity to improper learning complexity. *ACM Symposium on Theory of Computing* (2014), 441–448.
[7] Amit Daniely and Shai Shalev-Shwartz. 2016. Complexity Theoretic Limitations on Learning DNF's. *JMLP* 49 (2016), 1–16.
[8] G. Drmanac, F. Liu, and L-C. Wang. 2009. Predicting Variability in Nanoscale Lithography Processes. *ACM/IEEE Design Automation Conference* (2009).
[9] Janine Chen et al. 2009. Data learning techniques and methodology for Fmax prediction. *IEEE International Test Conference* (2009).
[10] Pedregosa et al. 2011. Scikit-learn: Machine Learning in Python. *JMLR* (2011), 2825–2830.
[11] Ian Goodfellow, Yoshua Benjio, and Aaron Courville. 2016. Deep Learning. *The MIT Press* (2016).
[12] David Haussler. 1998. Quantifying Inductive Bias: AI Learning Algorithms and Valiant's Learning Framework. *Artificial Intelligence* 36 (1998), 177–221.
[13] K-K. Hsieh, S. Siatkowski, Li-C. Wang, Wen Chen, and Jayanta Bhadra. Jan 2017. Feature Extraction from Design Documents to Enable Rule Learning for Improving Assertion Coverage. *ASP Design Automation Conference* (Jan 2017).
[14] K-K. Hsieh and Li-C. Wang. 2018. A Robust Learning Tool for Feature-Based Analytics with Limited Samples. *Tech. Report* (2018).
[15] Machael J. Kearns and Umesh Vazirani. 1994. Cryptographic limitations on learning Boolean formulae and finite automata. *JACM* 14, 1 (1994), 67–95.
[16] Machael J. Kearns and Umesh Vazirani. 1994. An Introduction to Computational Learning Theory. *The MIT Press* (1994).
[17] Rajeev Motwani and Prabhakar Raghavani. 1995. Randomized Algorithms. *Cambridge University Press* (1995).
[18] S. Siatkowski, Li-C. Wang, N. Sumikawa, and L. Winemberg. 2017. Learning the Process for Correlation Analysis. *IEEE VLSI Test Symposium* (2017).
[19] Carsten Sinz. 2005. Towards an optimal CNF encoding of boolean cardinality constraints. In *International Conference on Principles and Practice of Constraint Programming*. Springer, 827–831.
[20] Jeff Tikkanen, Sebastian Siatkowski, Nik Sumikawa, Li-C. Wang, and Magdy S. Abadir. 2014. Yield Optimization Using Advanced Statistical Correlation Methods. *IEEE International Test Conference* (2014).
[21] L. G. Valiant. 1984. A theory of learnable. *Communications of ACM* 27, 11 (1984), 1134–1142.
[22] Vladimir Vapnik. 2000. The Nature of Statistical Learning Theory. *Springer* (2000).
[23] Li-C. Wang. 2015. Data Mining in Functional Test Content Optimization. *ACM/IEEE Asian South Pacific Design Automation Conference* (2015).
[24] Li-C. Wang. 2017. Experience of Data Analytics in EDA and Test - Principles, Promises, and Challenges. *IEEE Trans. on CAD* 36, 6 (2017), 885–898.
[25] David H. Wolpert. 1990. The Relationship Between Occam's Razor and Convergent Guessing. *Complex System* 4 (1990), 319–368.
[26] David H. Wolpert. 1996. The Lack of A Priori Distinctions between Learning Algorithms. *Neural Compt.* 8, 7 (1996), 1341–1390.

Data Efficient Lithography Modeling with Residual Neural Networks and Transfer Learning

Yibo Lin
The University of Texas at Austin
yibolin@cerc.utexas.edu

Yuki Watanabe
Toshiba Memory Corporation
yuki9.watanabe@toshiba.co.jp

Taiki Kimura
Toshiba Memory Corporation
taiki2.kimura@toshiba.co.jp

Tetsuaki Matsunawa
Toshiba Memory Corporation
tetsuaki.matsunawa@toshiba.co.jp

Shigeki Nojima
Toshiba Memory Corporation
shigeki.nojima@toshiba.co.jp

Meng Li
The University of Texas at Austin
alfred@cerc.utexas.edu

David Z. Pan
The University of Texas at Austin
dpan@cerc.utexas.edu

ABSTRACT

Lithography simulation is one of the key steps in physical verification, enabled by the substantial optical and resist models. A resist model bridges the aerial image simulation to printed patterns. While the effectiveness of learning-based solutions for resist modeling has been demonstrated, they are considerably data-demanding. Meanwhile, a set of manufactured data for a specific lithography configuration is only valid for the training of one single model, indicating low data efficiency. Due to the complexity of the manufacturing process, obtaining enough data for acceptable accuracy becomes very expensive in terms of both time and cost, especially during the evolution of technology generations when the design space is intensively explored. In this work, we propose a new resist modeling framework for contact layers that utilizes existing data from old technology nodes to reduce the amount of data required from a target lithography configuration. Our framework based on residual neural networks and transfer learning techniques is effective within a competitive range of accuracy, i.e., 2-10X reduction on the amount of training data with comparable accuracy to the state-of-the-art learning approach.

ACM Reference Format:
Yibo Lin, Yuki Watanabe, Taiki Kimura, Tetsuaki Matsunawa, Shigeki Nojima, Meng Li, and David Z. Pan. 2018. Data Efficient Lithography Modeling with Residual Neural Networks and Transfer Learning . In *Proceedings of 2018 International Symposium on Physical Design (ISPD'18)*. ACM, New York, NY, USA, 8 pages. https://doi.org/10.1145/3177540.3178242

1 INTRODUCTION

Due to the continuous semiconductor scaling from $10nm$ technology node (N10) to $7nm$ node (N7) [10, 11], the prediction of printed pattern sizes is becoming increasingly difficult and complicated due to the complexity of manufacturing process and variations. However, complex designs demand accurate simulations to guarantee functionality and yield. Resist modeling, as a key component in

lithography simulation, is critical to bridge the aerial image simulation to manufactured wafer data. Rigorous simulations that perform physics-level modeling suffer from large computational overhead, which are not suitable when used extensively. Thus compact resist models are widely used in practice.

Figure 1(a) shows the process of lithography simulations where the optical model computes the aerial image from the input mask patterns and the resist model determines the output patterns from this. As the aerial image contains the light intensity map, the resist model needs to determine the slicing thresholds for the output patterns as shown in Figure 1(b). With the thresholds, the critical dimensions (CDs) of printed patterns can be computed, which need to match CDs measured from manufactured patterns. In practice, various factors may impact a resist model such as the physical properties of photoresist, design rules of patterns, process variations.

Accurate lithography simulation like rigorous physics-based simulation is notorious for its long computational time, while simulation with compact models suffers from accuracy issues [21, 25]. On the other hand, machine learning techniques are able to construct accurate models and then make efficient predictions. These approaches first take training data to calibrate a model and then use this model to make predictions on testing data for validation. The effectiveness of learning-based solutions has been studied in various lithography related areas including aerial image simulation [15], hotspot detection [13, 16, 22, 26, 28, 29], optical proximity correction (OPC) [5, 8, 14, 17], sub-resolution assist features (SRAF) [24, 27], resist modeling [21, 25], etc. In resist modeling, a convolutional neural network (CNN) that predicts slicing thresholds in aerial images is proposed [25]. The neural network consists of three convolution layers and two fully connected layers. Since the slicing threshold is a continuous value, learning a resist model is a regression task rather than a classification task. Around 70% improvement in accuracy is reported compared with calibrated compact models from Mentor Calibre [18]. Shim et al. [21] propose an artificial neural network (ANN) with five hidden layers to predict the height of resist after exposure. Significant speedup is reported with high accuracy compared with a rigorous simulation.

Although the learning-based approaches are able to achieve high accuracy, they are generally data-demanding in model training. In other words, big data is assumed to guarantee accuracy and generality. Furthermore, one data sample can only be used to train the

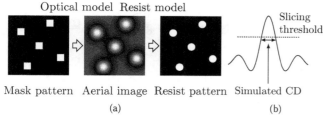

Figure 1: (a) Process of lithography simulation with optical and resist models. (b) Thresholds for aerial image determine simulated CD, which should match manufactured CD.

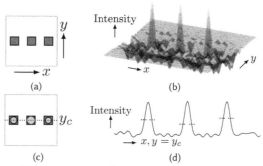

Figure 2: (a) Design target of 3 contacts and (b) the light intensity plot of aerial image. Assume that RETs such as SRAF and OPC have been already applied to the contacts before optical simulation. (c) A dotted line horizontally crosses the centers at $y = y_c$ and the circles denote the contours of printed patterns. (d) Light intensity profiling along the dotted line at $y = y_c$ extracted from the aerial image and different slicing thresholds for each contact.

corresponding model under the same lithography configuration, indicating a low data efficiency. Here data efficiency evaluates the accuracy a model can achieve given a specific amount of data, or the amount of data samples are required to achieve target accuracy. Nevertheless, obtaining a large amount of data is often expensive and time-consuming, especially when the technology node switches from one to another and the design space is under active exploration, e.g., from N10 to N7. The lithography configurations including optical sources, resist materials, etc., are frequently changed for experiments. Therefore, a fast preparation of models with high accuracy is urgently desired.

Different from previous approaches, in this work, we assume the availability of large amounts of data from the previous technology generation with old lithography configurations and small amounts of data from a target lithography configuration. We focus on increasing the data efficiency by reusing those from other lithography configurations and transfer the knowledge between different configurations. The objective is to achieve accurate resist models with significantly fewer data to a target configuration. The major contributions are summarized as follows.

- We propose a high performance resist modeling technique based on the residual neural network (ResNet).
- We propose a transfer learning scheme for ResNet that can reduce the amount of data with a target accuracy by utilizing the data from other configurations.
- We explore the impacts from various lithography configurations on the knowledge transfer.
- The experimental results demonstrate 2-10X reduction in the amount of training data to achieve accuracy comparable to the state-of-the-art learning approach [25].

The rest of the paper is organized as follows. Section 2 illustrates the problem formulation. Section 3 explains the details of our approach. The effectiveness of our approach is verified in Section 4 and the conclusion is drawn in Section 5.

2 PRELIMINARIES

In this section, we will briefly introduce the background knowledge on lithography simulation and resist modeling. Then the problem formulation is explained. We mainly focus on contact layers in this work, but our methodology shall be applicable to other layers.

2.1 Lithography Simulation

Lithography simulation is generally composed of two stages, i.e., optical simulation and resist simulation, where optical and resist models are required, respectively. In the optical simulation, an optical model, characterized by the illumination tool, takes mask patterns to

compute aerial images, i.e., light intensity maps. Then in the resist simulation, a resist model finalizes the resist patterns with the aerial images from the optical simulation. Generally, there are two types of resist models. One is a variable threshold resist (VTR) model in which the thresholds vary according to aerial images, and the other is a constant threshold resist (CTR) model in which the light intensity is modulated in an aerial image. We adopt the former since it is suitable to learning-based approaches [25].

Figure 2 shows an example of lithography simulation for a clip with three contacts. We assume that proper resolution enhancement techniques (RETs) such as OPC and SRAF have been applied before the computation of the aerial image [12]. The optical simulation generates the aerial image, as shown in Figure 2(b). Resist simulation then computes the thresholds in the aerial image to predict printed patterns. If we consider the horizontal sizes of contacts along the dotted line in Figure 2(c), the light intensity profiling can be extracted from the aerial image along the line and calculates the CDs for each contact with the thresholds.

2.2 Historical Data and Transfer Learning

Since the lithography configurations evolve from one generation to another with the advancement of technology nodes, there are plenty of historical data available for the old generation. As mentioned in Section 1, accurate models require a large amount of data for training or calibration, which are expensive to obtain during the exploration of a new generation. If the lithography configurations have no fundamental changes, the knowledge learned from the historical data may still be applicable to the new configuration, which can eventually help to reduce the amount of new data required.

Transfer learning represents a set of techniques to transfer the knowledge from one or multiple source domains to a target domain, utilizing the underlying similarity between the data from these domains. Various studies have explored the effectiveness of knowledge transfer in image recognition and robotics [6, 19, 20], while it is not clear whether the knowledge between different resist models is transferable or not.

In this work, we consider the evolution of the contact layer from the cutting edge technology node N10 to N7 [10, 11]. A large amount

Table 1: Lithography Configurations for N10 and N7

	N10	N7	
		$N7_a$	$N7_b$
Design Rule	A	B	B
Optical Source	A	B	B
Resist Material	A	A	B

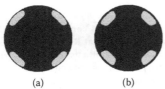

(a)   (b)

Figure 3: Optical sources (yellow) for (a) N10 and (b) N7.

of available N10 data are assumed. During the evolution to N7, different design rules for mask patterns, optical sources and resist materials for lithography are explored. Table 1 shows the lithography configurations considered for N10 and N7. Differences in letters A, B represent different configurations of design rules, optical sources, or resist materials. One configuration for N10 is considered, while two configurations are considered for N7, i.e., $N7_a$, $N7_b$, with two kinds of resist materials (about 20% difference in the slopes of dissolution curves). From N10 to N7, both the design rules and optical sources are changed. For N10, we consider a pitch of $64nm$ with double patterning lithography, while for N7, the pitch is set to $45nm$ with triple patterning lithography [10]. The width of each contact is set to half pitch. The lithography target of each contact is set to $60nm$ for both N10 and N7. Optical sources calibrated with industrial strength for N10 and N7 are shown in Figure 3, with the same type of illumination shapes.

Various combinations of knowledge transfer can be explored from Table 1, such as N10→N7, $N7_i$→$N7_j$, and N10+$N7_i$→$N7_j$, where $i \neq j, i, j \in \{a, b\}$.

2.3 Learning-based Resist Modeling

The thresholds of positions near the contacts are of significant importance since they usually determine the boundaries of printed contacts. Hence we consider the middle of the left, right, bottom and top edges for each contact, as shown in Figure 4(a), where the positions for prediction are highlighted with black dots. In addition, the threshold is mainly influenced by the surrounding mask patterns. Therefore, resist models typically compute the threshold using a clip of mask patterns centered by a target position. To measure the thresholds in Figure 4(a), we select a clip where the target position lies in its center, as shown in Figure 4(b) to Figure 4(e). The task of a resist model is to compute the thresholds for these positions of each contact [25].

Learning-based resist modeling consists of two phases, training and testing. In the training phase, training dataset with both aerial images and thresholds are used to calibrate the model, while in the testing phase, the model predicts thresholds for the aerial images from the testing dataset and compares with the golden thresholds to validate the model.

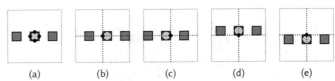

(a)   (b)   (c)   (d)   (e)

Figure 4: (a) The thresholds for the middle of the 4 edges of the center contact are predicted. (b) (c) (d) (e) The clip window is shifted such that the target position lies in the center of the clip.

2.4 Problem Formulation

The accuracy[1] of a model is evaluated with root mean square (RMS) error defined as follows,

$$\epsilon = \sqrt{\frac{1}{N} \sum_{i=1}^{N} (\hat{y} - y)^2}, \tag{1}$$

where N denotes the amount of samples, y denotes the golden values and $\hat{y}$ denotes the predicted values. We further define relative RMS error,

$$\epsilon_r = \sqrt{\frac{1}{N} \sum_{i=1}^{N} (\frac{\hat{y} - y}{y})^2}, \tag{2}$$

where a relative ratio of error from the golden values can be represented. Both metrics can refer to errors in either CD or threshold. Although during model training, the RMS error of threshold is generally minimized due to easier computation, the eventual model is often evaluated with the RMS error of CD for its physical meaning to the patterns. The RMS errors in threshold and CD essentially have almost the same fidelity, and usually yield consistent comparison. For convenience, we report relative RMS error in threshold (ϵ_r^{th}) for comparison of different models since it removes the dependency to the scale of thresholds, and use RMS error in CD (ϵ^{CD}) for data efficiency related comparison.

Definition 1 (Data Efficiency). *The amount of target domain data required to learn a model with a given accuracy.*

Given a specific amount of data from a target domain, if one can learn a model with a higher accuracy than another, it also indicates higher data efficiency. Thus improving model accuracy benefits data efficiency as well.

The resist modeling problem is defined as follows.

Problem 1 (Learning-based Resist Modeling). *Given a dataset containing information of aerial images and thresholds at their centers, train a resist model that can maximize the accuracy for the prediction of thresholds.*

In practice, accuracy is not the only objective. The amount of training data should be minimized as well due to the high cost of data preparation. Therefore, we propose the problem of data efficient resist modeling as follows.

Problem 2 (Data Efficient Resist Modeling). *Given datasets from N10 and N7 containing information of aerial images and thresholds, train a resist model for target dataset $N7_i$ that can achieve high accuracy and meanwhile minimize the amount of data required for $N7_i$, where $i \in \{a, b\}$.*

---

[1]Note that the accuracy we talk about in this paper refers to the accuracy at end of lithography flow including all RETs.

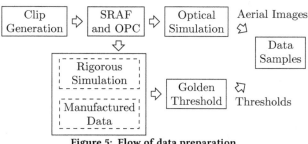

Figure 5: Flow of data preparation.

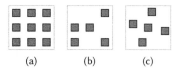

(a)   (b)   (c)

Figure 6: (a) A clip of 3×3 contact array. (b) A clip of 3×3 randomized contact array. (c) A clip of contacts with random positions.

3 ALGORITHMS

In this section, we will explain the structure of our models and then the details regarding the transfer learning scheme.

3.1 Data Preparation

Figure 5 gives the flow of data preparation. We first generate clips and perform SRAF insertion and OPC. The aerial images are then computed from the optical simulation, and at the same time, the golden thresholds need to be computed from either the rigorous simulation or the manufactured data. Each data sample consists of an aerial image and the threshold at its center.

3.1.1 Clip Generation. Following the design rules such as minimum pitch of contacts, we generate three types of $2 \times 2\mu m$ clips. It is necessary to ensure that there is a contact in the center of each clip since that is the target contact for threshold computation.

Contact Array. All possible $m \times n$ arrays of contacts within the dimensions of clips are enumerated. The steps of the arrays can be multiple times of the minimum pitch p, i.e., $p, 2p, 3p, \ldots$, in horizontal or vertical directions. An example of 3×3 contact array with a certain pitch is shown in Figure 6(a). It needs to mention that the same 3×3 contact array with different steps should be regarded as different clips due to discrepant spacing.

Randomized Contact Array. The aforementioned contact arrays essentially distribute contacts on grids and fill all the slots in the grid maps. The randomization of contact arrays is implemented by a random distribution of contacts in those grid maps. Fig 6(b) shows an example of randomized contact array from the 3×3 contact array in Figure 6(a). Various distribution of contacts can be generated even from the same grid maps.

Contacts with Random Positions. Contacts in this type of clips do not necessarily align to any grid map, as their positions are randomly generated, while the design rules are still guaranteed. An example is shown in Figure 6(c). No matter how the surrounding contacts change, the contact in the center of the clip should remain the same.

3.1.2 Data Augmentation. Due to the symmetry of optical sources in Figure 3, data can be augmented with rotation and flipping, improving the data efficiency [4]. Eight combinations of rotation and flipping are shown in Figure 7, where new data samples are obtained

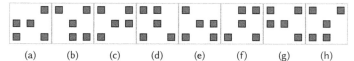

(a)   (b)   (c)   (d)   (e)   (f)   (g)   (h)

Figure 7: Combinations of rotation and flipping. (a) Original. (b) Rotate $90°$. (c) Rotate $180°$. (d) Rotate $270°$. (a) Flip. (b) Flip and rotate $90°$. (c) Flip and rotate $180°$. (d) Flip and rotate $270°$.

without new thresholds. Data augmentation inflates datasets to obtain models with better generalization.

3.2 Convolutional Neural Networks

Convolutional neural networks (CNN) have demonstrated impressive performance on mask related applications in lithography such as hotspot detection, and resist modeling [25, 29]. The structure of CNN mainly includes convolution layers and fully connected layers. Features are extracted from convolution layers and then classification or regression is performed by fully connected layers. Figure 10(a) illustrates a CNN structure with three convolution layers and two fully connected layers [25]. The first convolution layer has 64 filters with dimensions of 7×7. Although not explicitly shown most of the time, a rectified linear unit (ReLU) layer for activation is applied immediately after the convolution layer, where the ReLU function is defined as,

$$x^l = \begin{cases} x^{l-1}, & \text{if } x^{l-1} \geq 0, \\ 0, & \text{otherwise.} \end{cases} \quad (3)$$

Then the max-pooling layer performs down-sampling with a factor of 2 to reduce the feature dimensions and improve the invariance to translation [4]. After three convolution layers, two fully connected layers are applied where the first one has 256 hidden units followed with a ReLU layer and a 50% dropout layer, and second one connects to the output.

3.3 Residual Neural Networks

One way to improve the performance of CNN is to increase the depth for a larger capacity of the neural networks. However, the counterintuitive degradation of training accuracy in CNN is observed when stacking more layers, preventing the neural networks from better performance [7]. An example of CNNs with 5 and 10 layers is shown in Figure 8, where the deeper CNN fails to converge to a smaller training error than the shallow one due to gradient vanishing [2, 3], eventually resulting in the failure to achieve a better testing error either. The study from He et al. [7] reveals that the underlying reason comes from the difficulty of identity mapping. In other words, fitting a hypothesis $\mathcal{H}(x) = x$ is considerably difficult for solvers to find optimal solutions. To overcome this issue, residual neural networks (ResNet), which utilizes shortcut connections, are adopted to assist the convergence of training accuracy.

The building block of ResNet is illustrated in Figure 9, where a shortcut connection is inserted between the input and output of two convolution layers. Let the function $\mathcal{F}(x)$ be the mapping defined by the two convolution layers. Then the entire function for the building block becomes $\mathcal{F}(x) + x$. Suppose the building block targets to fit the hypothesis $\mathcal{H}(x)$. The residual networks train $\mathcal{F}(x) = \mathcal{H}(x) - x$, while the convolution layers without shortcut connections like that in CNN try to directly fit $\mathcal{F}(x) = \mathcal{H}(x)$. Theoretically, if $\mathcal{H}(x)$ can be approximated with $\mathcal{F}(x)$, then it can also be approximated with $\mathcal{F}(x) + x$. Despite the same nature, comprehensive experiments have

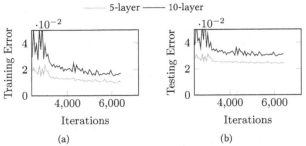

(a) (b)

Figure 8: Counterintuitive (a) training and (b) testing errors for different depth of CNN with epochs.

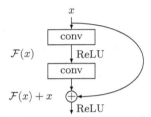

Figure 9: Building block of ResNet.

demonstrated a better convergence of ResNet than that of CNN for deep neural networks [7]. We also observe a better performance of ResNet with the transfer learning schemes than that of CNN in our problem, which has never been explored before.

The ResNet is shown in Figure 10(b) with 8 convolution layers and 2 fully connected layers. Different from the original setting [7], we add a shortcut connection to the first convolution layer by broadcasting the input tensor of $64 \times 64 \times 1$ to $64 \times 64 \times 64$. This minor change enables better empirical results in our problem. For the rest of the networks, 3 building blocks for ResNet are utilized.

3.4 Transfer Learning

Transfer learning aims at adapting the knowledge learned from data in source domains to a target domain. The transferred knowledge will benefit the learning in the target domain with a faster convergence and better generalization [4]. Suppose the data in the source domain has a distribution P_s and that in the target domain has a distribution P_t. The underlying assumption of transfer learning lies in the common factors that need to be captured for learning the variations of P_s and P_t, so that the knowledge for P_s is also useful for P_t. An intuitive example is that learning to recognize cats and dogs in the source task helps the recognition of ants and wasps in the target task, especially when the source task has significantly larger dataset than that of the target task. The reason comes from the low-level notions of edges, shapes, etc., shared by many visual categories [4]. In resist modeling, different lithography configurations can be viewed as separate tasks with different distributions.

Typical transfer learning scheme for neural networks fixes the first several layers of the model trained for another domain and finetune the successive layers with data from the target domain. The first several layers usually extract general features, which are considered to be similar between the source and the target domains, while the successive layers are classifiers or regressors that need to be adjusted. Figure 11 shows an example of the transfer learning scheme. We first train a model with source domain data and then use the source domain model as the starting point for the training of the target domain. During the training for the target domain, the first k layers

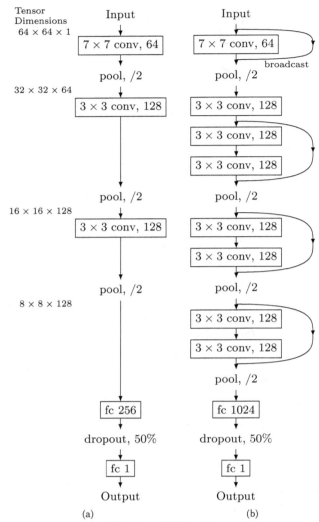

(a) (b)

Figure 10: (a) CNN and (b) ResNet structure.

are fixed, while the rest layers are finetuned. We denote this scheme as TF_k, shortened from "Transfer and Fix", where k is the parameter for the number of fixed layers.

4 EXPERIMENTAL RESULTS

Our framework is implemented with Tensorflow [1] and validated on a Linux server with 3.4GHz Intel i7 CPU and Nvidia GTX 1080 GPU. Around 980 mask clips are generated according to Section 3.1 for N10 and N7 separately following the design rules in Section 2.2, respectively. N7$_a$ and N7$_b$ use the same set of clips, but different lithography configurations. SRAF, OPC and aerial image simulation are performed with Mentor Calibre [18]. The golden CD values are obtained from rigorous simulation using Synopsys Sentaurus Lithography models [23] calibrated from manufactured data for N10, N7$_a$, and N7$_b$ according to Table 1. Then golden thresholds are extracted. Each clip has four thresholds as shown in Figure 4. Hence the N10 dataset contains 3928 samples and each N7 dataset contains 3916 samples, respectively. The data augmentation technique in Section 3.1.2 is applied, so the training set and the testing set will be augmented by a factor of 8 independently. For example, if 50% of the data for N10

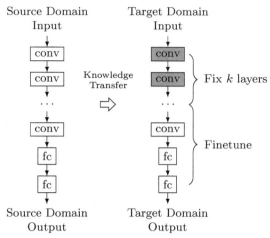

Figure 11: Transfer learning scheme with the first k layers fixed when training for target domain, denoted as TF_k.

are used for training, then there are 3928×50%×8 = 15712 samples. It needs to mention that always the same 50% portions are used during the validation of a dataset for fair comparison of different techniques. The batch size is set to 32 for training accommodating to the large variability in the sizes of training datasets. Adam [9] is used as the stochastic optimizer and maximum epoch is set to 200 for training.

The training time for one model takes 10 to 40 minutes according to the portions of a dataset used for training, and prediction time for an entire N10 or N7 dataset takes less than 10 seconds, while the rigorous simulation takes more than 15 hours for each N10 or N7 dataset. Thus we no longer report the prediction time which is negligible compared with that of the rigorous simulation. Each experiment runs 10 different random seeds and averages the numbers.

4.1 CNN and ResNet

We first compare CNN and ResNet in Figure 12(a). Column "CNN-5" denotes the network with 5 layers shown in Figure 10(a). Column "CNN-10" denotes the one with 10 layers that has the same structure as that in Figure 10(b) but without shortcut connections. Column "ResNet" denotes the one with 10 layers shown in Figure 10(b). When using 1% to 20% training data, ResNet shows better average relative RMS error ϵ_r^{th} than CNN-10, but CNN-5 provides the best error. We will show later that ResNet on the contrary outperforms CNN-5 when transfer learning is incorporated.

The impacts of depth on the performance of ResNet are further explored in Figure 12(b), where we gradually stack more building blocks in Figure 9 before fully connected layers. The x-axis denotes total number of convolution and fully connected layers corresponding to different numbers of building blocks. For instance, 0 building block leads to 4 layers and 3 building blocks result in 10 layers (Figure 10(b)). The testing error decreases to lowest value at 10 layers and then starts to increase, indicating potential overfitting afterwards [4]. Therefore, we use 10 layers for the ResNet in the experiment.

4.2 Knowledge Transfer From N10 to N7

We then compare the testing accuracy between knowledge transfer from N10 to N7 and directly training from N7 datasets in Figure 13(a). In this example, the x-axis represents the percentage of training dataset for the target domain $N7_a$, while the percentage of data

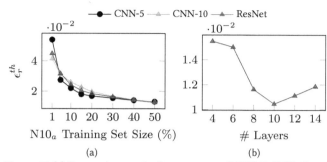

Figure 12: (a) Comparison on testing accuracy of CNN-5, CNN-10, and ResNet on N10. (b) Impact of depth on the testing accuracy of ResNet.

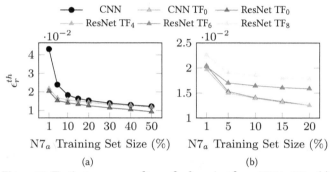

Figure 13: Testing accuracy of transfer learning from N10 to $N7_a$. (a) Comparison between CNN and transfer learning. (b) Comparison between transfer learning schemes where different numbers of layers are fixed.

from the source domain N10 is always 50%. Similar trends are also observed for $N7_b$. Curve "CNN" denotes training the CNN of 5 layers in Figure 10(a) with data from target domain only, i.e., no transfer learning involved. Curve "CNN TF_0" denotes the transfer learning scheme in Section 3.4 for the same CNN with zero layer fixed. Curve "ResNet TF_0" denotes applying the same scheme to ResNet. The most significant benefit of transfer learning comes from small training dataset with a range of 1% to 20%, where there are around 52% to 18% improvement in the accuracy from CNN. Meanwhile, ResNet TF_0 can achieve an average of 13% smaller error than CNN TF_0.

Figure 13(b) further compares the results of fixing different numbers of layers during transfer learning. In this case, ResNet TF_0 and ResNet TF_4 have the best accuracy, while the error increases with more layers fixed. It is indicated that the tasks N10 and N7 are quite different and both feature extraction layers and regression layers need finetuning.

4.3 Knowledge Transfer within N7

The transfer learning between different N7 datasets, e.g., from $N7_a$ to $N7_b$, is also explored in Figure 14. The x-axis represents the percentage of training dataset for the target domain $N7_b$, while the percentage of data from the source domain $N7_a$ is always 50%. Compared with the knowledge transfer from N10 to N7, we achieve even higher accuracy between 1% and 20% training datasets in Figure 14(a). For example, with 1% training dataset, there is around 65% improvement in accuracy from CNN, and with 20% training dataset, the improvement is around 23%. ResNet TF_0 keeps having lower errors than that of CNN TF_0 as well, with an average benefit around 15%.

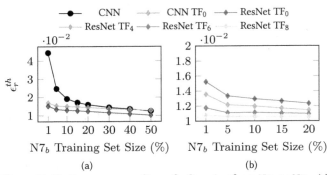

Figure 14: Testing accuracy of transfer learning from $N7_a$ to $N7_b$. (a) Comparison between CNN and transfer learning. (b) Comparison between transfer learning schemes where different numbers of layers are fixed.

The curves in Figure 14(b) show different insights from that of the knowledge transfer from N10 to N7. The accuracy of ResNet TF_0 can be further improved with more layers fixed, e.g., ResNet TF_8, by around 28% to 14%. This is reasonable since $N7_a$ and $N7_b$ have the same design rules and illumination shapes, and the only difference lies in the resist materials. Therefore, the feature extraction layers are supposed to remain almost the same. With the sizes of the training dataset increasing to 15% and 20%, the differences in the accuracy become smaller, because there are enough data to find good configurations for the networks.

4.4 Impact of Various Source Domains

In transfer learning, the correlation between the datasets of source and target domains is critical to the effectiveness of knowledge transfer. Thus, we explore the impacts of source domain datasets on the accuracy of modeling for the target domain. Figure 15 plots the testing errors of learning $N7_b$ using ResNet TF_0 with various source domain datasets. Curves "$N10^{50\%}$" and "$N7_a^{50\%}$" indicate that 50% of the N10 or the $N7_a$ dataset is used to train source domain models, respectively. Curve "$N10^{50\%} + N7_a^{1\%}$" describes the situation where we have 50% of the N10 dataset and 1% of the $N7_a$ dataset for training. In this case, as shown in Figure 16, we first use the 50% N10 data to train the first source domain model; then train the second source domain model using the first model as the starting point with the 1% $N7_a$ data; in the end, the target domain model for $N7_b$ is trained using the second model as the starting point with $N7_b$ data. Curves "$N10^{50\%} + N7_a^{5\%}$" and "$N10^{50\%} + N7_a^{10\%}$" are similar, simply with different amounts of $N7_a$ data for training.

The knowledge from $N7_a^{50\%}$ is the most effective for $N7_b$ due to the minor difference in resist materials between two datasets. For the rest curves, the accuracy of $N10^{50\%} + N7_a^{5\%}$ and $N10^{50\%} + N7_a^{10\%}$ is in general better than or at least comparable to that of $N10^{50\%}$. This indicates that having more data from closer datasets to the target dataset, e.g., $N7_a$, is still helpful.

4.5 Improvement in Data Efficiency

Table 2 presents the accuracy metrics, i.e., relative threshold RMS error (ϵ_r^{th}) and CD RMS error (ϵ^{CD}), for learning $N7_b$ from various source domain datasets. Since we consider the data efficiency of different learning schemes, we focus on the small training dataset for $N7_b$, from 1% to 20%. Situations such as no source domain data ($\emptyset$), only source domain data from N10 ($N10^{50\%}$), only source domain

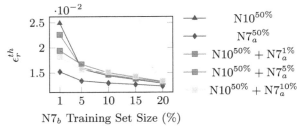

Figure 15: Testing accuracy of ResNet TF_0 for $N7_b$ from different source domain datasets.

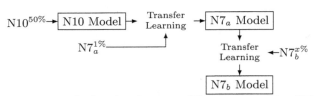

Figure 16: Transfer learning from 50% of N10 dataset and 1% of $N7_a$ dataset (i.e., $N10^{50\%} + N7_a^{1\%}$) to $N7_b$ with x% of $N7_b$ dataset.

data from $N7_a$ ($N7_a^{50\%}$), and combined source domain datasets, are examined. As mentioned in Section 2, the fidelity between relative threshold RMS error and CD RMS error is very consistent, so they share almost the same trends. Transfer learning with any source domain dataset enables an average improvement of 23% to 40% from that without knowledge transfer. In small training datasets of $N7_b$, ResNet also achieves around 8% better performance on average than CNN in the transfer learning scheme. At 1% of $N7_b$, combined source domain datasets have better performance compared with $N10^{50\%}$ only, but the benefits vanish with the increase of the $N7_b$ dataset.

In real manufacturing, models are usually calibrated to satisfy a target accuracy or target CD RMS error. Figure 17 demonstrates the amount of training data required in the target domain for learning the $N7_b$ model. Curve "CNN" does not involve any knowledge transfer, while curves "CNN TF_0" and "ResNet TF_0" utilize transfer learning in CNN and ResNet, respectively. The curves in Fig 17(a) assume the availability of N10 data. Consider the CD RMS error from $1.5nm$ to $2.5nm$, which is around 10% of the half pitch for N7 contacts. This range of accuracy is also comparable to that of the state-of-the-art CNN [25]. ResNet TF_0 requires significantly fewer data than both CNN and CNN TF_0. For instance, when the target CD error is $1.75nm$, ResNet TF_0 demands 5% training data from $N7_b$, while CNN requires 20% and CNN TF_0 requires 15%. Figure 17(b) considers the transfer from $N7_a$ to $N7_b$. Both ResNet TF_0 and CNN TF_0 only require 1% training data from $N7_b$ for most target CD RMS errors, where CNN TF_0 cannot achieve the accuracy unless given 30% data. Overall, ResNet TF_0 can achieve 2-10X reduction of training data within this range compared with CNN. It needs to mention that 1% of dataset only correspond to fewer than 40 samples owing to the data augmentation, indicating only thresholds of 40 clips are required.

5 CONCLUSION

A transfer learning framework based on residual neural networks is proposed for resist modeling. The combination of ResNet and transfer learning is able to achieve high accuracy with very few data from the target domains, under various situations for knowledge transfer, indicating high data efficiency. Extensive experiments demonstrate that the proposed techniques can achieve 2-10X reduction according to various requirements of accuracy comparable to the state-of-the-art

Table 2: Relative Threshold RMS Error and CD RMS Error for $N7_b$ with Different Source Domain Datasets

Source Datasets		$\emptyset$		$N10^{50\%}$				$N7_a^{50\%}$				$N10^{50\%} + N7_a^{5\%}$		$N10^{50\%} + N7_a^{10\%}$	
Neural Networks		CNN		CNN TF$_0$		ResNet TF$_0$		CNN TF$_0$		ResNet TF$_0$		ResNet TF$_0$		ResNet TF$_0$	
		ϵ_r^{th} (10^{-2})	ϵ^{CD}	ϵ_r^{th} (10^{-2})	ϵ^{CD}	ϵ_r^{th} (10^{-2})	ϵ^{CD}	ϵ_r^{th} (10^{-2})	ϵ^{CD}	ϵ_r^{th} (10^{-2})	ϵ^{CD}	ϵ_r^{th} (10^{-2})	ϵ^{CD}	ϵ_r^{th} (10^{-2})	ϵ^{CD}
$N7_b$	1%	4.44	4.76	2.34	2.48	2.29	2.39	1.69	1.79	1.52	1.60	1.94	2.03	1.82	1.91
	5%	2.78	2.96	1.73	1.86	1.60	1.70	1.53	1.64	1.34	1.43	1.67	1.78	1.57	1.67
	10%	1.92	2.04	1.63	1.76	1.47	1.57	1.50	1.60	1.30	1.38	1.50	1.60	1.51	1.61
	15%	1.72	1.84	1.56	1.68	1.39	1.47	1.48	1.55	1.27	1.35	1.41	1.50	1.43	1.52
	20%	1.60	1.71	1.50	1.61	1.31	1.39	1.44	1.55	1.23	1.31	1.32	1.41	1.34	1.43
ratio		1.00	1.00	0.77	0.77	0.70	0.69	0.69	0.69	0.60	0.60	0.69	0.69	0.69	0.68

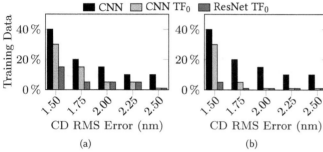

(a)   (b)

Figure 17: Amount of training data required for $N7_b$ given target CD RMS errors when (a) 50% N10 dataset is available or (b) 50% $N7_a$ dataset is available.

learning approach. It is also shown that the performance of transfer learning differs from dataset to dataset and is worth exploring to see the correlation between datasets. Examining the quantitative relation between the correlation of datasets and performance of transfer learning is valuable in the future.

ACKNOWLEDGE

This project is supported in part by Toshiba Memory Corporation, NSF, and the University Graduate Continuing Fellowship from the University of Texas at Austin. The authors would like to thank Memory Lithography Group from Toshiba Memory Corporation for helpful discussions and feedback.

REFERENCES

[1] Martín Abadi, Ashish Agarwal, Paul Barham, Eugene Brevdo, Zhifeng Chen, et al. 2015. TensorFlow: Large-Scale Machine Learning on Heterogeneous Systems. (2015). https://www.tensorflow.org
[2] Yoshua Bengio, Patrice Simard, and Paolo Frasconi. 1994. Learning long-term dependencies with gradient descent is difficult. *IEEE transactions on neural networks* 5, 2 (1994), 157–166.
[3] Xavier Glorot and Yoshua Bengio. 2010. Understanding the difficulty of training deep feedforward neural networks. In *Proceedings of the Thirteenth International Conference on Artificial Intelligence and Statistics*. 249–256.
[4] Ian Goodfellow, Yoshua Bengio, and Aaron Courville. 2016. *Deep learning*. MIT press.
[5] Allan Gu and Avideh Zakhor. 2008. Optical proximity correction with linear regression. *IEEE Transactions on Semiconductor Manufacturing (TSM)* 21, 2 (2008), 263–271.
[6] Josiah P Hanna and Peter Stone. 2017. Grounded Action Transformation for Robot Learning in Simulation.. In *AAAI*. 3834–3840.
[7] Kaiming He, Xiangyu Zhang, Shaoqing Ren, and Jian Sun. 2016. Deep residual learning for image recognition. In *Proceedings of the IEEE conference on computer vision and pattern recognition*. 770–778.
[8] Ningning Jia and Edmund Y Lam. 2010. Machine learning for inverse lithography: using stochastic gradient descent for robust photomask synthesis. *Journal of Optics* 12, 4 (2010), 045601.
[9] Diederik Kingma and Jimmy Ba. 2014. Adam: A method for stochastic optimization. *arXiv preprint arXiv:1412.6980* (2014).
[10] Lars Liebmann, Albert Chu, and Paul Gutwin. 2015. The daunting complexity of scaling to 7nm without EUV: Pushing DTCO to the extreme. In *Proceedings of SPIE*, Vol. 9427.
[11] Lars Liebmann, Jia Zeng, Xuelian Zhu, Lei Yuan, Guillaume Bouche, and Jongwook Kye. 2016. Overcoming scaling barriers through design technology CoOptimization. In *VLSI Technology, 2016 IEEE Symposium on*. IEEE, 1–2.
[12] Lars W Liebmann, Scott M Mansfield, Alfred K Wong, Mark A Lavin, William C Leipold, and Timothy G Dunham. 2001. TCAD development for lithography resolution enhancement. *IBM Journal of Research and Development* 45, 5 (2001), 651–665.
[13] Yibo Lin, Xiaoqing Xu, Jiaojiao Ou, and David Z Pan. 2017. Machine learning for mask/wafer hotspot detection and mask synthesis. In *Photomask Technology*, Vol. 10451. International Society for Optics and Photonics, 104510A.
[14] Rui Luo. 2013. Optical proximity correction using a multilayer perceptron neural network. *Journal of Optics* 15, 7 (2013), 075708.
[15] Xu Ma, Xuejiao Zhao, Zhiqiang Wang, Yanqiu Li, Shengjie Zhao, and Lu Zhang. 2017. Fast lithography aerial image calculation method based on machine learning. *Applied Optics* 56, 23 (2017), 6485–6495.
[16] Tetsuake Matsunawa, Shigeke Nojima, and Toshiya Kotani. 2016. Automatic Layout Feature Extraction for Lithography Hotspot Detection Based on Deep Neural Network. In *Proceedings of SPIE*.
[17] Tetsuaki Matsunawa, Bei Yu, and David Z Pan. 2016. Optical proximity correction with hierarchical Bayes model. *Journal of Micro/Nanolithography, MEMS, and MOEMS* 15, 2 (2016), 021009–021009.
[18] Mentor Graphics. 2008. Calibre Verification User's Manual. (2008).
[19] Sinno Jialin Pan and Qiang Yang. 2010. A survey on transfer learning. *IEEE Transactions on knowledge and data engineering* 22, 10 (2010), 1345–1359.
[20] Andrei A Rusu, Neil C Rabinowitz, Guillaume Desjardins, Hubert Soyer, James Kirkpatrick, Koray Kavukcuoglu, Razvan Pascanu, and Raia Hadsell. 2016. Progressive neural networks. *arXiv preprint arXiv:1606.04671* (2016).
[21] Seongbo Shim, Suhyeong Choi, and Youngsoo Shin. [n. d.]. Machine Learning-Based Resist 3D Model. In *Proc. of SPIE Vol*, Vol. 10147. 101471D–1.
[22] Moojoon Shin and Jee-Hyong Lee. 2016. Accurate Lithography Hotspot Detection Using Deep Convolutional Neural Networks. In *Journal of Micro/Nanolithography, MEMS, and MOEMS (JM3)*.
[23] Synopsys. 2016. Sentaurus Lithography. https://www.synopsys.com/silicon/mask-synthesis/sentaurus-lithography.html. (2016).
[24] Chin Boon Tan, Kar Kit Koh, Dongqing Zhang, and Yee Mei Foong. 2015. Sub-resolution assist feature (SRAF) printing prediction using logistic regression. In *Proceedings of SPIE*. 94261Y–94261Y.
[25] Yuki Watanabe, Taiki Kimura, Tetsuaki Matsunawa, and Shigeki Nojima. 2017. Accurate lithography simulation model based on convolutional neural networks. In *SPIE Advanced Lithography*. International Society for Optics and Photonics, 101470K–101470K.
[26] Jen-Yi Wuu, Fedor G Pikus, and Malgorzata Marek-Sadowska. 2011. Efficient approach to early detection of lithographic hotspots using machine learning systems and pattern matching. In *SPIE Advanced Lithography*. International Society for Optics and Photonics, 79740U–79740U.
[27] Xiaoqing Xu, Yibo Lin, Meng Li, Tetsuaki Matsunawa, Shigeki Nojima, Chikaaki Kodama, Toshiya Kotani, and David Z. Pan. 2017. Sub-Resolution Assist Feature Generation with Supervised Data Learning. *IEEE Transactions on Computer-Aided Design of Integrated Circuits and Systems (TCAD)* PP, 99 (2017).
[28] Haoyu Yang, Yajun Lin, Bei Yu, and F.Y. Evangeline Young. 2017. Lithography Hotspot Detection: From Shallow to Deep Learning. In *IEEE International System-on-Chip Conference (SOCC)*.
[29] Haoyu Yang, Jing Su, Yi Zou, Bei Yu, and F.Y. Evangeline Young. 2017. Layout Hotspot Detection with Feature Tensor Generation and Deep Biased Learning. In *ACM/IEEE Design Automation Conference (DAC)*.

Compact-2D: A Physical Design Methodology to Build Commercial-Quality Face-to-Face-Bonded 3D ICs

Bon Woong Ku, Kyungwook Chang, and Sung Kyu Lim
School of ECE, Georgia Institute of Technology, Atlanta, GA
{bwku,k.chang,limsk}@ece.gatech.edu

ABSTRACT

The recent advancement of wafer bonding technology offers fine-grained and silicon-space overhead-free 3D interconnections in face-to-face (F2F) bonded 3D ICs. In this paper, we propose a full-chip RTL-to-GDSII physical design solution to build high-density and commercial-quality two-tier F2F-bonded 3D ICs. The state-of-the-art flow named Shrunk-2D (S2D) [10] requires shrinking of standard cells and interconnects by a factor of 50% to fit into the target 3D footprint of a two-tier design. This, unfortunately, necessitates commercial place/route engines that handle one node smaller geometries, which can be challenging and costly. Our flow named Compact-2D (C2D) does not require any geometry shrinking. Instead, C2D implements a 2D IC with scaled interconnect RC parasitics, and contracts the layout to the F2F design footprint. In addition, C2D offers post-tier-partitioning optimization that is shown to be effective in fixing timing violations caused by inter-tier 3D routing, which is completely missing in S2D. Lastly, we present a methodology to recycle the routing result of post-tier-partitioning optimization for final GDSII generation. Our experimental results show that at iso-performance, C2D offers up to 26.8% power reduction and 15.6% silicon area savings over commercial 2D ICs without any routing resource overhead.

CCS CONCEPTS

• **Hardware → 3D integrated circuits**; **Physical design (EDA)**;

KEYWORDS

Compact-2D; Physical Design Methodology; Wafer-level Bonding; Face-to-Face (F2F) Bonded 3D ICs

ACM Reference Format:
Bon Woong Ku, Kyungwook Chang, and Sung Kyu Lim. 2018. Compact-2D: A Physical Design Methodology to Build Commercial-Quality Face-to-Face-Bonded 3D ICs. In *ISPD '18: 2018 International Symposium on Physical Design, March 25–28, 2018, Monterey, CA, USA.* ACM, New York, NY, USA, 8 pages. https://doi.org/10.1145/3177540.3178244

1 INTRODUCTION

Face-to-face (F2F) bonding technology involves 3D integration of two pre-fabricated dies in a face-to-face fashion. In F2F bonding,

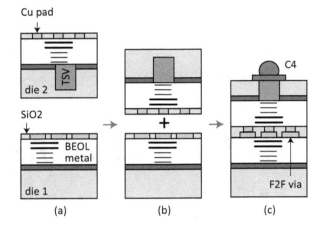

Figure 1: F2F integration using hybrid W2W bonding technology [3]. (a) Wafers are fabricated in parallel before bonding. One wafer contains via-middle TSVs for the I/Os. The wafer surface is flattened by chemical-mechanical planarization. (b) Wafers are aligned, bonded at room temperature, and annealed at < 250 °C. (c) F2F vias are formed at the locations of direct metal-to-metal bonding. The top wafer is thinned to reveal TSVs for bumping.

electrical connections between the dies are made by F2F vias, and the minimum pitch of these F2F vias defines the density of 3D interconnections. As 2D interconnects become denser along with logic device scaling, it calls for a tighter 3D interconnect pitch to improve the functional density and power-performance-area benefit of F2F-bonded 3D ICs. To enable smaller F2F via pitches, R&D has focused on enhancing the bonding precision of F2F integration lately. Among several notable achievements, hybrid wafer-to-wafer (W2W) bonding technology has emerged as a promising solution.

Hybrid W2W bonding is a wafer-level integration technology that enables direct metal-to-metal (damascene-pad) and dielectric-to-dielectric bonding between the back-end-of-lines (BEOLs) of pre-fabricated wafers [9, 12]. After an annealing process at a low temperature (< 250 °C) to strengthen the inter-facial bonding, F2F vias are naturally formed at the locations of direct metal-to-metal bonding. Thanks to the high precision of wafer-level integration, a $1.8 \mu m$ F2F via pitch has been demonstrated. In addition, the minimum pitch is projected down to $0.8 \mu m$ in the near future [3, 6]. This allows designers to utilize fine-grained and silicon-space overhead-free 3D interconnections in F2F-bonded 3D ICs.

Various studies have shown the benefits of F2F-bonded 3D ICs. Using a $5 \mu m$ F2F pitch, [5] demonstrated a test chip that achieves a high memory bandwidth ($63.8 GB/s$) in core-memory stacking architecture at $4W$ power consumption. [11] adopted F2F bonding technology for the heterogeneous integration of MEMS and SoCs, and reported 30% form factor savings. However, all these benefits are still based on a large F2F via pitch. To fully benefit from the advanced F2F integration technology, new design and CAD solutions are required. In this paper, we present a physical design methodology named Compact-2D (C2D) to build high-density and commercial-quality F2F-bonded 3D ICs.

2 MOTIVATION

The state-of-the-art in F2F full-chip design flow, Shrunk-2D (S2D) [10], proposed a unique method to build F2F-bonded 3D ICs. S2D requires shrinking of standard cells and interconnects by 50% to fit into the footprint of a two-tier F2F design with no silicon-area overhead. Then, the shrunk layout objects are used to implement the Shrunk-2D design, where the (X,Y) locations of cells are optimized with the same half perimeter wirelength (HPWL) as that of the target F2F design, assuming that the Z dimension is so small and thus negligible. To decide the Z location of each cell, tier partitioning is subsequently performed. Then, F2F via planning decides the actual F2F via locations based on the (X,Y,Z) placement solution. Although S2D shows how to use commercial 2D P&R engines to design F2F-bonded 3C ICs, it introduces the following new issues, especially in the advanced technology nodes.

- To handle shrunk geometries, S2D requires place/route (P&R) engines and design rule checkers that target one node smaller technology, which is both challenging and costly.[1]
- The shrunk dimension of interconnects leads to inaccuracy in RC parasitics of the S2D design unless the parasitic database is rebuilt for the shrunk geometries.[2]
- Tier partitioning in S2D ignores the fact that any inter-tier 3D route requires the *full* metal stacks for *both* tiers in F2F designs. Nevertheless, S2D does not support any optimization after tier partitioning. Therefore, it is prone to timing failure caused by inter-tier 3D routing overheads.

The physical design of monolithic 3D ICs [4, 7, 8] resembles that of F2F-bonded 3D ICs because the inter-tier vias are negligibly small. This offers similar freedom in constructing a (X,Y,Z) placement solution for both monolithic 3D and F2F designs. However, a notable difference lies in how inter-tier routing is done: in monolithic 3D ICs, only a single stack of BEOL is used, whereas both stacks are required in F2F-bonded 3D ICs. This motivates us to address the inter-tier 3D routing overheads efficiently (in both timing and power) for commercial-quality F2F designs. Thus, existing works on monolithic 3D ICs cannot be easily migrated to handle F2F designs.

3 DESIGN METHODOLOGY

This section presents our design methodology named Compact-2D (C2D) flow to build commercial-quality F2F-bonded 3D ICs. C2D

---

[1]Our conversations with S2D flow users at industry design houses revealed an exponential increase in design rule violations at the 7nm node. S2D suggests that designers ignore these errors. However, they reported that an excessive number of violations may cause commercial engines to terminate abruptly or produce low-quality layouts.
[2]Unless the resistivity and thickness of an interconnect are modified, the unit length resistance of a wire segment is not the same in S2D and F2F designs because the width of the interconnect is shrunk by 29.3%. Similarly, the shrunk width and spacing of the interconnect lead to inaccurate capacitance values in S2D designs.

Table 1: Terminologies in our Compact-2D (C2D) flow.

Compact-2D Design	An initial 2D design with unit length RC scaled by a factor of 0.707
Memory Expansion	Expanding the pin locations and memory macro boundaries by a facror of 1.414
Placement Contraction	Linearly contracting the placement solution of a Compact-2D design by a factor of 0.707
Compact F2F Via Planning	Performing timing, power, and F2F via location co-optimization to address inter-tier routing overhead
Incremental Routing	Recycling the routing result from Compact F2F Via Planning for the final GDSII generation

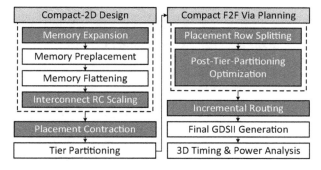

Figure 2: Our Compact-2D (C2D) flow. In color are the key steps proposed in this paper to build commercial-quality F2F-bonded 3D ICs using 2D IC implementation tools.

flow finds the (X,Y) placement solution of a F2F design using the original geometries of standard cells and interconnects. It also introduces an optimization capability to take the inter-tier 3D routing overheads into account correctly. The overall design methodology is shown in Figure 2.

3.1 Compact-2D Design

A Compact-2D design is a pseudo-3D design in C2D flow to find the optimal (X,Y) locations of standard cells in a target F2F design. The floorplan of the Compact-2D design is two times as large as the final 3D footprint in the same aspect ratio to accommodate all the synthesized gates in the two-tier F2F design with their original geometries. However, the HPWL of a net in the F2F design is 29.3% shorter than the corresponding net in the Compact-2D design when both are projected on the X-Y plane. To match the electrical length despite the difference in geometrical length, Figure 3 illustrates the need for interconnect RC scaling in the Compact-2D design. By Scaling the unit RC per length by a factor of 0.707, we avoid the redundant buffer insertions caused by increased geometrical length in the Compact-2D design while still using the original geometries of standard cells and interconnects. Then, we perform all the required implementation steps of the conventional 2D ICs in the Compact-2D design.

3.2 Placement Contraction

Once the Compact-2D design is implemented, the cell locations are linearly mapped to the 3D design footprint to finalize the optimal

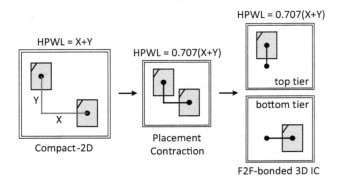

Figure 3: The need for interconnect RC scaling in a Compact-2D design. The length of interconnects will be reduced to 0.707X in the final F2F layout. In order to reflect this, we reduce the unit length RC to 0.707X in the Compact-2D design. The red line in the most left figure indicates an interconnect with reduced parasitics.

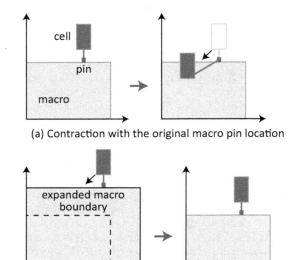

(a) Contraction with the original macro pin location

(b) Contraction with the expanded macro pin location

Figure 4: The need for the expansion of memory boundaries in C2D flow. (a) The original macro pin location causes placement contraction to introduce unwanted routing change and cell overlap, (b) The macro boundary and its pin locations are expanded by a factor of 1.414 to resolve this issue.

(X,Y) locations of cells in the F2F design. This is called placement contraction. Considering the linearly contracted HPWL of a net, the scaled interconnect RC parasitics of the Compact-2D design are the same as those of the F2F design in the original unit length RC. Also, it implies that the (X,Y) solutions based on the shrinking idea from S2D and interconnect RC scaling / placement contraction ideas from our C2D are ideally the same. However, C2D necessitates the P&R engines that handle the target technology node only while S2D relies on the CAD engines for the next technology node.

3.3 Handling Memory Macros

In the conventional 2D IC design, memory macros are preplaced in the floorplan without any overlaps, and none of standard cells is placed inside the memory macros. However, the Compact-2D design needs to allow overlaps of memory macros when they share the same (X,Y) location, but at different Z locations. Moreover, P&R engines should be allowed to place the standard cells inside the memory macro regions unless the memory macros fully occupy the regions in both tiers. Previously, S2D proposed shrinking the footprint of memory macros down to the minimum placement unit, and use placement blockages at its original boundary. Full placement blockages are used in the fully overlapped regions of memory macros, and restrict the standard cell placement. To enable the standard cell placement at partially vacated regions, 50% partial placement blockages are used. The pin locations of memory macros are retained, which serve as anchors for the standard cell placement regardless the footprint change of memory macros.

C2D follows the same way, but requires an additional step. Considering that the boundary of placement blockages should be the same as the original boundary of memory macros after placement contraction, the placement blockages for memory macros needs to be expanded by a factor of 1.414 for the Compact-2D design. The pin locations of memory macros also should be expanded to correctly anchor the standard cells around the placement blockages as shown in Figure 4. Therefore, at the floorplan stage of the Compact-2D design, we should prepare for the expanded memory

macro Library Exchange Format (LEF) files (Memory Expansion), assign their tier locations, and preplace them manually considering the inter-module connectivity (Memory Preplacement), and generate placement blockages on the expanded memory regions while flattening the tier locations of memory macros (Memory Flattening).

3.4 Tier Partitioning

Since the tier locations of memory macros are preassigned manually, the standard cells within the memory macro boundaries move to the tier where memory macros do not occupy. To determine the Z location of each standard cell outside the memory macro boundaries, C2D introduces tier partitioning that utilizes bin-based placement-driven Fiduccia-Mettheyses (FM)-mincut partitioning algorithm [10]. Each partitioning bin is defined in a regular fashion on the final F2F footprint, and we run the algorithm based on the (X,Y) solution derived from placement contraction.

Bin-based placement-driven FM-mincut partitioning helps balance the area skew over the entire design footprint, otherwise resulting in huge white spaces or displacement from the optimal (X,Y) locations during placement legalization. The number of cutsize, which turns into the minimum number of inter-tier connections, is controlled by the size of partitioning bins. Too many cutsize leads to routing congestion, while too few cutsize decreases the power-performance benefits of F2F-bonded 3D ICs. Therefore, a sweet spot exists along the partitioning-bin size. Once tier partitioning determines the Z location of each cell, a placement engine legalizes the overlaps caused by placement contraction, and a Design Exchange Format (DEF) file for each die is created.

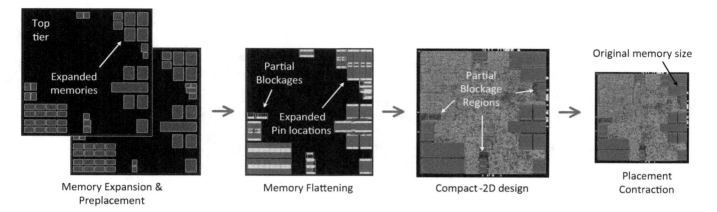

Figure 5: Our C2D flow demonstrated with OpenSparc T2 [1] single core design: memory expansion and preplacement, memory flattening, Compact-2D design, and placement contraction. Tier partitioning and Compact F2F via planning follow next.

3.5 Compact F2F Via Planning

After we decide the (X,Y,Z) locations of standard cells, we should determine the F2F via locations. This is called F2F via planning. In this step, inter-tier 3D routing overhead, which is not accounted by the Compact-2D design, starts to affect the design closure. S2D is not only susceptible to this degradation, but none of 3D-routing-aware optimization is introduced after tier partitioning. In order to support post-tier-partitioning optimization (post-TP opt) to compensate the inter-tier routing overhead, C2D presents a unique stage named Compact F2F via planning. Compact F2F via planning consists of two steps, and following subsections describe them in detail.

3.5.1 Placement Row Splitting. Compact F2F via planning performs based on the 3D technology LEF which includes the definition and design rules of metal stacks in both tiers. 3D macro LEFs are required for the commercial router to distinguish the pin layer of macros based on their tier locations. Next, our in-house program creates a DEF and a Verilog file by instantiating the cells with 3D macro LEFs while flattening the tier location of cells. However, in order to fully utilize the optimization capabilities, the flattened DEF file should not have the placement overlaps although all synthesized gates are accommodated in the final F2F design footprint. Therefore, we split a placement row into the top and bottom rows, and change the height of standard cells in 3D macro LEFs to the half of the original to fit into the split rows.

In Figure 6, Row0 and Row1 are two adjacent placement rows to be split. Row1 is vertically flipped over to share the power rail with Row0. Now, placement row splitting turns each row into two horizontally split rows. In Row0, the bottom half is reserved for the bottom tier placement, and the top half for the top tier. However, in Row1, the bottom half is reserved for the top tier placement and the top half for the bottom tier due to the flipped orientation of Row1. As a result, the placement overlap is fully legalized while accommodating every cell in the design on the final F2F footprint. It is worth noting that the pin locations of standard cells are preserved regardless of splitting placement rows. Based on the retained pin locations and the same width of standard cells, accurate post-TP opt proceeds.

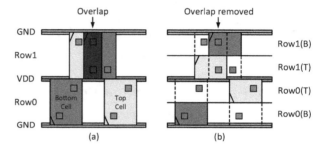

Figure 6: (a) Shrunk-2D flow [10] does not offer post-tier-partitioning optimization because of the placement overlap. (b) Placement row splitting in our C2D flow enables the optimization by fully legalizing the placement overlap.

3.5.2 Post-Tier-Partitioning Optimization. C2D performs timing, power, and F2F via location co-optimization to close the design under inter-tier 3D routing overhead. Post-TP opt requires RC corners for the full 3D metal stack including the F2F via, and the timing corners for both top and bottom tiers. Thanks to placement row splitting, full optimization capabilities, including insertion, deletion, move, and resizing, are employed. Once the optimization is done, our in-house binaries create a DEF file for each die that introduces the F2F vias as I/O ports (F2F ports) and contains the final cell locations by restoring the original cell height. Since the pin locations of cells are preserved regardless of having the cell height, we can easily retrieve the correct (X,Y) locations of cells based on the original cell height. Also, we generate a Verilog file for each die that presents the connectivity among F2F ports and the cells within a die. A top Verilog file that defines the connections between F2F ports in separate tiers is created, and lastly, we generate a top Standard Parasitic Exchange Format (SPEF) file that presents the RC parasitics of F2F vias.

3.6 Incremental Routing

Incremental routing is a CAD solution to preserve the routing result of Compact F2F via planning for the final GDSII file generation of each die. We first construct a graph for each net that consists of vertices and edges representing individual routing objects and their connectivities. Routing objects include a wire, a via, an I/O port, or a cell pin. The X/Y locations where those routing objects cross each other are kept along with their edge definitions. Next, if the graph contains a F2F via vertex, we convert it into two vertices without an edge between them representing I/O ports for the top and bottom tier. Each vertex is only connected to the adjacent vertices that shares the same tier. As a result, the graph turns into a group of disconnected subgraphs, and each subgraph represents a 2D subnet on the specific die. Now, we reproduce the routing result for each subgraph based on the actual connection points defined in each edge. A depth-first search ordering is used to make the output in the format of DEF syntax. Finally, the routing information for each subgraph is delivered to the DEF for a corresponding die.

In the final GDSII file generation step, we use this routing information as an initial solution for sign-off physical design rule violation (DRV) fixing. The reason why DRV fixing is necessary is that tools built for 2D ICs do not support full DRV fixing for the pins outside the macro boundary while employing placement row splitting. When the sign-off DRV fixing is done, RC parasitics of each die are extracted, and we proceed the final 3D timing & power analysis.

4 STATE-OF-THE-ART COMPARISON

In Table 2, we compare the timing & power savings of C2D with those of S2D based on the OpenSparc T2 [1] single core (SPC) design at $1.0GHz$ clock frequency. We use dual-Vt cell libraries in 28nm commercial-grade technology process design kit (28nm PDK). Six metal layers are used for 2D, and the top and bottom tiers for F2F implementations. The F2F via diameter, pitch, resistance and capacitance are assumed to be $0.5\mu m$, $1.0\mu m$, 0.5Ω, and $0.2fF$, respectively. For the static power analysis, we set the switching activity as 0.1 for primary input ports and register output pins, and 2.0 for a clock port.

We observe that both C2D and S2D designs significantly decrease the net switching power thanks to the huge wirelength savings in F2F designs. Following buffer reduction contributes to the cell internal power savings. The total power reduction of C2D is 11.3% while S2D offers a 11.0% savings over 2D IC at iso-performance. In addition, it is remarkable that C2D reduces the total negative slack violations by 83.6% while S2D worsens the timing. This result not only shows that C2D offers comparable power reduction as the state-of-the-art S2D, but also proves that C2D builds timing-robust F2F designs. Most of all, C2D is more scalable than S2D in that <u>our C2D flow performs with P&R engines, technology files, and design rules for the target technology and does not require handling of the next smaller node.</u>

5 EXPERIMENTAL RESULTS

In this section, we analyze the impact of each design step in C2D flow with LDPC, AES-128, and JPEG from OpenCore benchmark suites [2]. Assumptions on the technology and analysis are the same as Section 4 made. The initial utilization density for AES-128 and JPEG is 60%, while 40% for wire-dominated LDPC. The maximum clock frequency for each benchmark is 2.0GHz for LDPC,

Table 2: Timing & power comparison among 2D, S2D [10], and C2D using OpenSparc T2 [1] single core (28nm). Δ% shows % improvement over 2D. Target clock period is 1ns. C2D offers comparable power reduction and significant performance savings compared with S2D.

	2D	S2D	Δ%	C2D	Δ%
Total WL (m)	15.36	11.77	23.4%	11.55	24.8%
F2F Via #	-	154,127	-	193,487	-
Footprint (mm^2)	2.53	1.26	50.2%	1.26	50.2%
Total Power (mW)	338.20	300.87	**11.0%**	299.88	**11.3%**
Cell Power (mW)	82.12	79.11	3.7%	79.07	3.7%
Net Power (mW)	183.26	153.33	16.3%	150.86	17.7%
Leak. Power (mW)	72.83	68.43	6.0%	69.95	4.0%
Mem. Power (mW)	45.98	44.94	2.3%	44.77	2.6%
Comb. Power (mW)	171.30	140.90	17.7%	139.90	18.3%
Reg. Power (mW)	67.72	67.68	0.1%	69.80	-3.1%
Clk Tree Power (mW)	53.17	47.34	11.0%	45.40	14.6%
Worst Neg. Slack (ps)	-27.65	-52.52	**-89.9%**	-25.99	**6.0%**
Total Neg. Slack (ps)	-832.85	-846.94	**-1.7%**	-136.75	**83.6%**
Total Pos. Slack (ps)	35988.60	38884.50	8.0%	39422.20	9.5%

5.4GHz for AES-128, and 2.16GHz for JPEG. Figure 7 shows the GDSII layouts of 28nm 2D and C2D-based F2F implementations for each benchmark including SPC at their maximum frequency.

5.1 Impact of Interconnect RC Scaling

In a Compact-2D design, we scale interconnect RC parasitics by a factor of 0.707 to imitate the parasitics of wirelength in the final F2F design based on that the footprint of the F2F design is exactly 50% of the 2D footprint. However, the RC scaling factor can be generalized and set to be 0.6 in case the F2F design footprint is 36% of the 2D footprint. Table 3 shows Compact-2D design results with various 3D/2D footprint ratios.

With a low RC scaling factor, such as 0.548, all benchmarks has huge power and standard cell area savings because of the reduced interconnect parasitics and the less number and lower drive-strength of buffers. However, since the target footprint is way smaller than the standard cell area savings, it results in the impractical placement utilization per each die in the F2F design. Assuming placement utilization in [70%, 80%] range is allowed, our footprint savings reach up to 65% for LDPC, and 56% for both AES-128 and JPEG. In case of wire-dominated LDPC design, since the 2D footprint is determined by the routability, the huge wirelength reduction in the F2F design helps increase the footprint savings more.

When the same placement utilization in both 2D and F2F-bonded 3D ICs should be considered, we observe that 53-57% footprint savings are good target for all designs due to the buffer savings from the interconnect RC scaling. With a constraint on the exact 50% footprint savings, we find that 4-12% of placement utilization savings in F2F designs. In summary, sweeping the interconnect RC scaling helps to set the practical and optimal F2F design assumption. This also shows that C2D is incredibly flexible to design and find the optimal footprint of F2F designs for logic benchmarks thanks to the usage of original geometries for standard cells. For the rest of experiments, we keep the 50% footprint savings in F2F designs for all benchmarks to factorize the impact of other steps clearly.

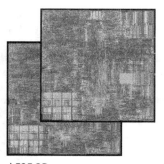

(b) LDPC 2D and F2F 3D

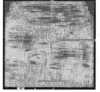

(a) SPC 2D and F2F 3D   (c) AES-128 2D and F2F 3D   (d) JPEG 2D and F2F 3D

Figure 7: 28nm GDSII die images of 2D and F2F-bonded 3D implementations using our C2D flow. (a) SPC (1.0GHz), (b) LDPC (2.0GHz), (c) AES-128 (5.4GHz), (d) JPEG (2.16GHz).

Table 3: Impact of target 3D footprint. Assuming placement utilization in [70%, 80%] range is allowed, our footprint savings reach up to 65% for LDPC, and 56% for both AES-128 and JPEG

Footprint ($3D/2D$)	50%	45%	40%	35%	30%
RC Scaling	0.707	0.671	0.632	0.592	0.548
LDPC					
Std. Cell Area (mm^2)	0.180	0.178	0.177	0.172	0.169
3D Place. Util. per Die	58.31%	63.92%	72.03%	79.69%	91.29%
Place. Util ($3D/2D$)	87.83%	96.30%	108.50%	120.04%	137.51%
Total Power (mW)	179.23	174.48	167.70	158.03	153.85
Footprint ($3D/2D$)	50%	47%	44%	41%	38%
RC Scaling	0.707	0.686	0.663	0.640	0.616
AES-128					
Std. Cell Area (mm^2)	0.359	0.356	0.355	0.355	0.355
3D Place. Util. per Die	70.10%	73.88%	78.99%	84.58%	91.43%
Place. Util ($3D/2D$)	95.09%	100.22%	107.15%	116.15%	124.03%
Total Power (mW)	331.68	330.49	324.54	323.39	322.18
JPEG					
Std. Cell Area (mm^2)	0.943	0.941	0.939	0.936	0.933
3D Place. Util. per Die	70.71%	70.71%	80.07%	85.65%	92.16%
Place. Util ($3D/2D$)	96.03%	101.78%	108.73%	116.32%	125.15%
Total Power (mW)	579.17	573.52	565.84	563.80	560.10

5.2 Impact of Tier Partitioning

While placement contraction is deterministic in that the (X,Y) locations of cells are scaled by 0.707, bin-based tier partitioning is heuristic w.r.t the size of partitioning bins. Depending on the partitioning-bin size, the number of cells applied to the algorithm varies, resulting in different cut sizes between the dies. Table 4 shows how the different partitioning-bin sizes change the number of 3D connections (F2F vias) and the wirelength of a design. F2F utilization indicates the F2F via usage out of the maximum available number of F2F vias inside the F2F design footprint. While the small bin size leads to the large number of F2F vias, the large bin size allows the algorithm to find the minimum cut size.

To explore the impact of the different number of 3D connections on the wirelength savings, a net is defined as either a 2D or a 3D net based on their F2F usage, and compare its wirelength with that in the Compact-2D design. We observe that the average wirelength

per net is correlated to the optimal partitioning-bin size. If the bin size is way smaller ($5\mu m$) than the average net wirelength, most of the nets become 3D, causing congestion and detour to meet the design rules for F2F vias. This is the reason that the wirelength savings of 3D nets decreases at $5\mu m$ bin, lowering the total wirelength savings. On the other hand, if the bin size is too large, then most of the nets remain at 2D, requiring huge legalization caused by placement contraction. Therefore, embracing too much 2D nets again degrades the wirelength savings. LDPC shows the best wirelength savings (27.3%), which is almost ideal (29.3%), when the bin size is in the range of 20 to $80\mu m$, while AES-128, and JPEG, which has short wirelength per net (gate-dominant), have 22.15% and 20.47%, respectively at $10\mu m$ bin. It is noteworthy that gate-dominant circuits steeply loose the wirelength savings along with increasing the bin size over the sweet spots. We determine the size of partitioning bins as $40\mu m$ for LDPC, $10\mu m$ for both AES-128 and JPEG, and proceed Compact F2F via planning.

5.3 Impact of Compact F2F Via Planning

Using LDPC, Table 5 demonstrates that how negatively inter-tier 3D routing affects the timing, and how effectively post-TP opt fixes the timing violations. Since the Compact-2D design does not account the inter-tier routing overheads when it is implemented, we observe that the worst negative slack (WNS) is degraded to 5.87x, and 7.71x for the total negative slack (TNS) after the inter-tier 3D routing is done. All of these timing violations are fixed after we perform post-TP opt. The WNS is improved by 44.4% and the TNS is restored by 91.5% with the negligible power overhead. This proves that post-TP opt in Compact F2F via planning is critical to implement timing-robust F2F designs. In general, post-TP opt restores the timing by inserting or up-sizing the buffers while minimizing the power increase. However, if the power overhead becomes the issue, then post-TP opt can start to delete or down-size the buffers at the expense of the timing margin.

5.4 Impact of Incremental Routing

Table 6 shows how final DRV fixing and tier-by-tier 2D routing affects the design result from post-TP opt, and how much better our incremental routing performs than the existing iterative tier-by-tier

Table 4: Impact of tier partitioning bin size. Smaller bins cause more F2F vias to be used and tend to improve WL saving for 3D. Saving values are w.r.t. 2D results.

Bin Size (μm)	5	10	20	40	80
LDPC					
Bin #	6,169	1,542	386	96	24
Avg. Cell # / Bin	11	42	169	677	2,707
F2F Via #	55,468	26,999	20,850	19,802	19,726
F2F Util. (%)	34.20	16.65	12.86	12.21	12.16
Avg. WL / net (μm)	39.16	38.85	38.83	38.84	38.82
3D Net # (%)	61.41	24.71	17.73	16.89	16.75
3D Net WL Savings (%)	26.73	27.58	27.87	27.87	27.95
2D Net WL Savings (%)	26.60	26.93	26.80	26.79	26.77
Total WL Savings (%)	26.70	27.28	27.32	27.30	27.33
AES-128					
Bin #	10,247	2,562	640	160	40
Avg. Cell # / Bin	14	55	219	877	3,507
F2F Via #	104,306	61,902	51,460	22,311	10,824
F2F Util. (%)	39.16	23.24	19.32	8.38	4.06
Avg. WL / net (μm)	16.45	16.24	16.56	18.16	18.83
3D Net # (%)	59.67	28.11	22.91	11.14	5.96
3D Net WL Savings (%)	20.57	22.10	21.50	18.45	16.73
2D Net WL Savings (%)	22.74	22.20	19.95	11.46	8.76
Total WL Savings (%)	21.14	22.15	20.60	12.94	9.71
JPEG					
Bin #	26,680	6,670	1,668	417	104
Avg. Cell # / Bin	11	43	171	682	2,729
F2F Via #	240,301	120,921	94,868	71,353	53,810
F2F Util. (%)	35.17	17.70	13.88	10.44	7.88
Avg. WL / net (μm)	14.54	14.57	14.76	15.06	15.67
3D Net # (%)	61.36	25.19	18.42	13.27	10.10
3D Net WL Savings (%)	20.69	21.73	21.61	21.39	19.11
2D Net WL Savings (%)	19.76	19.01	17.66	15.53	12.17
Total WL Savings (%)	20.47	20.31	19.29	17.60	14.28

Table 5: Impact of post-tier-partitioning optimization. $\Delta\%$ indicates its savings. Inter-tier 3D routing (A vs. B) introduces huge timing violations, and our optimization (B vs. C) fixes the timing violations with the negligible power overhead.

Design	LDPC			
Stage	Before	After 3D Routing		
	3D Routing (A)	NO-Opt (B)	YES-Opt (C)	$\Delta\%$
Total Cell (#)	65,187	65,187	65,271	-0.1
Worst Neg. Slack (ps)	-7.42	-43.57	-24.23	44.4
Total Neg. Slack (ps)	-341.86	-2637.13	-222.99	91.5
Total Pos. Slack (ps)	19194.40	17042.80	27072.40	58.8
Violated Path (#)	20	383	27	93.0
Total Power (mW)	179.23	178.25	178.49	-0.1

routing method in S2D. Iterative routing starts the tier-by-tier routing from scratch on top of the placement result of post-TP opt. This leads to a different routing result from post-PT opt due to the final DRV fixing, and perturbs the design closure. We observe that the worst negative slack is degraded to 1.86x, and 25.88x for the total negative slack after using iterative routing. However, our incremental routing preserves the worst negative slack in the acceptable

Table 6: The impact of Final DRV fixing and tier-by-tier 2D routing after post-TP opt. We note that the incremental routing (Incr-R) used in C2D preserves the timing closed by post-TP opt (A vs. C) better than the iterative routing (Iter-R) in S2D [10] (A vs. B). Incr-R also offers smaller wirelength and power overheads for the tier-by-tier routing than Iter-R. $\Delta\%$ indicates the savings from Incr-R over Iter-R.

Design	LDPC			
Stage	Before	After 2D Routing		
	2D Routing (A)	Iter-R (B)	Incr-R (C)	$\Delta\%$
Total WL (m)	2.721	2.754	2.750	0.1
Worst Neg. Slack (ps)	-24.23	-45.17	-25.16	44.3
Total Neg. Slack (ps)	-222.99	-5771.74	-1599.73	72.3
Total Pos. Slack (ps)	27072.40	11257.00	15107.10	34.2
Violated Path (#)	27	734	402	45.2
Total Power (mW)	178.49	179.53	179.15	0.2

Table 7: Runtime comparison (in minutes): Intel(R) Xeon(R) CPU E5-2640 @ 2.50GHz, 16 cores usage for Cadence Innovus run.

Design	LDPC			AES-128			JPEG		
Runtime (min)	2D	S2D	C2D	2D	S2D	C2D	2D	S2D	C2D
Placement	3	3	3	3	3	3	7	7	7
Pre-CTS Opt.	44	19	22	33	29	28	59	54	55
Clock Tree Syn.	3	5	3	5	6	5	15	17	13
Post-CTS Opt.	8	6	6	12	9	7	15	12	12
Routing	6	8	6	5	7	5	9	11	8
Post-route Opt.	11	10	10	8	8	8	20	19	19
Place. Contr.	-	-	1	-	-	1	-	-	2
Tier Part.	-	1	1	-	3	3	-	11	11
F2F Via Plan.	-	10	10	-	10	10	-	19	19
Post-TP Opt.	-	-	20	-	-	15	-	-	39
Iter. Routing	-	11	-	-	12	-	-	20	-
Incr. Routing	-	-	7	-	-	7	-	-	11
Signoff Analysis	2			3			10		
Final Total	77	75	91	69	90	95	135	180	206

level (less than 25ps under 0.5ns clock period), and retains the total wirelength and power results close to the optimization result (less than 1% overheads).

5.5 Runtime Analysis

In Table 7, we tabulate runtime for each design step of 2D, S2D, C2D flows to build LDPC, AES-128, and JPEG. Intel(R) Xeon(R) CPU E5-2640 @ 2.50GHz is used, and 16 cores are employed while running Cadence Innovus. Thanks to the reduced interconnect loads and HPWL savings, Compact-2D designs take 34% less time than 2D until the post-route optimization is done (Compact-2D designs take 10% less time than Shrunk-2D designs at best). However, the total runtime of C2D is longer than that of 2D by a maximum 50% (JPEG), due to the additional steps starting from placement contraction. Although incremental routing achieves a huge runtime savings up to 60% compared with iterative routing in S2D, post-TP opt takes a large portion of the F2F design flow, resulting in 21% runtime overhead in C2D over S2D at worst.

5.6 Commercial 2D vs. C2D

Based on the optimal footprint derived from Section 5.1, we compare the design results of commercial 2D with C2D-based F2F designs. The total area savings of F2F designs over the 2D is 57.8% for LDPC, and 53.0% for both AES-128, and JPEG. As shown in Table 8, our C2D flow offers a 20-34% wirelength savings and a 4-13% standard cell area savings. Therefore, the wire-dominated LDPC, which shows the highest wirelength to standard cell area ratio, benefits most from C2D in terms of the total power savings at iso-performance (26.8%), whereas the lowest wirelength to standard cell area ratio benchmark, JPEG, gains the lowest total power savings (5.7%). An interesting trend is that the standard cell area reduction depends on the ratio of sequential cell count to the total number of cells. Since the number of sequential cells in a design is not changed, only reduced drive strength for the sequential cells contributes to the power savings. On the other hand, buffers are optimized in both number and strength. Therefore, LDPC, which has the lowest sequential cell count to the total cell count ratio (2.7%), achieves the largest standard cell area savings (12.7%) in the F2F design.

6 CONCLUSIONS

To maximize the utilization of 3D interconnect and the power-performance-area benefit of F2F-bonded 3D ICs, in this paper, we proposed a full-chip RTL-to-GDSII physical design solution named Compact-2D (C2D) that offers a commercial-quality F2F-bonded 3D IC physical layout. We presented interconnect RC scaling, placement contraction, and memory expansion idea, which allows us to utilize the original technology files and design rules of the target technology node for a F2F-bonded 3D IC implementation. We also introduced placement row splitting idea to enable post-tier-partitioning optimization in our C2D flow, which is completely missing in the state-of-the-art F2F physical design solution. With our extensive experiments and analysis, we evaluated the impact of those ideas in the final F2F design results, and showed that using 28nm process design kit, F2F-bonded 3D ICs implemented by our C2D flow offers a maximum 26.8% of total power reduction with a maximum 15.6% silicon area savings compared to the 2D IC designs at iso-performance.

For the future directions, we will generalize C2D flow to handle more than two tiers. For example, we can adjust the scaling factors in interconnect RC scaling / placement contraction for multi-tier designs. Various multi-way balanced partitioning schemes can be applied to the tier partitioning, and placement row splitting in the Compact F2F via planning can be based on the number of dies. Lastly, we can adopt C2D to build commercial-quality TSV-based 3D ICs or monolithic 3D ICs as well with advanced tier partitioning algorithms for the given implementation and fabrication constraints. All these challenges are the future works for C2D flow.

REFERENCES

[1] http://www.opensparc.net/.
[2] http://www.opencores.org/.
[3] E. Beyne. The 3-d interconnect technology landscape. *IEEE Design Test*, 33(3):8–20, 2016.
[4] K. Chang, S. Sinha, B. Cline, R. Southerland, M. Doherty, G. Yeric, and S. K. Lim. Cascade2D: A Design-aware Partitioning Approach to Monolithic 3D IC with 2D Commercial Tools. In *Proc. IEEE Int. Conf. on Computer-Aided Design*, pages 130:1–130:8, 2016.
[5] D. H. Kim et al. Design and Analysis of 3D-MAPS (3D Massively Parallel Processor with Stacked Memory). *IEEE Transactions on Computers*, 64(1):112–125, 2015.
[6] S. W. Kim et al. Ultra-Fine Pitch 3D Integration Using Face-to-Face Hybrid Wafer Bonding Combined with a Via-Middle Through-Silicon-Via Process. In *Electronic Components and Technology Conference*, pages 1179–1185, 2016.
[7] B. W. Ku, P. Debacker, D. Milojevic, P. Raghavan, and S. K. Lim. How much cost reduction justifies the adoption of monolithic 3d ics at 7nm node? In *Proc. IEEE Int. Conf. on Computer-Aided Design*, pages 87:1–87:7, 2016.
[8] B. W. Ku, P. Debacker, D. Milojevic, P. Raghavan, D. Verkest, A. Thean, and S. K. Lim. Physical Design Solutions to Tackle FEOL/BEOL Degradation in Gate-level Monolithic 3D ICs. In *Proc. Int. Symp. on Low Power Electronics and Design*, pages 76–81, 2016.
[9] P. R. Morrow et al. Three-dimensional wafer stacking via Cu-Cu bonding integrated with 65-nm strained-Si/low-k CMOS technology. *IEEE Electron Device Letters*, 27(5):335–337, 2006.
[10] S. Panth, K. Samadi, Y. Du, and S. K. Lim. Design and CAD methodologies for low power gate-level monolithic 3D ICs. In *Proc. Int. Symp. on Low Power Electronics and Design*, pages 171–176, 2014.
[11] C. S. Premachandran et al. A novel, wafer-level stacking method for low-chip yield and non-uniform, chip-size wafers for MEMS and 3D SIP applications. In *Electronic Components and Technology Conference*, pages 314–318, 2008.
[12] T. Suga et al. Direct Cu to Cu Bonding and Other Alternative Bonding Techniques in 3D Packaging. *Springer*, pages 129–155, 2017.

Table 8: Iso-performance power comparison between commercial 2D vs. C2D. $\Delta\%$ indicates the savings over 2D designs.

Design	2D	C2D	$\Delta\%$
LDPC, 2GHz			
Footprint ($\mu m \times \mu m$)	555.7×555.1	361.2×360.8	57.8
F2F Via Count	-	21,575	-
Cell Count	77,024	64,610	16.1
Seq. Cell Count (%)	2,048 (2.7%)	2,048 (3.2%)	0.0
Standard Cell Area (μm^2)	204,782	178,876	12.7
Total Wirelength (m)	3.8	2.5	33.6
Tot. WL / Cell Area (m^{-1})	18.7	14.2	24.1
Switching Power (mW)	193.9	136.9	29.4
Cell Internal Power (mW)	33.0	28.8	12.7
Leakage Power (mW)	11.1	8.2	26.1
Total Power (mW)	237.8	174.0	26.8
AES-128, 5.4GHz			
Footprint ($\mu m \times \mu m$)	716×715.6	490.9×490.6	53.0
F2F Via Count	-	63,211	-
Cell Count	147,483	140,960	4.4
Seq. Cell Count (%)	10,688 (7.2%)	10,688 (7.6%)	0.0
Standard Cell Area (μm^2)	377,702	361,096	4.4
Total Wirelength (m)	2.9	2.2	22.9
Tot. WL / Cell Area (m^{-1})	7.7	6.2	19.5
Switching Power (mW)	250.8	223.7	10.8
Cell Internal Power (mW)	113.6	108.4	4.6
Leakage Power (mW)	17.5	16.1	8.0
Total Power (mW)	381.9	348.2	8.8
JPEG, 2.16GHz			
Footprint ($\mu m \times \mu m$)	1156.3×1153.7	792.8×791.0	53.0
F2F Via Count	-	121,357	-
Cell count	312,451	284,884	8.8
Seq. Cell Count (%)	37,538 (12.0%)	37,538 (13.2%)	0.0
Standard Cell Area (μm^2)	982,231	943,812	3.9
Total Wirelength (m)	5.8	4.6	20.2
Tot. WL / Cell Area (m^{-1})	5.9	4.9	16.9
Switching Power (mW)	415.8	385.9	7.2
Cell Internal Power (mW)	195.1	189.9	2.7
Leakage Power (mW)	30.2	28.5	5.6
Total Power (mW)	641.1	604.4	5.7

Analog Placement Constraint Extraction and Exploration with the Application to Layout Retargeting

Biying Xu
ECE Department, University of Texas at Austin
biying@utexas.edu

Bulent Basaran
Synopsys, Inc.
Bulent.Basaran@synopsys.com

Ming Su
Synopsys, Inc.
Ming.Su@synopsys.com

David Z. Pan
ECE Department, University of Texas at Austin
dpan@ece.utexas.edu

ABSTRACT

In analog/mixed-signal (AMS) integrated circuits (ICs), most of the layout design efforts are still handled manually, which is time-consuming and error-prone. Given the previous high-quality manual layouts containing valuable design expertise of experienced designers, exploring layout design constraints from the existing layouts is desirable. In this paper, we extract and explore analog placement constraints from previous quality-approved layouts, including regularity and symmetry (symmetry-island) constraints. For the first time, an efficient sweep line-based algorithm is developed to comprehensively extract the regularity constraints in a given analog placement, which can not only improve routability but also minimize the layout parasitics-induced circuit performance degradation. Furthermore, we propose a novel layout technology migration and performance retargeting framework, where we apply the constraint extraction algorithms to improve the placement quality while preserving previous design expertise. Experimental results show that the proposed techniques can preserve the symmetry and regularity constraints, and also reduce the placement area by 7.6% on average.

ACM Reference Format:
Biying Xu, Bulent Basaran, Ming Su, and David Z. Pan. 2018. Analog Placement Constraint Extraction and Exploration with the Application to Layout Retargeting . In *ISPD '18: 2018 International Symposium on Physical Design, March 25–28, 2018, Monterey, CA, USA*. ACM, New York, NY, USA, 8 pages. https://doi.org/10.1145/3177540.3178245

1 INTRODUCTION

Analog/mixed-signal (AMS) integrated circuits (ICs) are used widely and heavily in many emerging applications, including consumer electronics, automotive, and Internet of Things (IoT). The increasing demand of these applications calls for a shorter design cycle and time-to-market of AMS ICs. However, most of the design efforts in AMS ICs are still handled manually, which is time-consuming and error-prone, especially as the design rules are becoming more

and more complicated in nanometer-scale IC era, and as the circuit performance requirements are becoming more and more stringent. Despite the progress in the AMS IC layout design automation field [1–6], the automatic layout tools have not been widely used among AMS IC layout designers. The AMS IC design automation level is far from meeting the need for fast layout-circuit performance iterations for the rapid growth of the market.

Given the vast amount of previous high-quality analog layouts, it is desirable to explore the layout design constraints from them. The extracted layout constraints can be applied in layout technology migration [7, 8], retargeting to updated design specifications (performance retargeting) [9, 10], and knowledge-based layout synthesis [11], etc., to preserve experts' knowledge across designs, shorten design cycle and reduce design efforts. Layout technology migration and performance retargeting are called *layout retargeting*.

In [7], a layout technology migration tool Migration Assistant Shape Handler (MASH) was proposed, which addressed the geometry scaling between technologies and corrected design rule violations with minimum layout perturbations. Nevertheless, it did not consider the layout design constraints in AMS ICs, including symmetry (symmetry-island [3]), regularity, matching, etc. Then, in [8], N. Jangkrajarng *et al.* presented an intellectual property reuse-based analog IC layout automation tool, IPRAIL, that could automatically retarget existing analog layouts for new process technologies and new design specifications. [9] and [10] further improved the analog layout retargeting algorithm by considering layout parasitics and circuit performance degradation. The above-mentioned prior works [8–10] extracted the topological template from the existing layout so that the target layout had the same layout topology, and they automatically detected symmetry in the existing layouts and carried the symmetry constraints to the target layout, as well. More recently, P.-H. Wu *et al.* proposed a knowledge-based analog physical synthesis methodology to generate new layouts by integrating existing design expertise [11]. It extracted common sub-circuits between previous designs and the target design and reused quality-approved layout topologies.

However, the previous works on analog layout retargeting had the following limitations. Firstly, although symmetry constraints were extracted from the existing layouts and preserved in the target layout, regularity constraints were not considered, including topological rows, columns, arrays, and repetitive structures, which are common in AMS ICs. Regular structures in AMS IC layouts not only improve routability, but also minimize the number of vias and bends of wires that are critical, and reduce the layout parasitics-induced

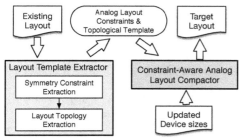

Figure 1: The conventional analog layout retargeting framework.

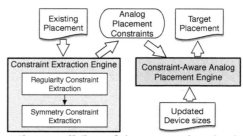

Figure 2: The overall flow of the proposed analog layout retargeting framework.

Figure 3: An example of AMS circuit placement. Orange: row constraint; Blue: column constraint; Red: array.

circuit performance degradation [12, 13]. Thus, it is beneficial to take regularity constraints into account. Secondly, previous works extracted a topological template from the existing layout to preserve the entire layout topology. Nevertheless, it may introduce unnecessary extra topological constraints and limit the solution space. In fact, due to new process technologies or updated design specifications, the device sizes may not scale proportionally during layout retargeting, and it may be more desirable to adopt a different layout topology. To address these limitations, in this paper, we extract and explore the regularity and symmetry (symmetry-island) constraints from previous quality-approved layouts. The extracted constraints are applied to a novel analog layout retargeting framework to preserve the design expertise. An efficient sweep line-based algorithm is developed to extract the regularity constraints from a given analog placement. Our main contributions include:

- We extract and explore symmetry and regularity constraints in previous high-quality layouts.
- For the first time, an efficient sweep line-based algorithm is developed to extract all the regularity constraints in an analog placement.
- We propose a novel analog layout retargeting framework based on the extracted constraints, which reduces the placement area compared with the conventional approach while preserving the design expertise.
- Experimental results show the effectiveness and efficiency of the proposed techniques.

The rest of this paper is organized as follows. Section 2 shows the overall flow of the proposed analog layout retargeting framework. Section 3 describes the algorithms to extract analog placement constraints. Section 4 describes the regularity and symmetry constraint-aware analog placement algorithm used in the proposed layout retargeting framework. Section 5 shows the experimental results. Finally, Section 6 concludes the paper.

2 OVERALL FLOW

Conventionally, most of the prior works on analog layout retargeting extract symmetry (symmetry-island) constraints and a topological template of the existing layout, followed by a constraint-aware layout compactor to preserve the extracted constraints and the entire layout topology. The conventional analog layout retargeting framework is shown in Fig. 1, where only symmetry constraints were considered. The layout compactor only generates the layout with the same topology as the existing one.

The proposed analog layout retargeting flow based on placement constraint extraction is shown in Fig. 2. First, the constraint extraction engine explores various analog placement constraints in the existing placement, including regularity and symmetry constraints. Different from the conventional framework that only detects symmetry constraints, we are the first to propose an efficient sweep line-based algorithm to extract the regularity constraints, which will be described in Section 3. Then, given the extracted constraints and the updated device sizes due to new process technologies or new design specifications, a constraint-aware analog placement is performed such that the design expertise is preserved. Adopting constraint-aware analog placement engine instead of analog layout compactor with fixed layout topology provides the potential to explore various different placement topologies, which may result in the placement quality improvement. The constraint-aware analog placement algorithm will be described in Section 4.

3 LAYOUT CONSTRAINT EXTRACTION

3.1 Regularity Constraint Extraction

3.1.1 Problem Definition. AMS IC placements often contain *regular structures* which are also called *regularity constraints* [12]. A regular structure is composed of a group of devices forming a slicing structure whose rectangular bounding box in the placement does not cut any device bounding box. Fig. 3 shows an example of an analog placement with regularity constraints. Each rectangle represents the bounding box of a placement device (e.g. a transistor). The orange bounding boxes indicate row constraints. For example, devices {10, 11} form a row. The blue bounding boxes indicate column constraints. For example, devices {1, 2, 3}, {4, 5, 6} and devices 7, 8 are four rows in a column. The array constraints are indicated by red bounding boxes. For instance, devices {1, 2, 3, 4, 5, 6} form a 2-row-by-3-column array. If all the devices in row/column/array A are inside another bigger row/column/array B, and the set of slicing lines of A is a subset of that of B, we say that row/column/array A is *dominated* by row/column B. As an example, the row consisting

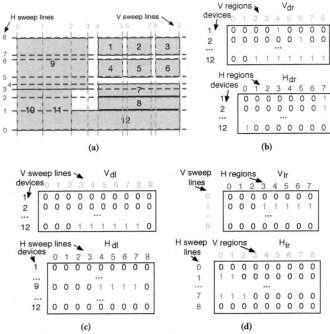

Figure 4: (a) The example analog placement in Fig. 3 with the grids. (b) LUT V_{dr} and H_{dr}. (c) V_{dl} and H_{dl}. (d) V_{lr} and H_{lr}.

of devices {1, 2} is dominated by the row consisting of devices {1, 2, 3}, and the row consisting of devices {1, 2, 3} is dominated by the array consisting of devices {1, 2, 3, 4, 5, 6}. The regularity constraint extraction problem is to find all the regular structures which are non-dominated by any other regular structure in an analog placement.

3.1.2 Lookup Table Construction. We first turn the placement into a grid-based representation. A device bounding box can be represented by the x (horizontal) coordinates of its left and right edges, and the y (vertical) coordinates of its bottom and top edges. The entire placement can be divided by the Hanan grid of all device bounding boxes, which is built based on the horizontal and vertical sweep lines. We construct the sets of horizontal and vertical sweep lines as follows. For each device bounding box in the placement, a *vertical sweep line* is added for the x coordinate of its left edge, and another vertical sweep line is added for the x coordinate of its right edge. For the vertical sweep lines with the same x coordinate, only one is added to the set. Therefore, the total number of vertical sweep lines is less than two times of the number of placement devices. Similarly, two *horizontal sweep lines* are added for the y coordinates of the bottom and top edges of a device, respectively. Fig. 4a shows the placement of Fig. 3 with the Hanan grid. In Fig. 4, "H/V" stands for "horizontal/vertical", respectively.

Then, several Boolean lookup tables (LUTs) are constructed which will be used by the sweep line-based algorithm in Section 3.1.3. For the subscripts of the LUTs, "d" stands for "device", "l" is for "sweep line", and "r" is for "region". For example, the LUT V_{dr} tells us the relationship between a device and a vertical region. The

LUTs V_{dr} and H_{dr} shown in Fig. 4b indicate which *region* each device bounding box in Fig. 4a lies in. A region is defined as the range between adjacent sweep lines. For example, a *vertical region* i is between vertical sweep lines i and $i + 1$. The number of vertical regions is one less than the number of vertical sweep lines. Each row in V_{dr} indicates which vertical region a device bounding box occupies. As an example, device 12 lies between vertical sweep lines 2 and 9, i.e. it occupies vertical regions {2, 3, ⋯, 8}. Hence, there are 1's at indices {2, 3, ⋯, 8} and 0's elsewhere on the row corresponding to device 12 in V_{dr}. Similarly, the *horizontal region* is defined and H_{dr} is constructed.

The LUTs V_{dl} and H_{dl} shown in Fig. 4c indicate the vertical or horizontal sweep lines a device bounding box strictly intersects. We say that an *HR/VR/HSL/VSL* (see Table 1) strictly intersect with a device when there is at least some portion of the *HR/VR/HSL/VSL* that is strictly inside the device bounding box, not including the borders of the bounding box. For instance, device 1 does not strictly intersect any vertical sweep line nor horizontal sweep line, so the rows corresponding to device 1 have all 0's in V_{dl} and H_{dl}. Device 9 strictly intersects horizontal sweep lines {4, 5, 6, 7}, so there are 1's at indices {4, 5, 6, 7} and 0's elsewhere on the row corresponding to device 9 in H_{dl}. The first and the last columns in V_{dl} and H_{dl} consist of all 0's, since the first and the last sweep lines will not strictly intersect with any device. Once we have constructed V_{dr} and H_{dr}, V_{dl} and H_{dl} can be computed by bitwise operations efficiently:

$$V_{dl}[d] = V_{dr}[d]\&(V_{dr}[d] \ll 1)$$

$$H_{dl}[d] = H_{dr}[d]\&(H_{dr}[d] \ll 1)$$

where "d" is the device index, "&" stands for the bitwise *and* operation, and "$\ll$" is the bitwise left shift operation.

The LUTs V_{lr} and H_{lr} shown in Fig. 4d indicate whether a sweep line strictly intersects any device bounding box in a region. Each row in the LUT corresponds to a sweep line, and each column in the LUT corresponds to a region. For example, the vertical sweep line 1 strictly intersects device 9 in horizontal regions 3 to 7. Therefore, in LUT V_{lr}, row 1 has 1's in columns {3, 4, ⋯, 7}. Note that the first and the last rows in V_{lr} and H_{lr} are all 0's, since the first and the last sweep lines will not strictly intersect with any device in any region. LUTs V_{lr} and H_{lr} can be computed from V_{dr}, H_{dr}, V_{dl} and H_{dl} as follows:

$$V_{lr}[i][j] = \bigvee_d (V_{dl}[d][i] \wedge H_{dr}[d][j])$$

$$H_{lr}[i][j] = \bigvee_d (H_{dl}[d][i] \wedge V_{dr}[d][j])$$

where "d" is the device index, "$\wedge$" is the logical conjunction operator, and "$\bigvee$" is the logical disjunction operator. Overall, the time complexity for LUT construction is $O(n)$, where n is the number of placement devices.

3.1.3 Sweep Line-Based Algorithm. A sweep line-based algorithm is proposed to extract all the regularity constraints in an analog placement. The notations used are listed in Table 1. The overall algorithm is described in Alg. 1. The algorithm is based on the observation that if there is a slicing line segment between point A and point B for the placement (i.e., the line segment AB does not strictly intersect any device bounding box), then for every point

Table 1: Notations

HSL	Horizontal sweep line.
VSL	Vertical sweep line.
HR	Horizontal region.
VR	Vertical region.
VR_j	The j-th VR.
R_{fin}	All regular structure results.
R_{par}	Intermediate/partial regular structures.
r_h, r_v	Consecutive HRs and VRs in the intermediate/final regular structure.
l_h, l_v	Slicing $HSLs$ and $VSLs$ in the intermediate/final regular structure.
(r_h, l_h, r_v, l_v)	Represents an intermediate or final regular structure.
f_v	Indicates if the consecutive HRs are slicing at a VSL.
f_h	Indicates if a set of $HSLs$ are slicing at a VR.
Q	A set of consecutive HRs that are slicing at a VSL.

C on AB, AC and CB must also be slicing for the placement. The terminology is defined as follows:

Definition 1 (Slicing Region). *If an HR/VR does not strictly intersect with any device bounding box at a VSL/HSL, it is a slicing HR/VR at that VSL/HSL.*

Definition 2 (Sweep Line within a Region). *An HSL/VSL is within a HR/VR (or a region covers a sweep line) when the coordinate of the HSL/VSL is within the region or at the region endpoints.*

Fig. 5a, Fig. 5b, Fig. 5c and Fig. 5d show the intermediate steps after Alg. 1 proceeds to $VSLs$ 1, 2, 3 and 4, respectively, when the algorithm is applied to the analog placement example in Fig. 3.

Lines 1-2 in Alg. 1 initialize the set of final regular structures R_{fin} and the set of intermediate (partial) regular structures R_{par}. For each $VSL\ j$, in line 4, we obtain the set of consecutive slicing HRs, Q, at the j-th VSL. We also initialize all consecutive HRs in Q to be irredundant, and will use this indicator in subsequent operations. Q can be obtained from the consecutive 0's on the j-th row of LUT V_{lr}, which is explained in Lemma 1. Lemma 1 is correct by construction of the LUT V_{lr}.

Lemma 1. *The consecutive HRs are slicing at a $VSL\ j$ iff the corresponding indices of the consecutive HRs have consecutive 0's on the row $V_{lr}[j]$ in V_{lr}.*

Each intermediate or final regular structure can be represented by its (r_h, l_h, r_v, l_v) (see Table 1). For each intermediate regular structure in R_{par}, r_v is updated to contain the j-th VR (line 7 of Alg. 1). We define two indicator variables f_v and f_h, as shown in lines 11 and 12 and in Table 1.

f_v can be obtained in a way similar to the way of obtaining Q. f_v indicates whether all the consecutive HRs in r_h are slicing at $VSL\ j$. If it is true, one and only one q in Q will overlap with r_h, and Alg. 2 will be executed. In Alg. 2, we first add j to the set of $VSLs$ in the intermediate result. Let q be the consecutive slicing HRs at j that overlap with r_h, and let l_h^q be the set of $HSLs$ within q at which the j-th VR is slicing. If l_h^q is the same as l_h in the intermediate result under consideration, then q will be marked as redundant, and no new intermediate regular structure needs to be created for q, since it is contained in the existing intermediate result. This can be illustrated by Fig. 5b. Before processing $VSL\ 2$, $R_{par}[1]$ (in green) has $r_h = \{0, 1, 2\}$ and $l_v = \{0, 1\}$. The set of consecutive slicing HRs Q at $VSL\ 2$ only has one element $q = \{0, 1, 2\}$. Therefore, f_v is true for $R_{par}[1]$ at $VSL\ 2$, and $VSL\ 2$ is added to l_v which makes l_v {0, 1,

---

Algorithm 1 Regularity Constraint Extraction Algorithm

Input: H_{lr}, V_{lr}
Output: All regular structures R_{fin}
1:   $R_{fin} \leftarrow \emptyset$;
2:   $R_{par} \leftarrow \emptyset$;
3:   **for** each $VSL\ j$ except the last one **do**
4:     $Q \leftarrow$ The set of consecutive slicing HR at j;
5:     Mark each q in Q as irredundant;
6:     **for** each (r_h, l_h, r_v, l_v) in R_{par} **do**
7:       $r_v \leftarrow r_v \cup VR_j$;
8:       $f_v \leftarrow$ Whether r_h are all slicing at $VSL\ j$;
9:       **if** f_v is true **then**
10:        UpdateC1$((r_h, l_h, r_v, l_v), R_{par}, R_{fin}, Q)$;
11:       **else**
12:        UpdateC2$((r_h, l_h, r_v, l_v), R_{par}, R_{fin}, Q)$;
13:       **end if**
14:       $f_h \leftarrow$ Whether VR_j is slicing at every HSL in l_h;
15:       **if** f_h is false **then**
16:        $l_h^{rh} \leftarrow$ The set of $HSLs$ within r_h at which VR_j is slicing;
17:        $l_h' \leftarrow l_h^{rh} \cap l_h$;
18:        $r_h' \leftarrow$ The minimal consecutive HRs covering l_h';
19:        Check (r_h, l_h, r_v, l_v) before adding to R_{fin};
20:        $r_h \leftarrow r_h'$;
21:        $l_h \leftarrow l_h'$;
22:       **end if**
23:     **end for**
24:     **for** each irredundant $HRs\ q$ in Q **do**
25:       $l_h^{new} \leftarrow$ The set of $HSLs$ within q where VR_j is slicing;
26:       $r_v^{new} \leftarrow$ the j-th VR;
27:       $l_v^{new} \leftarrow VSL\ j$;
28:       Add $(q, l_h^{new}, r_v^{new}, l_v^{new})$ to R_{par};
29:     **end for**
30:   **end for**
31:   **for** each (r_h, l_h, r_v, l_v) in R_{par} **do**
32:     $l_v \leftarrow l_v \cup$ the last VSL;
33:     Check (r_h, l_h, r_v, l_v) before adding to R_{fin};
34:   **end for**
35:   **return** R_{fin};

2}. Since $l_h^q = \{0, 1, 2, 3\}$ is not the same as $l_h = \{0, 3\}$, q is not marked as redundant when processing $R_{par}[1]$ at $VSL\ 2$.

Otherwise, if f_v is false, there may be zero or more HRs in Q overlapping with r_h, and Alg. 3 will be executed. In Alg. 3, for each consecutive slicing $HRs\ q$ overlapping with r_h, l_h^q is obtained as in the case where f_v is true. Then l_h', which is the intersection between l_h^q and l_h, is calculated and compared with l_h^q. If they are the same, then no new intermediate result for q needs to be added to R_{par}, and q is marked as redundant. After that, we find the minimal HRs r_h' covering l_h' and add that intermediate result with $VSL\ j$ to the set R_{par}. This process can be illustrated by Fig. 5a. Before processing $VSL\ 1$, $R_{par}[0]$ (in red) has $r_h = \{1, 2, \cdots, 7\}$, but Q only consists of one element which is $q = \{0, 1, 2\}$. Hence, f_v is false for $R_{par}[0]$. $l_h^q = \{0, 3\}$, and l_h' is the same as l_h^q. Therefore, q is marked as redundant

Algorithm 2 UpdateC1$((r_h, l_h, r_v, l_v), R_{par}, R_{fin}, Q)$

1: $l_v \leftarrow l_v \cup j$;
2: $q \leftarrow$ The consecutive slicing HRs in Q overlapping r_h;
3: $l_h^q \leftarrow$ The set of HSLs within q at which VR_j is slicing;
4: **if** $l_h == l_h^q$ **then**
5:      Mark q as redundant;
6: **end if**

Algorithm 3 UpdateC2$((r_h, l_h, r_v, l_v), R_{par}, R_{fin}, Q)$

1: **for** each consecutive slicing HRs q in Q overlapping r_h **do**
2:      $l_h^q \leftarrow$ The set of HSLs within q where VR_j is slicing;
3:      $l_h' \leftarrow l_h^q \cap l_h$;
4:      **if** $l_h' == l_h^q$ **then**
5:          Mark q as redundant;
6:      **end if**
7:      $r_h' \leftarrow$ The minimal HRs covering l_h';
8:      Add $(r_h', l_h', r_v, l_v \cup j)$ to R_{par};
9: **end for**

and no new intermediate result needs to be created for it. We find the minimal HRs $r_h' = \{0, 1, 2\}$, and create a new intermediate result with $(r_h', l_h', r_v, l_v \cup j)$ (see $R_{par}[1]$ in green in Fig. 5a). Lines 9 to 13 in Alg. 1 call the two functions "UpdateC1" (Alg. 2) and "UpdateC2" (Alg. 3) depending on f_v.

f_h can be obtained from the j-th column of LUT H_{lr} (see Lemma 2, and line 14 of Alg. 1). Similar to Lemma 1, Lemma 2 also holds by construction of H_{lr}.

Lemma 2. *VR j is slicing at an HSL i iff $H_{lr}[i][j]$ is 0.*

If f_h is true, it means the slicing HSLs in l_h continues to be slicing at the j-th VR. For instance, In Fig. 5a, before processing VSL 1, the r_v of $R_{par}[0]$ (in red) is $\{0\}$ (only VR 0 is in r_v). Since all the three HSLs in $l_h = \{0, 3, 8\}$ are slicing at VR 1, f_h is true and VR 1 is added to r_v which becomes $\{0, 1\}$ after processing VSL 1 (see Fig. 5a).

Otherwise, if f_h is false, it means at least one of the HSLs in l_h is no longer slicing at the j-th VR, and we will add the previous intermediate result to the final result after trimming and checking whether the resulting regular structure is valid (line 19 in Alg. 1). That is, r_h and r_v will be trimmed such that they are the minimal regions covering l_h and l_v (see Definition 2). We also check to ensure that each of the rectangular regions formed by l_h and l_v contains at least one device. This can be done by bitwise operations on V_{dr} and H_{dr}. We further prune the final result such that the regular structure contains more than 2 HSLs or more than 2 VSLs to form a valid regular structure. Finally, the resulting regular structure will be compared against the existing ones in R_{fin} to ensure that each regular structure is non-dominated by any other regular structure. After that, the existing intermediate result is updated to contain only the continuing slicing VR (lines 20 to 21 in Alg. 1). Fig. 5d shows the case where f_h is false. Before processing VSL 4, $R_{par}[1]$ (in green) have two HSLs $l_h = \{0, 3\}$ (as in Fig. 5c). However, the VR 4 is not slicing at HSL 3, resulting in f_h being false. We trim the r_v from $\{0, 1, 2, 3\}$ to $\{0, 1\}$ (since $l_v = \{0, 1, 2\}$), and make sure that each of the 2 columns in the row contains at least one device

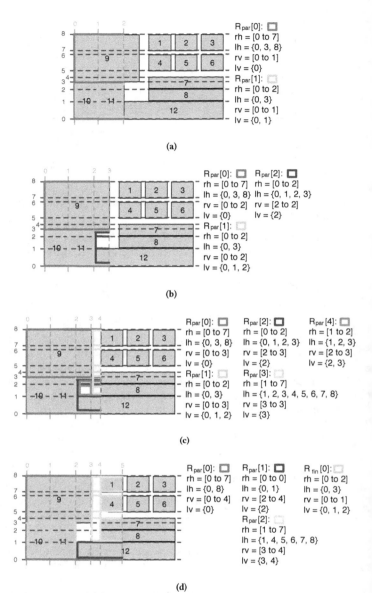

(a)

(b)

(c)

(d)

Figure 5: Applying Alg. 1 to the placement in Fig. 3 after processing (a) *VSLs 0 and 1.* **(b)** *VSL 2.* **(c)** *VSL 3.* **(d)** *VSL 4.*

(devices 10 and 11, respectively). Therefore, $R_{fin}[0]$ is added the final result (see Fig. 5d). Since there is only one HSL remaining in the original intermediate result which will no longer form a regular structure, it will be removed. Similarly, for $R_{par}[3]$ in Fig. 5c (in cyan), its l_h changes from $\{1, 2, 3, 4, 5, 6, 7, 8\}$ to $\{1, 4, 5, 6, 7, 8\}$. It remains in R_{par} but becomes $R_{par}[2]$ in Fig. 5d since the original intermediate result $R_{par}[1]$ in Fig. 5c (in green) is removed. The resulting candidate to add to R_{fin} with $l_h = \{1, 2, 3, 4, 5, 6, 7, 8\}$ and $l_v = \{3, 4\}$ is not valid because it contains no device. Thus it is not added to R_{fin}.

After iterating through all the intermediate regular structures in R_{par}, for each of the consecutive slicing HRs q in Q that remains irredundant (i.e. that is not marked as redundant by the algorithm), a new intermediate regular structure is added to R_{par}, as can be seen in lines 24-29 in Alg. 1. The new intermediate result has q, the j-th VR, and the VSL j. Its $HSLs$ can be obtained from H_{lr} similarly to the way of getting f_h. Fig. 5b shows an example of adding a new intermediate regular structure for the irredundant consecutive slicing HRs in Q. The set of consecutive slicing HRs Q at VSL 2 only has one element $q = \{0, 1, 2\}$. It turns out that q remains irredundant after processing both $R_{par}[0]$ and $R_{par}[1]$. Therefore, a new intermediate result $R_{par}[2]$ (in purple) with $r_h = \{0, 1, 2\}$, $l_h = \{0, 1, 2, 3\}$, $r_v = \{2\}$ and $l_v = \{2\}$ is added to the set R_{par}.

The above procedure is performed for all the $VSLs$ except the last one. Finally, in lines 31-34 in Alg. 1, the last VSL is added to the l_v for all the intermediate results in R_{par}, and the updated regular structures (r_h, l_h, r_v, l_v) are checked and trimmed before they are added to the R_{fin}, as already described above.

3.1.4   Algorithm Analysis. The proposed sweep line-based algorithm is, in essence, a smart enumeration algorithm with pruning, and is guaranteed to find all the regularity constraints.

Lemma 3. *Alg. 1 finds all regular structures that are non-dominated by any other regular structure in an analog placement.*

PROOF. We begin with the proof that the results found by Alg. 1 are slicing structures and are non-dominated by any other regular structure. The proof is by induction. For the first VSL, the entire VSL is slicing, and it must be irredundant. Therefore, the first intermediate result in R_{par} is obviously slicing (lines 24-29 in Alg. 1). Now assume that the intermediate results in R_{par} are slicing just before the algorithm proceeds to the j-th VSL. There are two cases depending on f_v (lines 9-13 in Alg. 1). In Alg. 2, VSL j is slicing and is added to l_v, thus the intermediate regular structure is still slicing. In Alg. 3, $(r'_h, l'_h, r_v, l_v \cup j)$ is a slicing structure, and after it is added to R_{par}, the slicing property of the intermediate regular structure still holds. When l'_h is assigned to l_h (line 21 in Alg. 1), the slicing property is maintained. When $(q, l_h^{new}, r_v^{new}, l_v^{new})$ is added to R_{par} (line 28 in Alg. 1), the slicing property is still maintained. As a result, we know that after processing the j-th VSL, the intermediate results in R_{par} are all slicing. For the last VSL, the entire VSL is slicing, after adding it to the l_v of every intermediate regular structure, the results are still slicing. Note that before adding to R_{fin}, the regular structure is compared against other regular structures to ensure the non-dominance condition. Therefore, the results found by Alg. 1 are slicing structures and are non-dominated by any other regular structure.

Next, we show that any regular structure that is non-dominated by other regular structures will be found by Alg. 1. Let $(r_h^*, l_h^*, r_v^*, l_v^*)$ be any of these regular structures. Let j^* be the first VSL in l_v^*. VSL j^* must be slicing at some irredundant HRs q and $r_h^* \subseteq q$, since otherwise the regular structure must be in a larger regular structure, which contradicts with the non-dominance condition. Lines 24-29 in Alg. 1 adds the intermediate result $(q, l_h^{new}, r_v^{new}, l_v^{new})$ to R_{par}, where $r_h^* \subseteq q$, $l_h^* \subseteq l_h^{new}$, $r_v^{new} = VR j^*$, $l_v^{new} = VSL j^*$. Then, before processing the last VSL in l_v^*, for every HSL in l_h^{new} but not in l_h^*, there must be some VR where it is not slicing, therefore, f_h will be false and the HSL will be removed from l_h of the intermediate result. In contrast, all HSL in l_h^* will remain in l_h. As for the $VSLs$,

from j^* until the last VSL in l_v^*, if the $VSL \notin l_v^*$, f_v must be false, it is not added to the l_v of the intermediate result. On the contrary, if the $VSL \in l_v^*$, there are two cases depending on f_v. If f_v is true, in Alg. 2, the VSL is added to l_v of the intermediate result. Otherwise, if f_v is false, in Alg. 3, there must be some $q \in Q$ overlapping r_h^*. r'_h must contain r_h^*, and l'_h must contain l_h^*, hence the newly added intermediate result by line 8 in Alg. 3 will continue to produce $(r_h^*, l_h^*, r_v^*, l_v^*)$. Before processing the last VSL in l_v^*, the intermediate result contains exactly l_h^* and all the $VSLs$ in l_v^* except the last one. For the last VSL in l_v^*, f_v must be true and f_h must be false. The last VSL in l_v^* is added to the l_v of the intermediate regular structure which makes it the same as l_v^*, thus the regular structure $(r_h^*, l_h^*, r_v^*, l_v^*)$ is added to R_{fin}. Therefore, any regular structure that is non-dominated by other regular structures will be found by Alg. 1.   □

Most of the operations in the proposed algorithm are bitwise operations and efficient. Let n be the number of placement devices. The outer loop of Alg. 1 is executed $O(n)$ times. In each iteration of the outer loop, the number of intermediate regular structures is $O(n^3)$. Inside the inner loop, with bitwise operations and parallelization, the run-time is $O(1)$. Therefore, the time complexity of the proposed algorithm is $O(n^4)$.

3.2   Symmetry Constraint Extraction

The symmetry and symmetry-island constraint extraction algorithm we used is similar to that in [8, 14]. The main steps are sorting the devices by the edges, widths, and heights. Due to the page limit, we will skip the details of the algorithm.

4   CONSTRAINT-AWARE PLACEMENT

After the regularity constraints and symmetry (symmetry-island) constraints are extracted from the existing layout, the next step is to perform constraint-aware analog placement considering the extracted constraints and updated device sizes. The extracted constraints are general and can be applied to any constraint-aware analog placement engine that can handle regularity constraints and symmetry (symmetry-island) constraints, e.g., [2, 6, 12, 15]. The analog placement engine used in our layout retargeting flow is based on the Mixed-Integer Linear Programming (MILP) formulation, and the non-overlapping constraints and symmetry-island constraints are formulated similarly to [6].

As for the regularity constraints, we have the following conditions:

1) Conditions for devices inside the constraint: The devices inside the regularity constraint are separated by slicing lines. The devices in the i-th row and j-th column of the regular structure must lie inside the box formed by the i-th and $(i + 1)$-th horizontal slicing lines and the j-th and $(j + 1)$-th vertical slicing lines.

Let $D_{i,j,k}$ be the set of devices in the i-th $(i < i^k)$ row and j-th $(j < j^k)$ column in the regularity constraint k, where i^k is the number of rows and j^k is the number of columns in the regular structure, respectively. Let x_d be the x coordinate and y_d be the y coordinate of device d. For a regularity constraint with i^k rows and j^k columns, there should be $i^k + 1$ $HSLs$ and $j^k + 1$ $VSLs$ separating the rows and columns. We introduce $i^k + 1$ auxiliary

Table 2: Benchmark AMS IC placements

Placement	#Devices	#Row Const.	#Column Const.	#Array Const.	#Sym. Const.
1	45	3	9	3	14
2	50	5	14	0	18
3	200	20	56	1	72

variables, i.e., $y_r^{k,0}, y_r^{k,1}, \ldots, y_r^{k,i^k}$, to represent the y coordinates of the *HSLs*. Similarly, we introduce $j^k + 1$ auxiliary variables, i.e., $x_r^{k,0}, x_r^{k,1}, \ldots, x_r^{k,j^k}$, to represent the x coordinates of the *VSLs*. Assuming that the rows and *HSLs* are ordered from bottom to top, and that the columns and *VSLs* are ordered from left to right, the devices in $D_{i,j,k}$ must lie inside the box formed by $x_r^{k,j}$, $x_r^{k,j+1}$, $y_r^{k,i}$, and $y_r^{k,i+1}$:

$$x_d \geq x_r^{k,j}, x_d \leq x_r^{k,j+1}, y_d \geq y_r^{k,i}, y_d \leq y_r^{k,i+1}, \forall d \in D_{i,j,k}$$

2) Conditions for devices outside of the constraint: The devices outside of the regularity constraint must not overlap the bounding box formed by the devices inside the regularity constraint.

For each $d' \notin D_{i,j,k}$, we introduce a pair of auxiliary binary variables $s_{d'}^k$ and $t_{d'}^k$ to ensure the non-overlapping property. The following inequalities must be satisfied:

$$\begin{cases} x_{d'} + M_W(s_{d'}^k + t_{d'}^k) \geq x_r^{k,j^k} \\ x_{d'} + w_{d'} - M_W(1 + s_{d'}^k - t_{d'}^k) \leq x_r^{k,0} \\ y_{d'} + M_H(1 - s_{d'}^k + t_{d'}^k) \geq y_r^{k,i^k} \\ y_{d'} + h_{d'} - M_H(2 - s_{d'}^k - t_{d'}^k) \leq y_r^{k,0} \end{cases} \forall d' \notin D_{i,j,k}$$

where M_W and M_H are sufficiently large constants (big-M method [16]), such that no matter what binary values $s_{d'}^k$ and $t_{d'}^k$ are, only 1 out of the 4 inequalities takes effect, while other inequalities are left ineffective.

In the implementation, the orientations of the devices inside a regularity constraint are preserved during retargeting. Also, our placement engine takes the layout compaction result of the conventional layout retargeting approach as a starting point so that our placement quality will not be worse than the conventional approach.

5 EXPERIMENTAL RESULTS

All algorithms are implemented in C++ and all experiments are performed on a Linux machine with 3.4GHz CPU and 32GB memory. Table 2 lists the benchmark information used in our experiments, including small to medium scale analog circuits. In this section, "const." stands for constraints, "sym." stands for symmetry (symmetry-island), and the placement area unit is μm^2. The numbers of rows, columns and arrays can be obtained by a naïve exhaustive enumeration algorithm (with exponential complexity) which searches over all the possible combinations of *HSLs* and *VSLs* and guarantees to find all the regularity constraints.

5.1 Layout Constraint Extraction Results

For all benchmarks, our algorithm can correctly find all the regular structures, which are the same as those found by the naïve

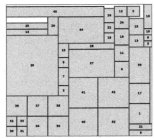

Figure 6: Regularity constraints in benchmark #1.

Table 3: Placement result comparison between the approach in [10] and our layout retargeting framework

Benchmark placement	[10]		Our work		Area reduction
	Area	Run-time	Area	Run-time	
1	23068	1.4s	20586	200s	10.8%
2	36248	2.0s	32752	200s	9.6%
3	134400	5.0s	131040	1200s	2.5%

exhaustive enumeration algorithm. As an example, Fig. 6 shows the benchmark placement #1, with the regularity constraints found by the proposed algorithm indicated in blue boxes. For instance, devices {2, 7, 9, 15} form a column, and {30, 31, 32, 33} form a 2-by-2 array. Symmetry (symmetry-island) constraints are also extracted as in [8–10]. For all benchmarks, the run-time of the constraint extraction engine is very fast (less than 0.01 seconds), which demonstrates the efficiency of the proposed algorithms.

5.2 Layout Retargeting Results

We implemented the layout topology extraction and layout compaction algorithms in [10] for comparison. For our constraint-aware analog placement engine, we implement it to take the layout compaction result of the approach in [10] as initial starting point so that we will only generate equal or better results. The change of device sizes due to different process technologies or updated design specifications is simulated by deviating the widths and heights from the original values by random percentages. According to the industrial designs, the percentages of the deviation are generated uniformly randomly in the range from -30% to +30% in our experiments. The size deviation percentage of the devices in a symmetry pair should be the same such that they have the same sizes.

The layout retargeting results are shown in Table 3, where for benchmark #1 and #2, we set the run-time limit to be 200s, and for benchmark #3, it is set to 1200s (see Fig. 8 for the selection of the run-time limit). In practice, users can set the run-time limit for our algorithm to achieve run-time and result quality tradeoff. Compared with the approach of [10], our framework explores more layout topologies and consistently achieves placement area reduction for all benchmarks. The layout retargeting results of benchmark #1 are shown in Fig. 7a and Fig. 7b, benchmark #2 in Fig. 7c and Fig. 7d, and benchmark #3 in Fig. 7e and Fig. 7f, respectively. We can see that the regularity and symmetry constraints are preserved for both approaches. However, our approach can achieve more compact placement than that of [10].

lines are the convergence curves of our framework, and the red lines indicate the result area of the approach in [10], which is also the initial starting point used by our placement engine. Although the approach in [10] finishes in a shorter period of time, it only returns one result with the same layout topology as the existing layout, which limits the solution space and may lead to inferior results. Currently, only symmetry and regularity constraints are captured in our method. Other features that are important to AMS circuits (e.g., signal integrity) should also be considered as the future work.

6　CONCLUSION

In this paper, we extract and explore the layout constraints and preserve the design expertise in the previous high-quality AMS IC layouts. Besides considering symmetry constraints as in the prior works, we further develop an efficient sweep line-based algorithm to extract the regularity constraints in an AMS circuit placement. We also propose a novel analog layout retargeting framework based on the extracted constraints, which can provide more flexibility and achieve better placement quality. Experimental results show the effectiveness of the proposed techniques.

ACKNOWLEDGMENT

This work is supported by the National Science Foundation under Grant No. 1527320.

REFERENCES

[1] K. Lampaert, G. Gielen, and W. M. Sansen, "A performance-driven placement tool for analog integrated circuits," *IEEE Journal Solid-State Circuits*, vol. 30, no. 7, pp. 773–780, 1995.
[2] M. Strasser, M. Eick, H. Gräb, U. Schlichtmann, and F. M. Johannes, "Deterministic analog circuit placement using hierarchically bounded enumeration and enhanced shape functions," in *Proc. ICCAD*, 2008, pp. 306–313.
[3] P.-H. Lin, Y.-W. Chang, and S.-C. Lin, "Analog placement based on symmetry-island formulation," *IEEE TCAD*, vol. 28, no. 6, pp. 791–804, 2009.
[4] Q. Ma, L. Xiao, Y.-C. Tam, and E. F. Young, "Simultaneous handling of symmetry, common centroid, and general placement constraints," *IEEE TCAD*, vol. 30, no. 1, pp. 85–95, 2011.
[5] H.-C. Ou, K.-H. Tseng, J.-Y. Liu, I.-P. Wu, and Y.-W. Chang, "Layout-dependent effects-aware analytical analog placement," *IEEE TCAD*, vol. 35, no. 8, pp. 1243–1254, 2016.
[6] B. Xu, S. Li, X. Xu, N. Sun, and D. Z. Pan, "Hierarchical and analytical placement techniques for high-performance analog circuits," in *Proc. ISPD*, 2017, pp. 55–62.
[7] F.-L. Heng, Z. Chen, and G. E. Tellez, "A vlsi artwork legalization technique based on a new criterion of minimum layout perturbation," in *Proc. ISPD*, 1997, pp. 116–121.
[8] N. Jangkrajarng, S. Bhattacharya, R. Hartono, and C.-J. R. Shi, "IPRAIL–intellectual property reuse-based analog ic layout automation," vol. 36, no. 4, pp. 237–262, 2003.
[9] L. Zhang, N. Jangkrajarng, S. Bhattacharya, and C.-J. R. Shi, "Parasitic-aware optimization and retargeting of analog layouts: A symbolic-template approach," *IEEE TCAD*, vol. 27, no. 5, pp. 791–802, 2008.
[10] Z. Liu and L. Zhang, "A performance-constrained template-based layout retargeting algorithm for analog integrated circuits," in *Proc. ASPDAC*, 2010, pp. 293–298.
[11] P.-H. Wu, M. P.-H. Lin, T.-C. Chen, C.-F. Yeh, X. Li, and T.-Y. Ho, "A novel analog physical synthesis methodology integrating existent design expertise," *IEEE TCAD*, vol. 34, no. 2, pp. 199–212, 2015.
[12] S. Nakatake, M. Kawakita, T. Ito, M. Kojima, M. Kojima, K. Izumi, and T. Habasaki, "Regularity-oriented analog placement with diffusion sharing and well island generation," in *Proc. ASPDAC*, 2010, pp. 305–311.
[13] S. Nakatake, "Structured placement with topological regularity evaluation," in *Proc. ASPDAC*, 2007, pp. 215–220.
[14] Y. Bourai and C.-J. Shi, "Symmetry detection for automatic analog-layout recycling," in *Proc. ASPDAC*, 1999, pp. 5–8.
[15] P.-H. Lin and S.-C. Lin, "Analog placement based on hierarchical module clustering," in *Proc. DAC*, 2008, pp. 50–55.
[16] S. Sutanthavibul, E. Shragowitz, and J. Rosen, "An analytical approach to floorplan design and optimization," *IEEE TCAD*, vol. 10, no. 6, pp. 761–769, 1991.

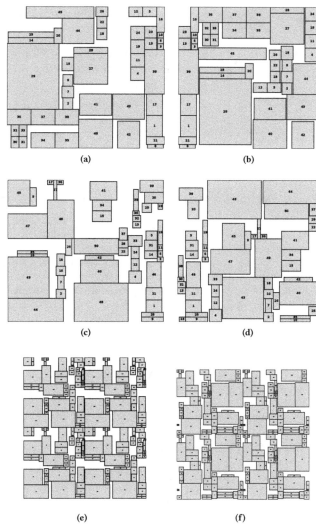

Figure 7: Layout retargeting results: benchmark #1 by (a) [10], and (b) our appoach; benchmark #2 by (c) [10], and (b) our appoach; benchmark #3 by (e) [10], and (f) our appoach.

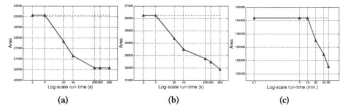

Figure 8: Layout retargeting result area and run-time trade-off of benchmark (a) #1, (b) #2, and (c) #3.

We further plot the convergence curves of running our layout retargeting framework on all benchmarks in Fig. 8. In Fig. 8, the run-time is plotted in logarithmic-scale. In Fig. 8a and 8b, the run-time unit is in "s", while in Fig. 8c the run-time unit is in "min.". The blue

Pin Assignment Optimization for Multi-2.5D FPGA-based Systems

Wan-Sin Kuo
National Tsing Hua University
Hsinchu, Taiwan
ws_kuo@gapp.nthu.edu.tw

Shi-Han Zhang
National Tsing Hua University
Hsinchu, Taiwan
ted21018@gmail.com

Wai-Kei Mak
National Tsing Hua University
Hsinchu, Taiwan
wkmak@cs.nthu.edu.tw

Richard Sun
Synopsys Inc.
Mountain View, CA
Richard.Sun@synopsys.com

Yoon Kah Leow
Synopsys Inc.
Mountain View, CA
YOON.LEOW@synopsys.com

ACM Reference Format:
Wan-Sin Kuo, Shi-Han Zhang, Wai-Kei Mak, Richard Sun, and Yoon Kah Leow. 2018. Pin Assignment Optimization for Multi-2.5D FPGA-based Systems. In *ISPD '18: 2018 International Symposium on Physical Design, March 25–28, 2018, Monterey, CA, USA.* ACM, New York, NY, USA, 8 pages. https://doi.org/10.1145/3177540.3178246

Abstract— Advanced 2.5D FPGAs with larger logic capacity and higher pin counts compared to conventional FPGAs are commercially available. Some multi-FPGA systems have already utilized 2.5D FPGAs. Commercial 2.5D FPGA consists of multiple dies connected through an interposer. The interposer provides a fraction of the amount of interconnect resources with increased delay compared to that within individual dies. A recent study has shown the benefits of reducing signal crossings between dies on routability and timing when a circuit is mapped to a 2.5D FPGA. In a multi-2.5D FPGA system with multiplexed hardwired inter-FPGA connections, there can be tens of thousands of inter-FPGA signals incident with each FPGA and their pin assignment can greatly affect the amount of signal crossings between dies. In this paper, we formulate the pin assignment problem for such system with the objective of minimizing signal crossings between dies within the individual FPGAs. Taking into consideration of the multi-die structure of 2.5D FPGA, we propose an effective and efficient iterative improvement algorithm based on integer linear programming to the pin assignment problem. Experimental results show that our algorithm can reduce signal crossings between dies in the individual FPGAs by over 30% on average compared to two heuristic approaches.

This work was supported in part by the Ministry of Science and Technology under grant MOST 104-2628-E-007-003-MY3.

1 INTRODUCTION

Multi-FPGA (field-programmable gate arrays) systems are widely used for logic emulation and rapid prototyping of large designs, and as reconfigurable custom computing platforms[1]. A multi-FPGA system consists of multiple FPGAs which are connected using direct hardwired connections or a programmable interconnection network that may consist of one or more field-programmable interconnect chips (FPICs).

The majority of multi-FPGA systems have some or all of their FPGAs directly connected[2]. In practice, the available pin counts of the FPGAs can greatly limit the utilization of FPGA logic resources in a mulit-FPGA system. So, time-division-multiplexing (TDM) which multiplexes the use of FPGA pins and inter-FPGA physical wires among multiple inter-FPGA signals is commonly deployed[3]. In this way, the number of pins available in each FPGA can be effectively increased leading to higher logic utilization per FPGA.

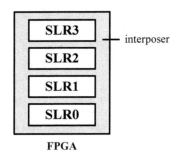

Figure 1: Structure of a commercial 2.5D FPGA.

2.5D FPGAs are commercially available and they have much larger capacity compared to traditional FPGAs[4]. For example, Xilinx's Virtex-7 2.5D FPGA is made up of four dies (also known as super logic regions or SLR) arranged linearly on an interposer as shown in Fig.1. Since building multi-FPGA systems with the largest available FPGAs enables the implementation of larger designs or the implementation of the same design with higher execution speed due to reduced need of inter-FPGA communication, 2.5D FPGAs are quickly adopted inside multi-FPGA systems[5].

It is known that the amount of interconnect resources between dies in a 2.5D FPGA is considerably less than that within a die and there is increased delay to cross the interposer. When a circuit is implemented on a 2.5D FPGA, [6] showed the importance of incorporating a die partitioning step during physical synthesis to reduce signal crossings between super logic regions. By reducing the SLR crossings, both routability and circuit speed can be enhanced significantly[6].

[6] focused on reducing the total SLR crossings by SLR partitioning in a stand-alone 2.5D FPGA. However, the problem of pin assignment in the context of a multi-FPGA system and its impact on the amount of SLR crossings were not addressed in [6]. When a large scale design is implemented on a multi-FPGA system with multiplexed hardwired connections, the I/O signal counts per FPGA is in the order of tens of thousands and their I/O pin assignment can have a big impact on the overall SLR crossings. Hence, pin assignment for multi-FPGA system should consider SLR relationship to maximize system performance. In our experiments, we found that our SLR-aware pin assignment approach can reduce the I/O signal induced SLR crossings by more than 30% compared to heuristic approaches.

In this paper, we formulate the SLR-aware pin assignment problem for modern multi-FPGA system utilizing high capacity 2.5D FPGAs, and propose an efficient and effective approach to solve the problem. To the best of our knowledge, ours is the first work to consider minimizing the number of SLR crossings in a multi-2.5D FPGA-based system during pin assignment.

The rest of the paper is organized as follows. In Section 2, we provide more relevant preliminary information for the multi-FPGA system compilation flow and the SLR-aware pin assignment problem. Our SLR-aware pin assignment algorithm is introduced in Section 3. In Section 4, we report the experimental comparisons against two other approaches and analyze the proposed approach. We conclude the paper in Section 5. A small example is given in the appendix.

2   PRELIMINARIES

In this section, we first describe the assumed multi-FPGA system architecture and the overall compilation flow. Then we discuss the previous works for pin assignment in multi-FPGA systems. Finally, we define the SLR-aware pin assignment problem.

2.1   Targeted Architecture and Compilation Flow

We consider a multi-FPGA system with multiplexed hardwired inter-FPGA connections. We assume that each FPGA in the system is a 2.5D device like the Virtex-7/UltraScale device which consists of multiple super logic regions (SLRs) connected through a silicon interposer. Fig. 2 depicts a system with four 2.5D FPGAs where each consists of four super logic regions. We say that two FPGAs are adjacent if they are directly connected in the system. We can divide the physical wires between two adjacent FPGAs into distinct groups according to the pair of SLRs they connect. For example, there are a total of 120 physical wires between FPGAs A and B, they are divided into three groups where the first group is between SLR1 of A and SLR1 of B which contains 50 wires, the second group is between SLR3 of A and SLR2 of B which contains 50 wires, the

third group is between SLR3 of A and SLR3 of B which contains 20 wires.

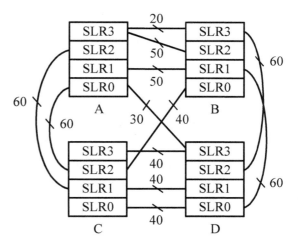

Figure 2: A multi-2.5D FPGA system.

A typical compilation flow for a multi-FPGA system[7] is shown in Fig. 3. The first step of the compilation flow is logic synthesis and technology mapping. Technology mapping maps the given circuit into a netlist of primitive elements such as Lookup-tables (LUTs), flip-flops, RAM slices, etc. The technology mapped netlist is then divided into partitions such that each partition can fit into a single FPGA subject to the constraints on its resources. The partitioning step tries to minimize the required inter-FPGA connections. Next, board level placement puts each partition into a distinct FPGA on the board. After board level placement, inter-FPGA global routing is performed.

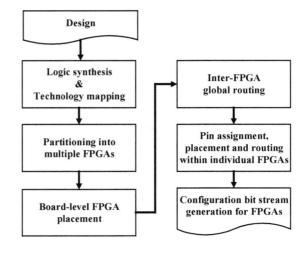

Figure 3: A typical compilation flow for a multi-FPGA system.

Inter-FPGA global routing determines the routing path/tree for every inter-FPGA net subject to the available board interconnect resources. An inter-FPGA route passing through multiple FPGAs induces multiple inter-FPGA 2-pin subnets. The time-division-multiplexing (TDM) factor for each inter-FPGA 2-pin subnet is decided during global routing based on its timing criticality. The board level global router has to ensure that the number of inter-FPGA 2-pin subnets between any two adjacent FPGAs will not require more physical wires than available under their TDM specification. Then, the pin assignment step chooses the specific physical wire and pins to use for each inter-FPGA 2-pin subnet subject to the TDM constraints imposed by the board level global router. Finally, the placement and routing of individual FPGAs can be performed.

2.2 Previous Works on Pin Assignment

It was noted in [7, 8] that early multi-FPGA systems generally ignored the issue of pin assignment, and simply randomly assigned signals to physical wires and pins. A disadvantage of such an approach is that it may lead to increased routing congestion and wirelength within the FPGAs. [8] is a pioneering work trying to improve individual FPGA placement and routing quality and runtime by proposing a specialized pin assignment algorithm. Unfortunately, the algorithm in [8] is for the special case that each physical wire can only accommodate one signal, in other words, no time-division-multiplexing is allowed since it is unable to account for TDM constraints. Moreover, it targeted much older FPGA architectures instead of 2.5D FPGAs. Nowadays, for 2.5D FPGAs, optimizing routing resource usage across SLRs is the dominant factor in improving the quality and runtime of individual FPGA placement and routing.

It is worth mentioning that there are different forms of pin assignment problem that have been studied in other contexts of VLSI design which differ from ours. For example, [9] considered a generic pin assignment problem for multiple components to be interconnected by a wiring substrate in order to optimize the routability and cost of the wiring substrate. [10–12] considered the pin assignment for a FPGA when it has to be integrated into a PCB with other ASIC chips utilizing a mixture of different I/O standards subject to the FPGA I/O banking constraints.

2.3 SLR-Aware Pin Assignment

For 2.5D FPGAs consisting of multiple super logic regions, the routing usage across SLRs depends on both the SLR partitioning and pin assignment of each FPGA. We assume SLR partitioning[6] that minimizes the SLR crossings due to connections between logic elements within the same FPGA has been performed prior to pin assignment, and place & route. In other words, when performing pin assignment, we already know which SLR each logic element belongs to. Eventually, both the SLR partitioning and pin assignment results of a FPGA are propagated to the FPGA P&R tool so that all logic elements will be placed within their desired SLRs and all I/O pins at their specified locations[1].

Below we elaborate on the SLR-aware pin assignment problem which is the focus of this work. Fig. 4 shows an inter-FPGA global routing result of an instance containing two inter-FPGA nets p

---

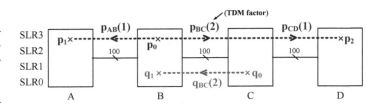

Figure 4: A global routing result. Net p induces three inter-FPGA 2-pin subnets p_{AB}, p_{BC}, and p_{CD}. Net q induces one inter-FPGA 2-pin subnet q_{BC}.

and q. Net p 's source is logic element p_0 and its sinks are logic elements p_1 and p_2. Net q 's source is logic element q_0 and its sink is logic element q_1. Note that even though net p does not have any terminal in FPGA C, it routes through FPGA C. Suppose die partitioning has put the logic elements into the SLRs as shown in Fig. 5. A feasible pin assignment solution with seven SLR crossings under the given inter-FPGA global routing result is illustrated in Fig. 5. The number of crossings within FPGAs A, B, C, and D are 2, 2, 2, and 1, respectively.

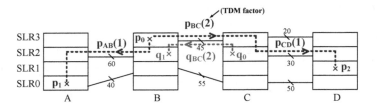

Figure 5: A feasible pin assignment with 7 SLR crossings.

We make a few remarks about our pin assignment problem by referencing the example in Fig. 5. First, even though the TDM factors for both subnets p_{BC} and q_{BC} are 2, they cannot share a physical wire since their directions are different. In Fig. 5, they are assigned to two distinct physical wires between SLR3 of B and SLR3 of C. Second, which two out of the forty-five physical wires between SLR3 of B and SLR3 of C are used do not affect the final SLR crossing value. Finally, in order to correctly count the SLR crossings of a specific pin assignment solution, it is important to know which 2-pin subnets originated from the same net. For example, the number of SLR crossings made by net p inside FPGA B depends on how its 2-pin subnets p_{AB} and p_{BC} are assigned. There are four different combinations of assignment for p_{AB} and p_{BC} which yield different amounts of SLR crossings inside FPGA B.

The SLR-aware pin assignment problem is defined below. We are given a set of 2-pin inter-FPGA subnets with their corresponding TDM factors and directions, and the knowledge of which 2-pin subnets originate from the same net. The goal is to assign all these 2-pin subnets to physical wires and pins to minimize the total SLR crossings subject to the constraints on the TDM factors and directions. Therefore, only 2-pin subnets between two adjacent FPGAs in the same direction with identical TDM factor can share a physical wire, and the number of signals sharing a physical wire

---

[1] Such constraints are supported by FPGA P&R tools like Vivado.

cannot exceed the TDM factor of the wire which is equal to the TDM factor of the signals it is carrying.

3 ALGORITHM

3.1 Overview

As observed in the last section, the SLR crossings caused by each inter-FPGA net is solely determined by the assignment of its 2-pin inter-FPGA subnets to physical wire groups without regard to which wires in the wire groups are used. So, the SLR-aware pin assignment problem can be reduced to the following problem. For each 2-pin inter-FPGA subnet, determine which group of wires it should be assigned to. At the same time, determine how many wires in each wire group is reserved for each particular type of 2-pin inter-FPGA signals between two neighboring FPGAs such that each type of 2-pin inter-FPGA signals has enough wires reserved. For example, if there are thirty-eight 2-pin inter-FPGA subnets directed from FPGA u to v with TDM factor of 10 assigned to the group between SLR1 of u and SLR2 of v, then there must be at least $\lceil 38/10 \rceil = 4$ wires in that group reserved for them. Moreover, the assignment of 2-pin inter-FPGA subnets to wire groups should be done in such a way that minimizes the total SLR crossings.

One major difficulty of the SLR-aware pin assignment problem is that the effect on SLR crossings when a 2-pin subnet is assigned to a particular physical wire group is not fixed but depends on the assignment of other subnets that belong to the same net. To overcome this difficulty, we propose an integer linear programming(ILP)-based iterative improvement approach to the problem as shown in Fig. 6. We start with a random initial assignment of all 2-pin inter-FPGA subnets to physical wires subject to the direction and TDM constraints (recall that the existence of a feasible assignment is guaranteed by the prior inter-FPGA global routing step). If there are n FPGAs in the system, each round of optimization consists of n iterations. At the beginning of a new round, we order the FPGAs in decreasing order of their current SLR crossings. In each iteration, we pick an FPGA according to this order and construct an ILP to re-assign all 2-pin inter-FPGA subnets between it and its neighboring FPGAs to optimally reduce the total number of SLR crossings in it and its neighboring FPGAs while assuming the assignment of all other 2-pin inter-FPGA subnets in the rest of the system is fixed. As a result, the overall SLR crossings of the whole system is guaranteed to decrease monotonically at each iteration. In practice, the above process converges quickly in just a few rounds. Moreover, experimental results show that the quality of result is very stable, i.e., there is very little variation in the final total number of SLR crossings when different initial feasible pin assignments are used.

3.2 Initial Feasible Pin Assignment Generation

We may generate an initial feasible pin assignment solution subject to the constraints of TDM factors and directions as follows. For any two adjacent FPGAs u and v in the system, we first classify all the inter-FPGA 2-pin subnets between them into different connection types according to their TDM factors and directions (i.e., from u to v, or from v to u). Second, we compute the minimum number of physical wires between u and v required by each connection type. For example, if 74 2-pin subnets belong to a connection type

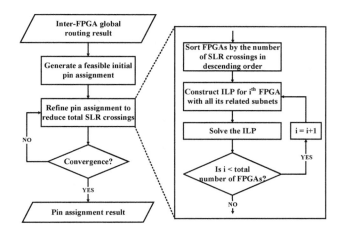

Figure 6: Overview of our pin assignment optimization algorithm.

with TDM factor of 5 which is directed from v to u, then the minimum number of physical wires between u and v required by this connection type is $\lceil 74/5 \rceil = 15$. Then, we randomly reserve the minimum number of physical wires required by each connection type between u and v. Recall that the inter-FPGA global routing step has ensured that the minimum total number of physical wires required by all connection types between two adjacent FPGAs does not exceed the number of physical wires available between the two FPGAs. Finally, all the 2-pin subnets of each connection type are distributed randomly to the physical wires reserved for the type subject to the TDM constraints.

3.3 Pin Assignment Refinement

In this subsection, we describe the details of each iteration of refinement. In each iteration, we want to optimally re-assign all 2-pin inter-FPGA subnets between a particular FPGA u and its neighboring FPGAs to reduce the total number of SLR crossings in u and its neighboring FPGAs without changing the assignment of all other 2-pin inter-FPGA subnets in the rest of the system. Suppose FPGA v is a neighbor of FPGA u. Since the 2-pin inter-FPGA subnets between FPGA u and v have different TDM factors and two different directions, we classify them into different connection types according to their TDM factors and directions. Only 2-pin inter-FPGA subnets between FPGAs u and v that are of the same connection type can share the same physical wire. Let TDM_t denote the TDM factor of connection type t.

Let α_{uv} denote a 2-pin inter-FPGA subnet between FPGAs u and v originated from net α. The required connection type of subnet α_{uv} is denoted by $TYPE_{\alpha_{uv}}$. The set of all connection types required by the 2-pin inter-FPGA subnets between FPGAs u and v is denoted by $TYPES_{uv}$. Moreover, we divide the physical wires between FPGAs u and v into groups according to the pair of SLRs they connect. Let $G_{u_i v_j}$ denote the group of physical wires between FPGA u's SLR i and FPGA v's SLR j.

Let α_u denote an ordered list[2] of all 2-pin inter-FPGA subnets incident with FPGA u originated from net α. Consider the instance in Fig. 5. Net p passes through FPGAs A, B, C, and D, we have $p_A = (p_{AB})$, $p_B = (p_{AB}, p_{BC})$, $p_C = (p_{BC}, p_{CD})$, and $p_D = (p_{CD})$. Net q passes through FPGAs B and C, we have $q_B = (q_{BC})$, and $q_C = (q_{BC})$.

Recall that we want to re-assign all 2-pin inter-FPGA signals between a particular FPGA u and its neighboring FPGAs to reduce the total number of SLR crossings in u and its neighboring FPGAs without changing the assignment of all other 2-pin inter-FPGA signals in the rest of the system. We use M_{α_u} to denote the set of all feasible mappings of α_u to physical wire groups. Refer to the current pin assignment shown in Fig. 5, and suppose u is now C. We have $M_{p_C} = \{(G_{B_1C_0}, G_{C_0D_0}), (G_{B_1C_0}, G_{C_2D_2}), (G_{B_1C_0}, G_{C_3D_3}), (G_{B_3C_3}, G_{C_0D_0}), (G_{B_3C_3}, G_{C_2D_2}), (G_{B_3C_3}, G_{C_3D_3})\}$ since $p_C = (p_{BC}, p_{CD})$ where subnet p_{BC} can be assigned to wire group $G_{B_1C_0}/G_{B_3C_3}$ and subnet p_{CD} can be assigned to wire group $G_{C_0D_0}/G_{C_2D_2}/G_{C_3D_3}$. Similarly, we have $M_{q_C} = \{(G_{B_2C_1}), (G_{B_3C_3})\}$ since $q_C = (q_{BC})$ where subnet q_{BC} can be assigned to wire group $G_{B_2C_1}/G_{B_3C_3}$. Note that the number of SLR crossings caused by net α inside FPGA u and its neighboring FPGAs depends on which mapping in M_{α_u} is chosen, and it is a known constant if the assignment of all other 2-pin inter-FPGA signals in the rest of the system is fixed. Consider the current pin assignment in Fig. 5 and suppose subnet p_{AB} is fixed to wire group $G_{A_2B_2}$. Currently, p_{BC} is mapped to $G_{B_3C_3}$ and p_{CD} to $G_{C_2D_2}$, the number of SLR crossings caused by net p inside FPGAs B, C, and D are 1, 1, and 1, respectively. If we re-map p_{BC} to $G_{B_1C_0}$ and p_{CD} to $G_{C_0D_0}$, then the number of SLR crossings caused by net p inside FPGAs B, C, and D will be equal to 2, 0, and 1, respectively. For each mapping m in M_{α_u}, we define its cost as the number of SLR crossings caused by net α inside FPGA u and its neighboring FPGAs under this mapping. And we denote the cost of mapping m by $COST_m$.

Table 1: Notations

TDM_t	The TDM factor for connection type t
α_{uv}	A 2-pin subnet between FPGAs u and v originated from net α
$TYPE_{\alpha_{uv}}$	The required connection type of subnet α_{uv}
$TYPES_{uv}$	The set of connection types required by all 2-pin subnets between FPGAs u and v
$G_{u_iv_j}$	The group of physical wires between FPGA u's SLR i and FPGA v's SLR j
α_u	An ordered list of 2-pin subnets incident with FPGA u originated from net α
M_{α_u}	The set of all feasible mappings of α_u to physical wire groups
$COST_m$	The number of SLR crossings caused by net α inside FPGA u and its neighboring FPGAs under mapping $m \in M_{\alpha_u}$

---

[2]Note that the cardinality of α_u is bounded by the number of neighboring FPGAs of u.

For our ILP formulation, we introduce binary variable $x_{\alpha_{uv}G_{u_iv_j}}$ to indicate if 2-pin subnet α_{uv} is assigned to physical wire group $G_{u_iv_j}$ or not. We also introduce integer variable $n^t_{G_{u_iv_j}}$ for the number of physical wires in wire group $G_{u_iv_j}$ designated for connection type t. Finally, we use binary variable y_m to indicate if a mapping $m \in M_{\alpha_u}$ is chosen. All the notations and decision variables are summarized in Table 1 and Table 2.

Table 2: Decision Variables of the ILP Formulation

$x_{\alpha_{uv}G_{u_iv_j}}$	$= \begin{cases} 1, & \text{if 2-pin subnet } \alpha_{uv} \text{ uses a physical wire in } G_{u_iv_j} \\ 0, & \text{otherwise} \end{cases}$
$n^t_{G_{u_iv_j}}$	number of physical wires designated for connection type t in $G_{u_iv_j}$
y_m	$= \begin{cases} 1, & \text{if mapping } m \in M_{\alpha_u} \text{ is chosen} \\ 0, & \text{otherwise} \end{cases}$

The objective and constraints of our ILP are listed below.
Minimize
$$\sum_{\alpha_u} \sum_{m \in M_{\alpha_u}} COST_m * y_m$$
subject to
$$\sum_{t \in TYPES_{uv}} n^t_{G_{u_iv_j}} = |G_{u_iv_j}|, \quad \forall neighbor\ v\ of\ u; \forall i,j \quad (1)$$

$$\sum_{\forall \alpha_{uv}: TYPE_{\alpha_{uv}}=t} x_{\alpha_{uv}G_{u_iv_j}} \leq TDM_t * n^t_{G_{u_iv_j}},$$
$$\forall neighbor\ v\ of\ u; \forall t \in TYPES_{uv}; \forall i,j \quad (2)$$

$$\sum_{i,j} x_{\alpha_{uv}G_{u_iv_j}} = 1, \quad \forall neighbor\ v\ of\ u; \forall \alpha_{uv} \quad (3)$$

$$n^t_{G_{u_iv_j}} \in \mathbb{N}, \quad \forall neighbor\ v\ of\ u; \forall t \in TYPES_{uv}; \forall i,j \quad (4)$$

$$\sum_{m \in M_{\alpha_u}} y_m = 1, \quad \forall \alpha_u \quad (5)$$

$$x_{\alpha_{uv}G_{u_iv_j}} = \sum_{m \in M_{\alpha_u}\ s.t.\ m[\alpha_{uv}]=G_{u_iv_j}} y_m,$$
$$\forall neighbor\ v\ of\ u; \forall \alpha_{uv}; \forall i,j \quad (6)$$

$$y_m = 0\ or\ 1, \quad \forall m \quad (7)$$

The objective of our ILP is to minimize the total number of SLR crossings in FPGA u and its neighboring FPGAs by re-assigning all 2-pin inter-FPGA signals between u and its neighbors while assuming the assignment of all other 2-pin inter-FPGA signals in the rest of the system is fixed. Constraint (1) ensures that the total number of physical wires in group $G_{u_iv_j}$ designated for different connection types is equal to the number of physical wires available in $G_{u_iv_j}$. Constraint (2) ensures that there are enough physical wires designated as connection type t in group $G_{u_iv_j}$ for all subnets of connection type t assigned to $G_{u_iv_j}$. We use constraint (3) to force each 2-pin subnet between FPGAs u and v to be assigned to exactly one physical wire group. Constraint (4) specifies that the number of physical wires in group $G_{u_iv_j}$ designated for any connection type must be a non-negative integer. Constraint (5) makes sure exactly one mapping will be chosen for α_u for each inter-FPGA net α related to FPGA u. Constraint (6) ensures that $x_{\alpha_{uv}G_{u_iv_j}}$ is 1 if and only if the chosen mapping for α_u assigns subnet α_{uv} to wire group $G_{u_iv_j}$. Constraint (7) specifies that y_m is a binary decision variable.

4 EXPERIMENTAL RESULTS

We implemented our algorithm using C++ programming language, and conducted the experiments on a Linux workstation with an Intel Xeon 2.6GHz CPU and 64GB memory. We used Gurobi7.0.2[13] as our ILP solver. We assumed each 2.5D FPGA had four super logic regions (SLRs) as in Fig.1. Since there is no public benchmark circuits large enough for our experiments, we generated six text cases. Three of them for a system with ten 2.5D FPGAs and another three for a system with twenty 2.5D FPGAs. The characteristics of the test cases are listed in Table 3. Note that without time-division-multiplexing, the total number of FPGA I/O pins consumed by the inter-FPGA signals would be two times the number of 2-pin inter-FPGA subnets in each test case. For example, for test case 1, the total number of FPGA I/O pins consumed by inter-FPGA subnets without time-division-multiplexing would be over 75K implying an average of 7.5K I/O pins required per FPGA while the largest Virtex-7 device only has 1.2K I/O pins. The inter-FPGA interconnection topology assumed mimics that of a commercial system.

Table 3: Test case characteristics.

Test case	#FPGAs	#Inter-FPGA nets	#2-pin subnets
1	10	10,000	37,851
2	10	20,000	75,208
3	10	30,000	113,636
4	20	20,000	71,506
5	20	30,000	106,320
6	20	50,000	177,790

In order to show the effectiveness of our proposed algorithm, we compared it against two other approaches. The first approach for comparison is picking the best from random sampling. We used the procedure described in section 3.2 to generate different feasible pin assignment solutions. Therefore, for any pair of adjacent FPGAs, we randomly select sufficient physical wires for each connection type and then randomly distribute each type of inter-FPGA 2-pin subnets to the physical wires reserved for them under the corresponding capacity. In our experiments, we generated one thousand feasible pin assignment solutions for each test case and finally picked the one with the minimum amount of SLR crossings.

In addition, we also implemented a heuristic pin assignment approach to minimize the expected number of SLR crossings. The intuition of the heurisitc is as follows. We note that connecting a pin in SLR1/SLR2 of a FPGA with some element in another SLR of the same FPGA will incur at most two SLR crossings (i.e., SLR1 to SLR3, or SLR2 to SLR0), while connecting a pin in SLR0/SLR3 with some element in another SLR of the same FPGA will incur three SLR crossings in the worst case (i.e., SLR0 to SLR3, or SLR3 to SLR0). So, for each pair of adjacent FPGAs, the heuristic tries to route as many inter-FPGA 2-pin subnets as possible using wires incident with

SLR1/SLR2 on both ends. Then, it routes as many of the remaining inter-FPGA 2-pin subnets as possible using wires incident with SLR1/SL2 on one end and SLR0/SLR3 on the other end. Finally, the rest of the inter-FPGA 2-pin subnets are routed using wires incident with SLR0/SLR3 on both ends. This can be done by routing the inter-FPGA 2-pin subnets in the order of their connection types where all connection types are sorted in decreasing TDM values.

Table 4 compares the results obtained by the three methods. Column 2 shows the results of picking the best assignment out of 1000 random feasible pin assignments. Column 3 shows the results by the heuristic pin assignment approach. Column 4 shows the results by our algorithm. It can be seen that both the method of picking the best from random sampling and the pin assignment heuristic are far from optimal. Our algorithm produced feasible pin assignments that incurred 28 to 45% less SLR crossings than the method of picking the best from random sampling, and 21 to 42% less SLR crossings than the pin assignment heuristic.

Table 4: Comparing our proposed algorithm against two other approaches.

Test case	#SLR crossings			$\frac{A-C}{A}$	$\frac{B-C}{B}$
	Best of 1000(A)	Heuristic(B)	Ours(C)		
1	65,612	59,720	46,934	28.44%	21.41%
2	129,309	113,930	81,021	37.32%	28.89%
3	198,570	178,757	140,465	29.29%	21.42%
4	123,565	113,685	70,508	42.94%	37.98%
5	184,030	171,157	101,475	44.88%	40.71%
6	307,620	290,695	168,859	45.11%	41.91%

We report some execution statistics of our algorithm in Table 5. We show the numbers of SLR crossings of the initial feasible pin assignment generated in the first phase, and the reduction after the integer linear programming-based iterative refinement phase. The number of rounds of refinement and the total runtime for each test case are also shown. In our experiments, we terminated our program when the numbers of SLR crossings between two consecutive rounds was less than 0.1%. It can be seen that it only took a few rounds for the iterative refinement phase to converge.

Finally, we wanted to check the stability of our algorithm. We ran ten trials of our algorithm on each test case where each trial had a different initial feasible pin assignment generated in the first phase. The results are shown in Table 6. It can be observed that while the quality of the initial feasible pin assignment solutions may vary by a few percent, the variation of the quality after iterative refinement is very little. In other words, our algorithm is very stable and its final solution quality is insensitive to the initial solution.

5 CONCLUSIONS

We introduced the SLR-aware pin assignment problem for modern multi-FPGA system utilizing high capacity 2.5D FPGAs. We proposed an iterative improvement algorithm based on integer linear programming to minimize the total number of SLR crossings in all FPGAs. Experimental results showed that the amount of SLR crossings can be significantly reduced by over 30% on average compared to two other approaches. Moreover, another advantage of

Table 5: Execution statistics of our algorithm.

Test case	#SLR crossings			#rounds	Runtime(sec)
	Initial	Final	Reduction (%)		
1	67,889	46,934	30.87	4	43.34
2	134,407	81,021	39.72	5	110.99
3	204,376	140,465	31.27	4	107.37
4	126,795	70,508	44.39	4	103.26
5	186,807	101,475	45.68	5	182.68
6	310,660	168,859	45.65	5	278.82

Table 6: Comparing 10 trials of our algorithm using different initial feasible pin assignments on each test case.

Test case	#SLR crossings			
	Initial		Final	
	Range	Variation	Range	Variation
1	67,262-70,030	3.953%	46,931-46,974	0.092%
2	132,839-136,201	2.468%	81,040-81,120	0.099%
3	204,990-209,537	2.170%	140,400-140,527	0.090%
4	125,122-126,833	1.349%	70,463-70,532	0.098%
5	185,555-188,480	1.552%	101,439-101,532	0.092%
6	308,957-314,968	1.908%	168,937-169,035	0.058%

our approach is that instead of minimizing the total number of SLR crossings in all FPGAs, it can be easily adapted to handle other objectives by adjusting the objective function in our integer linear program accordingly. For example, for timing-aware pin assignment, we may change the objective function into a weighted sum of SLR crossings incurred by the inter-FPGA nets where timing-critical inter-FPGA nets receive higher weights.

REFERENCES

[1] S. Hauck. The roles of FPGAs in reprogrammable systems. *Proceedings of the IEEE*, 86(4):615–638, Apr 1998.
[2] S. Hauck. *Multi-FPGA Systems*. Ph.D. dissertation, University of Washington Seattle, WA, USA, 1995.
[3] J. Babb, R. Tessier, M. Dahl, S. Hanono, D. Hoki, and A. Agarwal. Logic emulation with virtual wires. *IEEE transactions on computer-aided design of integrated circuits and systems*, 16(6):609–626, 1997.
[4] Kirk Saban. Xilinx stacked silicon interconnect technology delivers breakthrough FPGA capacity, bandwidth, and power efficiency. Xilinx, 2012. https://www.xilinx.com/support/documentation/white_papers/wp380_Stacked_Silicon_Interconnect_Technology.pdf.
[5] ZeBu server-3. Synopsys. https://www.synopsys.com/verification/emulation/zebu-server.html.
[6] E. Nasiri, J. Shaikh, A.H. Pereira, and V. Betz. Muliple dice working as one: CAD flows and routing architectures for silicon interposer FPGAs. *IEEE transactions on very large scale integration systems*, 24(5):1821–1834, May 2016.
[7] M. A. S. Khalid. *Routing Architecture and Layout Synthesis for Multi-FPGA Systems*. Ph.D. dissertation, University of Toronto, 1999.
[8] S. Hauck and G. Borriello. Pin assignment for multi-FPGA systems. *IEEE transactions on computer-aided design of integrated circuits and systems*, 16(9):956–964, 1997.
[9] T. Meister, J. Lienig, and G. Thomke. Novel pin assignment algorithms for components with very high pin counts. In *Proc. of the conference on Design, Automation and Test in Europe*, pages 837–842, 2008.
[10] W.K. Mak. I/O placement for FPGAs with multiple i/o standards. *IEEE transactions on computer-aided design of integrated circuits and systems*, 23(2):315–320, 2004.
[11] W.K. Mak and C.L. Lai. On constrained pin mapping for FPGA-PCB co-design. *IEEE transactions on computer-aided design of integrated circuits and systems*, 25(11):2393–2401, 2006.
[12] S.I. Lei and W.K. Mak. Simultaneous constrained pin assignment and escape routing considering differential pairs for FPGA-PCB co-design. *IEEE transactions on computer-aided design of integrated circuits and systems*, 32(12):1866–1878, 2013.
[13] Gurobi Optimization. Gurobi optimizer reference manual, 2016. http://www.gurobi.com.

A ILLUSTRATIVE EXAMPLE

We give an example to illustrate how our algorithm works. Suppose an initial feasible pin assignment as shown in Fig. 5 has been generated. In this instance, there are a total of four inter-FPGA connection types utilized. Let $\overrightarrow{AB(1)}$ denote the connection type from FPGA A to FPGA B with TDM factor equals to 1. $\overrightarrow{BC(2)}$ denotes the connection type from FPGA B to FPGA C with TDM factor equals to 2. $\overrightarrow{CB(2)}$ denotes the connection type from FPGA C to FPGA B with TDM factor equals to 2. $\overrightarrow{CD(1)}$ denotes the connection type from FPGA C to FPGA D with TDM factor equals to 1.

The total number of SLR crossings is seven with two crossings in each of FPGAs A, B, and C, and one crossing in D. We sort the FPGAs in descending order of their SLR crossings and get the order $A - B - C - D$.

In the first iteration, we take FPGA A as u to perform refinement. We have $M_{p_A} = \{(G_{A_0 B_1}), (G_{A_2 B_2})\}$ where $COST_{(p_{AB} \to G_{A_0 B_1})} = 2$ and $COST_{(p_{AB} \to G_{A_2 B_2})} = 3$. The ILP for pin assignment refinement with FPGA A as u is given below.

Minimize

$$3 * y_{(p_{AB} \to G_{A_0 B_1})} + 2 * y_{(p_{AB} \to G_{A_2 B_2})}$$

subject to

$$n^{\overrightarrow{AB(1)}}_{G_{A_0 B_1}} = 40$$

$$n^{\overrightarrow{AB(1)}}_{G_{A_2 B_2}} = 60 \tag{1}$$

$$x_{p_{AB} G_{A_0 B_1}} \le 1 * n^{\overrightarrow{AB(1)}}_{G_{A_0 B_1}}$$

$$x_{p_{AB} G_{A_2 B_2}} \le 1 * n^{\overrightarrow{AB(1)}}_{G_{A_2 B_2}} \tag{2}$$

$$x_{p_{AB} G_{A_0 B_1}} + x_{p_{AB} G_{A_2 B_2}} = 1 \tag{3}$$

$$n^{\overrightarrow{AB(1)}}_{G_{A_0 B_1}}, n^{\overrightarrow{AB(1)}}_{G_{A_2 B_2}} \in \mathbb{N} \tag{4}$$

$$y_{(p_{AB} \to G_{A_0 B_1})} + y_{(p_{AB} \to G_{A_2 B_2})} = 1 \tag{5}$$

$$x_{p_{AB} G_{A_0 B_1}} = y_{(p_{AB} \to G_{A_0 B_1})}$$

$$x_{p_{AB} G_{A_2 B_2}} = y_{(p_{AB} \to G_{A_2 B_2})} \tag{6}$$

$$y_m = 0 \ or \ 1, \ \forall m \tag{7}$$

Solving the above ILP, we get $y_{(p_{AB} \to G_{A_0 B_1})} = 1$. So, we reassign subnet p_{AB} to wire group $G_{A_0 B_1}$ as shown in Fig.7. The total number of SLR crossings is reduced to 6.

In the second iteration, we take FPGA B as u to conduct refinement. The pin assignment result remains the same as Fig. 7.

In the third iteration, we take FPGA C as u to conduct refinement. We have $M_{p_C} = \{(G_{B_1 C_0}, G_{C_0 D_0}), (G_{B_1 C_0}, G_{C_2 D_2}), (G_{B_1 C_0}, G_{C_3 D_3}), (G_{B_3 C_3}, G_{C_0 D_0}), (G_{B_3 C_3}, G_{C_2 D_2}), (G_{B_3 C_3}, G_{C_3 D_3})\}$ and

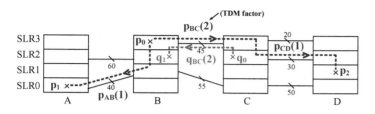

Figure 7: Pin assignment after iteration 1 (iteration 2).

$M_{q_C} = \{(G_{B_1C_0}), (G_{B_3C_3})\}$ where $COST_{(p_{BC}\to G_{B_1C_0}, p_{CD}\to G_{C_0D_0})} = 3$, $COST_{(p_{BC}\to G_{B_1C_0}, p_{CD}\to G_{C_2D_2})} = 5$, $COST_{(p_{BC}\to G_{B_1C_0}, p_{CD}\to G_{C_3D_3})} = 7$, $COST_{(p_{BC}\to G_{B_3C_3}, p_{CD}\to G_{C_0D_0})} = 6$, $COST_{(p_{BC}\to G_{B_3C_3}, p_{CD}\to G_{C_2D_2})} = 4$, $COST_{(p_{BC}\to G_{B_3C_3}, p_{CD}\to G_{C_3D_3})} = 4$, $COST_{(q_{BC}\to G_{B_1C_0})} = 3$, $COST_{(q_{BC}\to G_{B_3C_3})} = 2$. The ILP for pin assignment refinement with FPGA C as u is given below.

Minimize

$$3 * y_{(p_{BC}\to G_{B_1C_0}, p_{CD}\to G_{C_0D_0})} + 5 * y_{(p_{BC}\to G_{B_1C_0}, p_{CD}\to G_{C_2D_2})} +$$
$$7 * y_{(p_{BC}\to G_{B_1C_0}, p_{CD}\to G_{C_3D_3})} + 6 * y_{(p_{BC}\to G_{B_3C_3}, p_{CD}\to G_{C_0D_0})} +$$
$$4 * y_{(p_{BC}\to G_{B_3C_3}, p_{CD}\to G_{C_2D_2})} + 4 * y_{(p_{BC}\to G_{B_3C_3}, p_{CD}\to G_{C_3D_3})} +$$
$$3 * y_{(q_{BC}\to G_{B_1C_0})} + 2 * y_{(q_{BC}\to G_{B_3C_3})}$$

subject to

$$n^{\overrightarrow{BC(2)}}_{G_{B_1C_0}} + n^{\overrightarrow{CB(2)}}_{G_{B_1C_0}} = 55$$

$$n^{\overrightarrow{BC(2)}}_{G_{B_3C_3}} + n^{\overrightarrow{CB(2)}}_{G_{B_3C_3}} = 45$$

$$n^{\overrightarrow{CD(1)}}_{G_{C_0D_0}} = 50$$

$$n^{\overrightarrow{CD(1)}}_{G_{C_2D_2}} = 30$$

$$n^{\overrightarrow{CD(1)}}_{G_{C_3D_3}} = 20 \tag{1}$$

$$x_{p_{BC}G_{B_1C_0}} \le 2 * n^{\overrightarrow{BC(2)}}_{G_{B_1C_0}}$$

$$x_{p_{BC}G_{B_3C_3}} \le 2 * n^{\overrightarrow{BC(2)}}_{G_{B_3C_3}}$$

$$x_{q_{BC}G_{B_1C_0}} \le 2 * n^{\overrightarrow{CB(2)}}_{G_{B_1C_0}}$$

$$x_{q_{BC}G_{B_3C_3}} \le 2 * n^{\overrightarrow{CB(2)}}_{G_{B_3C_3}}$$

$$x_{p_{CD}G_{C_0D_0}} \le 1 * n^{\overrightarrow{CD(1)}}_{G_{C_0D_0}}$$

$$x_{p_{CD}G_{C_2D_2}} \le 1 * n^{\overrightarrow{CD(1)}}_{G_{C_2D_2}}$$

$$x_{p_{CD}G_{C_3D_3}} \le 1 * n^{\overrightarrow{CD(1)}}_{G_{C_3D_3}} \tag{2}$$

$$x_{p_{BC}G_{B_1C_0}} + x_{p_{BC}G_{B_3C_3}} = 1$$

$$x_{q_{BC}G_{B_1C_0}} + x_{q_{BC}G_{B_3C_3}} = 1$$

$$x_{p_{CD}G_{C_0D_0}} + x_{p_{CD}G_{C_2D_2}} + x_{p_{CD}G_{C_3D_3}} = 1 \tag{3}$$

$$n^{\overrightarrow{BC(2)}}_{G_{B_1C_0}}, n^{\overrightarrow{BC(2)}}_{G_{B_3C_3}}, n^{\overrightarrow{CB(2)}}_{G_{B_1C_0}}, n^{\overrightarrow{CB(2)}}_{G_{B_3C_3}},$$
$$n^{\overrightarrow{CD(1)}}_{G_{C_0D_0}}, n^{\overrightarrow{CD(1)}}_{G_{C_2D_2}}, n^{\overrightarrow{CD(1)}}_{G_{C_3D_3}} \in \mathbb{N} \tag{4}$$

$$y_{(p_{BC}\to G_{B_1C_0}, p_{CD}\to G_{C_0D_0})} + y_{(p_{BC}\to G_{B_1C_0}, p_{CD}\to G_{C_2D_2})} +$$
$$y_{(p_{BC}\to G_{B_1C_0}, p_{CD}\to G_{C_3D_3})} + y_{(p_{BC}\to G_{B_3C_3}, p_{CD}\to G_{C_0D_0})} +$$
$$y_{(p_{BC}\to G_{B_3C_3}, p_{CD}\to G_{C_2D_2})} + y_{(p_{BC}\to G_{B_3C_3}, p_{CD}\to G_{C_3D_3})} = 1$$

$$y_{(q_{BC}\to G_{B_1C_0})} + y_{(q_{BC}\to G_{B_3C_3})} = 1 \tag{5}$$

$$x_{p_{BC}G_{B_1C_0}} = y_{(p_{BC}\to G_{B_1C_0}, p_{CD}\to G_{C_0D_0})} +$$
$$y_{(p_{BC}\to G_{B_1C_0}, p_{CD}\to G_{C_2D_2})} +$$
$$y_{(p_{BC}\to G_{B_1C_0}, p_{CD}\to G_{C_3D_3})}$$

$$x_{p_{BC}G_{B_3C_3}} = y_{(p_{BC}\to G_{B_3C_3}, p_{CD}\to G_{C_0D_0})} +$$
$$y_{(p_{BC}\to G_{B_3C_3}, p_{CD}\to G_{C_2D_2})} +$$
$$y_{(p_{BC}\to G_{B_3C_3}, p_{CD}\to G_{C_3D_3})}$$

$$x_{q_{BC}G_{B_1C_0}} = y_{(q_{BC}\to G_{B_1C_0})}$$

$$x_{q_{BC}G_{B_3C_3}} = y_{(q_{BC}\to G_{B_3C_3})}$$

$$x_{p_{CD}G_{C_0D_0}} = y_{(p_{BC}\to G_{B_1C_0}, p_{CD}\to G_{C_0D_0})} +$$
$$y_{(p_{BC}\to G_{B_3C_3}, p_{CD}\to G_{C_0D_0})}$$

$$x_{p_{CD}G_{C_2D_2}} = y_{(p_{BC}\to G_{B_1C_0}, p_{CD}\to G_{C_2D_2})} +$$
$$y_{(p_{BC}\to G_{B_3C_3}, p_{CD}\to G_{C_2D_2})}$$

$$x_{p_{CD}G_{C_3D_3}} = y_{(p_{BC}\to G_{B_1C_0}, p_{CD}\to G_{C_3D_3})} +$$
$$y_{(p_{BC}\to G_{B_3C_3}, p_{CD}\to G_{C_3D_3})} \tag{6}$$

$$y_m = 0 \text{ or } 1, \quad \forall m \tag{7}$$

Solving the above ILP, we get $y_{(p_{BC}\to G_{B_1C_0}, p_{CD}\to G_{C_0D_0})} = 1$, and $y_{(q_{BC}\to G_{B_3C_3})} = 1$. So, we re-assign subnets p_{BC} to wire group $G_{B_1C_0}$, and p_{CD} to wire group $G_{C_0D_0}$. Subnet q_{BC} is re-assigned to wire group $G_{B_3C_3}$. The new pin assignment result after this iteration is shown in Fig. 8 The total number of SLR crossings is reduced to 5.

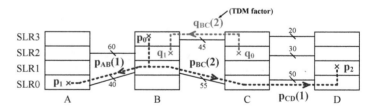

Figure 8: Pin assignment after iteration 3 (iteration 4).

Finally, we take FPGA D as u to carry out refinement. The pin assignment result remains the same as in Fig. 8. Since the total number of SLR crossings has been reduced in the first round of refinement, another round of refinement will be performed. The order in the second round is $B - C - D - A$ and it can be easily checked that the total number of SLR crossings at the end of the second round is identical to that at the end of the first round, so our algorithm will terminate then. Note that for simplicity, the example above only consists of two signals, but for practical instances the integer linear program constructed at each iteration will optimally re-assign a large number of 2-pin subsets simultaneously.

Influence of Professor T. C. Hu's Works on Fundamental Approaches in Layout

Andrew B. Kahng

UCSD Departments of CSE and ECE, La Jolla, CA 92093 USA

abk@ucsd.edu

ABSTRACT

Professor T. C. Hu has made numerous pioneering and fundamental contributions in combinatorial algorithms, mathematical programming and operations research. His seminal 1985 IEEE book *VLSI Circuit Layout: Theory and Design*, coedited with Prof. E. S. Kuh, shaped algorithmic and optimization perspectives, as well as basic frameworks, for IC physical design throughout the following decades [44]. Indeed, Professor Hu gave a keynote address at the very first International Symposium on Physical Design, in April 1997 [41]. His research approach of (i) studying small and/or extremal cases first, (ii) always seeking to establish error bounds or other properties of heuristic outcomes (hence, always seeking to understand optimal solutions), (iii) approaching new problems from as fresh a perspective as possible, and (iv) pursuing simplicity and beauty in both formulation and exposition, has influenced generations of researchers. This paper complements [20] in recounting highlights of Professor Hu's contributions to, and impacts on, physical design. The focus is on several problems of "connection", as well as the concept of "shadow price", as they relate to layout.

ACM Reference Format:
Andrew B. Kahng. 2018. Influence of Professor T. C. Hu's Works on Fundamental Approaches in Layout. In *ISPD'18: 2018 International Symposium on Physical Design, March 25–28, 2018, Monterey, CA, USA*. ACM, New York, NY, USA, 6 pages. https://doi.org/10.1145/3177540.3177563

1 INTRODUCTION

VLSI layout encompasses floorplanning, placement and routing, and is at the heart of integrated-circuit physical design. The pursuit of the "science" of VLSI layout has provided an important nexus of mathematics, graph theory, computer science, combinatorial algorithms, electrical engineering, device physics and optimization. Layout is where weighted hypergraphs and grid-graphs meet modules, signal nets, design rules, and a host of variant objectives and constraints that evolve continuously with semiconductor technology.

Professor T. C. Hu's works on VLSI layout, as well as his 1985 coedited book *VLSI Circuit Layout: Theory and Design* [44], have made a number of highly influential contributions to the field of physical design. Starting over 30 years ago, his works brought combinatorial

optimization and mathematical programming formulations and methods that had not been previously applied to layout problems. As reviewed in [20], numerous works of Professor Hu study the tree representation of inherent structure in VLSI circuits, as well as applications of duality (flows and cuts; shadow price). To this day, [44] remains a key reference work for hypergraph and graph models that underlie VLSI layout formulations, and for fundamental approaches to routing.

Professor Hu's papers and books consistently reflect his unique ability to combine geometric, graph-theoretic and combinatorial-algorithmic concepts. His novel framing of VLSI layout problems can be seen in his keynote address [41] at the very first ISPD in 1997, and in his 1982 book *Combinatorial Algorithms* [40], extended with M. T. Shing in 2002 [47]. The latter presents unifying treatments of (i) the minimum spanning tree and shortest-paths tree constructions, (ii) the discovery of underlying cut structure in networks without maximum flow [60] [63], and (iii) the unification of breadth- and depth-first traversals of a given graph. These ideas are visible throughout the IC physical design literature, e.g., in (i) the Prim-Dijkstra tradeoff of [8]), (ii) the ESC clustering method of [24]), and (iii) the "window" method [11].

In the following, Section 2 reviews Professor Hu's concept of "TACP" (Tentative Assignment, Competitive Pricing), whose application can be seen particularly in the floorplanning and global placement literatures. Section 3 examines the 1973 result of Adolphson and Hu, which was the first to propose a cut-based placement approach (in the context of linear placement), and which moreover established early bounds on achievable wirelength minimization based on the cut structure of a given circuit. Section 4 discusses the 1985 Hu-Moerder hyperedge net model, its original motivation of capturing flow properties of a circuit hypergraph, and its modern use in analytic placement. Section 5 concludes with a review of the 1993 Prim-Dijkstra routing tree construction, which has been widely used in industry IC design tools for over 20 years. Section 6 discusses the problem of finding a "wide path", and a network flow-based method that is an outgrowth from a 1992 result on the Plateau's minimum surface problem. These works share common themes of duality and "connection", in addition to their application to fundamental layout formulations of floorplanning, placement and routing.

2 "TACP" AND SHADOW PRICE

The "classical" floorplanning formulation studied in much of the academic literature seeks to shape and pack all blocks, such that no blocks overlap and the enclosing layout region has minimum area while satisfying aspect ratio constraints. By contrast, *fixed-outline floorplanning* (FOFP) [49] is motivated by the modern fixed-die (as opposed to variable-die) layout context: the aspect ratio of the floorplan is fixed, but the aspect ratios and indeed the shapes of the blocks can vary. At ISPD-2000, [49] proposed a *perfect rectilinear floorplanning* formulation that seeks zero-whitespace, perfectly packed rectilinear floorplans in a fixed-die regime. In the FOFP regime, floorplanning regains its proper focus on *connectivity*, timing and performance; packing itself becomes a non-issue.

FOFP provides a continuum between floorplanning and coarse placement in its support of global interconnects and performance optimizations. To avoid overconstraining, there is no restriction on block shapes. It is even possible for blocks to overlap, as long as there is no violation of bounds on the cell area (i.e., contents of given blocks) that is assigned to any region of the layout. This concept was originated by Professor Hu in the 1980s. Footnote 9 of [49] writes, "For example, two blocks with equal amounts of cell area could be placed into adjacent disjoint regions, with each block having depth = 1 in its respective region. An alternative would be to place each block with uniform depth = 1/2 into the union of the two regions. This idea was first proposed in 1987 by Prof. T. C. Hu in the context of a "TACP" (tentative assignment and competitive pricing) approach to placement." Figure 1 illustrates the above idea.

Based on the FOFP formulation, Adya et al. [2] suggest new objective functions to drive simulated annealing and new types of moves that better guide local search in hierarchical design to improve wirelength and aspect ratios of blocks. Liu et al. [57] propose an algorithm that uses sequence-pair representation and instance augmentation to optimize the floorplan. Lin et al. [54] develop an evolutionary search method to minimize the area. More recent works of [22][58][66] propose several other FOFP optimizations, including a two-stage convex optimization methodology, insertion-after-remove (IAR) technique, and deferred decision making. These methods improve runtime, wirelength and area over previous approaches.

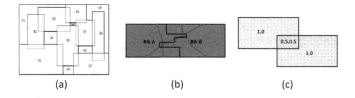

(a)   (b)   (c)

Figure 1: Fixed-Outline Floorplanning: (a) coarse placement-like global floorplanning; (b) irregular block shapes; and (c) example of tentative assignment.

The concept of competitive pricing in a TACP iteration is based on the *shadow price* in linear programming duality. As discussed in [20], column generation and shadow price have been applied to VLSI global routing, with primal-dual iterations being widely studied approximately 20 years ago [18] [4] [5]. Shadow price has subsequently been used in global placement, which lies on the placement continuum with FOFP. Equation (1) shows the classical analytical global placement objective, where $W(\mathbf{v})$ is the approximated total half-perimeter wirelength, and $D(\mathbf{v})$ represents the global density cost. These two terms are connected using a global Lagrangian multiplier λ.

The authors of the recent RePlAce global placement framework [21] propose a new constraint-oriented local-density function that incorporates a constraint-oriented local-density penalty factor for each placement bin i, as shown in Equation (2). Compared to the global density penalty factor which balances wirelength and cell spreading using only once coefficient, the new local-density function comprehends local density overflow at per-bin granularity, thus accelerating cell spreading for overflowed bins to resolve cell overlapping, while preserving the wirelength elsewhere. The concept of iterative pricing and (spatial location) assignment will no doubt continue to find further applications in physical design, e.g., co-optimization of power delivery network and placement. Further, the "fixed-outline floorplanning" problem of determining block shapes, utilizations, pin locations, etc. in an SOC floorplan remains a critical challenge for IC design teams.

$$\min_{\mathbf{v}} f(\mathbf{v}) = W(\mathbf{v}) + \lambda D(\mathbf{v}) \qquad (1)$$

$$\min_{\mathbf{v}} f(\mathbf{v}) = W(\mathbf{v}) + \Sigma_i \lambda_i D_i(\mathbf{v}) \qquad (2)$$

3 LINEAR PLACEMENT

Placement is a fundamental problem in many applications. The module placement problem, originating from Steinberg's backboard wiring problem, dates from 1961 and is one of the classical problems of VLSI layout. In this formulation, a set of n pins connected by wires should be placed into n holes, one pin per hole, such that total cost (wirelength) is minimized. A special case of the problem is the *optimal linear ordering* (O. L. O.) problem, where all holes are in a line, and are unit distance apart. The problem can be described using a graph, where each node represents a pin, and each edge represent a wire between pins. Each edge can be associated with a capacity representing the number of connections between its two nodes. The work of Adolphson and Hu [1] provided fundamental insights and bounds for the linear ordering problem, based on theory of maximum flows and minimum cuts in networks.

Gomory and Hu [31] show that $n(n-1)/2$ max flow values between any two source, sink nodes can be obtained with only $n-1$ max flow problems, giving $n-1$ "fundamental cuts". Adolphson and Hu [1] show that the sum of the values of the $n-1$ fundamental cuts is a lower bound on the total wirelength of the O.L.O. problem, and is the solution to the O.L.O. problem if the Gomory-Hu cut tree is a chain. The above is stated by Cheng [19] as:

Theorem 1. The min-cut defines an ordered partition that is consistent with an optimal vertex order in the linear placement problem.

Adolphson and Hu [1] also study the O.L.O. for *two-/k-chain* instances, and propose an efficient $O(n \log n)$ algorithm in the special case where the graph is a rooted tree. A rooted tree can also represent a job sequencing problem where each non-root node i represents a job, and has an associated linear delay cost $V(i)$ as well as a time $T(i)$ needed to finish the job. The objective of job sequencing is to find the job execution sequence ρ that minimizes the sum of linear delay costs when only one machine executes all jobs and all precedence constraints in the tree are satisfied. More precisely, the goal is to minimize the cost $c(\rho) = \sum_i V(i) \sum \{T(j) : \rho(j) \le \rho(i)\}$. Adolphson and Hu prove equivalence to the job sequencing problem with tree-like precedence relationships and linear delay costs, as well as the method of Horn [35]. Based on the work of Adolphson and Hu [1], Cheng in 1987 [19] proposed a recursive partitioning algorithm for arbitrary graphs which generates provably optimal placement solutions.

Minimum Cuts (Maximum Flows) in Placement. The early works of [1] [19] presage the universal application of the recursive min-cut approach to VLSI placement within commercial tools up through at least the mid-2000s. (In later years, min-cut has been often applied in conjunction with analytic methods.) Capo [16] uses a top-down, min-cut bisection algorithm, seeking to decompose a given placement instance into smaller instances by subdividing the placement region, assigning modules to subregions and inducing corresponding netlist sub-hypergraphs. Multiple types of min-cut partitioner are used that facilitate partitioning and improve efficiency; terminal propagation and whitespace management methods are also enabling to Capo solution quality. Numerous other works such as [3] also develop general-purpose global placers – applicable to both standard cell-based and mixed-size contexts – based on the min-cut paradigm.

The duality between maximum flows and minimum cuts is explicitly applied by Yang and Wong [67], who approach finding a balanced minimum cut in a netlist hypergraph from a maximum-flow perspective. Their work models the circuit netlist by a flow network, and heuristically achieves a balanced bipartition using repeated max-flow min-cut computations. Works such as [17] examine the time-quality tradeoff continuum from multilevel KL-FM partitioning, to flat KL-FM partitioning, to flow-based approaches, to implicit enumeration (branch-and-bound) within the top-down placement framework. Since the number of cell rows in a standard-cell block is often smaller than the number of cells per row, the "one-dimensional" linear placement problem is of special interest even within top-down placement of a "two-dimensional" layout.

Linear Placement Today. Since [1], there have been many linear placement-related problem formulations and results in the physical design literature. Indeed, today there is a tremendous renewal of attention to the linear placement problem. This is a consequence of increasingly intrusive manufacturing-induced placement constraints (minimum implant area, avoidance of OD notches, etc.) as well as heightened interference between the placement problem and various details of power delivery and pin access. Another driver for attention to linear placement is that it is an obvious opportunity for "end-case" recovery of layout quality, as noted in [17].

The work of [50] studies a type of linear placement problem in detailed placement. The authors propose a *single-row placement problem* which differs from classical linear placement in three ways: (i) cells (modules) have variable width; (ii) each row has fixed length with free sites; and (iii) cell ordering is fixed. The objective is to legalize all cells while minimizing the wirelength, given that all cells in other rows are fixed, as shown in Figure 2. In the figure, $C_1, \ldots, C_n$ gives the fixed left-to-right order of movable cells. For each legal position s_j of each movable cell C_i, since the optimal ordering is given and fixed, a minimum-cost constrained prefix placement $C_1, C_2, ..., C_i$, subject to the position of C_i being at or to the left of s_j, can be obtained. [50] gives a dynamic programming technique with time complexity $O(m^2)$ where m is the number of nets incident to cells in the given row. The dynamic programming is applied by using the prefix placement solution $P_{i-1}(s_j)$ to compute

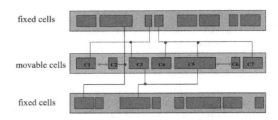

Figure 2: Ordered single-row placement.

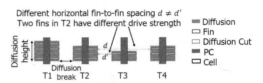

Figure 3: Neighbor diffusion effect caused by diffusion steps.

$P_i(s_{j'})$. A $O(m \log m)$ 'clumping' technique further exploits the convexity of the wirelength objective. Iterative improvement of cell ordering within a row can be run before applying this methodology.

Recent developments in linear placement reach beyond the ordered single-row placement, to multi-row detailed placement considering layout-dependent effects [27][32][55][56]. The work of [32] considers the neighbor diffusion effect caused by diffusion steps between adjacent standard cells, as shown in Figure 3. An optimal single-row dynamic programming-based approach is proposed to minimize the inter-cell diffusion cost and support cell variants, relocating and reordering. The authors further extend to an optimal double-row detailed placement supporting movable double-height cells.

One might speculate that "disconnects" between placer turn-around requirements and the runtime complexity of maximum flow or minimum cut calculation, as well as between the linear ordering problem and the two-dimensional nature of layout, led the physical design field to bypass the use of flow network "structure" in VLSI placement. Yet, the clear trend in recent years has been toward mathematical programming and combinatorial-algorithmic approaches that pay high runtime complexity as the price of solving real-world objectives and constraints. Looking forward, known mappings between one- and two-dimensional problem embeddings, as in [10], may help reconnect linear placement to the global placement and floorplanning problems. It may also be possible for flow- and cut-based frameworks to rejoin the toolkit for placement optimization in the future.

4 NET MODELING

In their 1985 paper, Hu and Moerder [45] propose a new hyperedge *net model* which use p pin nodes and one *star* node, to represent a p-pin hyperedge. A given netlist hypergraph is transformed by adding one star node for each signal net, and connecting the star node via a graph edge to each of the net's pin nodes. In the Hu-Moerder net model, we again see the motivation of network flows: specifically, it enables extension of network flow techniques to placement of modules on a chip. Figure 4(b) shows the Hu-Moerder hypergraph model of the set of modules and nets shown in Figure 4(a). The authors of [45] show that the max-flow min-cut theorem [53] can be used to find a minimum-cut bipartitioning of a hypergraph. They further describe an algorithm to construct a tree that is flow-equivalent to a given hypergraph.[1]

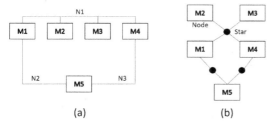

Figure 4: (a) Example circuit with 5 modules and 3 nets. (b) After transformation using the Hu-Moerder hyperedge net model.

The Hu-Moerder hyperedge model gives a very early, elegant answer to a question that challenges the VLSI layout community even today. Namely, how should a hyperedge of a hypergraph be *fairly* modeled by graph edges in a graph model of the hypergraph? This question is crucial to the application of analytic placement and to the ability to exploit sparse-matrix codes for layout applications.

Many works have proposed net models to represent hypergraphs as graphs. Weighted clique ($C(p, 2)$ edges), directed star ($p-1$ edges from the source to sink pins), spanning tree, etc. models have all been considered, but have respective disadvantages and advantages according to considerations of sparsity, whether the context is placement (based on half-perimeter wirelength) or partitioning (based on net cut), etc. A number of noted works on analytic placement, such as PROUD [65], Gordian [51] and BonnPlace [14], discuss the challenges of applying hyperedge net models in recursive placement and/or placement-based partitioning. Ihler et al. [48] proved in 1993 that it is impossible to achieve a net model that fairly represents the net cut properties of a hyperedge with more than three nodes. The star net model itself has been separately realized and used over the years, e.g., Brenner and Vygen describe a star net model in [15] and subsequently apply it in BonnPlace global placement [14].

Since its publication 33 years ago, the Hu-Moerder model arguably has not received the attention that it deserves. The model has important, useful qualities: it is sparse and symmetric, and it enables exact representation of net cut cost. It may be that in an era before 64-bit addressing, and before the emergence of sophisticated memory pool management and containers, the notion of rewriting the netlist to have essentially double the original number of vertices may have been unappealing. However, with today's ubiquitous tight loops involving buffer/inverter insertion, fanout clustering, and other on-the-fly netlist topology changes during physical optimization, it may be that past obstacles to the use of the star net model no longer exist.

5 PRIM-DIJKSTRA

The 1993 Prim-Dijkstra (PD) algorithm [8] has has been used extensively in industry for construction of spanning trees with good

balance between tree wirelength (WL) and source-to-sink pathlengths (PLs). Leading electronic design automation (EDA) tools and semiconductor company methodologies have used the *PD* algorithm extensively in their design flows, as evidenced by a number of patents assigned to IBM, Synopsys, Cadence, etc. [33] [13] [34] [29] [30] [62] [9] [7].

The *PD* algorithm merges the Prim and Dijkstra spanning tree constructions [61][26] to explicitly trade off tree WL (lightness) and source-to-sink PLs (shallowness). In their paper, the authors of [8] describe two versions of the algorithm, *PD1* and *PD2*.

Starting with just the source node v_0, *PD1* iteratively adds the edge e_{ij} and sink v_j to the tree such that $d_{ij} + \alpha \cdot l_i$ is minimized, where node v_i is in the current tree and v_j is not in the current tree. Here, d_{ij} is the distance between nodes v_i and v_j; l_i is the pathlength from the source v_0 to v_i in the current tree; and α is a weighting factor with $0 \le \alpha \le 1$. When $\alpha = 0$, *PD1* constructs Prim's minimum spanning tree (MST) [61], and with $\alpha = 1$, *PD1* constructs a shortest-path tree (SPT), identically to Dijkstra's algorithm [26]. As α increases from 0 to 1, *PD1* constructs trees with larger WLs and shorter PLs.

The *PD2* construction gives a second Prim-Dijkstra tradeoff, by iteratively adding the edge e_{ij} and sink v_j to the tree such that $(l_i{}^p + d_{ij})^{1/p}$ is minimized. Here, p is a parameter whose value satisfies $1 \le p < \infty$. When $p = \infty$, *PD2* produces a tree identical to Prim's MST, and when $p = 1$, *PD2* yields an SPT. Figure 5 shows *PD1* and *PD2* trees obtained with various parameter values for a 9-terminal net.

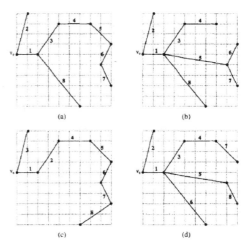

Figure 5: Tree constructions with *PD1* and *PD2* for a 9-terminal net. The edge labels give the order in which the algorithms add the edges into the tree. *PD1* constructions with $\alpha = 1/3$ and $= 2/3$ are shown in (a) and (b), respectively. *PD2* constructions with $p = 3$ and $= 3/2$ are shown in (c) and (d), respectively.

Prim's and Dijkstra's algorithms are well-known, fundamental graph algorithms that are basic to undergraduate discrete math and computer science curricula. The *PD* heuristic that blends these two greedy algorithms could very well be placed beside them in the same textbook. *PD* is very effective in practice, but simple enough to be implemented as homework in an algorithms course. The

---
[1]This cut-tree is similar to the Gomory-Hu cut-tree and result on multi-terminal maximum flows [31] that is reviewed in [20]. Professor Hu's work [37] subsequently applies the Gomory-Hu cut-tree in the context of multicommodity flows.

approach has also found broad appeal outside of IC design, with myriad applications including flood control [25], biomedical [68], military [59], wireless sensor networks [64], etc. At the same time, discovery and exploitation of the *PD* tradeoff took place 30+ years after the Prim and Dijkstra algorithms were published, suggesting non-obviousness and non-triviality.

It should be noted that the *PD* algorithm's construction of a |em spanning tree, as opposed to a *Steiner tree*, is advantageous in today's physical design tool chain. Spanning trees are widely used for global routing, since they provide an obvious way for the global router to decompose multi-fanout nets into two-pin nets. Even though rectilinear Steiner trees are required for actual realization of interconnect wires, Steiner trees are not preferred during the early routing stages because: (i) constructing Steiner trees is more time-consuming due to the added complexity of handling Steiner points, and (ii) Steiner points become unnecessary constraints that restrict the freedom of the global router to resolve congestion. Hence, spanning trees are typically preferred to Steiner trees.

Since the publication of [8], a number of researchers have continued to explore the tradeoff between lightness and shallowness of interconnection trees. The work of [28] achieves optimal (up to constant factors) tradeoffs of tree depth, tree weight, maximum degree and shallowness in a "narrow-shallow-low-light" construction. The merits of the *PD spanning* tree construction have also been revisited over the years. These merits are reasserted in the DAC-2006 work [12], whose authors argue that the *PD* WL is sufficiently close to minimal that it is practically 'free'. Their work concludes that *PD* obtains the best tradeoff between WL and PL compared to other spanning tree constructions such as BRBC [23], KRY [52], etc.

Finally, the scaling of power, performance, and area density has been exceptionally challenging in recent process nodes. This has brought renewed attention to the challenge of minimizing routing cost while optimizing delay or skew metrics. Indeed, for today's designs that are highly power-sensitive, even a 1% reduction in power provides considerable benefits. Consequently, even a small WL savings can have a high impact on value. A recent work [6] follows this motivation and proposes a new *PD-II* construction which directly improves upon the original *PD* construction by repairing the tree to simultaneously reduce both WL and PL. It seems inevitable that further research will be needed to similarly improve required arrival time, skew, prescribed-delay, per-sink radius, and other tradeoffs with tree cost that arise in physical design.

6   FINDING A WIDE PATH

Professor Hu has also made early contributions to connection-finding, which is a basic element of any routing approach. For example, the α-β routing of [46] finds connections when there exist both edge and vertex costs along a routing path. Notably, when the cost of traversing a vertex depends on whether a turn is being made at that vertex, this induces a "history-dependence" left unaddressed in previous works. The method of [46] unifies elements of Dijkstra's algorithm and best-first (A*) search.

The 1993 work [43] studies the problem of *robust* path finding (e.g., for a mobile agent in a general environment), which seeks a minimum-cost source-destination path *having prescribed width*. Figure 6 gives a cartoon of a source-destination (i.e., *s-t*) path with

prescribed width d, as might be required by a robot that has finite width.

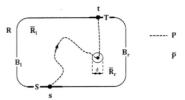

Figure 6: A d-separating path $\overline{P}$ of width d between two points $s \in S$ and $t \in T$ of the boundary of a region R. When the path has width d, every point of $\overline{R_l}$ is separated from every point of $\overline{R_r}$ by a distance of at least d.

Hu et al. [43] exploit the duality between cuts and flows to find a minimum-cost *robust* (i.e., a wide path) in a routing environment between given source and terminal nodes, s and t. A flow network is constructed based on a discretized (grid-graph) representation of the routing environment. By construction, a minimum cut between two appropriately chosen other vertices in this network will contain all vertices and edges inside a (minimum-cost) robust path between s and t. (A similar discretization is used in [42] to solve the discrete version of Plateau's problem of finding a minimum surface with given boundary.)

So that a maximum-flow computation will return a robust path, Hu et al. [43] superimpose a mesh network topology over region R. After assigning node weight to each node in the network, they connect each node to every neighboring node that is within distance d. Finally, they connect the source s' and sink t' to part of the boundary of region R such that a minimum $s'-t'$ cut corresponds to a wide path between s and t. Figure 7 illustrates the transformation from motion planning instance to network flow instance.

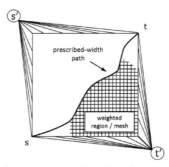

Figure 7: A robust motion planning instance transformed into a network flow instance.

Today, *wide paths* are relevant to many difficult and time-consuming connection formulations, such as top-level bus routing, bus feedthrough determination, etc. Also, as illustrated in Figure 8, IC package routing problems usually use traces of various width for different nets, depending on respective power integrity and signal integrity requirements. Most existing commercial package routers do not support such freedom of trace width. However, in a sequential routing scheme, *wide path* finding can provide routes with specified width in order to meet package power and signal integrity requirements.

Figure 8: Clip from chip package routing showing traces of various widths.

7　CONCLUSIONS

This paper has reviewed several fundamental contributions of Professor T. C. Hu to the field of VLSI layout, focusing on topics of connection and duality that are at the heart of modern floorplanning, placement and routing. The works reviewed here provide very early formulations and algorithmic solutions based on mathematical programming and network flows. As today's layout problems become more complex and challenging, the combinatorial frameworks and approaches proposed by Professor Hu become more compelling, and may be enabling to future physical design innovations.

8　ACKNOWLEDGMENTS

Above all, many thanks are due to Professor Hu for his guidance, inspiration, patience and help that has been given so generously to students and colleagues. I also thank Sriram Venkatesh, Lutong Wang and Bangqi Xu for their help in compiling and drafting the above material.

REFERENCES

[1] D. Adolphson and T. C. Hu, "Optimal Linear Ordering", *SIAM J. Appl. Math.* 25(3) (1973), pp. 403-423.
[2] S. N. Adya and I. L. Markov, "Fixed-Outline Floorplanning: Enabling Hierarchical Design", *IEEE TVLSI* 11(6) (2003), pp. 1120-1135.
[3] A. R. Agnihotri, S. Ono and P. H. Madden, "Recursive Bisection Placement: Feng Shui 5.0 Implementation Details", *Proc. ISPD*, 2005, pp. 230-232.
[4] C. Albrecht, "Provably Good Routing by a New Approximation Algorithm for Multicommodity Flow", *Proc. ISPD*, 2000, pp. 19-25.
[5] C. Albrecht, A. B. Kahng, I. Mandoiu and A. Zelikovsky, "Floorplan Evaluation with Timing-Driven Global Wireplanning, Pin Assignment, and Buffer/Wire Sizing", *Proc. ASP-DAC*, 2002, pp. 580-587.
[6] C. J. Alpert, W.-K. Chow, K. Han, A. B. Kahng, Z. Li, D. Liu, S. Venkatesh, "Prim-Dijkstra Revisited: Achieving Superior Timing-driven Routing Trees", *Proc. ISPD*, 2018, to appear.
[7] C. J. Alpert, R. G. Gandham, J. Hu, S. T. Quay and A. J. Sullivan, "Apparatus and Method for Determining Buffered Steiner Trees for Complex Circuits", *US Patent 6591411*, Jul. 2003.
[8] C. J. Alpert, T. C. Hu, J. H. Huang, A. B. Kahng and D. Karger, "Prim-Dijkstra Tradeoffs for Improved Performance-driven Routing Tree Design", *IEEE TCAD* 14(7) (1995), pp. 890-896.
[9] C. J. Alpert, J. Hu and P. H. Villarrubia, "Practical Methodology for Early Buffer and Wire Resource Allocation", *US Patent 6996512*, Feb. 2006.
[10] C. J. Alpert and A. B. Kahng, "Multi-Way Partitioning Via Geometric Embeddings, Orderings, and Dynamic Programming", *IEEE TCAD* 14(11) (1995), pp. 1342-1358.
[11] C. J. Alpert and A. B. Kahng, "A General Framework for Vertex Orderings, With Applications to Circuit Clustering", *IEEE TVLSI* 4(2) (1996), pp. 240-246.
[12] C. J. Alpert, A. B. Kahng, C. N. Sze and Q. Wang, "Timing-driven Steiner Trees are (Practically) Free", *Proc. DAC*, 2006, pp. 389-392.
[13] S. Bose, "Methods and Systems for Placement and Routing", *US Patent 8332793*, Dec. 2012.
[14] U. Brenner, M. Struzyna and J. Vygen, "BonnPlace: Placement of Leading-edge Chips by Advanced Combinatorial Algorithms", *IEEE TCAD* 27(9) (2008), pp. 1607-1620.
[15] U. Brenner and J. Vygen, "Worst-case Ratios of Networks in the Rectilinear Plane", *Networks* 38(3) (2001), pp. 126-139.
[16] A. E. Caldwell, A. B. Kahng and I. L. Markov, "Can Recursive Bisection Alone Produce Routable Placements?", *Proc. DAC*, 2000, pp. 477-482.
[17] A. E. Caldwell, A. B. Kahng and I. L. Markov, "Optimal Partitioners and End-case Placers for Standard-cell Layout", *IEEE TCAD* 19(11) (2000), pp. 1304-1313.
[18] R. C. Carden, J. Li and C. K. Cheng, "A Global Router with a Theoretical Bound on the Optimal Solution", *IEEE TCAD* 15(2) (1996), pp. 208-216.
[19] C.-K. Cheng, "Linear Placement Algorithms and Applications to VLSI Design", *Networks* 17(4) (1987), pp. 439-464.
[20] C. K. Cheng, R. Graham, I. Kang, D. Park and X. Wang, "Tree Structures and Algorithms for Physical Design", *Proc. ISPD*, 2018.
[21] C. K. Cheng, A. B. Kahng, I. Kang and L. Wang, "RePlAce: Advancing Solution Quality and Routability Validation in Global Placement", *manuscript in submission*, 2017.
[22] S. Chen and T. Yoshimura, "Fixed-Outline Floorplanning: Block-Position Enumeration and a New Method for Calculating Area Costs", *IEEE TCAD* 27(5) (2008), pp. 858-871.

[23] J. Cong, A. B. Kahng, G. Robins and M. Sarrafzadeh, "Provably Good Performance-driven Global Routing", *IEEE TCAD* 11(6) (1992), pp. 739-752.
[24] J. Cong and S. K. Lim, "Edge Separability-based Circuit Clustering with Application to Multilevel Circuit Partitioning", *IEEE TCAD* 23(3) (2004), pp. 346-357.
[25] P. Dickinson, J. Hulshof and A. Ran, "Optimal Flood Control" (2011).
[26] E. W. Dijkstra, "A Note on Two Problems in Connexion with Graphs", *Numerische Mathematik* 1 (1959), pp. 269-271.
[27] Y. Du and M. D. F. Wong, "Optimization of Standard Cell Based Detailed Placement for 16nm FinFET Process", *Proc. DATE*, 2014, pp. 1-6.
[28] M. Elkin and S. Solomon, "Narrow-Shallow-Low-Light Trees with and without Steiner Points", *SIAM J. Discrete Math.* 25(1) (2011), pp. 181-210.
[29] G. M. Furnish, M. J. LeBrun and S. Bose, "Node Spreading Via Artificial Density Enhancement to Reduce Routing Congestion", *US Patent 7921392*, Apr. 2011.
[30] G. M. Furnish, M. J. LeBrun and S. Bose, "Tunneling as a Boundary Congestion Relief Mechanism", *US Patent 7921393*, Apr. 2011.
[31] R. E. Gomory and T. C. Hu, "Multi-Terminal Network Flows", *J. SIAM* 9(4) (1961), pp. 551-570.
[32] C. Han, K. Han, A. B. Kahng, H. Lee, L. Wang and B. Xu, "Optimal Multi-Row Detailed Placement for Yield and Model-Hardware Correlation Improvements in Sub-10nm VLSI", *Proc. IC-CAD*, 2017, pp. 667-674.
[33] L. He, S. Yao, W. Deng, J. Chen and L. Chao, "Interconnect Routing Methods of Integrated Circuit Designs", *US Patent 8386984*, Feb. 2013.
[34] R. F. Hentschke, M. de Oliveira Johann, J. Narasimhan and R. A. de Luz Reis, "Methods and Apparatus for Providing Flexible Timing-driven Routing Trees", *US Patent 8095904*, Jan. 2012.
[35] W. A. Horn, "Single-Machine Job Sequencing with Treelike Precedence Ordering and Linear Delay Penalties", *SIAM J. Appl. Math.* 23(2) (1972), pp. 189-202.
[36] T. C. Hu, "The Maximum Capacity Route Problem", *Operations Research* 9(6) (1961), pp. 898-900.
[37] T. C. Hu, "Multi-commodity Network Flows", *Operations Research* 11(3) (1963), pp. 344-360.
[38] T. C. Hu, "On the Feasibility of Simultaneous Flows in a Network", *SIAM J.*, 12(2) (1964), pp. 359-360.
[39] T. C. Hu, "Optimum Communication Spanning Trees", *SIAM J. Computing* 3(3) (1974), pp. 188-195.
[40] T. C. Hu, *Combinatorial Algorithms*, Addison-Wesley, 1982.
[41] T. C. Hu, "Math, Models and Methods", keynote address and paper, *Proc. 1st ACM Intl. Symp. on Physical Design*, April 1997, pp. 207-210.
[42] T. C. Hu, A. B. Kahng and G. Robins, "Solution of the Discrete Plateau Problem", *Proc. National Academy of Sciences* 89(10), October 1992, pp. 9235-9236.
[43] T. C. Hu, A. B. Kahng and G. Robbins, "Optimal Robust Path Planning in General Environments", *IEEE Trans. Robotics and Automation* 9(6) (1993), pp. 775-784.
[44] T. C. Hu and E. S. Kuh, eds., *VLSI Circuit Layout: Theory and Design*, New York, IEEE Press, 1985.
[45] T. C. Hu and K. Moerder, "Multiterminal Flows in a Hypergraph", in: T.C. Hu and E. Kuh (Eds.), *VLSI Circuit Layout: Theory and Design* (IEEE Press, New York, 1985) pp. 87-93.
[46] T. C. Hu and M. T. Shing, "The α-β Routing", in: T. C. Hu and E. Kuh (Eds.), *VLSI Circuit Layout: Theory and Design* (IEEE Press, New York, 1985) pp. 139-143.
[47] T. C. Hu and M. T. Shing, *Combinatorial Algorithms, Enlarged Second Edition*, New York, Dover Publications, 2002.
[48] E. Ihler, D. Wagner and F. Wagner, "Modeling Hypergraphs by Graphs with the Same Mincut Properties", *Information Processing Letters* 45(4) (1993), pp. 171-175.
[49] A. B. Kahng, "classical Floorplanning Harmful?", *Proc. ISPD*, 2000, pp. 207-213.
[50] A. B. Kahng, P. Tucker and A. Zelikovsky, "Optimization of Linear Placements for Wirelength Minimization with Free Sites", *Proc. ASP-DAC*, 1999, pp. 241-244.
[51] J. M. Kleinhans, G. Sigl, F. M. Johannes and K. J. Antreich, "GORDIAN: VLSI Placement by Quadratic Programming and Slicing Optimization", *IEEE TCAD* 10(3) (1991), pp. 356-365.
[52] G. Kortsarz and D. Peleg, "Approximating Shallow-light Trees", *Proc. SODA*, 1997, pp. 103-110.
[53] T. Leighton and S. Rao, "An Approximate Max-Flow Min-Cut Theorem for Uniform Multicommodity Flow Problems with Applications to Approximation Algorithms", *Foundations of Computer Science*, 1988, pp. 422-431.
[54] C.-T. Lin, D.-S. Chen and Y.-W. Wang, "Fixed-Outline Floorplanning Through Evolutionary Search", *Proc. ASP-DAC*, 2004, pp. 42-44.
[55] Y. Lin, B. Yu, X. Xu, J.-R. Gao, N. Viswanathan, W.-H. Liu, Z. Li, C. J. Alpert and D. Z. Pan "MrDP: Multiple-row Detailed Placement of Heterogeneous-sized Cells for Advanced Nodes", *Proc. ICCAD*, 2016, pp. 7:1-7:8.
[56] Y. Lin, B. Yu, B. Xu and D. Z. Pan. "Triple Patterning Aware Detailed Placement Toward Zero Cross-Row Middle-of-Line Conflict", *Proc. ICCAD*, 2015, pp. 396-403.
[57] R. Liu, S. Dong, X. Hong and Y. Kajitani, "Fixed-Outline Floorplanning with Constraints Through Instance Augmentation", *Proc. ISCAS*, 2005, pp. 1883-1886.
[58] C. Luo, M. F. Anjos and A. Vannelli, "Large-Scale Fixed-Outline Floorplanning Design Using Convex Optimization Techniques", *Proc. ASP-DAC*, 2008, pp. 198-203.
[59] G. K. Moy, "A Specific Network Link and Path Likelihood Prediction Tool", *AIR FORCE INST OF TECH WRIGHT-PATTERSON AFB OH*, 1996, No. AFIT/GCS/ENG/96D-21.
[60] H. Nagamochi and T. Ibaraki, "Computing Edge-connectivity in Multigraphs and Capacitated Graphs", *SIAM J. Discrete Math.* 5(1) (1992), pp. 54-66.
[61] R. C. Prim, "Shortest Connecting Networks and Some Generalizations", *Bell System Tech. J.* 36 (1957), pp. 1389-1401.
[62] P. Saxena, V. Khandelwal, C. Qiao, P-H. Ho, J. C. Lin and M. A. Iyer, "Interconnect-driven Physical Synthesis using Persistent Virtual Routing", *US Patent 7853915*, Dec. 2010.
[63] M. Stoer and F. Wagner, "A Simple Min Cut Algorithm", In *European Symposium on Algorithms*, Berlin, Springer, pp. 141-147.
[64] A. Surampudi and K. Kalimuthu, "An Energy Efficient Spectrum Sensing in Cognitive Radio Wireless Sensor Networks" *arXiv preprint arXiv:1711.09255* (2017).
[65] R. S. Tsay, E. S. Kuh and C. P. Hsu, "PROUD: A Sea-of-Gates Placement Algorithm", *IEEE Design and Test of Computers* 5(6) (1988), pp. 44-56.
[66] J. Z. Yan and C. Chu, "DeFer: Deferred Decision Making Enabled Fixed-Outline Floorplanning Algorithm", *IEEE TCAD* 29(3) (2010), pp. 367-381.
[67] H. H. Yang and D. F. Wong, "Efficient Network Flow Based Min-Cut Balanced Partitioning", *IEEE TCAD* 15(12) (1996), pp. 1533-1540.
[68] H. Zou, W. Zhang and Q. Wang, "An Improved Cerebral Vessel Extraction Method for MRA Images", *Bio-medical Materials and Engineering* 26(s1) (2015), pp. S1231-S1240.

Tree Structures and Algorithms for Physical Design

Chung-Kuan Cheng
Computer Science and Engineering
UC San Diego, La Jolla, California
ckcheng@ucsd.edu

Ronald Graham
Computer Science and Engineering
UC San Diego, La Jolla, California
graham@ucsd.edu

Ilgweon Kang
Computer Science and Engineering
UC San Diego, La Jolla, California
igkang@ucsd.edu

Dongwon Park
Electrical and Computer Engineering
UC San Diego, La Jolla, California
dwp003@ucsd.edu

Xinyuan Wang
Electrical and Computer Engineering
UC San Diego, La Jolla, California
xiw193@ucsd.edu

ABSTRACT

Tree structures and algorithms provide a fundamental and powerful data abstraction and methods for computer science and operations research. In particular, they enable significant advancement of IC physical design techniques and design optimization. For the last half century, Prof. T. C. Hu has made significant contributions to broad areas in computer science, including network flows, integer programming, shortest paths, binary trees, global routing, etc. In this article, we select and summarize three important and interesting tree-related topics (ancestor trees, column generation, and alphabetical trees) in the highlights of Prof. T. C. Hu's contributions to physical design.

CCS CONCEPTS

• **Hardware** → **Physical design (EDA)**; • **Theory of computation** → *Theory and algorithms for application domains*; • **Mathematics of computing**;

KEYWORDS

Tree structures, ancestor trees, column generation, alphabetical trees

ACM Reference Format:
Chung-Kuan Cheng, Ronald Graham, Ilgweon Kang, Dongwon Park, and Xinyuan Wang. 2018. Tree Structures and Algorithms for Physical Design. In *ISPD '18: 2018 International Symposium on Physical Design, March 25–28, 2018, Monterey, CA,* . ACM, New York, NY, USA, 6 pages. https://doi.org/10.1145/3177540.3177564

1 INTRODUCTION

A *tree* is a fundamental data structure in computer science. From operations research to VLSI integrated circuit (IC) design and their optimization, and even for artificial intelligence (AI) technologies and warehouse computing systems, a tree structure provides a simple but powerful data abstraction in various applications. Starting

with a *root* node on the top of all other nodes, a *tree* is composed of a set of linked nodes without any cyclic paths. In a tree structure, we define a *parent* as a node that directs to some other node (i.e., *child*), an *ancestor* as a node reachable by repeatedly going upward from child to parent, and a *leaf* as a node without any children.

The tree structure and its related algorithms are also widely used in IC physical layout design. In floorplanning, tree structures (e.g., twin binary trees [41, 42], O-trees [17], and B*-trees [5]) are popular methods to represent the given floorplan for the layout design. Ratio cut and replication cut provide breakthroughs for two-way partitioning [9, 32]. The column generation technique that reduces the linear program complexity can be applied to efficiently construct tree structures for global routing [4, 21]. Alphabetical trees can be used for synthesizing adders [33, 43] and interconnect design models [39]. Also clock tree synthesis (CTS) is a crucial procedure during physical design to build a tree having low skew, while delivering the same clock signal to every sequential gate [28].

For the past half a century, Prof. T. C. Hu has contributed significantly to the improvement of algorithms in operations research and computer science. His papers and journal articles have been incredibly important across broad topics, including network flows, integer programming, shortest paths, binary trees, etc [44]. Specifically, many of his research results on tree structures suggest better opportunities to observe and understand IC physical layout designs. One of his notable achievements is the paper with Gomory on multi-terminal flows [14]. The so-called Gomory-Hu tree of an undirected graph in combinatorial optimization is a weighted tree that represents the minimum source-sink cuts for all source-sink pairs in the graph [44]. They proved that we can use $n - 1$ computations through the ancestor tree since the Gomory-Hu cut tree uses $n - 1$ non-crossing minimum cuts to find all the ordinary maximum flow values between all nodes in a network [8, 9].

In this work, we present several tree structures and related algorithms in the highlights of Prof. Hu's contributions. The remaining sections are organized as follows. Section 2 introduces the Gomory-Hu cut tree and the ancestor tree. Section 3 describes the duality in linear programs and the column generation. Section 4 presents the alphabetical tree and Hu-Tucker algorithm. Section 5 concludes this article.

2 ANCESTOR TREES

For ancestor trees, we try to represent the partitioning structure of a network. The cost of the cut can be arbitrary and it is known that the general problem of the finding the optimal cut is NP complete. The formulation is inspired by the Gomory-Hu cut tree which starts with a maximum flow minimum cut partitioning. The multi-terminal maximum flow problem is to find the maximum flow values for all pairs of nodes in a network. By the Max-Flow Min-Cut Theorem of Ford and Fulkerson [11], the maximum flow between a given pair of nodes is equal to the capacity of the minimum cut separating the two nodes.

We are given an undirected network with node set V, $|V| = n$, and edge set E. Each edge $e_{ij} \in E$ connects nodes i and j with a non-negative capacity b_{ij}. The maximum flow value between nodes i and j is denoted by f_{ij}. We utilize the description in Prof. Hu's book [22] to state the following theorems and lemmas.

THEOREM 1. *A necessary and sufficient condition for a set of non-negative numbers $f_{ij} = f_{ji}$ ($i, j = 1, \cdots, n$) to be the maximum flow values of a network is*

$$f_{ik} \geq \min(f_{ij}, f_{jk}) \quad \forall i, j, k. \tag{1}$$

Once inequality (1) is established, then by induction we have

$$f_{ip} \geq \min(f_{ij}, f_{jk}, f_{kl}, \cdots, f_{op}), \tag{2}$$

where indices $i, j, \cdots, p$, represent an arbitrary sequence of nodes in the network. With inequality (1), the following lemma states that the maximum flow values of the network can be simplified.

LEMMA 1. *For any three nodes of the network, at least two of the maximum flow values between them must be equal.*

By induction following the inequality (2), we find that among the $n(n-1)/2$ maximum flow values $f_{ij} = f_{ji}$, there exist at most $n-1$ distinct values.

Note that we can generalize the above theorem and lemma by extending the cutting objective to arbitrary cost functions f as long as the cost is symmetric, i.e. $f_{ij} = f_{ji}$. We can prove the extended statement by enumeration, which is similar to the original proof.

2.1 The Gomory-Hu Cut Tree

Among all $\binom{n}{2}$ pairs of nodes, Gomory and Hu [14] showed that $n-1$ minimum cost cuts which do not cross each other are sufficient to separate all pairs of nodes. We call any two networks *flow-equivalent* if the maximum flow values between all pairs of nodes are the same.

THEOREM 2. *Any network is flow-equivalent to a cut tree.*

To construct the cut tree, we first shall describe a process called "condensing nodes". A set of nodes in original graph is replaced by a single node, and all the edges connecting any node not in the set are condensed to a single edge associated with the sum of capacities of original edges. Then we will have a simplified network which will reduce computations.

The *non-crossing minimum cuts* provide the condition as to whether any subset of nodes can be condensed while not affecting the maximum flow computation. In [22], Chapter 2.3.2 discusses related lemmas and their proofs in detail.

We adopt the algorithm of constructing the tree network from [14] and use a numerical example to demonstrate the technique. Consider the network with five nodes in Figure 1, the numbers associated with the edges are their corresponding capacities. We are

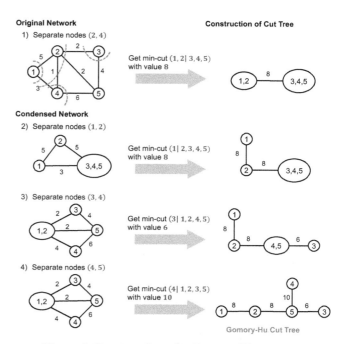

Figure 1: Construction of a Gomory-Hu cut tree.

going to find the maximum flow value between each pair of nodes in the network.

First let us arbitrarily choose a pair of nodes $(2, 4)$ and perform a maximum flow computation. A minimum cut $(1, 2 \mid 3, 4, 5)$ separates nodes 2 and 4 with flow 8. The set of nodes on each side of the cut can be represented with a terminal node as shown in the first step in Figure 1, and the cut value is assigned to the link of the cut tree.

Next choose any two nodes from a terminal node of the current cut tree. We pick the terminal node $\{1, 2\}$ and perform a maximum flow computation between nodes 1 and 2 on the condensed network (Figure 1.2)). The result gives a minimum cut $(1 \mid 2, 3, 4, 5)$ with value 8. The terminal nodes $\{1, 2\}$ are partitioned into two sets connected by a link with the cut value, which then replace the terminal node $\{1, 2\}$. The computation is repeated until there is only one node of original network in each terminal node of the cut tree.

After $n-1$ iterations, a tree diagram is obtained, which is termed a *Gomory-Hu cut tree* of this 5-node graph. The $n-1$ non-crossing minimum cuts are shown in red dashed lines in the original network.

2.2 The Construction of Ancestor Tree

The construction of the Gomory-Hu cut tree relies on the fact that there always exists a set of $n-1$ non-crossing minimum cuts. With arbitrary cut functions, the cuts may cross each other. However, Cheng and Hu [8, 9] show that we still need only $n-1$ computations by constructing a binary tree called an *ancestor tree*. This tree has $n-1$ internal nodes and each represents a cut, as well as n leaves and each of these represents a node of the original network. For each pair of leaves, their lowest common ancestor is the minimum cut of the corresponding pair of nodes. We call the $n-1$ distinct cuts an *essential cut set*.

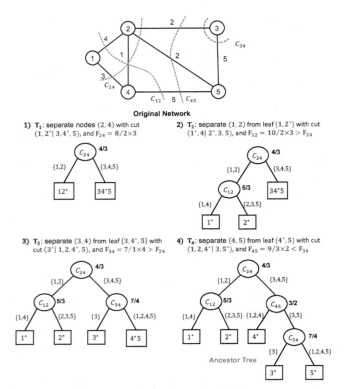

Original Network

1) T_1: separate nodes $(2, 4)$ with cut $(1, 2^* | 3, 4^*, 5)$, and $F_{24} = 8/2 \times 3$

2) T_2: separate $(1, 2)$ from leaf $\{1, 2^*\}$ with cut $(1^*, 4| 2^*, 3, 5)$, and $F_{12} = 10/2 \times 3 > F_{24}$

3) T_3: separate $(3, 4)$ from leaf $\{3, 4^*, 5\}$ with cut $(3^* | 1, 2, 4^*, 5)$, and $F_{34} = 7/1 \times 4 > F_{24}$

4) T_4: separate $(4, 5)$ from leaf $\{4^*, 5\}$ with cut $(1, 2, 4^* | 3, 5^*)$, and $F_{45} = 9/3 \times 2 < F_{34}$

Ancestor Tree

Figure 2: An example of constructing an ancestor tree.

In the construction of the tree, we define some nodes as *seeds*. Each cut C_{ij} in the tree is minimum cost cut separating seeds i and j. The tree structure that maintains the following three properties throughout the iterations is *admissible* [9].

- The cut value of an internal node is always no smaller than the value of its father.
- Each leaf L_i contains exactly one seed i.
- For any pair of leaves L_i and L_j with seeds i and j, let the internal node C_{pq} be their lowest ancestor.

Then C_{pq} with its two branches defines a minimum cut separating nodes i and j.

The algorithm to construct an ancestor tree gradually builds trees $T_0, T_1, \cdots, T_{n-1}$ by adding one more cut node and leaf [9] at a time. A numerical example is shown in Figure 2. The cost function is defined as $F_{ij} = \min \dfrac{C(X, \bar{X})}{|X| \cdot |\bar{X}|}$ with node $i \in X$ and node $j \in \bar{X}$. Seeds are postfixed with '*'.

Figure 2 illustrates an example of the process. We choose a pair of nodes $(2, 4)$ and separate them with minimum cost cut $\{1, 2^* | 3, 4^*, 5\}$. The cut cost is $F_{24} = 8/(2 \times 3) = 4/3$, then we have a cut node C_{24} with two branches and each is labeled with a partitioned subset of nodes. As shown in Figure 2:step 1, the tree has two leaves. One contains the subset $\{1, 2^*\}$ with seed 2^* and one contains $\{3, 4^*, 5\}$ with seed 4^*.

In the next iteration, we pick nodes $(1, 2)$ from the left leaf and compute the cut. The minimum cut $\{1^*, 4 \mid 2^*, 3, 5\}$ has value no smaller than its father $F_{12} = 10/(2) = 5/3 > F_{24}$, so we append the cut node C_{12} to the position of the old leaf and append new leaves to C_{12}. The leaves contain nodes by intersecting the labels

along the branches. For example, the left leaf of C_{12} contains nodes $\{1, 2\} \cap \{1, 4\} = \{1^*\}$.

There exists another case when the cost is smaller than its father. In Figure 2:step 4, the cut cost $F_{45} = 3/2 < F_{34}$. We find the highest ancestor of C_{45} with a larger cut cost which is C_{34}, so we place C_{45} at this position. Node C_{34} with its subtree is appended to C_{45} and the subsets of nodes are updated. Repeat these steps until there exists only one seeded node in each leaf. The cuts are shown in red dashed lines in the original network among which C_{12} and C_{24} cross each other.

Given an admissible tree T_k, we can prove the tree T_{k+1} is still admissible after an iteration. The correctness of the algorithm is proved by Theorem 3 [9].

THEOREM 3. *The cut tree algorithm derives an essential cut set with $n - 1$ minimum cut calls.*

2.3 Applications of the Ancestor Tree

The ancestor tree provides a natural hierarchical representation of a complicated network. The technique has been applied to solving complex multi-commodity network optimization problems [12] as well as network partitioning problems [7, 30]. This partitioning can be further applied to solve VLSI design problems for logic synthesis and physical layout [6]. An extension to directed graphs would be an interesting research problem.

3 COLUMN GENERATION

Column generation is a powerful technique utilizing the duality of the problem formulation. For example, in global routing, the original problem has a huge number of possible variables where each variable represents a tree structure. The search for an optimal routing tree is by itself an NP-complete problem in general. The competition among the trees for a limited routing resources complicates the issue. Column generation utilizes the shadow price of the dual formulation to provide a systematic guide in searching for the tree [4, 19].

3.1 Duality in Linear Programming

Formulations (3) and (4) represent the *primal* and *dual* of a linear programming problem, where $\mathbf{c}$ and $\mathbf{y}$ are row vectors, $\mathbf{x}$ and $\mathbf{b}$ are column vectors, and $\mathbf{A}$ is an $m \times n$ matrix. The primal (resp. dual) has n (resp. m) variables and m (resp. n) constraints. The variables $\mathbf{y}$ in the dual program are often denoted by π, and are called the *shadow prices*[1].

Maximize	$z = \mathbf{cx}$	(3)	Minimize	$w = \mathbf{yb}$	(4)
subject to	$\mathbf{Ax} \leq \mathbf{b}$		subject to	$\mathbf{yA} \geq \mathbf{c}$	
	$\mathbf{x} \geq 0$			$\mathbf{y} \geq 0$	

Figure 3 illustrates the relation between the primal and dual programs. For the primal program, the maximum $z = 4000$ occurs when $x_1 = 40$ and $x_2 = 80$. For the dual, the minimum $w = 4000$ occurs when $y_1 = 20$ and $y_2 = 5$. For the objective function in the linear program, we define the *reduced costs* (i.e., opportunity costs) as $\mathbf{c} - \mathbf{yA}$, implying that the current basis can be improved when the

---

[1]At the optimal solution of the linear program, the shadow price equals to the value of the *Lagrangian multiplier*.

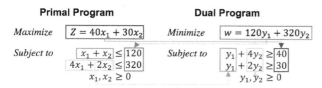

Figure 3: A primal program and its dual program [46].

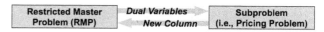

Figure 5: An overview of column generation.

reduced cost is negative. In other words, if all the reduced costs are non-negative, then the current solution is optimal. For the primal program in the figure, the reduced costs are $[0,0]$ at the optimal solution as $[40,30] - [20,5]\begin{bmatrix} 1 & 1 \\ 4 & 2 \end{bmatrix} = [0,0]$.

3.2 The Technique of Column Generation

For a routing problem, the primal formulation can have a huge number of variables which can far exceed the computational capability of a computer. The *column generation* technique offers an efficient technique to avoid this computational blowup. This technique allows us to reduce our attention to only a subset of the variables. Through primal-dual iterations, we swap improved choices through shadow prices.

Figure 4 demonstrates the variable reduction process. We partition columns into two groups (Figure 4(a)). From an initial solution of the linear program (3), we have (i) generated columns and (ii) non-generated columns. We only deal with a small subset of variables (i.e., generated columns) to solve the given linear program. By removing non-generated columns, we obtain the *master problem* composed of generated columns so that we can reduce the problem size (shown in Figure 4(b)).

Figure 5 shows an overview of the column generation technique and the relation between the master problem which gives the dual variables (i.e., the shadow prices) and the *subproblem* which identifies a new column (if it exists). Whenever the subproblem proposes a new variable to add, then the master problem adds a column to the

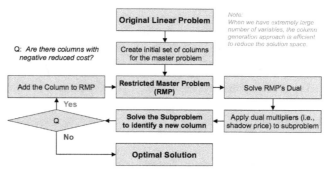

Figure 6: A flow chart for column generation.

matrix **A**. This is why this process is called column generation [45]. By alternating the two problems, the column generation efficiently approaches the optimal solution.

As mentioned above, if the minimum of all reduced costs is non-negative, then all the reduced costs are non-negative and the current solution is optimal. If the least reduced cost is negative (meaning that the current solution can be further improved), then we add the new column into the current basis. The iteration procedure of the column generation terminates when the least reduced cost is non-negative.

Figure 6 summarizes the overall flow of the column generation technique. From the original linear program, we first find a feasible solution and produce the restricted master problem. We then solve the dual of the master problem to obtain the shadow prices π as the sensitivity analysis effectively identifies the most critical variable. Through the dual feasible solution of the linear program, we try to find the column a_j which leads to the maximum πa_j. We can find the minimum reduced cost since the reduced cost is equal to $c_j - \pi a_j$. If there are no columns with the negative reduced cost, we end up with the optimal solution [20].

3.3 Applications of Column Generation

The column generation technique enables a large reduction of computation efforts when the number of variables is very large [15, 16]. For instance, we typically assign a variable for every possible route in vehicle routing problem. Thus, the number of variables is of the order of the factorial of the number of places to visit [45]. Some applications of the column generation technique are vehicle routing [10, 34], integrated circuit routing [4, 21, 26, 27], scheduling [25, 37], transportation [35], network design [2, 3], etc.

For physical design, our choice of the column generation approach for global routing [4, 18] is inspired by the discussion with Prof. Hu. The approach allows us to derive a theoretical bound from the optimal routing solution. Huang et al. [24] improved the circuit performance of the routing tree with timing cost in the formulation. Albrecht [1] incorporated the wirelength as part of the constraints in the primal problem. In [40], Wu et al. used the column generation to enumerate candidate routing trees and complete the tree selection using integer programming at local regions.

(a) Original linear problem with a very large number of variables

Maximize $[c_1 \cdots c_k \ c_{k+1} \cdots c_n][x_1 \cdots x_k \ x_{k+1} \cdots x_n]^T$

Subject to $\begin{bmatrix} A_{1,1} & \cdots & A_{1,k} & A_{1,k+1} & \cdots & A_{1,n} \\ \vdots & & \vdots & \vdots & & \vdots \\ A_{m,1} & \cdots & A_{m,k} & A_{m,k+1} & \cdots & A_{m,n} \end{bmatrix}\begin{bmatrix} x_1 \\ \vdots \\ x_k \\ x_{k+1} \\ \vdots \\ x_n \end{bmatrix} \leq \begin{bmatrix} b_1 \\ \vdots \\ b_m \end{bmatrix}$

Remove Non-generated Columns $[x_1 \cdots x_k \ x_{k+1} \cdots x_n] \geq \mathbf{0}$

(b) Master problem

Maximize $[c_1 \cdots c_k][x_1 \cdots x_k]^T$

Subject to $\begin{bmatrix} A_{1,1} & \cdots & A_{1,k} \\ \vdots & & \vdots \\ A_{m,1} & \cdots & A_{m,k} \end{bmatrix}\begin{bmatrix} x_1 \\ \vdots \\ x_k \end{bmatrix} \leq \begin{bmatrix} b_1 \\ \vdots \\ b_m \end{bmatrix}$

$[x_1 \cdots x_k] \geq \mathbf{0}$

Figure 4: An example of producing the master problem for the column generation procedure. The original figure can be found in [45].

4 ALPHABETICAL TREES

Alphabetical trees fit physical design very well because the tree construction respects the sequence of the nodes. In the formulation, the order of the nodes is given. We construct a tree to connect these nodes so that a depth-first traversal maintains the same order. Figure 7 shows an example of an alphabetical tree. In this tree structure, we can obtain the letters in the alphabetic order by scanning the leaves from left to right. For a binary tree, where left edges are assigned with 0 and right edges are assigned with 1, each leaf L_i can be associated to a binary number $n(L_i)$ along the path from the root node. For an alphabetical tree, and the following condition is always satisfied:

$$n(L_i) < n(L_{i+1}),$$

where i is the index of a leaf specified from left to right. For physical routing, a mismatch in the order indicates a crossing of the wires and a waste of routing resources.

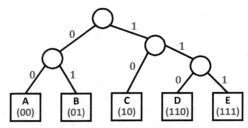

Figure 7: An alphabetical tree

4.1 The Hu-Tucker Algorithm

Several algorithms have been proposed to find optimum alphabetical trees. Gilbert and Moore constructed optimum alphabetical trees using dynamic programming techniques which has $O(n^3)$ in runtime and $O(n^2)$ in memory space [13]. Knuth [29] proposed a method that reduces the computation time to $O(n^2)$ but still has $O(n^2)$ in memory space. Hu and Tucker [23] further reduces the complexity to $O(n \log n)$ in runtime and $O(n)$ in memory space.

The Hu-Tucker algorithm has three phases which are the *combination*, *level assignment* and *reconstruction* phases as shown in Figure 8. In the combination phase, nodes are merged to produce the smallest weight when combined nodes are adjacent in the sense that there is no leaf between them. Note that between two adjacent leaves, we could have internal nodes, e.g., internal node labeled 10 between nodes 7 and 5 in Figure 8(a,b). The corresponding tree of the combinational phase is denoted by T' (Figure 8(a)), which is an optimum binary tree but not an alphabetical tree. To translate the optimum binary tree T' into an optimum alphabetical tree T'_N, the level assignment phase is required to identify the level of each leaf using the topology of T'. The level number is the path-length from the root node as shown in Figure 8(b). According to the result of the level assignment phase, an optimum alphabetical tree T'_N is composed by a level-by-level construction method from the bottom to the top in the reconstruction phase (Figure 8(c)).

4.2 Applications of Alphabetical Trees

Alphabetical trees have been applied in several applications such as adder synthesis, interconnect design problem and layout-driven

(a) Combination : T'

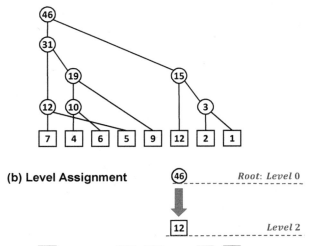

(b) Level Assignment

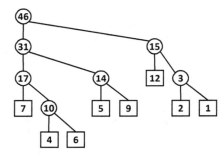

(c) Reconstruction : T'_N (Alphabetical Tree)

Figure 8: The Hu-Tucker algorithm [22].

logic synthesis. In generic parallel adders based on prefix computation, the computation structure of adders can be represented and simplified by an alphabetical tree [33, 43]. In [39], Vittal and Marek-Sadowska used the alphabetical tree with an analytical model to minimize the interconnect delay. In [36, 38], Vaishnav and Pedram adopted the alphabetical tree to optimize the fan-out in the layout-driven logic synthesis and technology decomposition.

5 CONCLUSION

In this article, we selected three tree-related topics, i.e., ancestor trees, column generation, and alphabetical trees. We then briefly described them in each section highlighting Prof. Hu's contributions. These techniques will certainly contribute to future innovation in these fundamental areas.

6 ACKNOWLEDGEMENT

This work was supported in part by the National Science Foundation (Grant CCF-1564302).

REFERENCES

[1] C. Albrecht, "Provably Good Global Routing by A New Approximation Algorithm for Multicommodity Flow", *Proc. ISPD*, 2000, pp. 19-25.

[2] F. Alvelos and J. M. V. de Carvalho, "An Extended Model and a Column Generation Algorithm for the Planar Multicommodity Flow Problem", *Networks* 50(1) (2007), pp. 3-16.

[3] W. Ben-Ameur and J. Neto, "Acceleration of Cutting-Plane and Column Generation Algorithms: Applications to Network Design", *Networks* 49(1) (2007), pp. 3-17.

[4] R. C. Carden, J. Li and C. K. Cheng, "A Global Router with a Theoretical Bound on the Optimal Solution", *IEEE Trans. on CAD* 15(2) (1996), pp. 208-216.

[5] Y. C. Chang, Y.-W. Chang, G. M. Wu and S. W. Wu, "B*-Trees: A New Representation for Non-Slicing Floorplans", *Proc. DAC*, 2000, pp. 458-463.

[6] S.-J. Chen and C. K. Cheng, "Tutorial on VLSI Partitioning", *VLSI Design* 11(3) (2000), pp. 175-218.

[7] C. K. Cheng, "The Optimal Partitioning of Networks", *Networks* 22(3) (1992), pp. 297-315.

[8] C. K. Cheng and T. C. Hu, "Ancestor Tree for Arbitrary Multi-Terminal Cut Functions", *Annals of Operations Research* 33(3) (1991), pp. 199-213.

[9] C. K. Cheng and T. C. Hu, "Maximum Concurrent Flows and Minimum Ratio Cuts", *Algorithmica* 8(1) (1992), pp. 233-249.

[10] C. Contardo, J.-F. Cordeau and B. Gendron, "An Exact Algorithm Based on Cut-and-Column Generation for the Capacitated Location-Routing Problem", *INFORMS Journal on Computing* 26(1) (2014), pp. 88-102.

[11] L. R. Ford and D. R. Fulkerson, "Maximal Flow through a Network", *Canadian Journal of Mathematics* 8(3) (1956), pp. 399-404.

[12] V. Gabrel, A. Knippel and M. Minoux, "Exact Solution of Multicommodity Network Optimization Problems with General Step Cost Functions", *Operations Research Letters* 25(1) (1999), pp. 15-23.

[13] E. N. Gilbert and E. F. Moore, "Variable Length Binary Encodings", *Bell System Technical Journal* 38 (1959), pp. 933-968.

[14] R. E. Gomory and T. C. Hu, "Multi-Terminal Network Flows", *Journal of SIAM* 9(4) (1961), pp. 551-570.

[15] J. Gondzio, P. González-Brevis and P. Munari, "New Developments in the Primal-Dual Column Generation Technique", *European Journal of Operational Research* 224(1) (2013), pp. 41-51.

[16] J. Gondzio, P. González-Brevis and P. Munari, "Large-Scale Optimization with the Primal-Dual Column Generation Method", *Mathematical Programming Computation* 8(1) (2016), pp. 47-82.

[17] P.-N. Guo, T. Takahashi, C. K. Cheng and T. Yoshimura, "Floorplanning Using a Tree Representation", *IEEE Trans. on CAD* 20(2) (2001), pp. 281-289.

[18] J. Hu and S. S. Sapatnekar, "A Survey on Multi-Net Global Routing for Integrated Circuits", *Integration, the VLSI Journal* 31(1) (2001), pp. 1-49.

[19] T. C. Hu, "Multi-Commodity Network Flows", *Operations Research* 11(3) (1963), pp. 344-360.

[20] T. C. Hu and A. B. Kahng, *Linear and Integer Programming Made Easy*, Springer, 2016.

[21] T. C. Hu and M. T. Shing, "A Decomposition Algorithm for Circuit Routing", *Mathematical Programming Study* 24 (1985), pp. 87-103.

[22] T. C. Hu and M. T. Shing, *Combinatorial Algorithms*, 2nd Ed., Dover Publications, 2002.

[23] T. C. Hu and A. C. Tucker, "Optimal Computer Search Trees and Variable-Length Alphabetical Codes", *Journal of SIAM* 21(4) 1971, pp.514-532.

[24] J. Huang, X. L. Hong, C. K. Cheng and E. S. Kuh, "An Efficient Timing-Driven Global Routing Algorithm", *Proc. DAC*, 1993, pp. 596-600.

[25] J. Janacek, M. Kohani, M. Koniorczyk and P. Marton, "Optimization of Periodic Crew Schedules with Application of Column Generation Method", *Transportation Research Part C: Emerging Technologies* 83 (2017), pp. 165-178.

[26] G.-W. Jeong, K. Lee, S. Park and K. Park, "A Branch-and-Price Algorithm for the Steiner Tree Packing Problem", *Computers & Operations Research* 29(3) (2002), pp. 221-241.

[27] D. G. Jørgensen and M. Meyling, "A Branch-and-Price Algorithm for Switch-Box Routing", *Networks* 40(1) (2002), pp. 13-26.

[28] A. B. Kahng, J. Lienig, I. L. Markov and J. Hu, *VLSI Physical Design: From Graph Partitioning to Timing Closure*, Springer, 2011.

[29] D. E. Knuth, "Optimum Binary Search Trees", *Acta Informatica 1* (1971), pp. 14-25.

[30] M. E. Kuo and C. K. Cheng, "A Network Flow Approach for Hierarchical Tree Partitioning", *Proc. DAC*, 1997, pp. 512-517.

[31] G. Laporte, "The Vehicle Routing Problem: An Overview of Exact and Approximate Algorithms", *European Journal of Operational Research* 59(3) (1992), pp. 345-358.

[32] L.-T. Liu, M.-T. Kuo, C. K. Cheng and T. C. Hu, "A Replication Cut for Two-Way Partitioning", *IEEE Trans. on CAD* 14(5) (1995), pp. 623-630.

[33] J. Liu, S. Zhou, H. Zhu and C. K. Cheng, "An Algorithmic Approach for Generic Parallel Adders", *Proc. ICCAD*, 2003, pp. 734-740.

[34] M. E. Lübbecke and J. Desrosiers, "Selected Topics in Column Generation", *Operations Research* 53(6) (2005), pp. 1007-1023.

[35] T. Nishi and T. Izuno, "Column Generation Heuristics for Ship Routing and Scheduling Problems in Crude Oil Transportation with Split Deliveries", *Computers & Chemical Engineering* 60 (2014), pp. 329-338.

[36] M. Pedram and H. Vaishnav, "Technology Decomposition Using Optimal Alphabetic Trees", *Proc. ECDA*, 1993, pp. 573-577.

[37] D. Potthoff, D. Huisman and G. Desaulniers, "Column Generation with Dynamic Duty Selection for Railway Crew Rescheduling", *Transportation Science* 44 (2010), pp. 493-505.

[38] H. Vaishnav and M. Pedram, "Alphabetic Trees - Theory and Applications in Layout-Driven Logic Synthesis", *IEEE Trans. on CAD* 42(2) (2002), pp. 219-223.

[39] A. Vittal and M. Marek-Sadowska, "Minimal Delay Interconnect Design Using Alphabetic Trees", *Proc. DAC*, 1994, pp. 392-396.

[40] T. H. Wu, A. Davoodi and J. T. Linderoth, "GRIP: Global Routing via Integer Programming", *IEEE Trans. on CAD* 30(1) (2011), pp. 72-84.

[41] B. Yao, H. Chen, C. K. Cheng and R. Graham, "Floorplan Representations: Complexity and Connections", *ACM Trans. on DAES* 8(1) (2003), pp. 55-80.

[42] E. F. Y. Young, C. C. N. Chu and Z. C. Shen, "Twin Binary Sequences: A Nonredundant Representation for General Nonslicing Floorplan", *IEEE Trans. on CAD* 22(4) (2003), pp. 457-469.

[43] Y. Zhu, J. Liu, H. Zhu and C. K. Cheng, "Timing-Power Optimization for Mixed-Radix Ling Adders by Integer Linear Programming", *Proc. ASP-DAC*, 2008, pp. 131-137.

[44] Brief Biography of Dr. Te Chiang Hu, *The Institute for Operations Research and the Management Sciences*, http://www.informs.org/Explore/History-of-O.R.-Excellence/Biographical-Profiles/Hu-Te-Chiang/.

[45] Column Generation and Dantzig-Wolfe Decomposition, *Group for Research in Decision Analysis (GERAD)*, http://www.science4all.org/article/column-generation/.

[46] Duality Theory in LP, http://www.slideshare.net/jyothimonc/duality-in-linear-programming/.

Pioneer Research on Mathematical Models and Methods for Physical Design

Chris Chu
Department of Electrical and Computer Engineering
Iowa State University
Ames, Iowa
cnchu@iastate.edu

ABSTRACT

In the inaugural International Symposium on Physical Design (ISPD) at 1997, Prof. Te Chiang Hu has delivered the keynote address "Physical Design: Mathematical Models and Methods" [1]. Without any question, Prof. Hu has made a lot of foundational and profound contributions to physical design automation and to computer science and mathematics in general. This paper highlights several of Prof. Hu's pioneer works related to flow and cut in a flow network to commemorate his achievements.

CCS CONCEPTS

• **Mathematics of computing → Network flows**; • **Theory of computation → Network flows**; • **Hardware → Physical design (EDA)**;

KEYWORDS

Physical design automation; Network flow; Cut

ACM Reference Format:
Chris Chu. 2018. Pioneer Research on Mathematical Models and Methods for Physical Design . In *ISPD '18: 2018 International Symposium on Physical Design, March 25–28, 2018, Monterey, CA, USA*. ACM, New York, NY, USA, 4 pages. https://doi.org/10.1145/3177540.3177565

1 INTRODUCTION

Finding a flow or a cut with specific property in a flow network has a lot of applications in diverse fields. In VLSI design, a circuit can be modeled as a network. A maximum flow in the network characterizes the connectivity between two components in the circuit. A minimum cut provides a partitioning of the circuit with the least dependency between the two partitions. In addition, many optimization problems in VLSI design can be transformed into either a flow or a cut problem. For example, the Lagrangian multiplier update problem in a Lagrangian relaxation based gate sizing algorithm is formulated as a minimum cost flow problem [2]. The layout decomposition problem in double patterning lithography is reduced to a maximum cut problem in a flipping graph [3].

Most researchers in design automation use network flow and cut algorithms as tools to solve various problems in the design flow. Prof. Hu is one of the few who has also made significant contributions to the fundamental and theoretical aspects of network flow and cut. In this paper, we will present a few selected works of Prof. Hu on network flow and cut to pay tribute to his achievements. Note that the selected papers is only a small subset of his work on flow network research, and flow network research is only one of his many research directions. Hopefully the selected papers can illustrate the insightfulness, mathematical rigor and substantial influence of his research.

2 MULTI-COMMODITY NETWORK FLOWS

The multi-commodity flow problem has many practical applications, e.g., modeling of messages in a communication network, different goods in a transportation system, and traffic in a road network. In VLSI design, routing in circuits can be modeled as a flow in a network. To handle the routing of multiple nets, we can use a multi-commodity flow model in which each of the nets is represented by one commodity. Multi-commodity flow based approaches have been applied to various formulations of VLSI routing problems (e.g., [4–8]).

Prof. Hu is one of the earliest researchers who works on the multi-commodity flow problem. He presented the seminal paper [9] which generalizes the max-flow min-cut theorem of Ford and Fulkerson [10] to the problem of finding the maximum simultaneous flows of two commodities.

Consider a connected network with positive arc capacities such that the arc capacity from node N_i to N_j is the same as that from node N_j to N_i. Suppose kth kind of flow is from node N_k to node $N_{k'}$ and is denoted by $F(k; k')$. Let $f(k; k')$ denote the value of $F(k; k')$. Let $c(k; k')$ denote the capacity of the minimum cut separating node N_k and node $N_{k'}$. As a generalization of cut, let a disconnecting set for k pairs of nodes N_i, $N_{i'}$ ($i = 1, 2, \ldots, k$) be a set of arcs, the removal of which will disconnect N_i from $N_{i'}$ ($i = 1, 2, \ldots, k$), and no proper subset of which will have this property. The value of a disconnecting set is the sum of capacities of the arcs in the set. Let $c(1, 2, \ldots, k; 1', 2', \ldots, k')$ be the value of the disconnecting set whose value is minimum among all those separating N_i from $N_{i'}$ ($i = 1, 2, \ldots, k$). Let $i - j$ denote that we condense N_i and N_j into one node in the network. Consider two kinds of flow.

THEOREM 1. **(Max Bi-Flows Min-Cut Theorem)** *Two flows $F(1; 1')$ and $F(2; 2')$ are feasible if and only if (1), (2), (3) below are* *all satisfied:*

$$f(1; 1') \leq c(1; 1') \tag{1}$$

$$f(2; 2') \leq c(2; 2') \tag{2}$$

$$f(1; 1') + f(2; 2') \leq c(1, 2; 1', 2') \tag{3}$$

The maximum sum of the two flows is equal to the minimum-cut capacity of all cuts separating the two pairs of nodes; i.e.,

$$max[f(1; 1') + f(2; 2')] = min[c(1 - 2; 1' - 2'), c(1 - 2'; 1' - 2)].$$

To prove this theorem, Prof. Hu has presented an algorithm similar to the labeling method for finding maximum flow of a single commodity to construct the two flows. The max-flow min-cut theorem is later extended to multicommodity flows by Onaga [11] and Iri [12].

3 MAXIMUM CONCURRENT FLOWS AND MINIMUM CUTS

In VLSI physical design and other applications, we often need to find the minimum cost cut separating a given pair of nodes. In [13], Prof. Hu together with Prof. Cheng have generalized the problem to finding all minimum cost cuts which separate all $\binom{n}{2}$ pairs of nodes. They showed that for arbitrary costs (e.g., usual cut [10], weighted sparsest cut [14], or flux cut [15]), there are only $n - 1$ essential minimum cuts out of all $2^{n-1} - 1$ possible cuts.

THEOREM 2. *Given a network with n nodes and an arbitrary cut cost function, we need at most $n - 1$ distinct cuts, such that for all pair of nodes, one of the $n - 1$ cuts is the minimum cut separating the pair.*

They have also presented an algorithm to find the set of essential cuts with only $n - 1$ calls to an oracle which generates the minimum cut for a given node pair with respect to a given cost function.

Among the distinct cuts in the essential cut set, we may find the global minimum cut which is the cut with minimum cost among all $2^{n-1} - 1$ possible cuts. In [13], Prof. Hu and Prof. Cheng focused on the ratio cut cost function, which is also called the weighted sparsest cut [14]. The problem of finding the global minimum ratio cut is NP-hard [16]. They proposed an approach by leveraging the relationship between global minimum ratio cut and the maximum concurrent flow [17]. The maximum concurrent flow problem, which maximizes the uniform flow demand between every pair of nodes, can be formulated as a linear programming problem and solved using column-generating techniques [18]. The saturated arcs in the maximum concurrent flow define a K-way partition of the network. Their key contribution is showing that if $K \leq 4$, then there exists a two-way partition of the partitioned K subsets which is the global minimum ratio cut.

4 A REPLICATION CUT FOR TWO-WAY PARTITIONING

In VLSI design, when a circuit is partitioned, it is often beneficial to allow some cells to be replicated. For example, when a large circuit is implemented by several FPGAs, the limited pin count of FPGA chips and the significant delay and power overhead for off-chip communications are often the bottleneck. By replicating

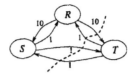 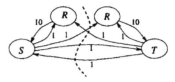

Figure 1: Effect of replication. (a) The min-cut has a cut cost of 13 without replication. (b) Replicating R results in a cut cost of 4. [19]

some cells into multiple FPGAs, the demand in pin count and off-chip communications can be reduced. The effect of replication in reducing interchip connections is illustrated in Figure 1.

In [19], Prof. Hu and his collaborators have investigated the problem of two-way min-cut partitioning with cell replication. They first considered networks with only two-pin nets and without constraints on partition size. Given two nodes s and t to be separated, they introduced a novel replication graph such that an optimal replication partition can be constructed from the maximum flow in the replication graph. The replication graph is derived by first formulating the replication partitioning problem as a linear program and next interpreting its dual linear program as a network flow problem. The replication graph corresponding to the network flow can then be constructed. The structure of the replication graph is illustrated in Figure 2 and an example is shown in Figure 3.

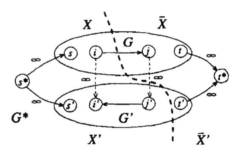

Figure 2: Structure of replication graph G^*. [19]

From Figure 2, we can see that the replication graph G^* basically consists of a copy of the original graph G and another copy G' similar to G but with all arcs reversed. Each node in G is connected to its corresponding nodes in G' with an arc with infinite capacity. A super source node s^* (a super sink node t^*) connecting to the source nodes (from the sink nodes) in G and G' with infinite capacity arcs is also added.

The optimum replication cut of G with respect to node pair s and t can be found by a maximum-flow minimum-cut solution of G^* with respect to node pair s^* and t^*. Suppose the maximum-flow minimum-cut solution partitions the nodes of G into X and $\bar{X}$ and the nodes of G' into X' and $\bar{X}'$ as illustrated in Figure 2. Let $S = X$, $T = \{i | i' \in \bar{X}'\}$ and $R = V - S - T$. Then the optimum solution is to replicate R such that the two subsets are $S \cup R$ and $T \cup R$.

To handle VLSI applications, the idea of replication graph is extended to release the requirement of separating two given nodes,

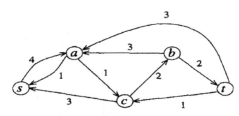

(a) A network with five nodes and nine arcs.

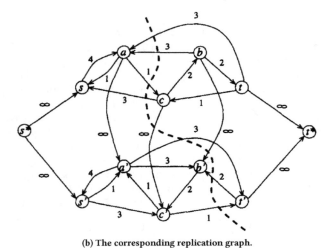

(b) The corresponding replication graph.

Figure 3: An example of replication graph. [19]

to allow multiple-pin nets, and to enforce size constraints on partitions. Then the FM algorithm is extended to minimize a directed cut cost under size constraints. The extended FM algorithm is applied to the proposed replication graph to find a minimum-cost replication cut.

The presented algorithms are both elegant and useful in practice that their contribution is recognized by the 1997 IEEE Circuit and System Society Best Paper Award.

5 OPTIMAL LINEAR ORDERING

A fundamental problem in VLSI placement is the optimal linear placement problem, in which the gates of a circuit are placed along a line with minimum total wirelength. A special version of optimal linear placement is optimal linear ordering in which a weighted graph is placed in uniformly spaced slots. The optimal linear ordering problem is useful for placement in chips with regular layout fabrics like FPGA and gate array as well as for non-VLSI applications. Unfortunately, it is NP-complete [20].

In the seminal paper [21], Prof. Hu and his collaborator have presented two interesting results on optimal linear ordering. First, for an arbitrary graph, based on non-trivial relationship between optimal linear ordering and network flow, they established a lower bound on the total wirelength.

THEOREM 3. *For an arbitrary graph, the total cut capacity of the* $n - 1$ *fundamental cuts constructed by the Gomory-Hu algorithm*

[22] *is a lower bound on the total wirelength of the optimal linear ordering.*

Second, they considered another case in which the graph is a rooted tree. The rooted tree imposes a partial ordering on the nodes. A node x should precedes a node y in the linear order if x is an ancestor of y in the rooted tree. For a rooted tree, they presented an algorithm which requires $O(n \log n)$ operations. They also showed the equivalence of the optimal linear ordering problem for a rooted tree to a job sequencing problem solved by Horn [23].

6 THE ORIENTATION OF MODULES BASED ON GRAPH DECOMPOSITION

After the placement of a VLSI circuit, the modules can be flipped to reduce wirelength and improve routability. This is a very practical problem and many heuristic algorithms have been proposed, e.g., analytical method [24], neural network approach [25], simulated annealing approach [26], simple greedy heuristics [27–30], linear programming / mixed integer linear programming based heuristics [31], and path-based optimization methodology [32]. An optimal symbolic algorithm based on Boolean Decision Diagram (BDD) has also been proposed but it can only be used for small size circuits as it is very slow [33].

Prof. Hu and his collaborators are among the earliest who have worked on the flipping problem [34]. They assumed that multi-pin nets have already been decomposed into two-pin nets. They have made several fundamental contributions.

First, they showed that the flipping problem can be transformed into the minimum cut problem of a graph with positive and negative capacities. Given a circuit with n modules, they constructed a graph with $n + 1$ nodes: n nodes represent the n modules which may be flipped, and a supernode T. The graph has an interesting property that for any cut, the cut value is equal to the change in the total wirelength if all nodes on the same side as T are unflipped and all those on the other side are flipped. Consequently, the minimum cut implies a flipping solution with minimum wirelength. To achieve this property, consider a net s connecting two modules u and v. Let

$C1$ be the change in wirelength when only v is flipped,
$C2$ be the change in wirelength when only u is flipped,
$C3$ be the change in wirelength when both u and v are flipped.

A triangle graph is devised as illustrated in Figure 4. The arc capacities c_{uT}, c_{vT}, and c_{uv} are uniquely determined by three simultaneous equations below:

$$c_{vT} + c_{uv} = C1 \tag{4}$$
$$c_{uT} + c_{uv} = C2 \tag{5}$$
$$c_{uT} + c_{vT} = C3. \tag{6}$$

It is clear that for any cut of the triangle graph, the cut value always equals to the wirelength change of s in the corresponding flipping solution. To construct the graph for the whole circuit, we just superimpose the triangle graphs of all nets.

Second, they also proved that the flipping problem is NP-complete by reducing the minimum cut problem of a graph with positive and negative capacities, which is NP-complete [20], to the flipping problem.

Third, to handle large circuits in practical applications, techniques were presented to decompose the graph into subgraphs and

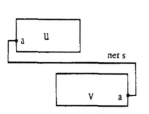 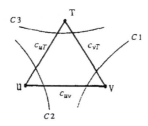

Figure 4: A net _s_ connecting modules _u_ and _v_ and its triangle graph. [34]

to condense the nodes to speed up the search for minimum cut without sacrificing optimality.

ACKNOWLEDGEMENT

I would like to thank Prof. C. K. Cheng and Prof. A. B. Kahng for their invaluable suggestions to this paper.

REFERENCES

[1] T. C. Hu. Physical design: Mathematical models and methods. In *International Symposium on Physical Design*, pages 207–210, 1997.

[2] J. Wang, D. Das, and H. Zhou. Gate sizing by lagrangian relaxation revisited. *IEEE Transactions on Computer-Aided Design of Integrated Circuits and Systems*, 28(7):1071–1084, July 2009.

[3] Yue Xu and Chris Chu. GREMA: Graph reduction based efficient mask assignment for double patterning technology. In *Proc. IEEE/ACM Intl. Conf. on Computer-Aided Design*, pages 601–606, 2009.

[4] E. Shragowitz and S. Keel. A global router based on a multicommodity flow model. *Integration. VLSI J.*, 5(1):3–16, March 1987.

[5] Robert C. Carden IV and Chung-Kuan Cheng. A global router using an efficient approximate multicommodity multiterminal flow algorithm. In *DAC*, pages 316–321, 1991.

[6] Christoph Albrecht. Provably good global routing by a new approximation algorithm for multicommodity flow. In *International Symposium on Physical Design*, pages 19–25, 2000.

[7] F. F. Dragan, A. B. Kahng, I. Mandoiu, S. Muddu, and A. Zelikovsky. Provably good global buffering by multiterminal multicommodity flow approximation. In *Asia and South Pacific Design Automation Conference*, pages 120–125, 2001.

[8] Xiaotao Jia, Yici Cai, Qiang Zhou, Gang Chen, Zhuoyuan Li, and Zuowei Li. Mcfroute: A detailed router based on multi-commodity flow method. In *IEEE/ACM International Conference on Computer-Aided Design*, ICCAD '14, pages 397–404, 2014.

[9] T. C. Hu. Multi-commodity network flows. *Operations Research*, 11(3):344–360, 1963.

[10] L. R. Ford, Jr. and D. R. Fulkerson. Maximal flow through a network. *Canadian Journal of Mathematics*, 8(3):399–404, 1956.

[11] K. Onaga. A multi-commodity flow theorem (in japanese). *Transactions of the Institute of Electronics and Communication Engineers of Japan*, 53-A(7):350–356, July 1970.

[12] Masao Iri. On an extension of the maximum-flow minimum-cut theorem to multicommodity flows. *J. Operations Research Soc. of Japan*, 13(3):129–135, January 1971.

[13] C. K. Cheng and T. C. Hu. Maximum concurrent flows and minimum cuts. *Algorithmica*, 8(1):233–249, Dec 1992.

[14] D. W. Matula. Concurrent flow and concurrent connectivity on graphs. In Y Alavi, G Chartrand, D R Lick, C E Wall, and L Lesniak, editors, *Graph Theory with Applications to Algorithms and Computer Science*, pages 543–559. John Wiley & Sons, Inc., 1985.

[15] David W. Matula. Determining edge connectivity in o(nm). In *Annual Symposium on Foundations of Computer Science*, pages 249–251, 1987.

[16] David W. Matula and Farhad Shahrokhi. Sparsest cuts and bottlenecks in graphs. *Discrete Applied Mathematics*, 27(1):113 – 123, 1990.

[17] T. Leighton and S. Rao. An approximate max-flow min-cut theorem for uniform multicommodity flow problems with applications to approximation algorithms. In *Annual Symposium on Foundations of Computer Science*, pages 422–431, Oct 1988.

[18] L. R. Ford, Jr. and D. R. Fulkerson. A suggested computation for maximal multicommodity network flows. *Management Science*, 5(1):97–101, 1958.

[19] Lung-Tien Liu, Ming-Ter Kuo, Chung-Kuan Cheng, and T. C. Hu. A replication cut for two-way partitioning. *IEEE Transactions on Computer-Aided Design of Integrated Circuits and Systems*, 14(5):623–630, May 1995.

[20] M. R. Garey and D. S. Johnson. *Computers and Intractability: A Guide to the Theory of NP-Completeness*. Freeman, NY, 1979.

[21] D. Adolphson and T. C. Hu. Optimal linear ordering. *SIAM Journal on Applied Mathematics*, 25(3):403–423, 1973.

[22] R. E. Gomory and T. C. Hu. Multi-terminal network flows. *Journal of the Society for Industrial and Applied Mathematics*, 9(4):551–570, 1961.

[23] W. A. Horn. Single-machine job sequencing with treelike precedence ordering and linear delay penalties. *SIAM Journal on Applied Mathematics*, 23(2):189–202, 1972.

[24] M. Yamada and C. L. Liu. An analytical method for optimal module orientation. In *IEEE Internation Symposium on Circuits and Systems*, pages 1679–1682, 1988.

[25] R. Libeskind-Hadas and C. L. Liu. Solutions to the module orientation and rotation problems by neutral computation network. In *ACM/IEEE Design Automation Conference*, pages 400–405, 1989.

[26] S. Nahar, E. Shragowitz, and S. Sahni. Simulated annealing and combinatorial optimization. In *International Journal of Computer Aided VLSI Design*, pages 1–23, 1989.

[27] K. Chong and S. Sahni. Flipping modules to minimize maximum wire length. In *International Conference on Computer Design*, 1991.

[28] K. Chong and S. Sahni. Minimizing total wire length by flipping modules. In *International Conference on VLSI Design*, pages 25–30, 1992.

[29] K. Chong and S. Sahni. Minimizing total wire length by flipping modules. In *IEEE Transactions on CAD of Integrated Circuits and Systems*, pages 167–175, 1993.

[30] K. Chong and S. Sahni. Flipping modules to improve circuit performance and routability. In *International Conference on VLSI Design*, pages 127–132, 1994.

[31] Chiu wing Sham, Evangeline F. Y. Young, and Chris Chu. Optimal cell flipping in placement and floorplanning. In *Proc. ACM/IEEE Design Automation Conf.*, pages 1109–1114, 2006.

[32] Y. A. Shih, T. H. Tsai, and H. M. Chen. Path-based cell flipping optimization for wirelength reduction and routability. In *IEEE Region 10 Conference*, pages 1535–1539, Nov 2010.

[33] X. Hao and F. Brewer. Wirelength optimization by optimal block orientation. In *IEEE Internation Conference on Computer-Aided Design*, 2005.

[34] C. K. Cheng, S. Z. Yao, and T. C. Hu. The orientation of modules based on graph decomposition. *IEEE Transactions on Computers*, 40(6):774–780, Jun 1991.

Theory and Algorithms of Physical Design

Chung-Kuan Cheng
Computer Science and Engineering
UC San Diego, La Jolla, California
ckcheng@ucsd.edu

T. C. Hu
Computer Science and Engineering
UC San Diego, La Jolla, California

Andrew B. Kahng
Computer Science and Engineering
UC San Diego, La Jolla, California
abk@ucsd.edu

ABSTRACT

Prof. T. C. Hu is a pioneer in combinatorial algorithms, mathematical programming and operations research. His works cover multicommodity flows, job scheduling, decomposition for distributed computation, integer programming, tree structures, matrix chain product, knapsack problems, routing, and many other fundamental topics. He also has contributed theory and algorithms to the field of physical design.

CCS CONCEPTS

• **Hardware** → **Physical design (EDA)**; • **Theory of computation** → *Theory and algorithms for application domains*; • **Mathematics of computing**;

KEYWORDS

T. C. Hu, ISPD-2018 Lifetime Achievement Award

ACM Reference Format:
Chung-Kuan Cheng, T. C. Hu, and Andrew B. Kahng. 2018. Theory and Algorithms of Physical Design. In *Proceedings of 2018 International Symposium on Physical Design (ISPD '18)*. ACM, New York, NY, USA, 2 pages.
https://doi.org/10.1145/3177540.3177566

1 INTRODUCTION

Prof. T. C. Hu is a pioneer in combinatorial algorithms, mathematical programming and operations research. He started his career as a Research Mathematician at IBM Research Center, where he published the Gomory-Hu cut tree on multi-terminal flows. His works cover multicommodity flows, job scheduling, decomposition for distributed computation, integer programming, tree structures, matrix chain product, knapsack problems, routing, and many other fundamental topics. In 1984, he and his Ph.D. student M. T. Shing applied routing to VLSI layout problems. Since then, he has contributed theory and algorithms to the field of physical design.

In 1985, he co-edited with Prof. E. S. Kuh an IEEE book entitled "VLSI Circuit Layout: Theory and Design" to describe the physical design with the perspective of theory and algorithms. The first article of the book raised the question, "Is there an algorithm which can be proved mathematically?" Since many physical design problems are NP-complete, most of the proposed ingenious algorithms tend to be heuristic. The question was met with a positive, "yes" response using an example of column-generating techniques for global routing. The analogy of traffic congestion was used to formulate the routing problem as a multicommodity network flow problem with duality and shadow price to reflect the cost of the traffic jams on each channel (street). The column generating technique was introduced to derive the error bound of the solution.

Through his career, Prof. Hu's contributions of mathematical programming and combinatorics have enriched the theory and methods of physical design. His works contribute to the physical design in tree representation, partitioning, and routing. Moreover, he also provided plenty of insight and recipes for successful researches. The shadow price highlights the importance to view problems from different angles. His motto, "always start with the simplest nontrivial cases," fits well with physical design, where the problem tends to be complex and complicated and at the same time the geometry of the layout provides us with insight into the solution.

2 BIOGRAPHY OF T. C. HU

2.1 EDUCATION

B.S. (Engineering),	National Taiwan University,	1953
M.S. (Engineering),	University of Illinois,	1956
Ph.D. (Applied Mathematics),	Brown University,	1960

2.2 POSITIONS

1954-1956	Programmer, University of Illinois
1964-1965	Visiting Associate Professor, Electrical Engineering and Operations Research Center, University of California, Berkeley (on leave from IBM)
1965-1966	Adjunct Associate Professor, Columbia University (Part-time)
1966-1968	Associate Professor, University of Wisconsin
1968-1974	Professor, Computer Sciences Department and Mathematics Research Center, University of Wisconsin-Madison
1974-1998	Professor, Department of Computer Science and Engineering, University of California, San Diego
1998-2007	Professor, Above-Scale, Department of Computer Science and Engineering, University of California, San Diego (Emeritus)

2.3   OTHER ACTIVITIES

Associate Editor, Journal of SIAM

Associate Editor, Journal of ORSA

Consultant, RAND Corporation, Summer 1965

Consultant, Office of Emergency Preparedness, Executive Office of
the President, 1968-1972

Visiting Professor, Stanford University, (Spring 2004, Summer 2006)

Editor, IEEE Transactions on Computers

Advisory Editor, Journal of Heuristics

Advisory Editor, Journal of Graphs and Applications

2.4   INVITED LECTURES AND HONORS

Workshop on VLSI Layout Theory, Dagstahl, Germany, September
9-11, 1991.

"Combinatorial Problems in VLSI," 16'th International Symposium
on Operations Research, Trier, Germany, September 9-11, 1991.

Second ORSA Telecommunications Conference, Boca Raton, Florida,
March 9-11, 1992, (90 minute tutorial).

Plenary lecture, 17'th Symposium on Operations Research, Hamburg, Germany, August 25-28, 1992.

Mathematische Optimierung, Mathematisches Forschungsinstitut
Oberwolfach, Germany, January 8-14, 1995.

John von Neuman Professorship, University of Bonn, Germany,
1994-1995.

Senior Professor, Fulbright, 1994-1995.

Keynote address: "Math, Models and Methods," Proceedings of 1st
International Symposium on Physical Design, April 14-16, 1997,
Napa Valley, CA, pp. 207-210.

IEEE Circuits and Systems Society, Best Paper Award, 1997.

Interconnect Optimization Considering Multiple Critical Paths

Jiang Hu
Department of ECE
Texas A&M University
College Station, Texas
jianghu@tamu.edu

Ying Zhou, Yaoguang Wei,
Steve Quay
IBM Corporation
Austin, Texas
nancyz@us.ibm.com

Lakshmi Reddy,
Gustavo Tellez, Gi-Joon Nam
IBM Research
Yorktown Heights, New York
gnam@us.ibm.com

ABSTRACT

Interconnect optimization, including buffer insertion and Steiner tree construction, continues to be a pillar technology that largely determines overall chip performance. Buffer insertion algorithms in published literature are mostly focused on optimizing only the most critical path. This is a sensible approach for the first order effect. As people strive to squeeze out more performance in the post Moore's law era, the timing of near critical paths is worth considering as well. In this work, a p-norm based Figure Of Merit (pFOM) is proposed to account for both the critical and near critical path timing. Accordingly, a pFOM-driven buffer insertion method is developed. Further, the interaction with timing driven Steiner tree is investigated. The proposed techniques are validated in an industrial design flow and the results confirm their advantages.

CCS CONCEPTS

• **Hardware** → **Physical design (EDA)**; *Interconnect*;

KEYWORDS

Buffer insertion; Steiner tree

ACM Reference Format:
Jiang Hu, Ying Zhou, Yaoguang Wei, Steve Quay, and Lakshmi Reddy, Gustavo Tellez, Gi-Joon Nam. 2018. Interconnect Optimization Considering Multiple Critical Paths. In *ISPD '18: 2018 International Symposium on Physical Design, March 25–28, 2018, Monterey, CA, USA*. ACM, New York, NY, USA, Article 4, 7 pages. https://doi.org/10.1145/3177540.3178237

1 INTRODUCTION

Despite the evident slowdown of VLSI technology scaling, market drive for fast yet low power chip designs has never ceased. Further performance and power-efficiency improvement rely on design optimizations more than ever before. For more than a decade, a main focus of design optimization is interconnect, which is a well known bottleneck for chip performance. To address the interconnect challenge, there have been many research studies on various interconnect optimization techniques including buffer insertion [17–19], wire sizing [6, 7], Steiner tree topology construction [1, 3–5, 8, 9], and integrated approaches [10–14].

Buffers can improve timing by regenerating signals with full strength and shielding capacitive load from timing-critical paths. Buffer insertion is so effective that it prevails in almost all modern chip designs [15]. Many practical buffer insertion tools are based on the dynamic programming framework that is originated by Van Ginneken [19] and later improved by Lillis, Cheng and Lin [12]. Although this framework has been quite successful and influential in practice, it has a hidden drawback. That is, its attention to timing performance is restricted to the most critical path. In this work, we show that it is important to consider near critical paths in addition to the most critical path. Then, a p-norm-based Figure Of Merit (pFOM) is suggested to capture this worthwhile effect. The pFOM is employed in buffer insertion and causes significant changes to the buffer insertion algorithm.

Steiner tree construction is another important part of interconnect optimization. It not only affects the signal propagation path but also restricts where buffers can be placed. Over the years, Steiner tree technology evolves through three stages. Early approaches [3, 5, 8] are directly timing driven without considering buffer insertion. Although they are often superior to wirelength driven Steiner trees, they would not necessarily lead to the best timing results after buffer insertion. The second stage is simultaneous Steiner tree construction and buffer insertion [13, 14], which produces highly timing optimized results but is too expensive to use in practice. The last stage is buffering aware Steiner tree construction [1, 9], which facilitates the best overall interconnect solutions with practical runtime. This work further investigates the interaction between buffer-aware Steiner tree construction and the pFOM-based buffer insertion.

Experiment is performed in an industrial design flow. The proposed techniques are evaluated on over one thousand nets in an industrial design. The results show that the new techniques can indeed remarkably improve the timing on near critical paths. Moreover, they can identify solutions that make the most critical path timing better but are neglected by a conventional buffer insertion tool. Further, the impact of pFOM-driven buffer insertion on entire design flow is tested on 6 industrial circuits, each of which has 0.3-1 million nets. The overall flow results indicate that the proposed techniques achieve 10% improvement on total negative slack with negligible area and power overhead.

2 CONVENTIONAL BUFFER INSERTION

2.1 Conventional Problem Formulation

The buffer insertion problem can be formulated in different ways and here we describe a few popular ones [12, 19]. The main input to buffer insertion is a Steiner tree $G = (V, E)$, where V is a set of vertices and E is a set of edges. This formulation assumes that the tree comes with a set of candidate buffer locations. There are three types of vertices: the source vertex v_0, a set of sink vertices V_{sink} and a set of vertices V_{buf} indicating candidate buffer locations, and $V = \{v_0\} \cup V_{sink} \cup V_{buf}$. Without loss of generality, one can treat a buffer vertex as a Steiner vertex. The input also includes a buffer library B, where each buffer type $b_i \in B$ is associated with distinct area and timing characteristics.

The decision in buffer insertion involves two factors: (1) whether or not to insert a buffer at each buffer vertex; (2) if the answer is yes, what buffer type in B to use. Each sink vertex $v_i \in V_{sink}$ has a required arrival time $q(v_i)$ and the signal propagation delay $d(v_i)$ from the source vertex. The slack at a sink is $s(v_i) = q(v_i) - d(v_i)$. The slack of entire tree is $s(G) = \min_{v_i \in V_{sink}} s(v_i)$. Without loss of generality, we can assume that the arrival time at the source is 0. Then, it can be proved that $s(G) = s_{dr}(v_0) = q_{dr}(v_0)$, where $s_{dr}(v_0)$ and $q_{dr}(v_0)$ are the slack and required arrival time at the source when the driver delay is included. The most basic formulation is to maximize the tree slack $s(G)$ [19]. When buffer area is considered, the formulation [12] can be minimizing total buffer area subject to no timing violation, i.e., satisfying constraint $s(G) \geq 0$. Sometimes, a safety margin (slack threshold) θ is added such that the constraint becomes $s(G) \geq \theta$, or alternatively a negative slack is treated as $\min(s - \theta, 0)$. Another popular formulation is to optimize a certain tradeoff between buffer area and the tree slack.

2.2 Conventional Buffering Algorithm

Conventional buffer insertion methods are mostly based on the dynamic programming framework [12, 19]. It first obtains a set of candidate solutions in a bottom-up traversal of the tree and then selects a solution at the source according to problem formulation.

A partial candidate solution $\psi(v_i)$ at vertex v_i is characterized by a 3-tuple $(c(v_i), q(v_i), w(v_i))$, where $c(v_i)$ denotes the downstream load capacitance, $q(v_i)$ represents the required arrival time and $w(v_i)$ is buffer area of this solution. The generation and propagation of candidate solutions are through the following operations.

- Solutions at sinks. The candidate solutions are started from sink vertices, where sink load capacitance and required arrival time are given.
- Extending a solution to its parent vertex through wire. When a solution is extended from vertex v_j to its parent vertex v_i, the solution is updated as $c(v_i) = c(v_j) + c(v_i, v_j)$ and $q(v_i) = q(v_j) - d(v_i, v_j)$, where $c(v_i, v_j)$ and $d(v_i, v_j)$ are the wire capacitance and additional signal propagation delay due to edge $(v_i, v_j) \in E$, respectively.
- Adding a buffer at a candidate location. If a buffer of type $b_k \in B$ is inserted at $v_i \in V_{buf}$, a new candidate solution $\psi_{b_k}(v_i)$ is generated with $c_{b_k}(v_i)$ being the input capacitance of b_k, $q_{b_k}(v_i) = q(v_i) - d(b_k, c(v_i))$, where $d(b_k, c(v_i))$ is the additional delay due to the buffer, and $w_{b_k}(v_i) = w(v_i) + w(b_k)$, where $w(b_k)$ is the area of b_k.
- Merging solutions from two children branches. Suppose v_i is a Steiner vertex with two children branches and the two solutions from the two branches are $\psi_l(v_i) = (c_l(v_i), q_l(v_i), w_l(v_i))$ and $\psi_r(v_i) = (c_r(v_i), q_r(v_i), w_r(v_i))$, respectively. The capacitance of the merged solution is $c_m(v_i) = c_l(v_i) + c_r(v_i)$.

The merged required arrival time is given by $q_m(v_i) = \min(q_l(v_i), q_r(v_i))$. The merged buffer area is $w_m(v_i) = w_l(v_i) + w_r(v_i)$.
- Solutions at the source. Since all solutions are driven by the same source driver, load capacitance becomes no longer relevant. The required arrival time (or slack) considering driver is $q_{dr}(v_0) = q(v_0) - d_{dr}$, where d_{dr} is the delay due to the driver.

A key ingredient of this dynamic programming framework is the solution pruning, where inferior candidate solutions are pruned during the propagation. For two solutions $\psi_i = (c_i, q_i, w_i)$ and $\psi_j = (c_j, q_j, w_j)$ at the same vertex, ψ_i is inferior if $c_i \geq c_j$, $q_i \leq q_j$ and $w_i \geq w_j$. If a solution is inferior to any other solution, it is pruned out without being further propagated. This buffer insertion problem is NP-hard and the runtime complexity of this dynamic programming framework is pseudo-polynomial [12].

3 MOTIVATION EXAMPLE

Conventional buffer insertion is focused on the most critical path or the worst slack $s(G)$. Consider the example in Figure 1, where small triangles indicate buffers, small squares represent sinks and the numbers by the sinks are slacks. The worst slack is -28 in (a) and improved to -24 in (b). As such, conventional buffer insertion may choose the solution in (b). However, the Total Negative Slack (TNS) is degraded from -61 to -67. For a tree with n sinks, its total negative slack is defined as

$$TNS = \sum_{i=1}^{n} \min(s_i - \theta, 0)$$

where θ is slack threshold and is equal to 0 in this example. Please note TNS is traditionally defined for an entire circuit, but we overload this term for individual nets in this work.

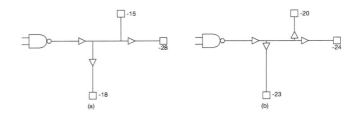

Figure 1: Comparing two buffer insertion solutions. TNS is -61 in (a) and -67 in (b).

A legitimate questions is: does TNS matter even when the worst slack is improved? The answer is yes for at least two reasons. First, the delay model used within buffer insertion is normally simple and not very accurate. Therefore, a near critical path perceived by buffer insertion may actually be the most critical path. Second, buffer insertion is often followed by other circuit optimizations and design steps. As such, having fewer negative slack paths is as important as having improvement on the worst slack. For example, the case of Figure 1(a) is easier to handle than (b) if gate sizing is subsequently performed as it can be focused on the only obvious critical path. Indeed, TNS instead of the worst slack is optimized in gate sizing algorithms [16].

4 P-NORM-BASED FIGURE OF MERIT

Section 3 shows the importance of near critical paths in term of TNS (Total Negative Slack). However, TNS treats all paths with negative slacks equally while paths with more negative slack are more important in practice. In other words, the worst slack still matters more than sinks with a little negative slacks. Then, the question is how to tradeoff the worst slack and TNS? The answer varies depending on different design scenarios. We propose to use p-norm to capture this tradeoff.

Given a vector of real numbers $\vec{x} = (x_1, x_2, ..., x_m)$, its p-norm is

$$||\vec{x}||_p = (\sum_{i=1}^{m} |x_i|^p)^{\frac{1}{p}} \qquad (1)$$

For a slack s, its generalized timing deficit is defined as

$$\hat{s} = \max(\theta - s, 0) \qquad (2)$$

where θ is a threshold parameter. When $\theta = 0$, $\hat{s}$ is equivalent to negative slack. The parameter θ allows designers a tuning knob for deciding how much slack is treated as near critical or placing a margin in evaluating timing slacks. Then, the p-norm-based Figure of Merit for m sinks is

$$pFOM = ||\vec{s}||_p = (\sum_{i=1}^{m} \hat{s}_i^p)^{\frac{1}{p}} \qquad (3)$$

If $p = \infty$

$$pFOM = ||\vec{s}||_\infty = \max(\hat{s}_1, \hat{s}_2, ..., \hat{s}_m) \qquad (4)$$

which corresponds to the worst negative slack. If $p = 1$

$$pFOM = ||\vec{s}||_1 = \sum_{i=1}^{m} \hat{s}_i \qquad (5)$$

which is equivalent to the TNS. Therefore, the value of p decides a tradeoff between the worst slack and TNS. Please note pFOM is a metric for considering both the worst slack and TNS in buffer insertion algorithm. Final solutions are still evaluated by the worst slack and TNS.

5 PFOM-BASED BUFFER INSERTION

In this section, we show how to incorporate pFOM with the Ginneken-Lillis buffer insertion framework. One can replace the worst slack (or required arrival time) with pFOM in characterizing candidate solutions. We use ψ_q and ψ_ϕ to represent solutions in conventional buffering and pFOM buffering, respectively. Then, solution $\psi_\phi(v_i)$ at vertex v_i is characterized by $(c(v_i), \phi(v_i), w(v_i))$, where ϕ denotes pFOM. This seemingly simple characterization change actually makes several significant differences in the buffer insertion algorithm.

First, in evaluating candidate solutions at a vertex $v_i \neq v_0$, the worst slack buffer insertion only needs to capture timing of the subtree rooted at v_i, while the pFOM evaluation requires estimating the delay from source to v_i, called upstream delay, in addition. This is because pFOM counts only the negative slacks while whether or not a sink slack is negative depends on the entire source-sink path delay. By contrast, the sign of the worst slack matters only

when all solution propagations reach the source, and therefore upstream delay estimation is not necessary. Since the Ginneken-Lillis buffer insertion is a bottom-up procedure, when solutions are propagated to a vertex $v_i \neq v_0$, the upstream part between v_i and v_0 is not buffered yet. Consequently, the upstream delay estimation is difficult to be accurate even under the Elmore delay model. This difference alone makes Lillis' algorithm [12] no longer optimal when the worst slack is replaced by pFOM. We use an analytical method [2] to predict buffered upstream delay from source to v_i. If the path length from v_0 to v_i is l, wire resistance and capacitance per unit length are R and C, respectively, and a typical buffer resistance and capacitance are R_b and C_b, respectively, then the buffered delay is estimated by

$$\tilde{d}(l) = (R_b C + R C_b + \sqrt{2 R_b C_b R C}) \cdot l \qquad (6)$$

Second, pFOM evaluation requires that all sink delays are propagated along with candidate solutions while the worst slack evaluation does not. In conventional buffering, a non-critical sink in a subtree can never become a critical sink and therefore can be ignored in solution propagations. However, a negative slack of a sink may vary and contribute differently to pFOM. Moreover, a sink may be regarded to have negative slack due to inaccurate upstream delay estimate at a vertex and later its slack turns out to be positive.

Third, there is numerical problem when p is large although it can theoretically achieve any tradeoff between the worst slack and TNS. In computing pFOM, the p_{th} power of timing deficit $\hat{s}$ is calculated as an intermediate result. When p is large and the number of sinks is not small, this calculation may lead to overflow. As such, the worst slack cannot be easily captured by ∞FOM, and must be explicitly tracked through max operation like in [12]. In other words, both pFOM-based solutions and the worst slack based solutions are required to be propagated.

The procedure of collecting candidate solutions for a vertex $v_i \in V$ is outlined in Algorithm 1. Lines 1-6 handle the case where v_i is a sink. Line 3 is to estimate the pFOM for v_i where $\tilde{d}(v_i)$ is the estimated buffered delay from source to v_i. Parameter θ, which is safety margin, determines the conservativeness of utilizing $\tilde{d}$. Since $\tilde{d}$ is an analytic approximation of the delay from source to v_i, it may lead to either over-estimate or under-estimate of pFOM. A large θ implies a conservative estimate of pFOM, i.e., less chance of under-estimate. Solution sets for pFOM and the worst slack based characterizations are denoted by Ψ_ϕ and Ψ_q, respectively. Lines 7-14 handle the case where v_i has a single child vertex v_l. It first recursively calls the function (line 8) to collect solutions at v_l, which are propagated to v_i by adding the wire delay and capacitance of edge $(v_i, v_l) \in E$ (line 9). Notation $\Psi_{\phi,l}(v_i)$ means the set of solutions propagated from v_l to v_i. Additional solutions are added by considering buffer insertion in line 10. If v_i has two children vertices, solutions from the other child v_r are propagated in lines 15-18. Since one can always make a tree to be binary by inserting dummy vertices, there is no need to consider cases of more than two children vertices. Solutions from the two children vertices are merged in lines 19 and 20. In line 21, inferior solutions are pruned out.

When candidate solutions are collected at source v_0, Algorithm 2 shows how to select a solution for this net. Driver delays are added in lines 2 and 3. The final solution selection (lines 4-10) depends

---

Algorithm 1: Collect solutions.

Input : $G = (V, E), B, v_i \in V$

1 **if** $v_i \in V_{sink}$ **then**
2     $\Psi_q(v_i) \leftarrow \{(c(v_i), q(v_i), 0)\};$
3     $\phi(v_i) \leftarrow \max(\theta - q(v_i) + \tilde{d}(v_i), 0);$
4     $\Psi_\phi(v_i) \leftarrow \{(c(v_i), \phi(v_i), 0)\};$
5   Return $(\Psi_\phi(v_i), \Psi_q(v_i));$
6 **end**
7 $v_l \leftarrow$ left child of $v_i;$
8 $(\Psi_\phi(v_l), \Psi_q(v_l)) \leftarrow CollectSolutions(G, B, v_l);$
9 $(\Psi_{\phi,l}(v_i), \Psi_{q,l}(v_i)) \leftarrow AddWire((v_i, v_l), \Psi_\phi(v_l), \Psi_q(v_l));$
10 $AddBuffer(\Psi_{\phi,l}(v_i), \Psi_{q,l}(v_i), B);$
11 **if** v_i *has single child* v_l **then**
12     $PruneSolutions(\Psi_{\phi,l}(v_i), \Psi_{q,l}(v_i));$
13   Return $(\Psi_{\phi,l}(v_i), \Psi_{q,l}(v_i));$
14 **end**
15 $v_r \leftarrow$ right child of $v_i;$
16 $(\Psi_\phi(v_r), \Psi_q(v_r)) \leftarrow CollectSolutions(G, B, v_r);$
17 $(\Psi_{\phi,r}(v_i), \Psi_{q,r}(v_i)) \leftarrow AddWire((v_i, v_r), \Psi_\phi(v_r), \Psi_q(v_r));$
18 $AddBuffer(\Psi_{\phi,r}(v_i), \Psi_{q,r}(v_i), B);$
19 $\Psi_\phi(v_i) \leftarrow merge(\Psi_{\phi,l}(v_i), \Psi_{\phi,r}(v_i));$
20 $\Psi_q(v_i) \leftarrow merge(\Psi_{q,l}(v_i), \Psi_{q,r}(v_i));$
21 $PruneSolutions(\Psi_\phi(v_i), \Psi_q(v_i));$
22 Return $(\Psi_\phi(v_i), \Psi_q(v_i));$

Algorithm 2: pFOM Buffer Insertion

Input : Steiner tree $G = (V, E)$, buffer library B

1 $(\Psi_\phi(v_0), \Psi_q(v_0)) \leftarrow CollectSolutions(G, B, v_0);$
2 $\Psi_\phi \leftarrow AddDriver(\Psi_\phi(v_0));$
3 $\Psi_q \leftarrow AddDriver(\Psi_q(v_0));$
4 $\psi_q \leftarrow KneeSolution(\Psi_q);$
5 **for** *each solution* $\psi \in \Psi_\phi$ **do**
6   **if** $slack(\psi) - slack(\psi_q) < \epsilon$ **then**
7   Remove ψ from $\Psi_\phi;$
8   **end**
9 **end**
10 $\psi^* \leftarrow KneeSolution(\Psi_\phi);$
11 Return $\psi^*;$

Figure 2: Illustration of knee solution.

on problem formulation, which further depends on design flow and methodology. We consider the case where buffer insertion is applied after cell placement and before wire routing. At this stage, circuit timing is not completely settled yet and subject to changes from optimizations and uncertainty of routing. Hence, the timing element in formulation is a soft objective instead of hard constraint. For conventional buffer insertion, one such formulation is to find a knee solution between the slack and buffer cost tradeoff. This is illustrated by Figure 2, where the slope of the tradeoff curve decreases with respect to buffer cost. The knee solution is selected by walking along the curve from the min-cost solution, stopping at a solution ψ^* where the slope is less than a parameter γ, and ψ^* is the selected knee solution and γ is the parameter for the tradeoff. When TNS is considered, the tradeoff is more complicated. In practice, when a new feature is added to an EDA tool, the basic requirement is that it would not significantly degrade in terms of traditional metrics. Although parameter p in pFOM is supposed to tradeoff the worst slack and TNS, it does not have direct guarantee on the conventional objective of the worst slack. To solve this issue, we first obtain solution ψ_q (line 4), which is the knee solution for conventional slack and buffer tradeoff. In order to *ensure* that pFOM solution is not too poor on the worst slack, a pruning is performed for the pFOM solution set Ψ_ϕ (lines 5-9), where ϵ is a constant parameter. In line 10, the knee solution for pFOM and buffer cost tradeoff is finally selected.

6 INTERACTIONS WITH TIMING-DRIVEN STEINER TREE

The effect of interconnect optimization, including buffer insertion, highly relies on Steiner tree topology. We study the interactions of pFOM buffer insertion with a couple of timing driven Steiner tree methods, both of which have been applied in industrial products.

The first method is CTree [1], where sinks are clustered according to their polarity, timing criticality and spatial proximity. The tree for each cluster and the top level tree that connects all clusters are constructed according to the AHHK algorithm [3]. AHHK uses a parameter to tradeoff between the Prim's minimum spanning tree and the Dijkstra's shortest path algorithm. As a result, it finds tradeoff between total wirelength and the maximum source-sink path length. In [1], the AHHK algorithm is performed for 5 times with different tradeoff parameter values, and then slacks are explicitly evaluated to choose the one with the best slack.

We made two methodological changes to this approach. An additional Steiner tree by SERT algorithm [5], which is a greedy algorithm driven by the Elmore delay, is evaluated along with the 5 AHHK trees. The SERT algorithm constructs Steiner tree by adding one sink to the partial tree at a time. Each time, all pairs between partial tree edges and unconnected sinks are evaluated. Then, the pair that leads to the minimum sink delay in the partial tree is selected. In the evaluation, slacks are estimated with anticipation of buffer insertion. Specifically, each edge delay is calculated by Equation (6). The driver delay is estimated by

$$d_{driver} = R_{driver} \cdot \sqrt{C_b \cdot C_{tree}} \qquad (7)$$

where C_{tree} is the total wire capacitance of the tree. This is in contrast to the conventional Elmore delay model where driver delay is $R_{driver} \cdot C_{tree}$. Evidently, the driver rarely sees the entire tree capacitance after buffer insertion. The over-emphasis on tree capacitance usually leads to choice of a tree topology with small wirelength or chain-like structure. As such, it is difficult for buffer insertion to separate paths of different criticalities. In the other extreme case, the driver only drives a buffer with capacitance C_b. The estimate in Equation (7) takes a geometric mean between one extreme of total tree capacitance and the other extreme of a single buffer capacitance. Thereby, a star-like topology, which is relatively easy for buffer insertion to take effect, is more likely to be selected.

The second method is a variant of the algorithm in [4], which is developed by Bonn University and we call it BTree. It first sorts all sinks in non-increasing order of a predicted slack. In [4], the sink delay prediction is proportional to wire capacitance assuming the sink is connected to the source directly. In this work, the delay from the source to each sink is predicted according to their distance and Equation (6). Since the required arrival time (RAT) of each sink is given, one can estimates its slack based on the RAT and predicated delay. In the tree construction, the sinks are added to the partial tree one by one following this order. When adding a sink, the connection point is selected in a way such that the worst slack of the partial tree is maximized.

7 EXPERIMENTAL RESULTS

Table 1: Results from 905 small nets with 2-5 sinks, where ΔTNS is the total negative slack improvement, ΔWS is the worst slack improvement, and $\Delta BufArea$ is the buffer area increase, all of which are compared with the baseline.

Buf	Steiner	ΔTNS (%)		ΔWS (ps)		$\Delta BufArea$ (%)	
		Ave	Max	Ave	Max	Ave	Max
Lite	CTree	0.67	54	0.06	9.5	0.91	69
	SERT	0.62	54	0.06	9.5	0.96	80
	BTree	0.60	54	0.05	9.5	0.97	80
p1	CTree	0.32	62	-0.04	40.2	0.35	50
	SERT	0.27	62	-0.06	40.2	0.37	50
	BTree	0.28	62	-0.06	40.2	0.44	50
p2	CTree	0.40	62	-0.01	40.2	0.05	75
	SERT	0.38	62	-0.03	40.2	0.16	75
	BTree	0.39	62	-0.03	40.2	0.20	75
p4	CTree	0.63	65	0.05	40.2	0.00	50
	SERT	0.56	65	0.04	40.2	0.09	50
	BTree	0.52	65	0.03	40.2	0.08	50
p6	CTree	0.63	65	0.07	40.2	-0.07	50
	SERT	0.66	65	0.06	40.2	0.07	50
	BTree	0.64	65	0.06	40.2	0.09	50
p8	CTree	0.73	65	0.06	40.2	-0.08	54
	SERT	0.68	65	0.04	40.2	-0.01	54
	BTree	0.66	65	0.04	40.2	0.01	54
p10	CTree	0.75	62	0.09	40.2	-0.03	50
	SERT	0.69	62	0.07	40.2	0.05	50
	BTree	0.67	62	0.07	40.2	0.07	50
p12	CTree	0.62	62	0.04	40.2	-0.07	50
	SERT	0.58	62	0.04	40.2	-0.03	50
	BTree	0.56	62	0.03	40.2	-0.01	50

Experiment is performed on 1112 nets of an industrial chip design with 14nm process technology. Single-sink nets are excluded

as the worst slack and TNS are the same for such nets. Even for nets with multiple sinks, the worst slack and TNS can be nearly equivalent if the difference between the most critical sink slack and near critical sink slack is very large. The buffer library has 8 buffer types. Circuit timing is evaluated by an industrial static timing analysis tool. The TNS is evaluated with slack threshold $\theta = 10ps$. In the experiment, the **baseline** is the conventional worst slack driven buffer insertion performed on CTree [1]. Different combinations of buffer insertion and Steiner tree options are evaluated by comparing with the baseline. For buffer insertion, besides the proposed pFOM buffer insertion with various p values, we also tested a light version of pFOM buffer insertion called "Lite". In "Lite", the bottom-up candidate collection is almost the same as the worst slack buffer insertion except that the best TNS solution is retained in addition to those solutions with $c - q - w$ tradeoffs. At the source, the solution selection is the same as our pFOM buffer insertion. We consider three Steiner tree options:

(1) CTree [1].
(2) SERT: an extension of CTree that considers additional candidate constructed by SERT [5] and has delay estimation change as described in Section 6.
(3) BTree: a variant of the timing driven Steiner tree in [4], which is also described in Section 6.

Table 2: Results from 147 medium nets with 6-15 sinks.

Buf	Steiner	ΔTNS (%)		ΔWS (ps)		$\Delta BufArea$ (%)	
		Ave	Max	Ave	Max	Ave	Max
Lite	CTree	1.26	27	0.41	18.0	2.61	44
	SERT	0.55	52	0.93	32.6	3.40	86
	BTree	1.66	46	0.76	31.6	3.55	83
p1	CTree	0.94	32	-0.30	18.3	1.47	54
	SERT	2.16	53	0.26	32.6	3.11	59
	BTree	2.60	52	0.11	29.0	1.97	62
p2	CTree	0.70	32	-0.26	18.3	0.72	54
	SERT	1.68	53	0.31	32.6	2.26	59
	BTree	2.04	52	0.16	31.8	1.18	80
p4	CTree	1.43	32	-0.05	18.7	0.99	54
	SERT	2.08	52	0.48	32.6	1.84	59
	BTree	2.80	52	0.39	31.8	1.53	78
p6	CTree	0.96	33	0.02	18.7	1.57	54
	SERT	1.64	52	0.40	32.6	1.49	56
	BTree	2.43	52	0.34	31.7	1.07	93
p8	CTree	1.38	44	0.20	19.3	1.68	47
	SERT	2.10	52	0.39	32.6	1.00	56
	BTree	2.60	52	0.37	32.5	0.32	62
p10	CTree	1.80	44	0.35	19.3	2.04	65
	SERT	2.33	52	0.53	32.6	1.52	65
	BTree	2.88	52	0.56	32.5	1.16	65
p12	CTree	1.44	44	0.24	19.3	1.45	47
	SERT	1.86	52	0.55	32.6	0.91	56
	BTree	2.45	52	0.62	32.5	0.97	62

The results from the small nets are summarized in Table 1, where ΔTNS indicates the improvement of TNS with respect to the baseline and an improvement means less negative result. In the leftmost column, $p2$ is for pFOM buffer insertion with $p = 2$. On average, all these methods always improve TNS and usually improve the worst slack as well. In the best case, our methods can usually improve the worst slack by 40*ps*, which is quite significant, and the TNS by over 60%. The average buffer area increase is always less than 1%. The "Lite" method tends to cause much greater buffer area than pFOM buffer insertion. The best timing results occur for pFOM buffer insertion when $p = 10$. When $p = 12$, total buffer area decreases along with the TNS and worst slack improvement. For the small nets, there is no obvious difference among CTree, SERT and BTree.

The results from 147 medium nets are shown in Table 2. For these nets, pFOM buffer insertion often achieves more than 2% TNS improvement on average while the improvement from the "Lite" is less than 2%. SERT always leads to the best maximal TNS improvement, which is over 50%. These methods usually improve the worst slack as well while SERT mostly performs better than the other two Steiner methods on the worst slack. Overall, the timing improvement and buffer cost increase of the medium nets are greater than those in small nets.

Table 3: Results from 60 large nets, each of which has more than 15 sinks.

Buf	Steiner	ΔTNS (%)		ΔWS (ps)		$\Delta Buf Area$ (%)	
		Avg	Max	Avg	Max	Avg	Max
Lite	CTree	3.12	69	1.47	32.8	8.22	88
	SERT	7.20	65	-2.07	60.4	7.53	98
	BTree	3.87	65	2.50	60.4	9.24	71
p1	CTree	7.15	65	0.50	42.8	5.58	85
	SERT	6.62	65	-5.37	35.5	4.55	57
	BTree	4.63	65	0.40	35.5	11.69	96
p2	CTree	7.06	65	0.38	39.5	5.16	82
	SERT	6.96	65	-4.92	35.5	2.76	57
	BTree	5.60	65	0.78	35.5	11.70	96
p4	CTree	6.67	65	1.03	39.5	4.18	57
	SERT	7.02	65	-4.46	40.5	3.60	57
	BTree	5.10	65	1.01	40.5	10.44	97
p6	CTree	4.87	70	0.50	39.5	5.26	59
	SERT	6.98	65	-4.06	40.5	4.39	92
	BTree	4.38	65	1.33	40.5	7.79	93
p8	CTree	5.53	70	0.90	39.5	6.71	66
	SERT	5.98	65	-4.18	40.5	3.32	57
	BTree	4.29	65	1.28	40.5	7.87	93
p10	CTree	4.11	65	0.74	39.5	3.57	70
	SERT	6.32	65	-4.08	41.8	4.06	99
	BTree	4.02	65	1.22	41.8	6.10	93
p12	CTree	4.44	65	0.84	39.5	3.98	70
	SERT	5.59	65	-4.16	41.8	4.09	99
	BTree	3.64	65	1.22	41.8	5.75	81

The results of large nets are listed in Table 3. For these nets, the TNS improvement is even more significant with greater buffer area overhead. The best TNS improvement is obtained when $p = 1, 2$. The "Lite" result is more comparable with the pFOM buffer insertion. Among the three Steiner tree methods, SERT tends to degrade the worst slack and BTree often causes large buffer area.

In Table 4, we take a close look at a particular large net with 64 sinks. This net initially has TNS $-7839ps$ and the worst slack $-196ps$ prior to buffer insertion. The rows with "WS" are results of conventional worst slack driven buffer insertion. The best timing improvement is obtained from pFOM buffer insertion with

$p = 16$ on SERT, with 13% TNS improvement and 26% worst slack improvement compared to the baseline, which is the worst slack buffer insertion on CTree. At the same time, this solution costs a large buffer area. In general, the timing results from SERT and BTree are better than those from CTree. With the same WS (worst slack) driven buffer insertion, SERT and BTree can improve TNS by around 500*ps* compared to CTree. This improvement is greater than applying pFOM buffer insertion on CTree. The pFOM buffer insertion entails much longer runtime than the worst slack buffer insertion and "Lite". However, the runtime on a 64-sink net is almost the worst case and is much less severe for small nets. Also, the pFOM buffer insertion is applied to a small subset of nets such that the overall runtime overhead for an entire circuit is still limited.

In Figure 3, we show the effect of knee solution selection described in Section 5. The results are from a 5-sink net, whose results are the solid dots, and a 7-sink net, whose results are shown as small triangles. The horizontal axis indicates the buffer area while the vertical axis is for the pFOM value when $p = 6$. These results are obtained by varying the knee selection parameter γ from large to small for pFOM buffer insertion on SERT Steiner tree. From Equation (3), we know that a large pFOM means more negative slack or worse timing. The results of Figure 3 indicate that parameter γ can largely control the timing and buffer area tradeoff as expected.

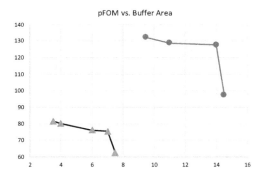

Figure 3: Tradeoff between pFOM and buffer area. The horizontal and vertical axis indicate buffer area and pFOM (p=6), respectively.

The impact of the proposed pFOM-driven buffer insertion on entire design flow is further evaluated on 6 industrial circuits, and the results are summarized in Table 5. In these experiments, $p = 4$ and the AHHK based Steiner tree construction is employed. The overall flow results demonstrate significant improvement on TNS with trivial effects on the worst slack, area and power.

8 CONCLUSIONS AND FUTURE WORK

In VLSI interconnect optimization, it is noticed that only considering the worst slack among all sinks is not adequate. In order to consider both the worst slack and total negative slack, a p-norm based figure of merit is proposed and the corresponding pFOM-driven buffer insertion technique is developed. At the same time, a few timing-driven Steiner tree algorithms and their interactions with buffer insertion are studied. The effect of timing improvement

Table 4: Results from a 64-sink net.

Steiner	Buf	$TNS(ps)$	$WS(ps)$	#Buffers	Buf Area	Runtime (s)
CTree	WS	-6610	-140	8	63	0.2
	Lite	-6444	-141	10	73	0.3
	p1	-6446	-141	11	77	1.1
	p4	-6465	-134	15	97	2.8
	p8	-6291	-134	20	121	2.8
	p16	-6311	-134	17	103	2.8
SERT	WS	-6152	-139	12	102	0.2
	Lite	-6152	-139	12	102	0.4
	p1	-6217	-141	10	94	2.7
	p4	-6059	-126	23	154	5.5
	p8	-6265	-142	8	86	4.7
	p16	-5764	-103	30	163	3.9
BTree	WS	-6083	-117	27	128	0.2
	Lite	-6260	-143	15	95	0.3
	p1	-6009	-121	22	108	5.7
	p4	-6280	-143	16	101	7.7
	p8	-5950	-113	35	168	5.4
	p16	-5899	-110	32	154	4.3

Table 5: Entire design flow results. ΔTNS is the total negative slack improvement, ΔWS is the worst slack improvement, $\Delta Area$ is the area increase and $\Delta Power$ is the power dissipation increase, all of which are compared with the baseline.

Circuit	#nets	ΔTNS	ΔWS	$\Delta Area$	$\Delta Power$
1	0.3M	23.6%	-8.1%	0.01%	-0.97%
2	0.6M	6.1%	2.4%	-0.17%	-0.16%
3	0.5M	6.7%	-0.7%	0.42%	-0.19%
4	0.5M	8.1%	6.2%	0.06%	0.27%
5	0.6M	8.6%	5.3%	0.16%	-0.26%
6	1M	4.4%	0.2%	0.15%	0.02%
Ave		10%	0.9%	0.11%	-0.22%

from the proposed techniques is validated on industrial circuits with both net-based and overall flow study.

Although the proposed techniques bring obvious benefits, they have room for further enhancement. The tradeoff between TNS and the worst slack by varying p value is not strong. Since this is an industrial tool, it contains other features, including slew constraints, layer assignment, speedup heuristic, all of which make the solution behaviors less predictable. In addition, the buffer insertion and Steiner tree construction use the Elmore delay model, which has discrepancy from the static timing analysis. In future research, we will conduct further study to solve these problems.

ACKNOWLEDGMENTS

This work is partially supported by NSF CCF-1525749.

REFERENCES

[1] C. J. Alpert, G. Gandham, M. Hrkic, J. Hu, A. B. Kahng, J. Lillis, B. Liu, S. T. Quay, S. S. Sapatnekar, and A. J. Sullivan. 2002. Buffered Steiner trees for difficult instances. *IEEE Transactions on Computer-Aided Design* 21, 1 (Jan. 2002), 3–14.
[2] C. J. Alpert, J. Hu, S. S. Sapatnekar, and C. N. Sze. 2006. Accurate estimation of global buffer delay within a floorplan. *IEEE Transactions on Computer-Aided Design* 25, 6 (June 2006), 1140–1145.
[3] C. J. Alpert, T. C. Hu, J. H. Huang, A. B. Kahng, and D. Karger. 1995. Prim-Dijkstra tradeoffs for improved performance-driven routing tree design. *IEEE Transactions on Computer-Aided Design* 14, 7 (July 1995), 890–896.
[4] C. Bartoschek, S. Held, D. Rautenbach, and J. Vygen. 2006. Efficient generation of short and fast repeater tree topologies. In *Proceedings of the ACM International Symposium on Physical Design.* 20–27.
[5] K. D. Boese, A. B. Kahng, B. A. McCoy, and G. Robins. 1995. Near-optimal critical sink routing tree constructions. *IEEE Transactions on Computer-Aided Design* 14, 12 (Dec. 1995), 1417–36.
[6] C. P. Chen, H. Zhou, and D. F. Wong. 1996. Optimal non-uniform wire-sizing under the Elmore delay model. In *Proceedings of the IEEE/ACM International Conference on Computer-Aided Design.* 38–43.
[7] J. Cong and K.-S. Leung. 1995. Optimal wiresizing under the distributed Elmore delay model. *IEEE Transactions on Computer-Aided Design* 14, 3 (March 1995), 321–336.
[8] H. Hou, J. Hu, and S. S. Sapatnekar. 1999. Non-Hanan routing. *IEEE Transactions on Computer-Aided Design* 18, 4 (April 1999), 436–444.
[9] M. Hrkic and J. Lillis. 2002. S-Tree: A technique for buffered routing tree synthesis. In *Proceedings of the ACM/IEEE Design Automation Conference.* 578–583.
[10] M. Hrkic and J. Lillis. 2003. Buffer tree synthesis with consideration of temporal locality, sink polarity requirements, solution cost, congestion and blockages. *IEEE Transactions on Computer-Aided Design* 22, 4 (April 2003), 481–491.
[11] J. Lillis, C. K. Cheng, T. T. Lin, and C. Y. Ho. 1996. New performance driven routing techniques with explicit area/delay tradeoff and simultaneous wire sizing. In *Proceedings of the ACM/IEEE Design Automation Conference.* 395–400.
[12] J. Lillis, C. K. Cheng, and T. Y. Lin. 1996. Optimal wire sizing and buffer insertion for low power and a generalized delay model. *IEEE Journal of Solid-State Circuits* 31, 3 (March 1996), 437–447.
[13] J. Lillis, C. K. Cheng, and T. Y. Lin. 1996. Simultaneous routing and buffer insertion for high performance interconnect. In *Proceedings of the Great Lake Symposium on VLSI.* 148–153.
[14] T. Okamoto and J. Cong. 1996. Interconnect layout optimization by simultaneous Steiner tree construction and buffer insertion. In *ACM Physical Design Workshop.* 1–6.
[15] P. J. Osler. 2004. Placement driven synthesis case studies on two sets of two chips: hierarchical and flat. In *Proceedings of the ACM International Symposium on Physical Design.* 190–197.
[16] M. Ozdal, S. Burns, and J. Hu. 2011. Gate sizing and device technology selection algorithms for high-performance industrial designs. In *Proceedings of the IEEE/ACM International Conference on Computer-Aided Design.* 724–731.
[17] Y. Peng and X. Liu. 2005. Freeze: engineering a fast repeater insertion solver for power minimization using the ellipsoid method. In *Proceedings of the ACM/IEEE Design Automation Conference.* 813–818.
[18] W. Shi and Z. Li. 2005. A fast algorithm for optimal buffer insertion. *IEEE Transactions on Computer-Aided Design* 24, 6 (June 2005), 879–891.
[19] L. P. P. P. van Ginneken. 1990. Buffer placement in distributed RC-tree networks for minimal Elmore delay. In *Proceedings of the IEEE International Symposium on Circuits and Systems.* 865–868.

Interconnect Physical Optimization

Arteris IP, Campbell, California
charlie.janac@arteris.com

ABSTRACT

The SoC Interconnect is one of the most important IPs in modern chips as it is the logical and physical instantiation of an SoC architecture and carries virtually all the SoC data. Interconnect IPs have to carry non-coherent, cache coherent, subsystem and service traffic. Another unique characteristic of SoC interconnect IP is that it changes many times per project and is unique for each project. Hence, the interconnect IP is the most configurable of all major IPs in a chip. The current state of the art in interconnect is the Network on Chip (NoC) distinguished by use of packetized transport and distributed arbitration. This interconnect IP approach is proven in billions of shipping SoCs. However, the world is changing. With the 16nm processes (and below), timing closure has become a major issue as there are valid logical architectures that are not timing closable in the place and route phase of the design. This has made it necessary to consider physical layout effects in the design of interconnect IPs at the architecture and RTL logic phases of chip development. Providing a timing-verified interconnect IP to the place and route group has become a new silicon success requirement. Interconnect Physical Optimization links the logic and physical design realms, providing a more optimal starting point for the place and route process to minimize the number of place and route iteration cycles. This paper will discuss an interconnect physical optimization capability, called PIANO, which addresses automation of the timing closure process in order to accelerate design of interconnect IPs and reduce the need to over-engineer the interconnect. The paper will also cover the inputs needed to make PIANO produce optimal results and outputs which enable optimization of latency-sensitive SoC connections.

ACM Reference format:

K. Charles Janac. 2018. Interconnect Physical Optimization In ISPD '18: 2018 International Symposium on Physical Design, March 25–28, 2018, Monterey, CA, USA. ACM, New York, NY, USA, 1 page.
https://doi.org/10.1145/3177540.3177558

BIOGRAPHY

K. Charles Janac is the Chairman, President and Chief Executive Officer of Arteris IP. Arteris pioneered the market for Network-on-Chip (NoC) interconnect IP and tools for semiconductor on-chip communications. ArterisIP products are designed into semiconductor chips used in the majority of currently shipping smart phones and latest car electronics for driving assistance (ADAS) and autonomous driving.

Charlie started his technology career as employee number two of Cadence Design Systems (originally SDA, Inc.), a publicly traded EDA software company. Subsequently, he served as President/CEO of HLD Systems, Smart Machines and Nanomix. Charlie also served as Entrepreneur-in-Residence at Infinity Capital, an early stage venture capital firm in Palo Alto, California.

He holds B.S. and M.S. degrees in Organic Chemistry from Tufts University and an MBA from the Stanford Graduate School of Business.

ISPD '18, March 25–28, 2018, Monterey, CA, USA
© 2018 Copyright is held by the owner/author(s).
ACM ISBN 978-1-4503-5626-8/18/03.
https://doi.org/10.1145/3177540.3177558

ISPD 2018 Initial Detailed Routing Contest and Benchmarks

Stefanus Mantik, Gracieli Posser, Wing-Kai Chow, Yixiao Ding, Wen-Hao Liu

Cadence Design Systems, USA

{smantik, gposser, wkchow, yxding, whliu}@cadence.com

ABSTRACT

In advanced technology nodes, detailed routing becomes the most complicated and runtime consuming stage. To spur detailed routing research, ISPD 2018 initial detailed routing contest is hosted and it is the first ISPD contest on detailed routing problem. In this contest, the benchmarks synthesized by industrial tool and library are released, which consider the design rules like spacing table, cut spacing, end-of-line spacing, and min-area rules. In addition, the global routing guide is provided associated to each benchmark, and detailed routers are required to honor the routing guides as much as possible meanwhile minimize design-rule-checking (DRC) violations. The biggest benchmark released in this contest has near-millions of nets, so the runtime and memory scalability for detailed routers need to be well addressed. To reduce routers' runtime, the deterministic multithreading framework is encouraged but optional in this contest.

ACM Reference Format:

Stefanus Mantik, Gracieli Posser, Wing-Kai Chow, Yixiao Ding, Wen-Hao Liu. 2018. *ISPD 2018 Initial Detailed Routing Contest and Benchmarks*. In *ISPD '18: 2018 International Symposium on Physical Design, March 25–28, 2018, Monterey, CA, USA*. ACM, New York, NY, USA, 4 pages. https://doi.org/10.1145/3177540.3177562

1 INTRODUCTION

Every new technology node comes with more complex design rules making the routing stage become more and more challenging, and so the routability awareness becomes more critical in the physical design flow [1-5]. Due to the enormous computational complexity, routing typically is divided into two stages: global routing and detailed routing.

In global routing, the entire routing region is divided into regular global cells and routing is performed based on these global cells. The obtained global routing results are used to generate detailed routing solution considering exact metal shapes and positions in the detailed routing stage.

The detailed routing stage can be further divided into two steps. First, an initial detailed routing step implements physical wires and vias from the global routing result while handling the major routing rules. Then, a detailed routing refinement step is performed to fix the remaining complicated DRC violations. The ISPD contest of this year focuses on the initial detailed routing step.

Assuming that a global routing result is already well optimized for certain metrics (e.g., congestion and timing [6, 7]), a detailed router needs to honor the global routing result in order to keep the optimized metrics. In addition, to minimize the net topology disturbance contributed by the later detailed routing refinement step, the initial detailed routing step needs to consider the major routing rules. If the initial detailed routing solution can meet the most common routing rules even it is not fully DRC clean, the later detailed routing refinement step will have less chance to largely disturb the routing solution. Therefore, the initial detailed routing need to obey the "guide" from global routing as much as possible and at the same time minimize DRC violations [8, 9, 10].

Although detailed routing has been studied extensively in the literature, there are still various challenges that make it difficult to apply the existing academic algorithms to modern industrial designs. The ISPD contest of this year aims at exposing some of the industrial detailed routing challenges to the academic community, while keeping the problem complexity reasonable to drive practical detailed routing researches. The contributions of this contest are listed below:

(1) Currently the detailed-routing researches take different objectives and test cases making hard to compare the performance of different routers [11-16]. This contest provides realistic industrial benchmarks with the common design rules as a standard to more fairly evaluate the effectiveness of the detailed-routing researches.

(2) This contest provides contestants the license of Cadence P&R tool Innovus [17] to evaluate and debug their routing solutions, which gives them the opportunity to combine their academic researches with industrial tool, producing more realistic results.

(3) In the physical design flow, detailed routing is one of the most complicated and time-consuming stages. Although the works [11-16] attempt to address the advanced routing issues, the problem instances adopted in these works are much smaller than the real industrial designs. By releasing the benchmarks with near millions of nets, this contest aims to drive detailed routing researches to have practical scalability in terms of runtime and memory.

(4) In this contest, the comprehensive routing issues and the common routing rules are considered. In order to obtain good routing solutions, contestants need to co-optimize routing strategy, pin access, DRC handling, routing guide honoring, and multithreading scheduling. Handling all of these constraints gives contestants a better understanding of the routing challenges on industrial designs.

The remaining sections are organized as follows. Section 2 describes the problem for the initial detailed routing contest. In Section 3, the evaluation metrics used in the contest are detailed. Section 4 introduces the benchmark information. Finally, acknowledgement is presented in Section 5.

ISPD'18, March 25–28, 2018, Monterey, CA, USA
© 2018 Association for Computing Machinery.
ACM ISBN 978-1-4503-5626-8/18/03...$15.00
https://doi.org/10.1145/3177540.3177562

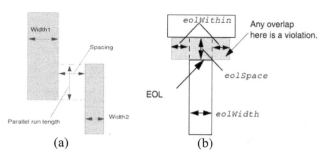

(a)   (b)

Fig. 1. (a) Example of spacing table; (b) Example of end-of-line (EOL) spacing.

2 PROBLEM DESCRIPTION

This contest evaluates the quality of detailed routing solutions from the following aspects:

(1) Connectivity constraints
(2) LEF routing rules
(3) Routing preference metrics

According to these constraints/rules/metrics, we will come out a score for a given detailed routing solution, and ranking of each participated team for the contest will be based on the scores. The details of these constraints/rules/metrics will be introduced in this section, and scoring method will be introduced in Section 3. Because this contest uses LEF/DEF format to represent the problem instances, the details of rule representation can be found in [18].

2.1 Connectivity Constraints

The connectivity constraints have to be satisfied in order to guarantee the valid signal and the routing wires that are able to be implemented. Therefore, the connectivity constraints have the highest priority to be obeyed.

2.1.1 Open

The pins of each net defined in DEF file need to be fully connected. If any pin in a net is disconnected, the net will be considered as an open net and the routing solution is invalid.

2.1.2 Short

A short violation will happen when either a via metal or wire metal overlaps with another object like via metal, wire metal, blockages, or pin shapes. The intersection part between two objects is the short area.

2.2 LEF Routing Rules

A detailed router need to consider many routing results defined in LEF files in order to meet the manufacturing requirements from foundries. Different technology nodes, different foundries, or different designs may have different routing rules. In this contest, we only consider the most common and major routing rules.

2.2.1 Spacing Table

Spacing table in LEF file specifies the required spacing between two objects according to the parallel-run length between two objects and the widths of the objects. Parallel-run length is the projection length between two objects. Figure 1(a) illustrates

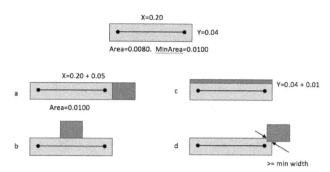

Fig. 2. Example of adding patch metal to satisfy min-area rule. (a), (b), and (c) are valid patch metal insertion solution, while (d) is an invalid solution.

how the width, parallel-run length, and the required spacing are defined in the spacing table. In general, the spacing table contains multiple length thresholds. Once the parallel-run length is over a bigger length threshold, larger required spacing will be triggered. For the simplicity of the contest, we reduce the number of length thresholds into one. Thus, the spacing value remain the same regardless of the parallel-run length as long as it is greater than zero. Namely, in this contest, the spacing value defined in the spacing table only depends on the width of the objects.

2.2.2 End-of-line Spacing

The end-of-line (EOL) spacing rule indicates that an edge that is shorter than *eolWidth*, noted as end-of-line edge requires spacing greater than or equal to *eolSpace* beyond the EOL anywhere within (that is, less than) *eolWithin* distance (see Figure 1(b)). Typically, *eolSpace* is slightly larger than the minimum allowed spacing on the layer. The *eolWithin* value must be less than the minimum allowed spacing.

2.2.3 Cut Spacing

The cut spacing rule specifies the minimum spacing allowed between via cuts on the same net or different nets.

2.2.4 Min Area Rule

The min area rule specifies the minimum metal area required for polygons on each layer. All polygons must have an area that is greater than or equal to the specified area value.

When a routed metal segment is small such that the whole polygon area does not satisfy the min area rule, a patch metal can be added to increase the area for the polygon. See Figure 2(a) to 2(c) for possible patch solution added to the existing metal routing to satisfy min area rule. However, the location and the size of the patch metal must be decided carefully so it will not cause any spacing or short violation. In addition, the overlapping region between patch and the existing metal routing must be greater or equal to the minimum *width* of the current routing layer (see Figure 2(d)).

2.3 Routing Preference Metrics

There are several metrics generally used to evaluate the quality of a detailed routing solution. Although they are not hard rules, the quality of a routing solution usually could be better in terms of timing, routability, and manufacturability if the detailed router considers these metrics.

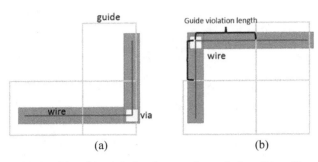

Fig. 3. (a) guide-violation-free routing solution; (b) guide-violation routing solution.

TABLE 1 EVALUATION METRICS

Metric	Weight
Short metal area	500
Number of spacing violations	500
Number of min-area violations	500
Total length of the wires outside of the routing guides	1
Total number of the vias outside of routing guides	1
Total length of off-track wires	0.5
Total number of off-track vias	1
Total length of wrong-way wires	1
Total number of vias	2
Total length of wires	0.5

2.3.1 Routing Guide Honoring

In the typical routing flow, global routing performs followed by detailed routing. A global routing result is usually well optimized for certain metrics, a detailed router needs to honor the global routing result as much as possible in order to minimize the disturbance to these metrics. In this contest, each benchmark has a guide file in which every net associates to a list of rectangles. The list of rectangles is called global routing guide (yellow rectangles in Fig. 3) to represent the regions passed by the global routing result of the associated net, and the global routing guide guarantees to contain at least a fully connected detailed routing solution for the net. If the center lines (red lines in Fig. 3) of wires or the coordinate of vias route outside of the guide, they will be considered as a guide violation; if wires or vias route inside or just on the boundaries of the rectangles, there is no guide violation. For example, Fig. 3(a) shows a routing solution without guide violations, while Fig. 3(b) shows a routing solution with guide violations for both via and wires. The score penalty will be applied based on the number of vias and the length of wires are routed out of guides. Note that, routing guide honoring does not consider patch metals. Namely, patch metals can put out of guides without the penalty.

2.3.2 Wrong-way Routing

Each metal layer has a preferred routing direction defined in LEF file, which is either horizontal or vertical. If a wire routes horizontally (vertically) on a vertical (horizontal) layer, the wire is considered as a wrong-way wire. The length of wrong-way wires will contribute as a penalty to the scoring function.

2.3.3 Off-track Routing

Each metal layer has a track structure defined in DEF files. The routing wires that align with tracks is so called on-track wires; otherwise, the wires are off-track wires. Also, a via is considered as an on-track via when the coordinate of the via aligns with the tracks on its both bottom and top layers. The length of off-track wires and the number of off-track vias will be considered as a penalty in the scoring function.

2.3.4 Multithreading Determinism

When design scale increases, the multithreading technique becomes an important feature to a detailed router. In this contest, we will evaluate the detailed routers on a machine with 8 CPUs, so multithreading technique is encouraged but optional. However, multithreading technique is easier to cause nondeterministic issue. Because nondeterministic behavior will increase the maintenance effort largely for a detailed router, it is better to be avoided.

3 EVALUATION METRICS

In this contest, a routing solution is treated as a valid solution only when the memory and runtime usage of the proposed router is respectively under 64G and 12 hours, and the solution has no open net. The quality of a valid routing solution is measured by Eq. (1). A router which can obtain a solution with a smaller scaled_score is considered as a better router in this contest.

$$\text{scaled\_score} = \text{original\_score} * (1 + np + rf), \qquad (1),$$

where original_score represents the result quality of a given detailed routing solution, np denotes the nondeterministic penalty, and rf denotes a runtime factor.

- The original score is measured by the weighted sum of the metrics shown in Table 1, which is computed by the released evaluator [19], and Cadence P&R tool Innovus [17] is used to verify DRC violations. Note that, the length unit used in Table 1 is the number of M2 pitches.
- The nondeterministic penalty is to reflect the debugging and maintenance difficulty for a nondeterministic router. We will run multiple times of a router for a benchmark, and pick the median scaled_score as the final score for the benchmark. If we observe nondeterministic results, nondeterministic penalty will be set to 3%; otherwise, it will be 0.
- The runtime factor rf is defined in Eqs. (2) and (3), where $rwt(b)$ represents the wall time of a detailed router for benchmark b, and $mwt(b)$ represents the median wall time of all submitted detailed routers from contestants for the benchmark b. The runtime factor is limited within 0.1 and -0.1.

$$rf = \min(0.1, \max(-0.1, f) \qquad (2),$$
$$f = 0.02 * \log_2(rwt(b) / mwt(b)) \qquad (3),$$

4 BENCHMARKS

The test cases used for the benchmark are derived from two real designs, a single-core 32-bit processor with four memory cores and a quad-core 32-bit processors with 16 on-chip memory blocks. The original size for the designs are 37k nets and 147k nets respectively. The designs are synthesized using generic 45nm and 32nm technology and cell libraries. Cadence Genus [20] and Innovus [17] are used to perform logic synthesis, floorplan, and placement on the designs. In order to be used as benchmarks for the contest, we simplify the designs so they pertain to the core essence of the contest while still maintaining

TABLE 2 BENCHAMRK INFORMATION

	#std	#blk	#net	#pin	#layer
ispd18_sample	22	0	11	0	9
ispd18_sample2	22	1	16	0	9
ispd18_sample3	5	1	7	5	16
ispd18_test1	8879	0	3153	0	9
ispd18_test2	35913	0	36834	1211	9
ispd18_test3	35973	4	36700	1211	9
ispd18_test4	72090	4	72410	1211	9
ispd18_test5	71946	8	72394	1211	9
ispd18_test6	107919	0	107701	1211	9
ispd18_test7	179865	16	179863	1211	9
ispd18_test8	191987	16	179863	1211	9
ispd18_test9	192911	0	178858	1211	9
ispd18_test10	290386	0	182000	1211	9

the accuracy of the initial design intent. The followings are the simplification steps done on the designs.

- Power and ground nets are removed due to the complexity of the special nets representation in DEF.
- Non-default rules are removed to reduce the additional complexity introduced by wide wires.
- Since the primary goal for this contest is DRC cleanliness and wirelength, timing related information are removed.
- For the purpose of the initial detailed routing contest, some design rules are also simplified into a regular spacing rule and an EOL spacing rule for the metal layers, and a simple cut-to-cut spacing rule for the cut layers.

Table 2 shows the benchmark information, where #std, #blk, #net, #pin, and #layer denote the number of standard cells, macro blockages, nets, IO pins, and metal layers, respectively. The sample benchmarks (ispd18_sample*) are derived from the original single-core design. The nets are selected randomly. A placement run is called for the selected instances that are connected to those selected nets to produce a compact floorplan. These test cases will be used as a sample for the contestants to make sure their binary is able to read the design data correctly and perform the initial detailed routing process. These sample tests will not be used for evaluation purpose. On the other hand, "ispd18_test*" are the official benchmarks used to evaluate and rank the detailed routers developed by the contestants.

5   ACKNOWLEDGEMENT

We thank the following people: Patrick Haspel, Cheryl Mendenhall, Angelos Athanasiadis, Anton Klotz and Tracy Zhu from Cadence Academic Network for the great support on the Innovus licenses; Neal Chang from Chip Implement Center (CIC) in Taiwan and Linda Dougherty from CMC Microsystems in Canada for helping Universities to setup Cadence licenses; Yufeng Luo, Mehmet C. Yildiz, Zhuo Li, Chuck Alpert, Jing Cheng, and Ismail S. Bustany for their insight and help on this contest; Guilherme A. Flach, Jucemar Monteiro and Mateus Fogaça for the adjustments on Rsyn academic tool to support the requirements for this contest and help students to get the setup easily.

REFERENCES

[1] V. Yutsis, *et al.* ISPD 2014 benchmarks with sub-45nm technology rules for detailed-routing-driven placement. In *International Symposium on Physical Design, ISPD'14*, 2014.

[2] W.-H Liu, *et al.* Routing congestion estimation with real design constraints. In *Design Automation Conference 2013, DAC '13*, 2013.

[3] W.-H. Liu, *et al.* Case study for placement solutions in ISPD11 and DAC12 routability-driven placement contests. In *International Symposium on Physical Design, ISPD'13*, 2013.

[4] D. Shi, *et al.* Dynamic planning of local congestion from varying-size vias for global routing layer assignment. In *IEEE Trans. on CAD of Integrated Circuits and Systems (TCAD'17)*, Vol. 36, No. 8, 2017.

[5] W.-K. Chow, *et al.* Placement: From Wirelength to Detailed Routability. In *IPSJ Trans. System LSI Design Methodology*, Vol. 9, 2016.

[6] W.-H Liu, *et al.* NCTU-GR 2.0: Multithreaded Collision-Aware Global Routing With Bounded-Length Maze Routing. In *IEEE Transactions on Computer-Aided Design of Integrated Circuits and Systems*, Vol. 32, no. 5, 2013.

[7] S. Held, *et al.* Global Routing with Timing Constraints. In *IEEE Transactions on Computer-Aided Design of Integrated Circuits and Systems*, Vol. PP, no. 99, 2017.

[8] X. Qiu, *et al.* Routing Challenges for Designs With Super High Pin Density. In *IEEE Transactions on Computer-Aided Design of Integrated Circuits and Systems*, Vol. 32, no. 9, 2013.

[9] T. Nieberg. Gridless pin access in detailed routing. In *Design Automation Conference, DAC'11*, 2011.

[10] X. Xu, *et al.* PARR: Pin access planning and regular routing for self-aligned double patterning. In *Design Automation Conference, DAC'15*, 2015.

[11] J.-R. Gao, *et al.* Flexible self-aligned double patterning aware detailed routing with prescribed layout planning. In *International Symposium on Physical Design, ISPD '12*, 2012.

[12] Y. Du, *et al.* Spacer-is-dielectric-compliant detailed routing for self-aligned double patterning lithography. In *Design Automation Conference DAC'13*, 2013.

[13] Y. Zhang, *et al.* RegularRoute: an efficient detailed router with regular routing patterns. In *International Symposium on Physical design, ISPD '11*, 2011.

[14] I.-J. Liu, *et al.* Overlay-aware detailed routing for self-aligned double patterning lithography using the cut process. In *IEEE Transactions on Computer-Aided Design of Integrated Circuits and Systems*, Vol. 35, no. 9, 2016.

[15] Y. Ding, *et al.* Self-aligned double patterning lithography aware detailed routing with color pre-assignment. In *IEEE Transactions on Computer-Aided Design of Integrated Circuits and Systems*, Vol. 36, no. 8, 2017.

[16] Y. H. Su, et al. Nanowire-Aware Routing Considering High Cut Mask Complexity. In *IEEE Transactions on Computer-Aided Design of Integrated Circuits and Systems*, Vol. 36, no. 6, 2017.

[17] Cadence P&R Tool Innovus: https://www.cadence.com/content/cadence-www/global/en_US/home/tools/digital-design-and-signoff/hierarchical-design-and-floorplanning/innovus-implementation-system.h

[18] Cadence, Inc. LEF/DEF 5.3 to 5.7 exchange format. 2009: www.si2.org/openeda.si2.org/projects/lefdef.

[19] Contest website: http://www.ispd.cc/contests/18/index.htm

[20] Cadence logic synthesis tool: https://www.cadence.com/content/cadence-www/global/en_US/home/tools/digital-design-and-signoff/synthesis/genus-synthesis-solution.html

The Pressing Need for Electromigration-Aware Physical Design

Jens Lienig, Matthias Thiele
Dresden University of Technology
Institute of Electromechanical and Electronic Design (IFTE)
01062 Dresden, Germany   www.ifte.de
Email: jens@ieee.org, matthias.thiele@tu-dresden.de

ABSTRACT

Electromigration (EM) is becoming a progressively intractable design challenge due to increased interconnect current densities. It has changed from something designers "should" think about to something they "must" think about, i.e., it is now a definite requirement. The on-going IC-down-scaling is producing physical designs with ever-smaller feature sizes, which can easily lead to current densities that exceed their maximum allowable values. This invited talk introduces the fundamentals of EM, its interactions with thermal and stress migration, and presents appropriate modelling and simulation methodologies. Following a summary of EM-inhibiting effects in physical design, we propose ways of facilitating EM-compliant layout design in future technology nodes.

CCS CONCEPTS

• **Hardware** → **Physical verification** • **Hardware** → **Electronic design automation** → Methodologies for EDA

KEYWORDS

Electromigration; current density; layout; interconnect reliability; short-line rules; short-length effects; Blech length; reservoir effect

ACM Reference format:

J. Lienig, M. Thiele. 2018. The Pressing Need for Electromigration-Aware Physical Design. In *Proc. of the Int. Symp. on Physical Design, March 25–28, 2018, Monterey, CA, USA*, March 2018, 8 pages.
DOI: 10.1145/3177540.3177560

1. INTRODUCTION

Excessive current density within interconnects – which if not effectively curtailed causes electromigration (EM) – is a growing reliability issue in modern integrated circuits (ICs) as a result of smaller feature sizes. Accordingly, the latest edition of the ITRS roadmap [1] indicates that all of today's minimum-sized interconnects are EM-affected (Fig. 1).

The trends towards smaller line widths and smaller cross-sectional areas will continue over the coming years (Table 1). These trends will be accompanied initially by a reduction in currents (Fig. 1, left and Table 1) due to lower supply voltages and shrinking gate capacitances. Given that current reduction is constrained by rising frequencies and will even be reversed beyond 2022, we witness an alarming trend towards increased current densities J in ICs going forward (Fig. 1, right and Table 1, bottom).

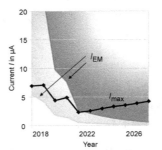 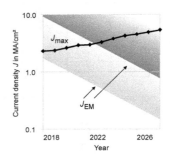

Figure 1: Projected development of currents (I_{max}, left) and current densities (J_{max}, right) needed for driving four inverter gates, according to ITRS [1,2] and Table 1. EM degradation must be considered inside the yellow areas for currents (I_{EM}) and current densities (J_{EM}). As of now, there are no known manufacturable solutions for the red areas.

Table 1: Predicted technology parameters based on the ITRS, 2015 edition [1]; maximum currents and current densities for copper at 105°C.

Year	2018	2020	2022	2024	2026	2028
Gate length (nm)	12.8	10.65	8.87	7.39	6.16	5.13
On-chip local clock frequency (GHz)***	6.69	7.24	7.83	8.47	9.16	9.91
DC equivalent maximum current (µA)*	6.92	4.41	2.33	2.98	3.56	4.24
Metal 1 properties						
Width – half-pitch (nm)	12	9	6	6	6	6
Aspect ratio	2.1	2.1	2.2	2.2	2.2	2.2
Layer thickness (nm)*	25.2	18.9	13.2	13.2	13.2	13.2
Cross-sectional area (nm²)*	302.4	170.1	79.2	79.2	79.2	79.2
DC equivalent current densities (MA/cm²)						
Maximum tolerable current density (w/o EM degradation)**	1.8	1.1	0.7	0.4	0.3	0.2
Maximum current density (beyond no known solutions)**	9.5	5.8	3.5	2.1	1.3	0.8
Required current density for driving four inverter gates***	2.29	2.59	2.94	3.76	4.50	5.35

*) Calculated values, based on given width W, aspect ratio A/R, and current density J in [1], calculated as follows: layer thickness $T = A/R \times W$, cross-sectional area $A = W \times T$ and current $I = J \times A$.
**) Approximated values from the ITRS 2015 figure INTC6 [1].
***) Values from the ITRS 2013 edition [2].
All remaining values are from the ITRS 2015 edition [1].

Due to smaller structure sizes, maximum tolerable current densities are shrinking, as well – giving further cause for concern. (Small voids and other material defects, which would have been tolerated in earlier technology nodes, increasingly cause dramatic damage to, or resistance change in, wires with shrinking metal structures.) Thus, the ITRS [1] states that all minimum-sized interconnects are EM-affected by 2018 (Fig. 1, yellow barrier).

Furthermore, the total length of interconnects per IC will continue to increase. As a consequence, reliability requirements per unit length of wire need to be *increased* in order to *maintain* overall IC reliability. But, as noted above, this accepted wisdom is set to be compromised by the prospective *drop* in interconnect reliability due to EM. And indeed, the ITRS states that no known solutions are available for the EM-related reliability requirements that we will face approximately 5 years from now (Fig. 1, red barrier).

Increased interconnect resistivity caused by scattering effects in small wires will raise further challenges [3]. Coupled with a rise in current densities, this will lead to large local temperature gradients inside the wire caused by Joule heating. This in turn will accelerate temperature-dependent EM and introduce additional thermal migration [4-5].

The tendency to replace SiO_2 with low-k dielectrics [1] with lower stiffness coefficients reduces the stress-induced atomic backflow [6] that counteracts EM in short lines. Another consequence of using low-k dielectrics is the increased likelihood of EM-induced compressive failures (extrusions) [7].

As already mentioned, the surge in current density is also driven by an increase in clock frequencies (Table 1), in response to the demand for enhanced performance and made possible by transistor miniaturization. Although higher frequencies will neither worsen nor improve EM issues in signal or clock nets [8], they will increase currents (and thus current densities) in (DC) supply nets, which are already sensitive to EM in state-of-the-art technologies.

As a consequence of these dramatic developments, any up-to-date physical design methodology must be EM-aware; how to achieve this is the subject of this paper. In Sect. 2, we introduce the physical EM process, followed by an outline of how EM interacts with thermal and stress migration (Sect. 3). Section 4 presents appropriate simulation approaches. Section 5 summarizes all known EM-inhibiting effects that can be exploited in physical design in order to reduce the negative impact of EM on circuit reliability. Section 6 sets out ways of facilitating EM-compliant layout design in the future.

2. ELECTROMIGRATION

Current flow through a conductor produces two forces to which the individual metal ions in the conductor are exposed. The first is an electrostatic force F_{field} caused by the electric field strength in the metallic interconnect. This force can be ignored in most cases, as the positive metal ions are shielded to some extent by the negative electrons in the conductor. The second force F_{wind} is produced by the momentum transfer between conduction electrons and metal ions in the crystal lattice. This force acts in the direction of current flow and is the main cause of EM (Fig. 2).

Hence, there is interaction between the moving electrons – a sort of "electron wind" – and the metal ions in the lattice structures. Atoms at the grain boundaries especially will be impacted by the electron wind, that is, they will be forced to move in the direction of the flow of electrons. Thus, in time, metal atoms will accumulate at individual grain boundaries, forming so-called "hillocks" in the direction of the current. At the same time, so-called "voids" can appear at grain boundaries (Fig. 3).

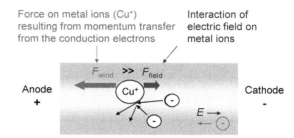

Figure 2: Two forces act on metal ions that make up the lattice of the interconnect material. EM is the result of the dominant force, that is, the momentum transfer from the electrons which move in the applied electric field.

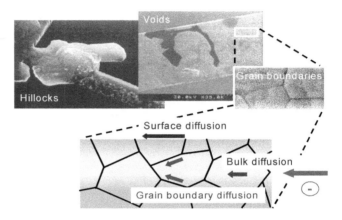

Figure 3: Hillock and void formations in wires due to EM, and illustration of various diffusion processes within the lattice (Photos courtesy of G. H. Bernstein und R. Frankovic, University of Notre Dame)

If the direction of an excessive current is constant over a longer period, these voids and hillocks appear in the wire. Analog circuits, or power supply lines in digital circuits, are therefore particularly susceptible to EM. In digital circuits, on the other hand, where the current direction varies with alternating capacitive charging and discharging in conductors, a certain amount of compensation occurs due to material backflow (self-healing effect). Nonetheless, interconnects can fail, with thermal migration playing a critical role.

There are three types of diffusion caused by EM: grain-boundary, bulk and surface diffusion (Fig. 3). In general, grain boundary diffusion is the main migration process in aluminum wires [9,10]; surface diffusion predominates in copper interconnects [11-13]. Detailed studies of the various EM failure mechanisms can be found in [10,11,14,15].

Many electronic interconnects in integrated circuits have a design median time to failure (MTF) of at least 10 years [16]. The failure of a single interconnect caused by EM can result in the failure of the entire circuit. At the end of the 1960s, the physicist J. R. Black developed an empirical model to estimate the MTF of a wire segment, taking EM into consideration [17]:

$$MTF = \frac{A}{J^n} \cdot \exp\left(\frac{E_a}{k \cdot T}\right) \tag{1}$$

where A is a constant based on the cross-sectional area of the interconnect, J is the current density, E_a is the activation energy (for example, 0.7 eV for grain boundary diffusion in Al [15,17], 0.9 eV for surface diffusion in Cu [18]), k is the Boltzmann constant, T is the temperature and *n* a scaling factor. Studies on Al and Cu interconnects show that void-growth-limited failure is characterized by $n = 1$, while void-nucleation-limited failure is best represented by $n = 2$ [11,19].

Equation (1) indicates that current density J and (to a lesser extent) the temperature T are deciding factors in the physical design process that affect EM.

3. INTERACTION OF EM, THERMAL AND STRESS MIGRATION

EM rarely acts alone. IC designers must also be aware of thermal and stress migration; both are introduced and described in this section in terms of their interaction with EM.

3.1 Thermal and stress migration

Temperature gradients produce *thermal migration*. In this case, high temperatures increase mean atomic speeds. The number of atoms diffusing from areas of high temperature to areas of lower temperature is greater than the number diffusing in the opposite direction. There is thus a net diffusion in the direction of the negative temperature gradient, which can lead to significant mass transport.

Stress migration describes a type of diffusion that balances mechanical stress. While there is a net atomic flow into areas subjected to tensile forces, metal atoms flow out of areas under compressive stress. Similar to thermal migration, this leads to diffusion in the direction of the negative mechanical tension gradient. The result is a balanced vacancy concentration that matches the mechanical tension.

3.2 Mutual interaction

Migration processes can produce an equilibrium state, where the limiting (or counteracting) process is another type of migration. For example, the equilibrium between electromigration (EM) and stress migration (SM) is named *Blech effect* as described next.

EM interacts directly with SM, as the dislocation of metal atoms induces mechanical stress, which is the driving force behind SM. SM works against EM, as its flow is directed from compressive to tensile stress, which is opposite to the EM flow direction. The resultant net flow is thus reduced and the damaging dislocation due to EM is abated or even halted (Blech effect).

Thermal migration (TM), on the other hand, is not a dedicated EM countermeasure, as it is less dependent on the current direction than EM. It may follow a different path than EM, depending on the temperature gradient, which may stem from sources other than current density.

While temperature accelerates EM as well as the other migration types, we are most likely to observe a mixture of all three types in a current-density hotspot. To effectively apply countermeasures, the dominant migration force must be known.

EM, TM and SM are closely coupled processes as their driving forces are linked with each other and with the resultant migration change, as discussed next.

Current density raises the temperature through Joule heating, and temperature change modifies mechanical stress through differences in expansion coefficients. Furthermore, temperature and mechanical stress affect the diffusion coefficient, which expresses the magnitude of the atomic flux. This, in turn, modifies the behavior of all three migration types. In addition, the mechanical stress is influenced by the change in atomic concentration caused by all migration types individually. These complex interactions are visualized in Fig. 4.

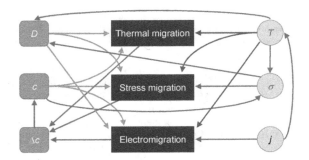

Figure 4: Interaction between TM, SM and EM through their driving forces temperature (T), mechanical stress (σ) and current density (j). The related migration parameters diffusion coefficient (D), concentration (c) and concentration change (Δc) are also shown

The effects of different combinations of EM, TM and SM are depicted in Figs. 5 and 6. Depending on the origins of the driving forces, several different amplifying and compensating results are observed.

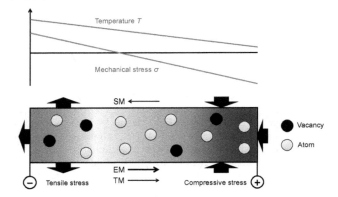

Figure 5: Example of coupled migration processes in a wire segment, where electromigration (EM) and thermal migration (TM) proceed from left to right, while stress migration (SM) flows in the opposite direction

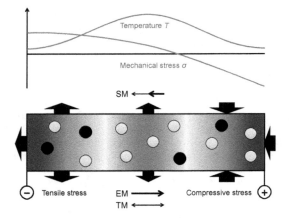

Figure 6: Another example of coupled migration processes. Here, thermal migration is induced through a hotspot in the middle of the segment, while the mechanical stress is a combination of tensile stress in the middle and EM-induced stress. This situation may occur near thermal vias or TSVs

Clearly, the causes and effects of migration are interrelated and at times self-reinforcing. For example, the void growth acceleration caused by positive feedback from a temperature rise is well known [20]. In general, the effects of different migration modes should be considered as interdependent. In particular, the material flows J_E (from EM), J_T (from TM), and J_S (from SM) can be calculated as follows [21]:

$$\vec{J_E} = \frac{c}{kT} \cdot D_0 \cdot \exp\left(-\frac{E_a}{kT}\right) \cdot z^* e\varrho \vec{j} , \qquad (2)$$

$$\vec{J_T} = -\frac{cQ}{kT^2} \cdot D_0 \cdot \exp\left(-\frac{E_a}{kT}\right) \cdot \operatorname{grad} T , \qquad (3)$$

$$\vec{J_S} = -\frac{c\Omega}{kT} \cdot D_0 \cdot \exp\left(-\frac{E_a}{kT}\right) \cdot \operatorname{grad} \sigma . \qquad (4)$$

In these equations, c is the atomic concentration, k the Boltzmann constant, T the absolute temperature, D_0 the diffusion coefficient at room temperature, E_a the activation energy, z^* the effective charge of the metal ions, e the elementary charge, ϱ the specific electrical resistance, j the electrical current density, Q the transported heat, Ω the atomic volume, and σ the mechanical tension (stress).

The resultant diffusion flux, defined as follows:

$$\vec{J_a} = \vec{J_E} + \vec{J_T} + \vec{J_S} , \qquad (5)$$

is the net effect of the combined driving forces.

In order to prevent EM effects, the net diffusion flow must be reduced to zero. For example, the EM diffusion flow and its associated SM flow (in the opposite direction) can cancel each other out (Blech effect).

3.3 Differentiation

The cause of a specific damage cannot be established by its appearance, as all damage, regardless of its origin, materializes as voids caused by diffusion processes. However, the locations and surroundings of these different damage types are pointers to their possible origin(s); this is exemplified in Fig. 8.

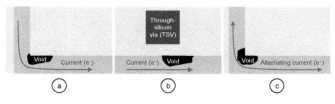

Figure 8: Different types of damage typically caused by EM (a), SM (b) and TM (c) (top view). In most cases, the cause of damage cannot be ascertained by its appearance, but rather by its location and surroundings

As discussed earlier, EM takes place inside wires and is driven by electric currents. Therefore, EM damage is most likely to be found in areas of high current density, that is, high currents and small cross-sections. Current crowding at wire bends and vias is a strong EM indicator.

TM correlates somewhat with EM, as large temperature differentials occur near locations of high current densities. Therefore, current crowding spots are also high temperature spots that are a potential TM driver. Here, large temperature differentials (in addition to current differentials) promote atomic motion.

There are many other causes of temperature gradients, such as external heating or cooling, and the heating of active circuit elements, like transistors. Thermal conduction can also dislocate

TM damage from hotspots in wires towards cooling spots or areas of low thermal conductivity. This, and alternating current directions might be TM indicators, whereas EM is always linked to locations of high current and a dominant current direction.

SM is often coupled with EM as a counteracting force. EM-transported atoms induce mechanical stress that consequently leads to SM in the opposite direction to the causal EM. Hence, SM has the potential to moderate EM damage in short wire segments (Sect. 5) and in locations of low current densities.

SM stems not only from EM, but also from fabrication, mismatches between different coefficients of thermal expansion (CTE), and induced stress from obstacles like through-silicon vias (TSV). With the increase in 3D-IC applications [22], stress-induced damage near structures such as TSVs in 3D-stacked ICs (Fig. 8 (b)) are rapidly raising concerns [20].

Finally, we would like to point out that hillocks (Fig. 3) and whiskers [20] usually point to EM as their cause. However, SM can also participate in the overall diffusion flow, and, hence, must be considered as well.

4. EM ANALYSIS THROUGH SIMULATION

4.1 Migration analysis

Migration is a complex problem that can be mathematically modeled by a system of differential equations. Several solution strategies are available for this type of mathematical problem:

- Analytical methods
- Quasi-continuous methods,
- Concentrated or lumped element methods, and
- Meshed geometry methods, such as
  - Finite element method (FEM),
  - Finite volume method (FVM), and
  - Finite differences method (FDM).

The last of these methods, *meshed geometry methods*, offer several advantages for migration analysis. The degrees of freedom can be spatially resolved in a flexible manner by adjusting the mesh granularity. The calculation effort is limited due to the bounded degrees of freedom – the mesh is finite. Using only basic geometries for the mesh elements further simplifies simulation.

The *finite element method* (FEM) is a universal tool for calculating elliptic and parabolic equation systems. It is a numerically very robust method suitable for a wide range of applications. The system of equations is built from degrees of freedom for nodes and elements.

For reduced problem sizes, such as the EM analysis of power and ground nets, FEM delivers precise results in reasonable calculation times. However, model preparation and calculation efforts are high when meshed methods are applied to complex geometries. These challenges are encountered in EM analysis due to the increasing complexity of geometries in VLSI circuits. Since signal nets are increasingly infected with EM, filtering only EM-critical nets, as proposed in [23], is no longer a viable option for reducing problem complexity.

4.2 Efficient FEM for EM analysis

Quick simulations are called for in physical design. These simulations are only one part of the verification phase; they must be repeated iteratively in the design flow. For example, applying FEM for use in the full-chip verification of complex integrated circuits is far too slow [16,23,24].

In order to maintain FEM precision despite the increasing number of structures and geometries to be analyzed, we propose that EM simulations are separated from the actual verification process. This means that FE analysis is performed prior to verification or even prior to layout synthesis. Routing, for example, will then be carried out exclusively with verified routing elements from a library. Hence, an entire library of routing elements with simplified parametric models attached will be verified by FE analysis. The complete chip can then be verified rapidly. The library should include all routing elements required to build a complete layout; the library size can be kept low by using only highly repetitive patterns. The verification is simplified to calculating only critical results from the actual boundary conditions by using the parametric models to check against current-density limits, or other migration metrics (Fig. 9).

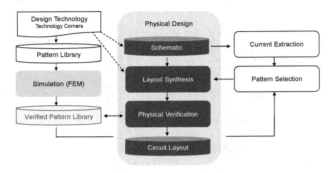

Figure 9: A full-chip EM simulation based on FEM should be uncoupled from the actual synthesis and verification process to compensate for the increasing circuit complexity. The resulting layout synthesis would then be restricted to pre-verified (routing) patterns to enable a fast pattern-based physical verification [24]

An important prerequisite for the above-mentioned verification method of combining several discrete FEM simulations is that the partial solutions equate with the respective parts of the complete solution. This requirement is met if the boundary conditions are transformed correctly between the full and partition models, as we discuss next.

The method's prerequisite can be best explained with a typical example, where a complete wire connection is simulated as a single entity and then split into separate parts. If we can transform the boundary conditions to the parts in a suitable manner, we will obtain equivalent simulation results.

There are several useful rules for finding the best locations to split the model. The best place to split is at locations where the boundary conditions are homogeneous, as they can easily be applied to FE models. Current-density regions in a straight wire some distance away from vias and branches are good places to split the model. If, however, the layout element of interest consists only of a via region, some adjuncts will have to be added to the wires in order to establish a homogeneous boundary condition.

The atomic flux, on the other hand, stops at diffusion barriers, that is, the transition from one material to another (this typically occurs near vias). These diffusion barriers provide ideal boundary conditions for this model.

Temperature influences and mechanical stress from "unmodeled" surroundings should not affect the simulation results. To this end, a sufficiently large volume surrounding a wire should be modeled, so that the difference between homogeneous model conditions and inhomogeneous real conditions can be neglected inside the wire.

The same applies when modelling temperature directly, as the surrounding dielectric distributes heat as well as the metal, only with lower conductivity.

Partitioning FE routing models without loss of accuracy is a prerequisite for applying FEM for full-chip current-density analysis. This is best done by comparing simulation results for generic sample patterns calculated both jointly and separately. Figures 10 and 11 visualize this using a T-shaped wire segment inside one metal layer and a via connection. Figure 10 (left) shows the current-density results from two separate (distinct) simulations. The simulation of both patterns combined is visualized in Fig. 10 (right); the combined results agree well with the individually calculated results. Figure 11 pictures the current-density distribution at the interface between the two patterns in a joint simulation; this is a measure of the error in the individual simulations. The maximum error is 3% in the visualized case; this is an acceptable value that has been verified for other patterns as well [24].

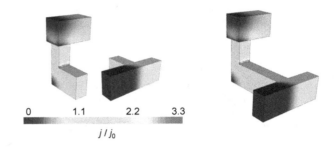

Figure 10: Current-density distribution using FEM for a T-shaped wire segment and a via connection. Results from separate simulations of the two individual patterns with homogeneous constraints at the cut surfaces are shown on the left. Joint FEM current-density simulation of the two patterns combined (on the right) produce a sufficiently similar outcome

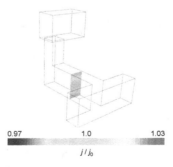

Figure 11: Verifying homogeneity of the current density at the cut surface between the two FEM sub-models (the maximum deviation is 3% here) can be used to ensure that joint and separate simulations show matching results

Evaluating interconnect structures in advance and building the layout exclusively from evaluated structures enables much faster verification: even a single circuit simulation, i.e., generating the (simulated) library patterns and using them only once, can be faster than a conventional, complete FEM simulation of the entire final layout [24].

With the aforementioned method of pre-verifying routing patterns, FEM, including its precision and spatial resolution, can be applied in the (full-chip) EM verification of complex, up-to-date circuit layouts.

4.3 Further simulation strategies

In addition to using FEM for current-density simulation, a host of other, more sophisticated simulation strategies are available for EM analysis (Fig. 12); please refer to [20] for a detailed description. Basically, the *atomic flux* can be calculated from current density and other driving forces to get a deeper insight into the damaging process. We can also simulate *mechanical stress* development as the driving force behind stress migration and compare it with the critical stress. *Void growth* can be simulated in order to better understand the damaging processes, in terms of both void nucleation (mechanical stress change) and void growth.

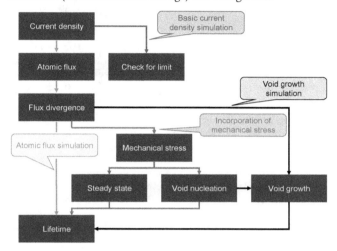

Figure 12: Overview of simulation strategies for EM analysis based on different parameters affecting migration; they are discussed in detail in [20]

5. MITIGATING EM IN PHYSICAL DESIGN

The most basic options for influencing current density and EM during the (physical) design of an electronic circuit are:

Wire material: Pure copper used for interconnect metallization is more EM-robust than aluminum at low temperatures.

Wire temperature: Interconnect MTF is greatly impacted by conductor temperature, as evidenced by Eq. (1) where it appears in the exponent. For an interconnect to remain reliable at high temperatures, the maximum tolerable current density of the conductor must necessarily decrease. On the other hand, lowering the temperature supports higher current densities while maintaining the reliability of the wire constant.

Wire width: Given that current density is the ratio of current I and cross-sectional area A, and given that most process technologies assume a constant thickness of the printed interconnects, it is the wire width that has a direct bearing on current density: the wider the wire, the lower the current density and the greater the resistance to EM.

The above mentioned three options have been discussed in detail in [25]. They are of limited use in today's technologies because they have been largely exploited and/or their application would be counter-intuitive to the new technology node itself, that is, its reduced structure size [26]. Therefore, tolerable current density limits need to be maximized by exploiting other EM-inhibiting measures, which we discussed in [20][27] and that are summarized next.

Bamboo effect: Diffusion typically occurs along the grain boundaries in a wire. High EM resilience can be achieved with conductor cross-sections smaller than grain sizes (in this case, grain boundaries are perpendicular to the direction of diffusion).

Short-length effect: Any wire length below a threshold length (Blech length) will not fail by EM. Here, mechanical stress buildup causes a reverse migration process which reduces, or even compensates for, the EM flow.

Reservoirs: Reservoirs increase the maximum permissible current density by supporting the stress-migration effect to partially neutralize EM. Reservoirs can, however, have an adverse effect on reliability in nets with current-flow reversals, as the (useful) stress migration is reduced in this case.

Via configurations: The robustness of interconnects fabricated with dual-Damascene technology depends on whether contact is made through vias from "above" (via-above) or "below" (via-below). It is easier to avoid EM with via-below configurations than with via-above configurations, as the former tolerate higher current densities due to their higher permissible void volumes.

Redundant vias: Multiple vias improve robustness against EM damage. They should be placed "in line" with the current direction so that all possible current paths have the same length. Current distribution is then uniform and there is no local detrimental increase in current density between vias.

Frequencies: The high frequencies normally encountered in signal nets reduce EM damage more than in power supply nets or very low-frequency nets under otherwise comparable operating conditions. Hence, different current-density boundary values (limits) must be assigned in EM analysis.

In order to prevent EM damage, the measures outlined above must be assessed with appropriate analysis tools, such as FEM (Sect. 4.2). Specifically, the impact of current density and other design parameters on the diffusion processes can be represented spatially by FEM, and the effects and measures analyzed by simulation. Many measures, such as the critical length effect, reservoirs, and the type of wire contacting, leverage stress migration as an effective EM inhibitor.

In summary, our investigations yield the following practical guidelines [20]:

- The critical length effect can be applied to obtain an EM-robust layout at the cost of no more than a slightly lower circuit performance.

- Reservoirs can be effective in power supply nets. However, signal nets do not significantly benefit from reservoirs due to the changing direction of the current; indeed on the contrary, incorporating them could negatively impact EM robustness, depending on the manufacturing process used.

- A via-below configuration, where the vias contact the critical segment from below, should be chosen in the dual-Damascene technology, if the layout permits.

- The product of length and current density must be bounded to a greater degree in the (remaining) via-above segments to compensate for their heightened EM susceptibility.

- Special care must be taken with multiple vias, as their geometrical configuration impacts time to failure. Redundant vias are generally better than an individual via. However, possible EM benefits depend on the inter-via configuration and the vias' relationships with the connected wire segments, as higher local current densities may adversely effect reliability.

6. OUTLOOK

This final section sketches a roadmap for EM-compliant layout design in future (EM-critical) technological nodes.

6.1 Segment lengths

The comparative evolutions of segment lengths and prospective Blech lengths due to IC downscaling are not encouraging. To illustrate this, technology-dependent, EM-robust segment lengths that are achievable solely with the short length effect (Blech length) are plotted in Fig. 13, based on data taken from the ITRS Roadmap [2]. These plots are based on maximum current densities predicted in the roadmap.

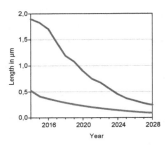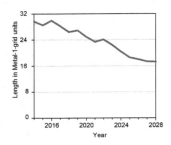

Figure 13: Segment lengths, up to which the short length effect alone suffices for EM robustness, depending on the respective technology node; absolute values in microns (red line on the left) and relative values in multiples of the routing grid (right) [20]. Also shown are the actual/expected mean segment lengths (blue line on the left) which fall off to a lesser degree. Values from ITRS [2] based on a maximum mechanical stress of 100 MPa

The red curves in Fig. 13 show that EM-robust segment lengths decrease significantly in pace with the structural miniaturization predicted in the ITRS Roadmap [2]. As can be seen as well, these Blech lengths drop more sharply than the actual mean segment lengths on the chip (blue line in Fig. 13 left). Furthermore, we can assume that the routing grid is almost proportional to the mean segment length, as the mainly short segment lengths are determined by the spacing between transistors. How alarmingly "less exploitable" EM-robust segment lengths really are becomes manifestly apparent if we plot these Blech lengths w.r.t. the routing grid, i.e., in multiples of the routing grid (Fig. 13 right).

Both observations imply that the number of nets benefiting from the short length effect drops with decreasing semiconductor scale. In other words, the Blech length is exceeded in an increasing proportion of the routing – up to approximately 5% by the year 2026 [20]. Countermeasures, such as the introduction of reservoirs, will be required for these segments.

6.2 Library of EM-robust elements

Increasingly, the required measures outlined in the preceding sections are being integrated in practical tools for layout design. However, these measures will need to be implemented as algorithms in the future, to automate the design of EM-robust integrated circuits.

One option to achieve this goal is to develop a *pattern generator* that produces routing elements for a given fabrication technology, that are EM robust when carrying a specified current density. These routing elements could be stored in a library, and the routing layout then drafted exclusively with routing elements from this library (Fig. 14).

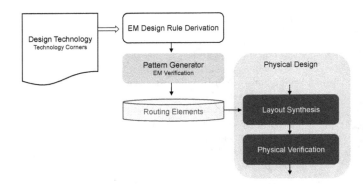

Figure 14: Improving the EM robustness of the generated layout by restricting physical design to EM-robust routing elements ("layout patterns") that have been generated for a given technology and verified with special emphasis on EM properties

Consequently, IC routing will be highly regulated, that is, *constraint-driven*, as only library elements may be used to create it. It will then be much easier to verify EM properties, as the robustness of individual elements is verified when the library is created. All that remains to be done in the complete layout is to examine the mutual interaction between elements when they are combined. The complexity of EM testing is thus reduced significantly, with the result that even for complex routing geometries no FE calculations are required for EM-robustness verification (Sect 4.2). Furthermore, parameters can be assigned to these analyses and the results stored in the library, allowing verification with a simplified (routing) model.

6.3 Constraint-driven physical design

Physical designs with ever-smaller feature sizes are subjected to a growing number of more complex constraints. These constraints are increasingly curtailing freedom in the design flow and are setting the boundaries of an ever-decreasing solution space. Hence, we are witnessing a slow, but steady evolution from a *constraint-correct* design flow to a *constraint-driven* one. In the latter case, design algorithms and methodologies are increasingly being governed by constraints instead of only verifying their correct implementation [28,29].

As has been shown throughout this paper, EM considerations are producing additional constraints in the design flow. The resultant reduction in the available solution space for physical design is illustrated in Fig. 15. Hence, a distinction must be made in the future between EM-robust and non-viable layout elements, whereby only EM-robust elements may be used for physical design. Thus, we expect constraint-driven physical design to predominate in future.

7. SUMMARY

EM has become an increasingly intractable design challenge due to IC-down-scaling. As has been shown, EM-aware design is no longer a design option; rather, it has become a prerequisite for producing reliable circuits. This paper summarizes our current understanding of EM and how its effects can be analyzed and moderated in practice. We also describe ways of facilitating EM-compliant layout design in future technology nodes.

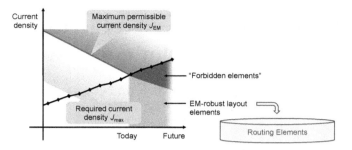

Figure 15: Projected evolution of the physical design (PD) solution space with falling current-density boundaries (red line) and increasing required current densities (black dots, cf. Fig. 1, right). The solution space for the allowed layout elements will be increasingly curtailed; hence, today's constraint-correct PD evolves into constraint-driven PD where only EM-robust layout elements may be used (see Fig. 14 for the generation of these elements)

REFERENCES

[1]   Int. Technology Roadmap for Semiconductors 2.0 (ITRS), 2015 Edition, http://www.itrs2.net/itrs-reports.html

[2]   *Int. Technology Roadmap for Semiconductors (ITRS)*, 2013 Edition, 2014. http://www.itrs2.net/itrs-reports.html

[3]   W. Steinhögl, G. Schindler, G. Steinlesberger, M. Engelhardt, "Size-dependent resistivity of metallic wires in the mesoscopic range," *Physical Review B*, 66 (2002) 075414. DOI: https://doi.org/10.1103/PhysRevB.66.075414

[4]   K. Jonggook, V. C. Tyree, C. R. Crowell, "Temperature gradient effects in electromigration using an extended transition probability model and temperature gradient free tests. I. Transition probability model," *IEEE Int. Integrated Reliability Workshop Final Report* (1999), 24–40. DOI: https://doi.org/10.1109/IRWS.1999.830555

[5]   X. Yu, K. Weide, "A study of the thermal-electrical- and mechanical influence on degradation in an aluminum-pad structure," *Microelectronics and Reliability* (1997), 37, 1545–1548. DOI: https://doi.org/10.1016/S0026-2714(97)00105-4

[6]   C. V. Thompson, "Using line-length effects to optimize circuit-level reliability," *15th Int. Symp. on the Physical and Failure Analysis of Integrated Circuits (IPFA)* (2008), 63–66. DOI: https://doi.org/10.1109/IPFA.2008.4588155

[7]   F. L. Wei, C. L. Gan, T. L. Tan, C. S. Hau-Riege, A. P. Marathe, J. J. Vlassak, C. V. Thompson, "Electromigration-induced extrusion failures in Cu/low-k interconnects," *J. Appl. Phys.* vol. 104 (2008), 023529-023529-10. DOI: https://doi.org/10.1063/1.2957057

[8]   J. Tao, N. W. Cheung, C. Hu, "Metal electromigration damage healing under bidirectional current stress," *IEEE Electron Device Letters* (1993), 14, 554–556. DOI: https://doi.org/10.1109/55.260787

[9]   A. G. Sabnis, "VLSI reliability," *VLSI Electronics—Microstructure Science*, London: Academic Press Ltd., vol. 22, 1990.

[10] A. Scorzoni, B. Neri, C. Caprile, F. Fantini, "Electromigration in thin-film inter-connection lines: models, methods and results," *Material Science Reports*, New York: Elsevier, vol. 7 (1991), 143–219. DOI: https://doi.org/10.1016/0920-2307(91)90005-8

[11] C. S. Hau-Riege, "An introduction to Cu electromigration," *Microel. Reliab.*, vol. 44 (2004), 195–205. DOI: https://doi.org/10.1016/j.microrel.2003.10.020

[12] M. Hayashi, S. Nakano, T. Wada, "Dependence of copper interconnect electromigration phenomenon on barrier metal materials," *Microel.*

[13] *Reliab.*, vol. 43 (2003), 1545–1550. DOI: https://doi.org/10.1016/S0026-2714(03)00273-7

[13] B. Li, T. D. Sullivan, T. C. Lee, D. Badami, "Reliability challenges for copper interconnects," *Microel. Reliab.*, vol. 44 (2004), 365–380. DOI: https://doi.org/10.1016/j.microrel.2003.11.004

[14] I. A. Blech, "Electromigration in thin aluminum films on titanium nitride," *J. Appl. Phys.*, vol. 47 (1976), 1203–1208. DOI: https://doi.org/10.1063/1.322842

[15] D. Young, A. Christou, "Failure mechanism models for electromigration," *IEEE Trans. on Reliability*, vol. 43(2) (June 1994), 186–192. DOI: https://doi.org/10.1109/24.294986

[16] G. Jerke, J. Lienig, "Hierarchical current-density verification in arbitrarily shaped metallization patterns of analog circuits," *IEEE Trans. on CAD of Integr. Circuits Sys.*, vol. 23(1) (Jan. 2004), 80–90. DOI: https://doi.org/10.1109/TCAD.2003.819899

[17] J. R. Black, "Electromigration – A brief survey and some recent results," *IEEE Trans. on Electronic Devices* (April 1969), 338–347. DOI: https://doi.org/10.1109/T-ED.1969.16754

[18] C.-K. Hu, L. Gignac, R. Rosenberg, "Electromigration of Cu/low dielectric constant interconnects," *Microelectronics and Reliability* (2006), 46, 213–231. DOI: https://doi.org/10.1016/j.microrel.2005.05.015

[19] M. A. Korhonen, P. Børgesen, K. N. Tu, C.-Y. Li, "Stress evolution due to electromigration in confined metal lines," *J. Appl. Phys.* 73 (1993), 3790. DOI: https://doi.org/10.1063/1.354073

[20] J. Lienig, M. Thiele, *Fundamentals of Electromigration-Aware Integrated Circuit Design*, Springer, Cham, ISBN 978-3-319-73557-3 (print), 978-3-319-73558-0 (ebook), 2018. DOI: https://doi.org/10.1007/978-3-319-73558-0

[21] K. Weide-Zaage, D. Dalleau, X. Yu, "Static and dynamic analysis of failure locations and void formation in interconnects due to various migration mechanisms," *Materials Science in Semiconductor Processing* (2003), 6 (1–3), 85–92. DOI: https://doi.org/10.1016/S1369-8001(03)00075-1

[22] R. Fischbach, J. Lienig, T. Meister, "From 3D circuit technologies and data structures to interconnect prediction," *Proc. of 2009 Int. Workshop on System Level Interconnect Prediction (SLIP)* (2009), 77–84. DOI: https://doi.org/10.1145/1572471.1572485

[23] G. Jerke, J. Lienig, "Early-stage determination of current-density criticality in interconnects," *Proc. 11th IEEE Int. Int. Symp. on Quality Electronic Design (ISQED)* (2010), 667–774. DOI: https://doi.org/10.1109/ISQED.2010.5450505

[24] M. Thiele, S. Bigalke, J. Lienig, "Exploring the use of the finite element method for electromigration analysis in future physical design", *Proc. of the 25th IFIP/IEEE Int. Conf. on Very Large Scale Integration (VLSI-SoC)* (2017), 1–6. DOI: https://doi.org/10.1109/VLSI-SoC.2017.8203466

[25] J. Lienig, "Introduction to electromigration-aware physical design," *Proc. Int. Symp. on Physical Design (ISPD'06)* (2006), 39–46. DOI: https://doi.org/10.1145/1123008.1123017

[26] G. Jerke, J. Lienig, J. Scheible, "Reliability-driven layout decompaction for electromigration failure avoidance in complex mixed-signal IC designs," *Proc. of the Design Automation Conf. (DAC'04)* (2004), 181–184. DOI: https://doi.org/10.1145/996566.996618

[27] J. Lienig, "Electromigration and its impact on physical design in future technologies," *Proc. of the ACM 2013 Int. Symposium on Physical Design (ISPD'13)* (2013), 33–40. DOI: https://doi.org/10.1145/2451916.2451925

[28] G. Jerke, J. Lienig, "Constraint-driven design — the next step towards analog design automation," *Proc. Int. Symp. on Physical Design (ISPD'09)* (2009) 75–82. DOI: https://doi.org/10.1145/1514932.1514952

[29] A. Nassaj, J. Lienig, G. Jerke, "A new methodology for constraint-driven layout design of analog circuits," *Proc. of the 16th IEEE Int. Conference on Electronics, Circuits and Systems (ICECS 2009)* (2009), 996–999. DOI: https://doi.org/10.1109/ICECS.2009.5410838

On Coloring and Colorability Analysis of Integrated Circuits with Triple and Quadruple Patterning Techniques

Alexey Lvov
IBM T. J. Watson Research Institute
Yorktown Heights, NY
lvov@us.ibm.com

Gustavo Tellez
IBM T. J. Watson Research Institute
Yorktown Heights, NY
tellez@us.ibm.com

Gi-Joon Nam
IBM T. J. Watson Research Institute
Yorktown Heights, NY
gnam@us.ibm.com

ABSTRACT

The continued delay of higher resolution alternatives for lithography, such as EUV, is forcing the continued adoption of multi-patterning solutions in new technology nodes, which include triple and quadruple patterning using several lithography-etch steps.

In the design space each pattern of a multi-patterning solution is modeled as a color on a shape. Designers or EDA tools must determine the colors that each shape is assigned so that the relative position of any two shapes of the same color does not violate the design rules. This results in a *shapes layout coloring problem* which is formulated as the traditional k-coloring problem in a graph. Because color interactions cross cell boundaries, coloring of a flat (as opposed to hierarchical) design becomes necessary, tremendously increasing the size of the input graph. If a color conflict occurs, any attempt to fix it may cause a chain reaction propagating through the whole design space which makes any approach of the type *color_greedily - fix_conflicts - loop_back* infeasible. Given the situation, it is extremely desirable to have a set of design rules which provably guarantee k-colorability and admit a practical coloring algorithm.

In this paper we formulate such sets of design rules for triple and quadruple patterning problems. For these sets of rules we provide proofs of colorability along with the coloring algorithms with the runtime upper bound of $O(n \cdot \log n)$. We also show that our sets of design rules are almost tight in the sense that even a very small relaxation of the formulated rules leads to existence of not k-colorable designs.

CCS CONCEPTS

• **Hardware** → **Design rules**;

KEYWORDS

multi patterning, integrated circuit, graph coloring

ACM Reference Format:
Alexey Lvov, Gustavo Tellez, and Gi-Joon Nam. 2018. On Coloring and Colorability Analysis of Integrated Circuits with Triple and Quadruple Patterning Techniques. In *ISPD '18: 2018 International Symposium on Physical Design, March 25–28, 2018, Monterey, CA, USA.* ACM, New York, NY, USA, 8 pages. https://doi.org/10.1145/3177540.3178241

1 INTRODUCTION

A few options of multi-patterning techniques exist, but in this paper we will focus on technologies with multiple lithography-etch steps, which we denote as *k-LE* multi patterning. The number k denotes the number of lithography-etch steps and the number of masks for a layer.

From the shapes layout perspective, *k-LE* multi-patterning requires that the shapes in a layer be subdivided into k masks, such that:

Two shapes i and j on the same mask must be spaced by distance $D_{i,j}$, $D_{i,j} \geq S_S$, where S_S is the minimum same mask spacing. Distance between two shapes on different masks must satisfy $D_{i,j} \geq S_D$, where S_D is the minimum different mask spacing and $S_D \leq S_S$.

To represent the masks in a shapes layout, the concept of a *color* was introduced. By coloring a shape, the mask of that shape is identified. The formulation of the *shape coloring problem* is as follows:

For a layout L, construct an undirected graph $G(V, E)$ with a vertex $v_i \in V$ for each shape $L_i \in L$. Edge $e_{i,j} \in G$ is present if and only if the distance between two shapes L_i and L_j is less than S_S. The shape layout coloring problem of L is the same as the k coloring problem of graph $G(V, E)$.

For $k = 2$ there exists a polynomial time algorithm for deciding if a given graph is 2-colorable and providing the coloring if the answer is positive : en.wikipedia.org/wiki/Bipartite_graph#Testing_bipartiteness

For $k \geq 3$ the general graph coloring problem is known to be NP-complete. More than that, for any number of colors k there exist non-colorable graphs, for example $(k + 1)$-cliques.

However not any adjacency graph can result from a planar layout with a given minimum same mask spacing. Also, for the sake of colorability, we can further restrict the set of possible adjacency graphs by introducing a number of additional design rules.

There are two distinct approaches in design automation towards coloring:

1) *correct-by-construction*, wherein an algorithm determines the color of shapes as the shapes are being created, while accepting some layout restrictions [5], and

2) *decomposition with post fix up*, wherein a coloring algorithm is invoked when the layout is completed, and a colored layout is generated, if possible.

In the correct-by-construction approach, a method is found that can be used to trivially color shapes, for example, coloring wires by track during routing and adopting unidirectional routing. Another example of correct-by-construction coloring is to color the shapes in the standard cells, and create cell boundary conditions, such that all placements of the standard cells are groundrule correct and do not create color spacing errors on the cell boundaries. The correct-by-construction method, when applied to standard cells, usually comes with a density penalty, which becomes prohibitive in the newest technology nodes. Dense standard cell designs contain shapes interactions across hierarchy, i.e. inter-cell interactions, which imply that correct-by-construction coloring at an intra-cell level is no longer possible, and *flat* decomposition coloring is necessary.

In the decomposition with post fix up method, the layout is completely constructed, and a coloring algorithm is run, generating colored shapes. If the coloring algorithm fails, then the layout has to be repaired, and coloring has to be attempted again. One method of local repair is to break an uncolorable shape into multiple shapes with multiple colors. This method is known as *color stitching* . Color stitching might introduce manufacturability problems and it is preferred to avoid it as much as possible.

In case of any not guaranteed coloring method, such as greedy coloring, the iteration between coloring and conflict repair can add significant time to design cycles, especially for flat designs, and is undesirable. The need for flat coloring significantly increase the number of possible color conflicts because some of the conflicts may result from neighbor cells placement, even though no such conflict exists inside the cells in the hierarchical representation of the design.

Standard cells are placed in rows, and therefore, shapes interactions between standard cells can be divided into two categories: *intra-row* interactions, and *inter-row* interactions. Past work produced an algorithm that solves the intra-row triple-patterning problem [7]. Other works consider practical methods for triple and quadruple patterning decomposition [8, 9]. Initial work in the area of triple patterning with layout restrictions is described in [3]. To our knowledge, no one has considered the implications to design flows, and more specifically to placement, resulting from the wholesale adoption of flat decomposition multi-patterning with the consideration of inter-row interactions.

We seek a practical strategy for the design of colorable layout, which does not impose density penalties and cannot result in coloring conflicts after cell placement. In other words, we seek layout and placement strategies which eliminate the possibility of decomposition failures.

In this paper we present some results on the complexity of coloring of the shape layout based graphs. From this analysis we derive some specific recommendations for design rules and restrictions that enable practical coloring methods. Model B, presented in section 2, is a practically usable colorable model for quadruple patterning. It is illustrated with a real design example and is shown to be almost minimally restricted in the sense that even a very small relaxation of model B rules leads to existence of not 4-colorable designs. More models for triple and quadruple patterning both colorable and not colorable are considered throughout the paper.

2   FOUR COLORABLE MODELS

Definition 2.1. *A model is a set of all layouts that follow specified design rules together with a definition of adjacency of a pair of shapes of a layout.*

Definition 2.2. *Call a model n-colorable if any layout that belongs to this model is colorable with $\leq n$ different colors so that no two adjacent shapes have the same color. Call a model not n-colorable otherwise.*

We start with a proof of four colorability of a fairly simple model:
Model A:
All shapes are vertical rectangles of width one aligned to a square grid and separated by space of width at least one. Call two shapes *adjacent* if l_∞ distance between them is equal to one, where l_∞ distance between two points (x_1, y_1) and (x_2, y_2) is defined as $\max(|x_1 - x_2|, |y_1 - y_2|)$, and distance between two shapes is defined as the minimum distance between any pair of points which belong to different shapes. An example of model A layer and its adjacency graph is shown on Figure 1.

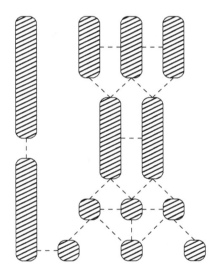

Figure 1: Model A. Dashed lines show adjacency.

Note that one *can not* use the famous Four Color Map theorem [1], which states that any planar graph is four colorable, for the proof of colorability of model A because model A admits a lot of non-planar adjacency configurations. In fact, each vertex of a graph in model A can have up to 8 edges. It makes it easy to construct a layer with a non-planar adjacency graph, as shown on Figure 2. The necessary condition for planarity based on Euler formula $\#EDGES \leq 3 * \#VERTEXES - 6$ is not satisfied for this graph. The existence of non-planar graphs rules out the possibility to refer to Four Color Map theorem to show four colorability of model A (or model B further in this section). However we still can prove that model A is four colorable and provide a coloring algorithm that runs in $O(n \log n)$ time.

Lemma 2.3. *Model A is four colorable.*

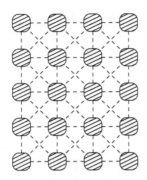

Figure 2: Non-planar example for model A. E = 55, 3*V − 6 = 54.

Algorithm:

(1) Split layout into columns of width 2.
(2) Split the set of available four colors into two pairs: {1, 2} and {3, 4}.
(3) Starting with the first column, label odd columns with {1, 2} and even columns with {3, 4}. See Figure 3a.
(4) In each column we will use only the colors from its label.
(5) By the design rules shapes are at least one square apart so they are linearly ordered in each column from top to bottom.
(6) Color the shapes in each column from top to bottom using the two colors from the columns label in alternating order. See Figure 3b.

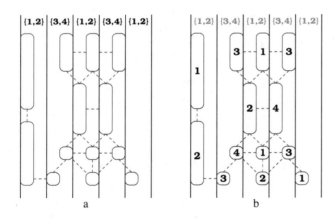

Figure 3: Coloring algorithm for Model A.

Runtime: The only operations required by this algorithm are ordering of the set of shapes by x coordinates and ordering of its disjoint subsets by y coordinate. Hence $O(n \log n)$ runtime upper bound.

Proof of correctness: Let S be a shape from the layer which belongs to column number N. All shapes from columns with numbers <= $N − 2$ and >= $N + 2$ are at least 2 squares apart from S so they contain no shapes adjacent to S. All shapes from columns $N − 1$ and $N + 1$ are colored differently than S because of (3). There can be at most two shapes adjacent to S in column N itself: one from

the top and one from the bottom of S. Because of (6) they are both of the same color and this color is different from the color of S. □

Now let us consider a more sophisticated model which can contain an additional type of shapes and is built to match the practical requirements on typical shapes from advanced technology nodes, such as 10nm.

Model B:
Shapes of two types are allowed:
  1) Vertical rectangles of width one as in model A.
  2) *Z-shapes*: A Z-shape occupies 5 squares exactly as shown on either Figure 4a or Figure 4b and can be adjacent only to four or less vertical rectangles which are located with respect to that Z-shape exactly as shown on either Figure 4a or Figure 4b.

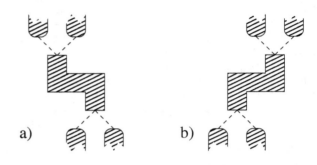

Figure 4: Definition of Z-shape for model B.

The same way as in model A all shapes must be aligned to a square grid and must be at l_∞ distance of ≥ 1 from each other. As before two shapes are *adjacent* if l_∞ distance between them is 1.

Lemma 2.4. *Model B is four colorable.*

Algorithm:

(1) Split layout into columns of width 2. Note that each column can contain parts of Z-shapes and only whole vertical shapes.
(2) Split the set of available four colors into two pairs: {1, 2} and {3, 4}.
(3) Starting with the first column, label odd columns with {1, 2} and even columns with {3, 4}.
(4) By the design rules shapes are at least one square apart so vertical shapes and parts of Z-shapes are linearly ordered in each column from top to bottom.
(5) Color the vertical shapes and the parts of Z-shapes in each column from top to bottom using the two colors from the columns label in alternating order. Then remove the colors from the parts of Z-shapes. Now only the vertical shapes are colored and any two consecutive vertical shapes not separated by a part of a Z-shape have different colors and any two consecutive vertical shapes separated by a part of a Z-shape have the same color. See Figure 5a.
(6) Color all Z-shapes without creating conflicts with the existing coloring of the vertical shapes. See Figure 5b.

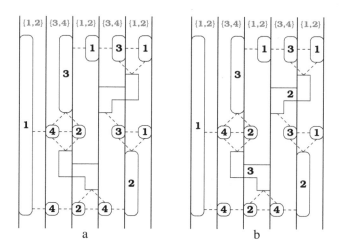

Figure 5: Coloring algorithm for Model B.

Runtime: The most expensive operation is the ordering of shapes by a coordinate. The runtime is $O(n \log n)$.

Proof of correctness: By the same argument as in the proof of Lemma 2.3 after (5) the vertical shapes are colored conflict free. We only have to show that (6) is always possible. In fact by definition a Z-shape can have at most four adjacent shapes all of which are vertical. By (5) the two of these shapes which lie on the vertical center line of Z-shape (if both are present) are colored in the same color. So the adjacent shapes have used up ≤ 3 colors and the remaining color can be used for the Z-shape. □

Figures 6 and 7 show an application of model B coloring algorithm to a real design CA layer.

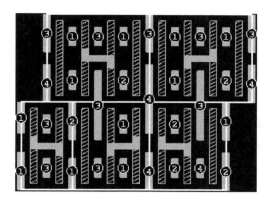

Figure 6: Four coloring of a real design CA layer, step 5 of 6. PC layer: shaded shapes. CA layer: solid shapes. Boundaries of cell instances: white lines.

We have presented a practically usable set of design rules (Model B) for quadruple patterning which guarantees splitting the design shapes into four separate masks without violating the minimum intra-mask distance requirement.

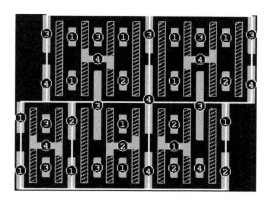

Figure 7: Four coloring of a real design CA layer, step 6 of 6.

3   NOT FOUR COLORABLE MODELS

Once we have a four colorable model it is a natural question to ask by how much can we relax the design rules without breaking the four colorability property. In this section we show that both models A and B are almost tight in that sense, namely:
• In model A:
Allowing only a few 3×1 horizontal rectangles breaks the four colorability.
• In model B:
Still enforcing the same upper limit on the number of neighbors of a Z-shape (a maximum of 4), but allowing the neighbors to be aligned differently with respect to Z-shapes, breaks the four colorability.

Model C:
Model C is model A with 3×1 horizontal rectangles allowed in addition to $1 \times n$ vertical rectangles.

LEMMA 3.1. *Model C is not four colorable.*

Example: It is sufficient to use only four 3×1 horizontal shapes to construct a not four colorable example for model C as shown on Figure 8.

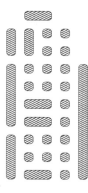

Figure 8: Not four colorable example for model C.

Proof: First color the 4-clique shown on Figure 9a. Without loss of generality denote the four colors by 1, 2, 3, 4, in the order shown on Figure 9a. Then color the 4-clique circled on Figure 9b. There are

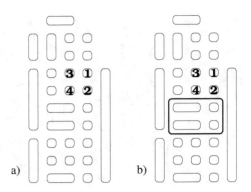

Figure 9

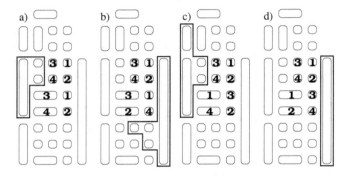

Figure 10

only four possibilities to do that as shown on Figure 10. For each of the four cases continue coloring to the circled region. For cases (a) and (d) this leads to a conflict immediately. Each of the cases (b) and (c) forks into two, see Figure 11. Again continue coloring to

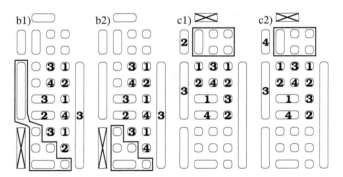

Figure 11

the circled regions. In each case it will surround the crossed shape by four different colors making the four coloring impossible. □

Model D:

Model D is model B with a relaxed restriction on the position of adjacent shapes with respect to Z-shapes: a Z-shape can be in any position with respect to its adjacent shapes as long as it has a

maximum of four (same maximum as in model B) adjacent shapes. As in model B the bounding boxes of all shapes must be at l_∞ distance of ≥ 1 from each other.

LEMMA 3.2. *Model D is not four colorable.*

Example: See Figure 12.

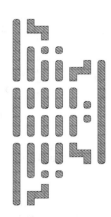

Figure 12: Not four colorable example for model D.

Proof: First color the 4-clique shown on Figure 13a. Without loss of generality denote the four colors by 1, 2, 3, 4, in the order shown on Figure 13a. Assume for the sake of contradiction that the

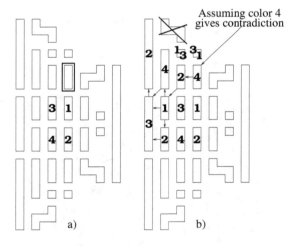

Figure 13

shape, which is circled on Figure 13a, has color 4. Then propagating colors along the arrows as shown on Figure 13b leads to a conflict: the crossed Z-shape can not be colored. So the circled shape must have color 2. The horizontally symmetric shape must have color 1 because the whole design is horizontally symmetric and assuming color 3 leads to a contradiction in the symmetric way. See Figure 14a.

Propagate coloring into the circled region. This can be done in four ways as shown on Figure 14b: in all 3/4 pairs choose either only the upper or only the lower color and in all 1/2 pairs choose

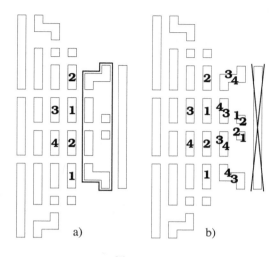

Figure 14

either only the upper or only the lower color. All these colorings lead to a conflict on the crossed shape. □

4 THREE COLORABILITY

Using only three masks instead of four gives obvious benefits for the manufacturing process. However it is intuitively clear that design restrictions sufficient to guarantee three colorability should be much stronger than the restrictions of four colorable models such as model A or model B. Theoretical results regarding planar and other related graphs without triangles are known [4, 6]. Unfortunately, graphs resulting from layouts contain triangles. It is also known that three coloring of planar graphs is an NP-complete problem [2].

In this section we define a number of models with more or less natural sets of design rules, each next model is more restricted than the previous. For each of these models except for the last one we find an example of not three colorable design, which examples become more and more complex as the models become more restricted. Finally for the last model we prove the three colorability.

Our first observation is that if, as in model A, we define adjacent shapes as shapes at l_∞ distance of one then any four one-by-one square shapes which centers are located at vertexes of a two-by-two square form a four-clique as on Figure 2. So, for three colorability we must introduce stricter requirements on mutual position of two shapes in order to count them adjacent. These requirements should be strict enough to prohibit diagonal interactions between shapes.

Model E:
• All shapes are vertical rectangles of width one separated by space of width at least one, which vertexes have integer coordinates and which vertical center lines are at divisible by two distances from each other.
• Two shapes are *adjacent* if l_∞ distance between them is equal to one and their projections on either a vertical or a horizontal axis intersect by a segment of length at least one. Some examples of adjacent and not adjacent pairs of shapes for model E are given on Figure 15.

LEMMA 4.1. *Model E is not three colorable.*

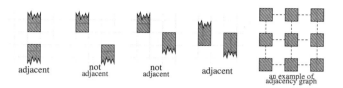

Figure 15: Adjacency for models for 3-colorability.

Example: See Figure 16a.

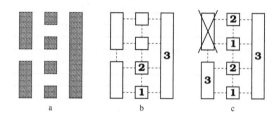

Figure 16: Not 3-colorable example for model E.

Proof: First color the three-clique shown on Figure 16b. Without loss of generality denote the three colors by 1, 2, 3. Then the coloring shown on Fig. 16c is forced and the crossed shape can not be colored without creating a conflict. □

This example is possible because coloring of a long vertical chain of small adjacent shapes is forced if they all are also adjacent to a long vertical shape to their left or right. Let us restrict model E to exclude this situation.

Model F:
• All shapes are vertical rectangles of width 1 at l_∞ distance ≥ 1 from each other with integer vertexes and with vertical center lines at divisible by two distances from each other.
• Two shapes are *adjacent* if l_∞ dist. between them is 1 and their proj. on vert. or horiz. axis intersect by a segment of length ≥ 1.
• A shape can have at most 2 shapes adj. to it from the left.
• A shape can have at most 2 shapes adj. to it from the right.

LEMMA 4.2. *Model F is not three colorable.*

Example: See Figure 17a.

Proof: First color the three-clique shown on Figure 17b. Without loss of generality denote the three colors by 1, 2, 3. The shapes of our example form a picture resembling a wheel. Keep propagating colors going around the empty center in both clockwise and counter clockwise directions. The length of the "wheel" is chosen so that when the colorings in the two directions meet we have a color conflict on the crossed shape as shown on Figure 17c. □

Let us further restrict the model by limiting the number of vertical interactions between shapes to just one per shape. This will rule out wheel-like examples.

Model G:
• All shapes are vertical rectangles of width 1 at l_∞ distance ≥ 1 from each other with integer vertexes and with vertical center lines at divisible by two distances from each other.

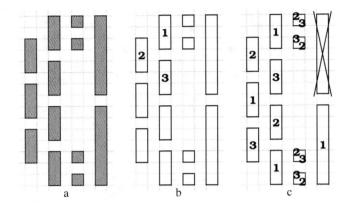

Figure 17: Not 3-colorable example for model F.

- Two shapes are *adjacent* if l_∞ distance between them is 1 and their projection on vert. or horiz. axis intersect by a segment of length ≥ 1.
- A shape can have at most 2 shapes adj. to it from the left.
- A shape can have at most 2 shapes adj. to it from the right.
- A shape can have at most 1 shape adjacent to it vertically.

LEMMA 4.3. *Model G is not three colorable.*

Note: However finding a not three colorable example for this model is not easy and the example is more complex.

Example: See Figure 18a.

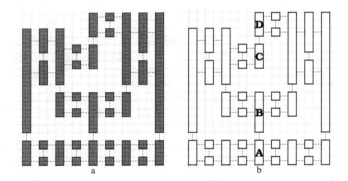

Figure 18: Not 3-colorable example for model G.

Proof: Color the four shapes in the central column and denote the colors (some of which may be the same) by A, B, C and D as shown on Figure 18b. Note that the leftmost and the rightmost shapes of a

configuration must have the same color. So the colors propagate as shown on Figure 19a.

The six interactions circled on Figure 19b force that

$$A \neq B, \quad A \neq C, \quad A \neq D, \quad B \neq C, \quad B \neq D, \quad C \neq D.$$

So the four colors in the central column must be pairwise different. A contradiction. □

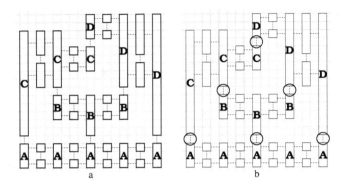

Figure 19: Proof of not 3-colorability of model G.

Now we have reached the point where any further reduction of limits on the number of interactions (horizontal or vertical) leads to a three colorable model. If we reduce the limit on the number of vertical interactions (which is already equal to one in model G) to zero then the model becomes two colorable as follows : just color the columns left to right in alternating order 1 - 2 - 1 - 2 - 1 - .... If we reduce the limit on the number of interactions from one side, say from the left, the model becomes three colorable as shown below.

Model H:
- All shapes are vertical rectangles of width 1 at l_∞ distance ≥ 1 from each other with integer vertexes and with vertical center lines at divisible by two distances from each other.
- Two shapes are *adjacent* if l_∞ dist. between them is 1 and their proj. on vert. or horiz. axis intersect by a segment of length ≥ 1.
- A shape can have at most 1 shape adj. to it from the left.
- A shape can have at most 2 shapes adj. to it from the right.
- A shape can have at most 1 shape adjacent to it vertically.

LEMMA 4.4. *Model H is three colorable.*

Algorithm and proof: Start coloring from the shapes in the leftmost column and continue through the columns from left to right. By the restrictions of model H each next uncolored shape is adjacent to at most two already colored shapes: at most one in its own column and at most one in the column to its left. Since we have three colors available each next uncolored shape can be colored conflict free. □

In this section we have analyzed a sequence of increasingly restricted models for triple patterning and found a nearly minimal set of restrictions necessary to guarantee a conflict free creation of three separate masks.

5 CONCLUSION

In this paper we have analyzed triple and quadruple coloring of various layout models, with the goal of developing robust layout methodologies. We have developed a very restricted layout model (Model H), in which all layouts are 3-colorable in $O(n \log n)$ time. We have also shown that even slightly less restricted layout models can yield layouts that are un-colorable when using triple patterning (Models E, F and G). We have also shown two layout models (Models A and B) which always result in layouts that are 4-colorable with a $O(n \log n)$ time algorithm, making them suitable for practical layouts. These 4-colorable layout models are particularly suitable for standard cell architectures, because their use enables worry-free placement. In the four color models we also find out that small relaxations (C and D) to the colorable models allow for layouts that are not colorable.

In future research we would like to determine the complexity of triple and quadruple coloring of the graphs that result from layouts which belong to models that are not generally colorable but some individual layouts of which still can be colored. This problem is of practical importance for the adoption of decomposition driven approaches.

REFERENCES

[1] Kenneth Appel and Wolfgang Haken. 1976. Every planar map is four colorable. *Bulletin of the American mathematical Society* 82, 5 (1976), 711–712.

[2] Michael R Garey, David S. Johnson, and Larry Stockmeyer. 1976. Some simplified NP-complete graph problems. *Theoretical computer science* 1, 3 (1976), 237–267.

[3] Michael S Gray, Matthew T Guzowski, Alexander Ivrii, Lars W Liebmann, Kevin W Mccullen, Gustavo E Tellez, and Michael Gester. 2015. Reducing color conflicts in triple patterning lithography. (Oct. 13 2015). US Patent 9,158,885.

[4] Herbert Grötzsch. 1959. Ein Dreifarbensatz für dreikreisfreie Netze auf der Kugel. *Wiss. Z. Martin-Luther-Univ. Halle-Wittenberg Math.-Natur. Reihe* 8 (1959), 109–120.

[5] L. W. Liebmann. 2003. Layout impact of resolution enhancement techniques: impediment or opportunity?. In *ISPD*. 110–117.

[6] Carsten Thomassen. 1994. GrötzschâĂš s 3-Color Theorem and Its Counterparts for the Torus and the Projective Plane. *Journal of Combinatorial Theory, Series B* 62, 2 (1994), 268–279.

[7] Haitong Tian, Hongbo Zhang, Qiang Ma, Zigang Xiao, and Martin DF Wong. 2012. A polynomial time triple patterning algorithm for cell based row-structure layout. In *Computer-Aided Design (ICCAD), 2012 IEEE/ACM International Conference on*. IEEE, 57–64.

[8] Bei Yu and David Z Pan. 2014. Layout decomposition for quadruple patterning lithography and beyond. In *Design Automation Conference (DAC), 2014 51st ACM/EDAC/IEEE*. IEEE, 1–6.

[9] Bei Yu, Kun Yuan, Duo Ding, and David Z Pan. 2015. Layout decomposition for triple patterning lithography. *Computer-Aided Design of Integrated Circuits and Systems, IEEE Transactions on* 34, 3 (2015), 433–446.

Standard CAD Tool-Based Method for Simulation of Laser-Induced Faults in Large-Scale Circuits

Raphael A. C. Viera
Ecole Nat. Sup. des Mines de St-Etienne
LIRMM, CNRS, UMR N5506
Univ. Grenoble Alpes, CNRS, TIMA
raphael.viera@emse.fr

Jean-Max Dutertre
Ecole Nat. Sup. des Mines de St-Etienne
Gardanne, France
dutertre@emse.fr

Philippe Maurine
LIRMM, CNRS, UMR N5506
Montpellier, France
philippe.maurine@lirmm.fr

Rodrigo Possamai Bastos
Univ. Grenoble Alpes, CNRS, TIMA
Grenoble, France
rodrigo.bastos@univ-grenoble-alpes.fr

ABSTRACT

Designing secure integrated systems requires methods and tools dedicated to simulating —at early design stages— the effects of laser-induced transient faults maliciously injected by attackers. Existing methods for simulation of laser-induced transient faults do not take into account IR drop effects that are able to cause timing failures, abnormal reset, and SRAM flipping. This paper proposes a novel standard CAD tool-based method allowing to simulate laser-induced faults in large-scale circuits. Thanks to a power-grid network modeled by a commercial IR drop CAD tool, an additional transient current component causing laser-induced IR drop is taken into consideration. This current component flows from v_{DD} to G_{ND} and may have a significant effect on the fault injection process. The method provides fault sensitivity maps that enable a quick assessment of laser-induced fault effects on the circuit under analysis. As shown in the results, the number of induced faults is underestimated by a factor as large as 3.1 if laser-induced IR drop is ignored. This may lead to incorrect estimations of the fault injection threshold, which is especially relevant for the design of countermeasure techniques for secure integrated systems. Simulation times regarding four different circuits are also presented in the results section.

ACM Reference Format:
Raphael A. C. Viera, Jean-Max Dutertre, Philippe Maurine, and Rodrigo Possamai Bastos. 2018. Standard CAD Tool-Based Method for Simulation of Laser-Induced Faults in Large-Scale Circuits. In *ISPD '18: 2018 International Symposium on Physical Design, March 25–28, 2018, Monterey, CA, USA.* ACM, New York, NY, USA, 8 pages. https://doi.org/10.1145/3177540.3178243

1　INTRODUCTION

Lasers have been used since the 1960s in order to emulate the effects caused by radiation on semiconductors [13]. In the early 2000s, [26] reported the use of laser illumination to induce faults

into secure integrated circuits, e.g., a bit-flip into a SRAM cell. This created a need for designing robust circuits against laser fault injection, consequently generating a demand for simulation tools capable of simulating the effects of laser shots on ICs. Although fault simulations can be performed at different abstraction levels of the design flow, i.e. transistor, gate, RTL and software, low abstraction levels provide the highest accuracy. At the electrical level, a double exponential current source has been demonstrated efficient for modeling a laser shot [16, 28]. This current source is added to the netlists of cells illuminated by the laser. Then an electrical level simulation, which takes into account the effects of the laser attack, can be performed.

The idea commonly accepted is that a laser shot generates parasitic currents [15]. These currents generate an undesired transient voltage that propagates through the logic toward the inputs of registers (D-type Flip Flops) and, if it is still present when the clock edge occurs, bits may be inverted, producing soft errors (SE). Due to the increasing transistor density, a laser shot will affect multiple gates at the same time. Thus, laser illumination also induces, in addition to the well known photoelectric effect, an IR drop phenomenon with a significant effect on the fault injection process that has to be taken into account while simulating laser fault injection [27]. These effects must be simulated at low abstraction levels taking into account the layout topology to better represent physical phenomenon in the scope of a whole system, i.e., the simulation must be performed in complex circuits and not just in one (or few) cells.

To the best of our knowledge, among the existent fault simulators [6, 12, 18, 21, 24], the most recent one is [19], which is based on the open-source Lifting [1]. The major issue with these fault simulators is that they rely on electrical models [8, 11, 25] that are technology dependent. For instance, in [14], the authors proposed a model that includes the vertical parasitic bipolar junctions inherent to MOSFETs in the fault injection process that may lead to IR drop effects. However, they did not extended their work beyond the scope of a single inverter. In fact, dimensioning the RC network of power/ground rails is a difficult task, since the RC values depend on the technology, the size of cells, the position of voltage taps on the rails, the RC parasitics, etc.

The issue being that, as far as we know, there is no tool capable to simulate laser-induced IR drop and its propagation in a large circuit. Thus, the first and main objective of this work is to introduce the devised methodology to simulate at the electrical level the effect of IR drop on the fault injection sensitivity using standard CAD tools; the second objective is to illustrate, on simulation grounds, that laser-induced IR drop has to be considered since it may result in underestimating the risk of fault injection.

2 STATE OF THE ART

2.1 Modeling laser effects on ICs

2.1.1 LASER INDUCED TRANSIENT CURRENTS. ICs are known to be sensitive to induced transient currents. These currents may be caused by laser shots passing through the device, creating electron-hole pairs along the path of the laser beam [15]. The induced charge carriers recombine without any significant effect, unless they reach the strong electric field found in the vicinity of reverse biased PN junctions. In this case, the electrical field puts these charges into motion and a transient current appears as well as a transient fault. The nature of this fault is similar to the ionization effect generated by energetic particles [13].

As an example (the cross section of an inverter), Fig. 1 illustrates where laser shots may generate parasitic currents. In case the inverter input is in low state ('0') the most laser-sensitive part of the inverter is the drain of the NMOS transistor since there is a reverse biased PN junction between the drain and the $P_{substrate}$. Thus, an induced transient current (I_{Ph}) flows from the drain of the NMOS to the $P_{substrate}$ biasing contact. A similar reasoning can be made when the inverter input is high ('1'). In that case, the susceptible part of the inverter is the drain of the PMOS transistor. In case of Fig. 1, a part of the induced photocurrent (I_{Ph}) charges the inverter output capacitance. As a result the inverter output undergoes a voltage transient.

Another transient current component flowing from V_{DD} to G_{ND} that may have a significant effect on the fault injection mechanism is taken into consideration by the model of Fig. 1 [27]. This transient current is induced in the reversed biased $Psub$-$Nwell$ junction that surrounds every $Nwell$. Even if the laser beam is directed towards a sensitive NMOS, the laser beam also induces charge carriers that will be sufficiently close to a $Psub$-$Nwell$ junction to induce a transient current in it flowing from V_{DD} to G_{ND}.

The $Psub$-$Nwell$ junction is always reversed biased and has a larger area than that of a transistor drain (the parameter S in (1)). Thus, it is no surprising that the authors of [9] reported on experimental basis that the transient current component flowing directly from V_{DD} to G_{ND} (IP_{Psub_nwell} in Fig. 1) may be more than an order of magnitude greater than those flowing in the drains of the sensitive transistors (I_{Ph} in Fig. 1). This transient V_{DD} to G_{ND} current may thus have a significant influence on the laser fault injection mechanism since it will produce a temporary supply voltage drop (IR drop) [9, 14, 27].

2.1.2 Spatial Distribution of Laser Beam Energy. The beam diameter is one of the most important propagation attribute of a laser beam in a class of commonly measured parameters (beam diameter, spatial intensity distribution, beam quality factor etc.). A commonly used definition of the laser beam diameter is derived from the bivariate normal distribution of its intensity leading to

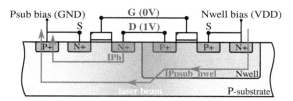

Figure 1: Laser-induced current components. Cross-section of a CMOS inverter.

measure the beam diameter at 86.5% of its maximum value [2], or a drop of $\frac{1}{e^2}$ from its peak value.

The effects of a Near Infrared laser beam have been modeled in [20] and later in [25]. In the latter work, it is shown that the induced photocurrent, which is spatially distributed as a bivariate normal distribution, has a peak amplitude I_{ph_peak} that follows the empirical equation:

$$I_{Ph\_peak} = (a \times V + b) \times \alpha_{gauss(x,y)} \times Pulse_w \times S \quad (1)$$

where V is the reverse-biased voltage of the exposed PN junction, a and b are constants that depend on the laser power, $\alpha_{gauss(x,y)}$ is a term related to the bivariate distribution of the laser beam amplitude in space, $Pulse_w$ is a term allowing to take into account the laser pulse duration and S is the area of the PN junction. One can refer to [25] for additional details of the above parameters.

By way of illustration, Fig. 2 shows a three-dimensional view of the normalized amplitude of a laser spot. Beam intensity at a given coordinate (x,y) represents the amount of power delivered by the laser source at this specific point.

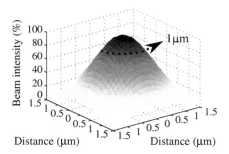

Figure 2: Three-dimensional view of a laser beam in terms of intensity per area. 100% of laser beam intensity represents the epicenter of the laser spot.

2.1.3 Electrical Model of a Cell Under Laser Illumination. Fig. 3a introduces, in case of an inverter, the classical model showing that the effect of a laser is modeled by a current source placed between the drain and the source of the laser-sensitive transistor (PMOS transistor in this example). Fig. 3b shows, in case of an inverter, the enhanced electrical model taking into account the laser-induced IP_{Psub_nwell} current. Without the power-grid model (i.e., considering V_{DD} and G_{ND} ideals), it would be impossible to take the current IP_{Psub_nwell} into account. Consequently, the laser-induced IR drop contribution also would not be taken into account during simulations. This work proposes in its flow the use of an

Electromigration/IR drop (EMIR) CAD tool to automatically provide the power-grid model for each cell in the circuit.

The current sources in Fig. 3a and Fig. 3b have a profile of a double exponential, such as the one illustrated in Fig. 4. The currents have a peak amplitude defined by (1). Since the parameter S (area of the PN junction) corresponds to the cell's *Nwell* area, thus, the current component IP_{Psub_nwell} is larger than that induced at a sensitive transistor drain (*IPh*) since the drain area is smaller than the *Nwell*'s area (see [9] for an experimental assessment).

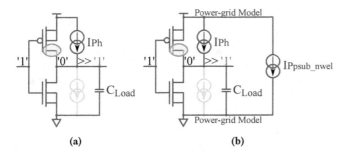

(a)   (b)

Figure 3: Laser-induced transient fault model applied to an inverter with its input biased at v_{DD}. (a) Classical model. (b) Improved model including the IR drop and ground bounce contribution induced by IP_{Psub_nwell} for a given power-grid model [27].

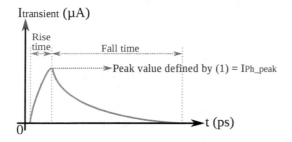

Figure 4: Double exponential profile with current peak defined by (1).

The IP_{Psub_nwell} current source is attached to the biasing contacts of the *Nwell* and the $P_{substrate}$ (for standard cells without embedded biasing contacts, the current source is connected to the closest). The various IP_{Psub_nwell} currents add up and flow from v_{ND} to G_{ND} trough the power and ground networks of the device under attack. Because the power grid exhibits both resistive and capacitive electrical behaviors, a local voltage drop and ground bounce occurs thus reducing the voltage swing seen by standard cells in the close vicinity of the laser spot. Considering the above, this paper provides a method based on standard CAD tools to take at chip level the effect of laser-induced IR drops into account.

2.2 Previous Works on Laser Fault Simulation

Laser fault injection may be anticipated or studied by using simulation tools at different abstraction levels: physical, electrical or

logical. In this section, previous works that proposed laser fault simulation tools are reviewed in order to justify the need for the methodology presented in this work.

2.2.1 Physical Level. Based on Technology Computer Aided Design (TCAD), the authors in [17] characterize and analyze photoelectric effects induced by static 1064 nm wavelength laser on a 90 nm technology NMOS transistor. In [10], Silicon-Germanium Heterojunction Bipolar Transistor (SiGe HBT) models are used in TCAD to investigate single event transients induced by heavy-ion broadbeam and pulsed-laser sources. Although TCAD is the ultimate tool to simulate laser effects on ICs, this simulator is extremely CPU consuming and can only be applied to individual transistors or small circuit areas.

2.2.2 Logic Level. The authors of [22] proposed a methodology for multiple fault injection at the Register Transfer Level (RTL). The methodology would reduce the fault space of laser fault injection campaigns by using the locality characteristic of laser fault, and through a partitioning of the RTL description of the circuit. Their efforts involve the development of an RTL fault injection approach more representative of laser attacks than random multi bits fault injection. Unfortunately, as a RTL fault simulator, the fault model is defined as a logic pulse with different widths, which is not sufficient to take into account neither the laser parameters nor IR drop effects.

2.2.3 Electrical Level. Laser fault simulation at the electrical level is a good tradeoff between speed (logic level) and accuracy (physical level). Therefore, it is possible to represent the laser physical phenomenon in the scope of a whole system. Although the simulation time might be an issue, today's electrical simulators are up to 100x faster than baseline SPICE simulators without loss of accuracy. Furthermore when large circuits are simulated, it is possible to profit by the use of hybrid simulation in which only the affected zone of the IC is simulated with SPICE accuracy while the non affected cells are simulated with gate level accuracy.

To the extent of our knowledge, the most recent fault simulator at the electrical level was proposed by [19]. Their simulator is based on the open-source Lifting [1], which allows both 0-delay and delay-annotated simulations of digital circuits using layout information to derive the laser spot location. They also use multi-level simulation, trading of speed for accuracy. The major issue with these fault simulators is that they to rely on electrical models [8, 11, 25] that are technology dependent. Even though it is possible to dimension these models, it is hard to obtain accurate results when dealing with new technologies.

For instance, the contribution of IR drop effects play a significant role in the fault injection process as reported in [27]. The authors of [14] modeled a RC network in the power/ground rails to demonstrated the significant contribution of the current induced by vertical parasitic bipolar junctions inherent to MOSFETs in the fault injection process. However, they did not study the effect of the IR drop induced by laser shots, i.e., its impact in the fault injection mechanism. They also did not extended their work beyond the scope of a single inverter since they manually dimensioned the values of the RC components, which would be a difficult task to do for a whole circuit.

2.2.4 Summary. What has been observed so far is that there is a great improvement of laser fault models. However the models were developed at the level of a single gate, ignoring thus the effects of laser-induced IR drops at chip level. Regarding laser fault simulators, they usually use the simple fault model in which current sources are attached to the drain and bulk of laser sensitive transistors [16, 28]. Unfortunately, this fault model was created at a time when laser sources with 1 μm to 5 μm spot diameter were used to target only one sensitive PN junction at the same time. For advanced technologies this model is questionable. For a 28 nm technology, the standard cells have a height value of about 1.2μm, meaning that even lasers with 1 μm spot diameter will also illuminate the *Psub-Nwell* junction (see Fig. 1) and thus induce significant IR drop in the area surrounding the laser spot.

In order to use a fault model that takes into account the IR drop contribution induced by the current component created between the *Psub-Nwell* junction, it is necessary to model by a RC network the power/ground rails. Modeling the RC network of a large circuit is not a task to be performed manually. In view of this limitation, i.e., that current laser fault simulators do not use complete and accurate fault models, we propose a fault simulation methodology that uses an EMIR CAD tool to automatically provide the RC network of the power/ground rails for a given design. It also provides the transient voltage that propagates along the power rails as a result of the IP_{Psub_nwell} current. The methodology can be used for any circuit designed in any technology supported by the standard CAD tools. Next section presents in details the proposed methodology.

3 PROPOSED METHODOLOGY FOR LASER FAULT SIMULATION

The diagram presented in Fig. 5 proposes a step by step simulation methodology that makes it possible to simulate laser fault injection in large scale circuits. This methodology, which is based on standard CAD tools (Cadence Voltus^{TM} [5] for EMIR simulation and Cadence Spectre XPS [4] for the electrical and hybrid simulation), allows to analyze the impact of laser shots on complex circuits by drawing laser-induced fault sensitivity maps.

The methodology can be easily adapted to provide other set of results besides the ones reported in this work. As far as we know, this is the first methodology able to simulate laser effects on ICs that takes into account laser-induced IR drop effects. Although Cadence tools were used, any other tools that are able to perform IR drop analysis and SPICE like simulations can be used. Fig. 5 is subdivided in numbers that represent each step described in the following sections.

3.1 Step 1: defining simulation parameters

In the first step, a shell script file (main.scr) defines parameters characterizing the laser shot. Among them, one can find: the laser beam diameter, the duration of the laser shot, the time at which begins the laser shot with regard to the operation of the IC, the (X,Y) displacement step of the laser spot when one aims to draw fault sensitivity maps (detailed in step 5), etc. This file is also responsible for calling the necessary tools and scripts for the correct execution of the simulation flow.

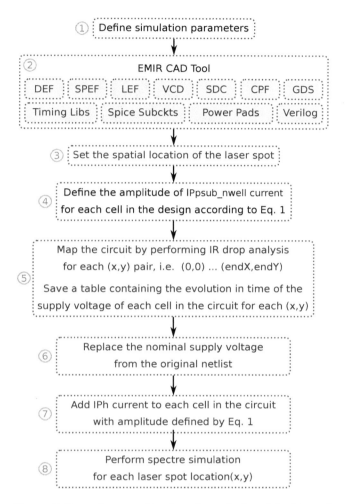

Figure 5: Procedure used to draw laser-induced fault sensitivity maps using the proposed methodology.

3.2 Step 2: data preparation for the EMIR CAD tool

Most of the inputs that are inside the dashed rectangle "EMIR CAD Tool" of Fig. 5 are files that were automatically generated by the design CAD tool (Cadence Innovus [3]). Other files were obtained from the design kit of the technology. It is out of scope of this work to explain each of these files in detail. It suffices to say that they are necessary to model the RC network in the power/ground rails and perform IR drop analysis in Cadence Voltus^{TM}, both necessary for the accomplishment of the proposed methodology.

3.3 Step 3: spatial location of the laser spot

In this step it is necessary to know the dimension of the design and the number of simulated laser shots that are going to be applied over the circuit. For this work, an ARM 7 with a 110 μm × 70 μm area was used (more details are provided in Section 4). If a displacement step of x, y: 5μm is set, then, in order to sweep the whole circuit, beginning at x, y: $(0, 0)$ and ending at x, y: $(110, 70)$, it would demand 345 laser shots as illustrate in Fig. 6.

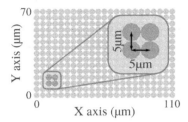

Figure 6: Spatial location of the laser spots. Each point corresponds to a laser shot at different positions (each point corresponds to a simulation).

This step allows to know where the laser spot illuminates the IC during each simulation. Next step shows which cells are illuminated by the laser spot for each x, y position and at which intensity.

3.4 Step 4: laser-induced fault injection

Faults induced by laser illumination can be simulated by specifying the current amplitude of the current sources that compose the laser-induced transient fault model (Fig. 3) of each standard cell in the circuit. Therefore, to simulate a circuit being attacked by means of laser fault injection it is necessary to know which cells will be affected by the laser.

Several ways can be adopted in order to discover the values to be assigned to the current sources in the fault model (Fig. 3). This methodology benefits from a feature present in Cadence Voltus^{TM}. This tool allows to apply an amount of current to a defined region, in this way, several small rectangular regions are defined and the current amplitude of that region follows the spatial distribution of the laser-induced photocurrent defined by (1). Fig. 7 illustrates how the rectangular regions can be used in order to apply the laser power (current induced by the laser) to each rectangle.

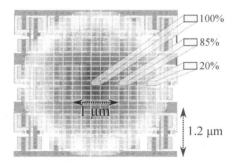

Figure 7: Laser-induced current regions applied over standard cells of a CMOS 28 nm technology. The current amplitude of each region is defined by (1).

The following code example represents the characterization of a rectangle (current region) located at the center of the laser spot (Fig. 7). Therefore its I_{Ph_peak} is maximum, 100% or 1 mA for this example. The double exponential has a step size of 5 ps, the peak is

thus found at it apex, i.e., 1.510ns, considering 10 ps of rise time and fault starting at 1.500 ns. Other parameters such as capacitances are extracted from .lib and .spi files of the technology for each affected cell. The resolution of each rectangle is 250 nm as shown by the last parameter: -region "x1 y1 x2 y2". The dimension of the rectangle can be changed according to the precision needed to model the laser spot.

```
create_current_region −current {1.500ns 0.000mA
1.505ns 0.820mA 1.510ns 1.000mA 1.515ns 0.950mA
...  1.800ns 0.000mA} −layer M2 −intrinsic_cap C
−loading_cap C  −region "1.50 1.50 1.75 1.75"
```

3.5 Step 5: mapping the circuit

In this step, Cadence Voltus^{TM} is used with the purpose to perform laser-induced IR drop simulations for the different laser spot locations calculated during step 3. All other simulation parameters being kept constant (spot diameter, intensity, etc.).

Clarifying, IR drop can be defined as the power supply noise induced by currents flowing through the resistive parasitic elements of the power distribution network. In this work, the laser-induced IR drop is also considered, meaning that the laser-induced current will accumulate with the dynamic current of a cell, thus increasing its IR drop while the laser is active ($IP_{Psub\_nwell} \neq \emptyset$).

For each iteration of this step, a table containing the evolution in time of each cell's voltage swing amplitude (v_{DD}-G_{ND}) is saved for future analysis since different cells are affected by the laser shot. It is also possible to save a table with the dynamic current in time, which translates directly to the amplitude of the current IP_{Psub_nwell} for each cell in the circuit. Table 1 illustrates for three different cells the remaining voltage swing when the laser effect reaches its apex (peak of the double exponential transient current from Fig. 4).

Table 1: List of cells of the circuit with their voltage swing at the apex of the laser shot.

Spot pos. 1 Voltage Swing	Spot pos. 2 Voltage Swing	Spot pos. 10 Voltage Swing
U232 0.619 V	U232 0.689 V	U232 0.926 V
U132 0.620 V	U132 0.678 V	U132 0.905 V
U271 0.621 V	U271 0.695 V	U271 0.932 V

Note in this example that, for the laser spot position 1 (cf. Table 1) the cells are more affected (lower voltage swing) as the epicenter of the laser spot is closer to these three cells. For laser spot positions 2 and 10, the cells are less affected since the epicenter of the laser spot is far away from the cells listed in the table.

3.6 Step 6: inserting IP$_{Psub\_nwell}$

The IP_{Psub_nwell} current component induces voltage drops in the power/ground rails. This effect is captured thanks to Cadence Voltus^{TM} in the previous steps. In this step a shell script replaces the ideal v_{DD} and G_{ND} in the original SPICE netlist by waveforms saved in step 5 for each cell in the circuit.

3.7 Step 7: inserting I_{ph}

A shell script is used in order to add a current source between the drain and bulk of PMOS and NMOS transistors. It models the laser-induced currents that may turn into faults. Note that only one of these current sources are activated depending on which drain's PN junction is reversely polarized. For this, it was necessary to run a fault free electrical simulation and save a golden table with all inputs and outputs of each cell as a function of time.

Knowing that the IP_{Psub_nwell} current is defined as a $factor \times I_{ph}$ because of the parameter S in (1), it is possible to compute the $factor$ value to be applied to each cell by analyzing the .lef file of each cell and to estimate the area of the affected PN junction of the transistor's drain as well as the $Nwell$ of the same cell.

3.8 Step 8: electrical/hybrid fault simulation

At this point, electrical simulations are performed for each laser shot with different locations as defined on step 3. Electrical simulations are time consuming depending mainly on the circuit's size and available computing resources. To circumvent this drawback, a hybrid simulation has to be performed. This simulation defines a region of the circuit where only the most affected cells are simulated with SPICE accuracy. For the hybrid simulation, Cadence Spectre XPS simulator is used. To define the cells that are going to be simulated at logical level, a threshold voltage is defined based on the V_{DD}-G_{ND} (IR drop + ground bounce) values provided by Table 2. If a cell's power/ground voltage is close to the nominal V_{DD} and G_{ND}, it is considered that this cell is not affected by the laser shot, since it is far away from the epicenter of the laser spot. For example, if a threshold voltage of 10% of the nominal V_{DD} = 1 V is defined, then all cells with IR drop + ground bounce lower than 100 mV are simulated at the logic abstraction level.

Table 2 shows the number of cells simulated with the logic abstraction level for different threshold voltages and different spot locations. The spot locations were selected by chance with the purpose to show that the number of affected cells changed depending on the location where the laser shot was applied.

Table 2: Number of cells simulated with the logic abstraction level for different threshold voltages and different spot locations. (5.21k cells in the circuit.)

Threshold (IR drop + bounce)	No. of cells (spot loc. 1)	No. of cells (spot loc. 2)
10%	2535	2625
15%	4510	4585
20%	4641	4620

4 LASER FAULT SIMULATION RESULTS

4.1 Testbench

In order to simulate the effects of laser-induced faults on complex systems, simulations were performed for different circuits, however only results for an ARM 7 processor (DUT) are shown in details. All circuits were synthesized using a 28 nm technology. The core nominal voltage of the DUT is 1 V and the clock period is 1 ns. The DUT has an area equal to 110 μm × 70 μm.

4.1.1 Circuit Inventory. The evaluated design is composed by 5.21 k cells, 5.34 k nets and 90 k nodes. The power-grid model generated by Cadence Voltus^{TM} has 100 k resistors and 90 k capacitors.

4.1.2 Laser Spot Diameter. Typical laser sources used to produce faults are characterized by a beam diameter equal to 1 μm, 5 μm or 20 μm and a wavelength of 1064 nm. Although the minimum diameter of a laser spot is 1 μm, given the laws of optic its effect area extends far beyond [7, 23]. Consequently, a laser spot does not induce a single transient current in a single cell, but several transient currents at different sensitive nodes of the target. Without loss of generality, a spot diameter of 1 μm has been chosen for the experiments reported below.

4.2 Simulation Performance

The performance of the simulation depends directly on the available computing resources and the complexity of the simulated circuit. The available processor used to perform simulations was an Intel Xeon E5630 @ 2.53 GHz with two cores and 16 GB of RAM. Since the proposed method deals with the simulation of laser-induced fault injection, other factors should be also taken into account, such as the laser spot diameter, its power and the duration of the laser shot. Considering the simulation performed using only Spectre accuracy, the simulation takes more time to be performed when comparing to the simulation of the same circuit in a fault free scenario. This happens as the cells no longer have ideal V_{DD} and G_{ND}, thus the simulator has to decrease the simulation step to account with laser-induced transient currents, which are in the ps range. Therefore, since the diameter of the laser spot determines how many cells are affected, it influences on the time required by the simulator to perform necessary calculations. When using hybrid simulation, it is possible to decrease the amount of cells simulated with Spectre accuracy, thus reducing simulation time.

Table 3 shows simulation times for different circuits using Spectre XPS (hybrid simulation). Simulation times for other simulators (Spectre accuracy only) are not shown as they take at least 22 times more to simulate. Simulations were also performed using Spectre and Spectre APS with the intention to compare results regarding the accuracy of Spectre XPS. In all cases the results were the same, i.e., the same sensitivity maps presented in the next section were obtained. In fact, for this kind of analysis there is no need to have the same precision as simulations for RF designs, in which the Spectre RF simulator is recommended.

4.3 Laser Propagation on the Circuit Surface

To illustrate how the IR drop propagates in the circuit, refer to Fig. 8a and Fig. 8b. In Fig. 8a, for which no laser effect is considered, the IR drop across the rails reach the maximum of 50 mV. In this figure, the voltage drop is uniquely due to normal switching activity. Even though not fully uniform, the IR drop affects almost the whole circuit. Fig. 8b (obtained in step 5 of the proposed method) illustrates how the laser effect propagates in the circuit. In presence of a single laser shot with a spot diameter of 1 μm at coordinates x=60 μm,

Table 3: Simulation performance for different circuits regarding one point of the fault sensitivity map (1 simulation out of 345 simulations to create a complete map).

Circuit	No. of cells	Simulation time
Arm7	5.210	1min 02s
S38584 (ISCAS'89)	20.705	1min 20s
B18 (ITC'99)	52.601	3min 05s
B19 (ITC'99)	105.344	6min 35s

y=35 μm, the effect area extends along the X axis of the power-grid main metal lines for more than 100 μm (the effect area has a shape that is stretched horizontally along the power supply rails as they provide a propagation path to the laser-induced IR drop and ground bounce). Whereas its extension along the Y axis is only approximately 3 μm, i.e., three times the laser spot diameter. The peak value of the induced voltage transient in the power lines is 400 mV (Fig. 8b). At this time, the voltage swing is reduced to 600 mV. This value is far below the nominal core voltage of 1 V. Thus laser-induced IR drop may induce faults in the circuit, such as timing errors or even data disruption.

There are hundreds of standard cells inside the area affected by the laser when considering a 28 nm technology, meaning that the cells inside the affected area will absorb the laser-induced current according to the surface distribution of the laser beam given by 1.

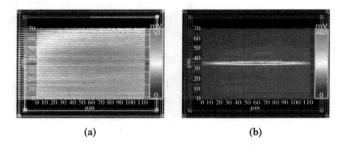

(a)   (b)

Figure 8: ARM 7 layout with 5k+ instances: (a) Maximum voltage drop (IR-Drop + ground bounce) in normal operation condition. (b) Maximum voltage drop in presence of a laser shot with spot diameter equal 1μm.

4.4 Simulated Scenarios

We report a total of 4 simulated scenarios among the ones studied. They are illustrated in Fig. 9 that shows in the first line the clock signal waveform used as a time reference. The two other lines give the typical evolutions observed during simulations, of the signal Q_x, the output of the cell 'x' of the design under illumination, in two different situations. These two situations represent the behavior when a laser pulse with 250 ps duration starts at 1.5 ns and 1.7 ns respectively. These times are thus closer and closer to the next rising clock edge that occurs at 2 ns.

The second line of Fig. 9 gives these evolutions when only the I_{Ph} current sources with a double exponential shape are considered

to model laser effects. In the third line, the curve has a smoother double exponential waveform when comparing with the profile of double exponential current pulse (c.f. second line) proposed by [20] due to the filtering effect (RC effect) of the supply voltage network. In fact, the profile proposed by [20] aims to model alpha-particle hits, which does not exactly correspond to charge generation and collection in PN junctions excited with pulsed infrared lasers as analyzed in [15].

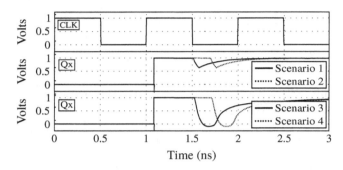

Figure 9: Typical waveforms observed during simulations at the output of gates illuminated by a laser beam. Line 1: clock signal. Line 2: waveforms observed when considering I_{Ph} contribution only. Line 3: waveforms observed when considering $I_{Ph} + IP_{Psub\_nwell}$ contributions.

4.5 Fault Injection Maps

For the purpose of assessing the contribution of laser-induced faults into the circuit, we drew fault sensitivity maps on simulation basis for different areas (considering the model presented in Section 2.1.3). These simulations were performed for locations of the laser spot sweeping the whole circuit area (110 μm x 70 μm) with X and Y displacement steps of 5 μm, resulting in 345 simulations for each figure (each dot location is that of a simulated laser shot). Fig. 10 reports the fault maps for which the model presented in Section 2.1.3 is used (i.e. with the power-grid model provided by the EMIR CAD tool). The red dots correspond to the occurrence of a fault (soft-error) and blue dots the absence of faults. Only bit-flip faults were considered, i.e. faults corresponding to the flipping (with reference to normal operation) of the output state of one or more flip-flops.

4.5.1 Contribution of $\mathbf{I_{ph}}$. Fig. 10a and Fig. 10b report simulations performed considering only the influence of I_{Ph} (laser-induced IR-drops are ignored). Having the transient current profile a width of 250 ps, when this current is applied at 1.5 ns and 1.7 ns, i.e., closer to the flip-flop sampling window (time window of width $t_{setup} + t_{hold}$ centered on the rising edge), more faults are observed.

4.5.2 Contribution of $\mathbf{I_{ph}}$ *and* $\mathbf{IP_{Psub\_nwell}}$. Fig. 10c and Fig. 10d report fault maps for which I_{Ph}, IP_{Psub_nwell} and the power-grid model are considered (scenarios 3 and 4). By comparison to the first line, it reveals that the fault areas are larger than expected for the considered laser shot times. It also unveiled an extension of the laser sensitivity in time, in which the number of faults are increased respectively by a factor of 2.6 and 3.1 for the laser applied at 1.5 ns and 1.7 ns. This demonstrates that IR drops induced by laser shots play an important role in the occurrence of faults. Not taking this effect into account leads to over optimistic results regarding the threshold of fault injection.

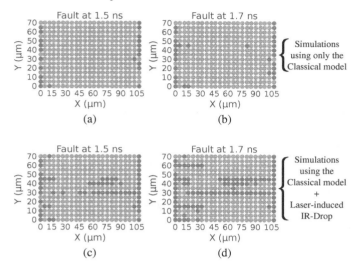

Figure 10: Maps of laser-induced faults for the simulated scenarios: (a-b) laser applied at 1.5 ns and 1.7 ns respectively, considering I_{Ph} contribution only. (c-d) laser applied at 1.5 ns and 1.7 ns respectively, considering $I_{Ph} + I_{P_{Psub\_nwell}}$ contributions.

5 CONCLUSIONS

This paper presented a new method that allows to simulate laser-induced faults at the electrical level in large-scale circuits by using standard CAD tools. Its main intent is to take into account the IR drop effects induced by laser shots: a key parameter in the fault injection process. For each cell in the circuit, a high accuracy electrical fault model that includes the voltage drop effects in the power and ground rails was used thanks to the use of an EMIR CAD tool. The method was applied to a test-chip in order to demonstrate how fault sensitivity maps can be drawn with the purpose of assessing the contribution of laser-induced faults into the circuit.

REFERENCES

[1] A. Bosio and G. D. Natale. 2008. LIFTING: A Flexible Open-Source Fault Simulator. In *2008 17th Asian Test Symposium*. 35–40. https://doi.org/10.1109/ATS.2008.17

[2] S.P. Buchner, F. Miller, V. Pouget, and D.P. McMorrow. 2013. Pulsed-Laser Testing for Single-Event Effects Investigations. *IEEE Transactions on Nuclear Science* (2013). https://doi.org/10.1109/TNS.2013.2255312

[3] Cadence. 2017. Innovus Implementation System. (2017). Retrieved December 3, 2017 from https://www.cadence.com/content/cadence-www/global/en_US/home/tools/digital-design-and-signoff/hierarchical-design-and-floorplanning/innovus-implementation-system.html

[4] Cadence. 2017. Spectre eXtensive Partitioning Simulator. (2017). Retrieved December 3, 2017 from https://www.cadence.com/content/cadence-www/global/en_US/home/tools/custom-ic-analog-rf-design/circuit-simulation/spectre-extensive-partitioning-simulator-xps.html

[5] Cadence. 2017. Voltus IC Power Integrity Solution. (2017). Retrieved December 3, 2017 from https://www.cadence.com/content/cadence-www/global/en_US/home/tools/digital-design-and-signoff/silicon-signoff/voltus-ic-power-integrity-solution.html

[6] Hungse Cha, E. M. Rudnick, J. H. Patel, R. K. Iyer, and G. S. Choi. 1996. A gate-level simulation environment for alpha-particle-induced transient faults. *IEEE Trans. Comput.* 45, 11 (Nov 1996), 1248–1256. https://doi.org/10.1109/12.544481

[7] F. Darracq, H. Lapuyade, N. Buard, F. Mounsi, B. Foucher, P. Fouillat, M. C. Calvet, and R. Dufayel. 2002. Backside SEU laser testing for commercial off-the-shelf SRAMs. *IEEE Transactions on Nuclear Science* (2002). https://doi.org/10.1109/TNS.2002.805393

[8] A. Douin, V. Pouget, D. Lewis, P. Fouillat, and P. Perdu. 2005. Electrical modeling for laser testing with different pulse durations. In *11th IEEE IOLTS*. 9–13. https://doi.org/10.1109/IOLTS.2005.27

[9] Jean-Max Dutertre, Rodrigo Possamai Bastos, Olivier Potin, Marie-Lise Flottes, Bruno Rouzeyre, Giorgio Di Natale, and Alexandre Sarafianos. 2014. Improving the ability of Bulk Built-In Current Sensors to detect Single Event Effects by using triple-well CMOS. *Microelectronics Reliability* 54 (Sept. 2014), 2289 – 2294. https://doi.org/10.1016/j.microrel.2014.07.151

[10] Z. E. Fleetwood, N. E. Lourenco, A. Ildefonso, J. H. Warner, M. T. Wachter, J. M. Hales, G. N. Tzintzarov, N. J. H. Roche, A. Khachatrian, S. P. Buchner, D. McMorrow, P. Paki, and J. D. Cressler. 2017. Using TCAD Modeling to Compare Heavy-Ion and Laser-Induced Single Event Transients in SiGe HBTs. *IEEE Transactions on Nuclear Science* 64, 1 (Jan 2017), 398–405. https://doi.org/10.1109/TNS.2016.2637322

[11] C. Godlewski, V. Pouget, D. Lewis, and Mathieu Lisart. 2009. Electrical modeling of the effect of beam profile for pulsed laser fault injection. *Microelectronics Reliability* (Aug. 2009).

[12] G. S. Greenstein and J. H. Patel. 1992. E-PROOFS: A CMOS bridging fault simulator. In *1992 IEEE/ACM International Conference on Computer-Aided Design*. 268–271. https://doi.org/10.1109/ICCAD.1992.279362

[13] D. H. Habing. 1965. The Use of Lasers to Simulate Radiation-Induced Transients in Semiconductor Devices and Circuits. *IEEE Transactions on Nuclear Science* 12, 5 (Oct 1965), 91–100. https://doi.org/10.1109/TNS.1965.4323904

[14] Laurent Hériveaux, Jessy Clédière, and Stéphanie Anceau. 2013. Electrical Modeling of the Effect of Photoelectric Laser Fault Injection on Bulk CMOS Design. In *39th ISTFA ASM*.

[15] A. H. Johnston. 1993. Charge generation and collection in p-n junctions excited with pulsed infrared lasers. *IEEE Trans. Nucl. Sci.* (1993). https://doi.org/10.1109/23.273491

[16] A. G. Jordan and A. G. Milnes. 1960. Photoeffect on diffused P-N junctions with integral field gradients. *IRE Transactions on Electron Devices* 7, 4 (Oct 1960), 242–251. https://doi.org/10.1109/T-ED.1960.14688

[17] R. Llido, A. Sarafianos, O. Gagliano, V. Serradeil, V. Goubier, M. Lisart, G. Haller, V. Pouget, D. Lewis, J. M. Dutertre, and A. Tria. 2012. Characterization and TCAD simulation of 90 nm technology transistors under continous photoelectric laser stimulation for failure analysis improvement. In *2012 19th IEEE International Symposium on the Physical and Failure Analysis of Integrated Circuits*. 1–6. https://doi.org/10.1109/IPFA.2012.6306298

[18] F. Lu, G. D. Natale, M. L. Flottes, and B. Rouzeyre. 2013. Laser-Induced Fault Simulation. In *2013 Euromicro Conference on Digital System Design*.

[19] F. Lu, G. D. Natale, M. L. Flottes, B. Rouzeyre, and G. Hubert. 2014. Layout-aware laser fault injection simulation and modeling: From physical level to gate level. In *2014 9th IEEE International Conference on Design Technology of Integrated Systems in Nanoscale Era (DTIS)*. 1–6. https://doi.org/10.1109/DTIS.2014.6850665

[20] G. C. Messenger. 1982. Collection of Charge on Junction Nodes from Ion Tracks. *IEEE Transactions on Nuclear Science* (1982). https://doi.org/10.1109/TNS.1982.4336490

[21] W. Meyer and R. Camposano. 1995. Active timing multilevel fault-simulation with switch-level accuracy. *IEEE Transactions on Computer-Aided Design of Integrated Circuits and Systems* 14, 10 (Oct 1995). https://doi.org/10.1109/43.466340

[22] A. Papadimitriou, D. Hély, V. Beroulle, P. Maistri, and R. Leveugle. 2014. A multiple fault injection methodology based on cone partitioning towards RTL modeling of laser attacks. In *2014 Design, Automation Test in Europe Conference Exhibition (DATE)*. 1–4. https://doi.org/10.7873/DATE.2014.219

[23] C. Roscian, A. Sarafianos, J. M. Dutertre, and A. Tria. 2013. Fault Model Analysis of Laser-Induced Faults in SRAM Memory Cells. In *FDTC, 2013 Workshop on*. 89–98. https://doi.org/10.1109/FDTC.2013.17

[24] M. B. Santos and J. P. Teixeira. 1999. Defect-oriented mixed-level fault simulation of digital systems-on-a-chip using HDL. In *Design, Automation and Test in Europe Conference and Exhibition, 1999. Proceedings (Cat. No. PR00078)*. 549–553. https://doi.org/10.1109/DATE.1999.761181

[25] A. Sarafianos, O. Gagliano, V. Serradeil, M. Lisart, J. M. Dutertre, and A. Tria. 2013. Building the electrical model of the pulsed photoelectric laser stimulation of an NMOS transistor in 90nm technology. In *IRPS, 2013 IEEE International*. 5B.5.1–5B.5.9. https://doi.org/10.1109/IRPS.2013.6532028

[26] Sergei P. Skorobogatov and Ross J. Anderson. 2002. Optical Fault Induction Attacks. In *4th International Workshop on Cryptographic Hardware and Embedded Systems*. Springer-Verlag, London, UK, 2–12.

[27] R. A. C. Viera, J. M. Dutertre, R. P. Bastos, and P. Maurine. 2017. Role of Laser-Induced IR Drops in the Occurrence of Faults: Assessment and Simulation. In *2017 Euromicro Conference on Digital System Design (DSD)*. 252–259. https://doi.org/10.1109/DSD.2017.43

[28] J. L. Wirth and S. C. Rogers. 1964. The Transient Response of Transistors and Diodes to Ionizing Radiation. *IEEE Transactions on Nuclear Science* 11 (1964).

Author Index

www.ingramcontent.com/pod-product-compliance
Lightning Source LLC
LaVergne TN
LVHW082127070326
832902LV00040B/2896